MW01097328

Let the Wind Speak

CAROL LOEB SHLOSS

LET
THE
WIND
SPEAK

Mary de Rachewiltz and Ezra Pound

PENN   PHILADELPHIA

Published by
University of Pennsylvania Press
Philadelphia, Pennsylvania 19104-4112
www.upenn.edu/pennpress

Printed in the United States of America on acid-free paper
10 9 8 7 6 5 4 3 2 1

Hardcover ISBN 9781512823257
Ebook ISBN 9781512823264

Library of Congress Control Number:
2022011664

The imagination is transnational.

Orhan Pamuk

To live in the world but outside of existing
conceptions of it.

Ezra Pound

I demand the honesty of forests.

Mary de Rachewiltz

CONTENTS

Photographs follow page 160

PREFACE

Who knows what loyalty is in the underworld?

Antigone to Creon

One world stood by you, one stood by me.

Antigone to Ismene

Different worlds, both equally offended.

Ismene to Antigone

If you were Mary de Rachewiltz, on whose side of history would you fall? In an alpine tower, there is time to reflect. She observes something small: a piece of straw on the floor; a cracked cup on the table; through the window she sees immensity: a gorge, a line of mountains, a summit, a path to the heights. She considers a discordant inheritance. There was her father, Ezra Pound; there, facing him, was the United States. Between them, a charge of treason. As the daughter of a gifted poet whose life ended in turmoil, she recognizes that her life has grown from epic talent even as it has chafed against lies, betrayal, and shifting fictions. Beauty and danger roil together on the steep slopes and in the mind.

I met her in 1992. When we sat down, the first thing she asked was, "What am I doing here?" We were drinking tea together in the high Italian Alps in a castle named Brunnenburg. I saw her choice of dwelling place as an immense act of courage and originality. "You chose it," I said, looking at turrets and winding staircases and terraces that hovered over steep chasms. But, as I was to learn, it was not a simple choice. She aligned character as well as fate with this dwelling place. What I considered "home" was, for her, also a place of exile, as if a familiar habitation could contain treacherous and isolated caverns within itself.

On one side, there was beauty: everything that made Brunnenburg familiar and beloved. She had lived in the Tyrol for most of her life; her children had been born here; her son, his wife and their family still inhabited another part of the castle; outside, vineyards were flourishing. The stone walls that sheltered us were filled with memory and manuscripts, artwork and archives, most of these things a testament to her father, the poet Ezra Pound. He had left her not only memory but vision. *The Cantos*, his poem "containing history," had taught her, shaped her, preoccupied her from childhood, informing her choices and understanding in the same way that a Bible might guide another person. It was a spiritual endowment. "Respect. Transcendental. I did not go as far as sewing fragments of cantos into my clothes, but I certainly wrapped them tightly around my mind."[1] Its mastery meant that one could somehow imbibe the father through his words and then enact the words in daily life.

In this poetic sense, Brunnenburg was not just an unusual house, but was founded as an ideal city, a terrestrial paradise, a place apart, above, imbued with principle. A shelter such as this was first conceived in imagination by her father against the ruin of Europe in the Great War ("As a lone ant from a broken ant-hill / from the wreckage of Europe, ego scriptor")[2] and then literally created by Mary against the collapse of her father in World War II. It represented escape from history ("against this ruin"),[3] an elevation from a broken Western civilization. And it actually tried to be a location without national ties. I was sitting in a remarkable place with a quiet but fiercely principled woman. In a certain sense, I was sitting in the aftermath of a poem.

In the way that Pound's cantos can be thought of as a construct of the mind—Pound building his "paradiso/terrestre"[4] word by word—Brunnenburg was the construct of a listening, receptive child building stone by stone an idea that had been implanted since understanding was first possible: poetry can heal the world. If poems are a "no place" and occupy "no time," their significance can still be reconfigured in the stones of houses, the limbs of children, and the roots of vines. They can become "placed" in the civic world; they can announce themselves in material form. They can assert moral and, in this case, even legal importance.

Brunnenburg was bought in 1948. By this time, World War II was over for most civilians, but Ezra Pound remained incarcerated in a mental hospital in the United States. He, too, had become an emblem: not only a person, but also the embodiment of values supposedly antithetical to the country of his birth. Languishing in a "bughouse" called St. Elizabeths, his name was, for most people, synonymous with "treason." He had spoken against the

American war effort on Rome Radio in the 1940s—an act construed as "aid and comfort to the enemy" by J. Edgar Hoover and later by President Franklin Delano Roosevelt. Few things that Mary did from Pound's capture in 1945 until his death in 1972 were, or could be, done apart from this filiation. Others might finesse the issue of Pound's politics by separating his personal views from his poetic genius. They might think him a great poet with an aberrant allegiance to Italian Fascism, but Mary could not. She grew up in the discordant neighborhood of this accusation. It was her heritage as much as *The Cantos*; and to a large extent, it explains the extraordinary step of buying a ruined castle and seeking territorial independence for it in the mid-twentieth century. Behind its acquisition lay an extraordinary conflict. Within its walls were answers to historical problems.

In thinking about this extraordinary human experiment, one can see that the castle was notable for what it excluded as much as for what it aspired to become: Italy, Mary's birthplace, was aligned with the Axis powers; the U.S., her father's country, took sides with the Allies. If Pound's downfall had been the result of unwanted national antagonisms, one could, at the least, imagine a place where differences were free to play out without devastating consequences. Before it was anything else, Brunnenburg was imagined as a haven for Ezra Pound, who had been captured and punished by the allies of World War II. As Mary put it in her autobiography, "Our dreams soared high: we would achieve extraterritoriality, we would fight for his extradition from the USA, and he could rule over a domain populated with artists."[5] She imagined that a stone building on a European mountainside could keep America imaginatively at bay.

Despite this idealism, Brunnenburg skirted danger. The castle was the measure of a serious prior exclusion. It was indeed an edifice that redefined political space, but the very need to extend imagination in this way was the mark of historical duress. Mary faced this squarely when she visited her father in the 1950s. Far from being "the land of the free," America positioned itself in her mind as captor, judge, and scourge. Pound's incarceration meant that he—and by extension she—was subject to laws far different from the rules that governed his poetic vision. Brunnenburg, in her eyes, stood as the embodiment of a deeply moral view of history's possibilities; the United States was governed by far different values. Thus, in Mary's journey to St. Elizabeths, two "cities" were enjoined. Two sets of laws were placed in opposition.

When Mary went to the hospital, she immediately saw a man "hit by history full blast."[6] Though Pound had persevered, the man she had known as a beloved father and teacher no longer existed. He wandered on psychiatric wards amid the disheartening chaos of disheveled minds. He spoke to ramshackle disciples on guarded lawns; he doled out pennies from a meager purse. As reduced as Pound was, she herself was even more diminished. No one took her seriously in the U.S. As long as she played the role of princess, a title derived from her marriage to Boris de Rachewiltz, lawyers could respond to her charm, but, in fact, she understood her own historical irrelevance. No one wanted to talk politics, least of all the politics of Pound's release.

Although she could see her own marginalization, she could not fully see the power of her adversaries. Against the clear-cut stone of Brunnenburg's idealism stood the assembled forces of the U.S. government, and though Americans were victors of war and could define their own narrative of conquest and virtue, the United States must have seemed terrible to her. From her perspective, it was a place of inquisition, secrecy, and corporately concealed loyalties. The pursuit of Ezra Pound extended far into a past that she could not imagine.

Long before it had sent Frank Amprim to Italy in 1943, the FBI had dispatched agents in search of Pound's perfidy to Birmingham, Alabama; Salt Lake City, Utah; Reno, Nevada; Butte, Montana; St. Paul, Minnesota; Hailey, Idaho; New Haven, Connecticut; Denver, Colorado; San Francisco, California; Springfield, Illinois; Chicago, Illinois; Boston, Massachusetts; New Orleans, Louisiana; Newark, New Jersey; Philadelphia, Pennsylvania; Baltimore, Maryland; New York City; and Washington, D.C.

Once Wendell Berge, assistant to Attorney General Francis Biddle, had labeled Pound's radio broadcasts "enemy propaganda" on 30 November 1942, there was no turning back. On American soil, the FBI had involved the Department of State, the Naval Investigative Service, the Foreign Broadcast Intelligence Service, the Office of War Information, and the Criminal Division of the Justice Department. They had asked assistance from the embassies of Genoa, Rome, Vienna, and Berlin; looked into the Philadelphia police department's criminal records on Pound (they had none); had lab reports made verifying Pound's handwriting, and had his letters examined for the presence of secret ink (negative results).

Why this was necessary is not clear. The case against Pound, as set forth by the Baltimore office of the FBI, was "giving aid and comfort to the enemy," and that case could only be made in Italy. Its steps were set out in a document dated 3 July 1945:

One needed proof that Italian Radio is Operated by the Italian Government; Proof that Broadcasts were Made by POUND; Admissions that he was Paid for Broadcasts and Made Them; Witnesses who Saw POUND in Italy and Heard Broadcasts and can Recognize his Voice; Witnesses who Saw POUND in Italy and can Recognize his Voice; Witnesses who Heard Broadcasts and can Recognize his Voice; Witnesses who can Recognize his Voice; Witnesses who saw POUND in Italy; Books, Writings and Statements showing POUND'S Fascist Sympathies; Other Potential Sources of Information.

None of these steps involved Pound's American friends; nonetheless, over a four-year period, the FBI contacted not only James Angleton and his father, but also drew into the investigation James Laughlin, John Slocum, Reed Whittemore, Nancy Cunard, Caresse Crosby, Richard Aldington, George Antheil and his wife, Ernest Hemingway, William Carlos Williams, Francis S. Bacon, Theodore Spencer, John Slocum, Archibald MacLeish, e. e. cummings and his wife, Marion Morehouse, Viola Baxter Jordan, Irving Fisher, Max Eastman and his wife Eliena Krylenko, Karl Shapiro, F. O. Matthiessen, Saxe Commins, Louis Untermeyer, Conrad Aiken, Reynolds Packard and his wife of the *United Press*, Bill Stoneman of the *Chicago Daily News*, Herbert Macken of the *New York Times*, and others. Though she could not know it, the people to whom Mary turned for help were sometimes the very people who had expressed willingness to testify against her father.[7]

With some vague realization of the wide reach of the state, with a clearer knowledge of her own curtailed powers to stand against it, Mary returned home to the Tyrol. She was not, in any case, placed to confront such raw immensities, for she was not even an American citizen. That much had become clear at the beginning of the war when Pound had walked from Rome to the northern mountains to explain that "family" was not, in her case, a simple matter. She was his natural child, the daughter of Olga Rudge. But papers had been falsified, documents ignored, the facts surrounding her birth hidden. Dissimulation abounded, and it did not stop there. Pound had a legal son, although that boy was not his natural son. That son, Omar, had enlisted in the U.S. Army. Whatever Ezra Pound family existed in the 1940s was a twisted skein of legalities that carried immensely complicated moral and civic implications.

* * *

Let's pause here. For these circumstances—a treason charge, a ritual exclusion, a divided family, a lone woman standing before the powers of the state with a moral claim provide echoes of an ancient story. From Mary's perspective, the United States was speaking with the voice of Creon, king of Thebes, as Sophocles imagined him in the fifth century. The times were modern, and the countries involved were diverse, but she stood, grief-stricken, playing a role like Antigone's, arguing on behalf of the humanity of a disgraced blood relative. What claim did she bring to the tale, so often told, of Ezra Pound, accused traitor to his country? And why is remembering an old story important?

We can see that the Greek drama clarifies the struggles of Mary's life. In making a comparison between Mary and Antigone, one sees that she no longer remains a powerless footnote to history, the young princess dismissed by Washington lawyers as a charming toy. Instead, she challenges us, as Antigone once did, to understand that morality has variations and that transgression can exist on two sides of a story. In this light, she becomes a voice opposing the state, uttering bold words, reminding us that laws underscored by hubris cannot support civic order. Antigone stood up for the integrity of her brother; Mary for that of her father, and in doing this, she resurrects Tiresias's question, "What is the bravery of killing a man over and over again?"[8] as we have "killed" Ezra Pound in our collective imagination. Sophocles recognized that his culture needed the voice of Antigone. In our time, we need Mary's perspective.

In Sophocles' play, Antigone was confronted with a great wrong, but a wrong that only she could initially see: her brother Polyneices had fought, much as Ezra Pound had fought, against the nation of his birth. Dying in his efforts against Thebes, he lay unburied and subject to a king's decree: no one should accord him burial rights; his body should lie exposed to birds and dogs. Two sisters, Antigone and Ismene, faced this circumstance: Ismene recognized that women were not citizens, considered that the king had made a decision, and, being subject to the king, she backed away from civic engagement. Antigone enjoined it . . . not in her own name, which by itself was equally without power . . . but in the name of the gods whom she worshiped. Their two responses defined two distinct worldviews. As Antigone said to her sister, "One world stood by you, one stood by me."[9] Their fates were divided. Having made her case for obedience to authority, Ismene withdrew, leaving Antigone to face Creon alone.

Her conversation with the king was about the complexity of moral beliefs in relation to the state. According to her, the law of the gods declared that all men were equal in death, that no man should be cast beyond the pale by simple decree. As Antigone said to Creon, after she had buried her brother, "I disobeyed because the law was not / The law of Zeus nor the law ordained / By Justice, Justice dwelling deep / Among the gods of the dead. What they decree / Is immemorial and binding for us all."[10]

Creon would have none of this. Not only did he let his decree stand, but he also condemned Antigone to a kind of living death. She should be taken to a cave or vault, closed within its walls and left there to die. Further events unfolded from this double ruling against a dissident family: the populace, their voices articulated by the chorus, did not perceive Antigone as a simple alien to be cast out: she was niece to the king; she was engaged to be married to his son, Haemon, and her claim rebounded against the king in ways Creon did not foresee. Instead of one right perspective, they saw two: "Different worlds, both equally offended."[11]

Sophocles' drama ended with all in accord: Antigone had been wrongly condemned for a right observance. As Tiresias observed, "You have buried her alive, and among the living / You have forbidden burial of one dead / One who belongs by right to the gods below. / You have violated their preroga- tives. / No earthly power, no god in upper air / Exerts authority over the dead. / Henceforth, therefore, there lie in wait for you / The inexorable ones, the furies who destroy. / Then tell me when the lamentation starts . . . here and now / The judgment is reversed."[12]

The modern version of this drama has no literal dead and no actual burial chambers, but we can see interesting equivalents. Mary claimed in her life and in her work that Pound, no matter what his political beliefs, deserved a "proper burial." That is, he deserved more than what the United States gov- ernment would give in the 1940s, which was, in its calculated negligence, the moral equivalent of leaving a citizen exposed to beasts of carrion, un- buried, unmourned, and beyond the pale of full humanity. What better way to consider Ezra Pound in the shambling, impotent years locked within St. Elizabeths Psychiatric Hospital? Like Polyneices, he was expelled from civic space, but never completely excluded. And what more imperative duty lies in acknowledging that we still hold him there in imagination, writing disparaging books like *In the Bughouse* and *Roots of Treason: Ezra Pound and the Secrets of Saint Elizabeths*, books that exile Pound intellectually in prose that seemingly comes to his sparse defense?

Mary also claimed that we are still governed by laws that exceed nation- alisms. In the aftermath of World War II, it was, perhaps, impossible for

Americans to hold this perspective. Now, looking back, in the midst of various kinds of globalism and the wandering of migrant populations, we can see the fragility of nation-states and the complications of defending or even defining them. We can appreciate Antigone's call to the "gods of the underworld" who judged by standards above or beyond the confines of human boundaries. And perhaps we can see that poetry has no boundaries that align with arbitrary walls and the divisions created by them. Pound lived by the rules of poetic possibility; he gave those rules to Mary, who believed them so much that she "planted" children and vineyards and poems in their name. Brunnenburg stood as a testament to a place beyond nationalistic rhetoric . . . and because it was in the Tyrolean Alps, it stood, quite literally, on land that had been freely traded among the victors of war, sometimes owing allegiance to the Austrian empire, sometimes to Italy, sometimes to Germany, and sometimes to American occupational authority. From her perspective, nationalism was not a call to absolute loyalty, but was a construct subject to change.

Creon's downfall had been initiated by pride, intransigence, and his failure to see the confluence of natural and divine law. A kingly decree then led to the deaths of family, leaving a stunted political order. Sophocles' gesture of ruin . . . Antigone, Haemon, and Eurydice sacrificed to Creon's failure . . . has no exact parallel in the Mary de Rachewiltz story. America has never relented in its view of Pound; it has never reevaluated its own blame in the hunt, the confrontation, or the judgment of the state. But it is not too late for us to see the stunting of values implicit in the hunt for Ezra Pound, "traitor." It lies in the list of names contained in the FBI Ezra Pound file and in the existence of the file itself. It consists of the practice of informing on fellow citizens and then hiding our complicity. In this hunt, and in this never-litigated "decree." lie the roots of secret government maneuvers, and false or double identities demanded by a scavenging state bent on unearthing the intimacies of poets and artists whose views are unorthodox.

By now, Mary knows the identities of many of the people who turned on Pound. The point is not to rehearse them again so much as it is to see them in the light of the "gods of the underworld." And it consists in facing Tiresias's question, "What is the bravery of killing a man over and over again?" What was accomplished by casting Pound out of the human circle? Which of our own proclivities did he articulate and which parts of ourselves have we denied by this collective rejection?

While I was writing this book, I would talk with Mary in the afternoons. We established a pattern or rhythm for our days. In the mornings, we both worked. Gathered into the arms of Brunnenburg's precarious shelter, I would make coffee and return to my room. Living on an edge, in the heights, I could watch birds fly beneath me. There was a kind of paucity here, but also great magnitude. In the afternoon, I would have tea with Olga Rudge, and only then would Mary and I settle into conversation. "They will hate you," she said. I could not imagine it.

But she, like Antigone, had had "wrong laid upon me wrongly," paying with her life experiences for the past of her father. And she, too, had chosen how to meet it. "Love that can't be withstood. / Love that scatters fortunes." Mary's version of heeding the gods was called "mercy." Of her father she said, "Acquit of evil intention."[13]

CHAPTER 1

Deep Cover

Hiding Children in the Tyrol, 1925–37

I

Mary Rudge de Rachewiltz was born on 9 July 1925 at the Sanitoria della citta Bressanone high in the Alto Adige. Although Bressanone had been ceded to Italy in 1919 by the Treaty of St. Germain, her American mother, Olga Rudge, had chosen it because she trusted the German medicine practiced by the clinic and because it was in a suitably obscure location in the Tyrolean mountains. The baby was premature and struggled to survive. On 20 July, Olga wrote to its father, who had not been present at the birth, "If you would like to see the child you had perhaps better come as it will probably not live—there is very little left of it—it is now in the 'couviuse'—it has no definite illness—only no appetite—it just doesn't catch on."[1]

Soon someone at the clinic, discerning the symmetry of fate, prevailed upon another patient, Johanna Marcher, to suckle the malingering baby. Still mourning her own stillborn son, she agreed. Many years later, imagining the scene of her own birth, Mary de Rachewiltz described Frau Marcher as a woman whose overflowing "milk, energy and compassion was diverted towards a small creature all skin and bones. . . . Like a starving nestling," she says, "did I stretch my long neck and open my beak wide. We had need of each other."[2]

For Hanne Marcher, there was, perhaps, consolation in this arrangement. For Olga Rudge, it was a godsend. A gifted but struggling violinist, she was unmarried, amid a complicated relationship with the American poet, Ezra Pound, and though she claims to have wanted the child, she had counted on having a boy. "I felt," she confided to her diary, "as if the boy had died."[3] She later reconciled herself to the child's gender, but she had no intention of raising it herself. Pound, as she well knew, would not leave his wife, Dorothy Shakespear, and though he had not turned his back on her during the pregnancy, had serious misgivings about artists without financial security bringing children into the world. Whether out of pride or an inarticulate hope that a son and heir might eventually coax Pound out of his current domestic arrangements, Rudge had insisted that she would bear full responsibility for the child, but full responsibility did not, apparently, entail parenting. Two days later, while discouraging Pound from visiting her ("There is no life or death reason why you should come here now"), she almost casually remarked, "I can't look after it, having no talent that way."[4]

She did not expect Pound to assume the child's rearing, but what she had in mind for the baby is hard to imagine. She had spent her confinement in Sirmione on Lago di Garde in complete seclusion, hiding her condition from even her closest friends. In April Pound had written to ask, "What am I to say re leoncina; where OFFICIALLY is she and what is she doing. I feel the reports shd. coincide."[5] Rudge had devised an elaborate set of ruses for each of her correspondents. To her father, who died in 1935 without knowing he had a grandchild, she wrote that she was only staying at the lake until her tenants left her Paris flat at the end of the summer. To George Antheil, her frequent musical partner who had professional reasons to know where she was, she intimated that she was having a frantic "affair" that was keeping her in Italy. For her good friend "Ramooh" (Renata Borgatti) she invented an elaborate itinerary: she was in Paris, then Rome, then back in Paris and "now" in England on a tour of the provinces. "The people in Paris" knew only that she had no definite address since she was "moving around the lake."[6] Pound agreed that it would be "imprudent" to explain things to Antheil "UNTIL one is ready to announce the matter in the Herald. STRANGE CASE of Lion cub, born in curious Circumstances."[7]

Having kept the curiosity of her friends and family at bay, Rudge's most pressing concern as she waited for the baby's arrival was another kind of deception: the falsification of documents. She had decided to claim that Arthur Rudge, the nineteen-year-old brother who had died in the Great War, was the child's father, and she was worried about the legal ramifications of making a false declaration. In June, Pound wrote a series of reassuring letters, suggesting that if she were caught by Italian authorities, she could somehow wiggle out of it. "Say they took you by surprise . . . or that you hadn't my permission. . . . All you appear to have done is to have declared a marriage that didn't happen and that has no relation to the product. THAT sant be a hanging offense." In the weeks that followed, he consulted Carlo Linati and continued to give Rudge advice. You can claim, he suggested, that you find that you don't have the proper certificates, that they might be in Paris, or that your "husband" still has them. He referred to his lover's supposed spouse as "E.R." (Edgar? Rudge) and wondered if Olga was going to "kill him off" as part of the imaginary (and obviously absent) identity, offering to write a letter saying that he had read about the "marito's" demise during a recent heat wave.[8]

But Rudge's concerns went beyond counterfeited paternity, for she was also worried about the child's nationality and its ability to get an American passport. On this matter, Pound was cavalier: "So long as it is IN Italy, it only needs passport to get out; and I don't think it had better get out, after all why leave Italy, I mean from its point of view." Later in the week, he was still insisting that nationality was insignificant: "I may be Italian myself by the time it wd. Matter."[9] For him the issue was not whether a piece of paper had false information, but whether one would hurt another person by "wishing it on someone who wasn't responsible." And he seemed also to think that the authorities would care only if the child eventually tried to claim a false inheritance. "That is WHY they have formalities, at least MOST law has property basis, and penalties are severe on THAT ground, NOT because the learned jurisconsults are shocked by bastardy."[10]

Having tried to allay Rudge's anxieties, he then made it clear that he was only participating in this masquerade for her sake. For his own part, he was willing to claim the child. On 9 June he wrote, "IF however, you want me to sign anything, perhaps better give em the 70 bis address," and he repeated this after he had gotten word from Carlo Linati, who apparently didn't respond clearly enough about the matter of false declaration. "Probably NOT his fault, as I went on to say that the padre was ready to declare himself." And he added that he could come to Bressanone if the declaration had to be made at the place of his child's birth.[11]

With motives known only to herself, Olga rejected Pound's willingness to declare paternity and identified herself on the birth certificate as Olga Stock (her grandmother's maiden name) and the father as Arthur Rudge. The authorities gave her no trouble in this respect, but they did need to record the infant's name immediately. Although she and Pound had corresponded for months about a name for the baby (Pound thought mythologically and phonetically, suggesting names like Polyxena, Calypso, Clymene, Alceste, Iseult), she also rejected his final suggestion ("ditta la Polyxena"). On 17 July, Pound was still in the dark, asking about "Polyxena or wottever 'er nyme iz," and he proposed that they discuss names in person if Olga didn't like any of his choices. The next day, Olga informed him that it was too late; the name M.Q.C. (Mary Quite Contrary) was official. "Yes very rude."[12]

She still didn't want to see him, though she did ask that Pound disguise his handwriting in various ways and send two or three letters of congratulations on the birth. When it was clear that the baby was improving with Frau Marcher's nursing, she began to consider the future. She met Pound's suggestion that they meet at Lago d'Iseo with incredulity ("does he expect her to travel with an infant?") and told him that the baby's health depended on remaining with her *contadina* until the end of August or "until I can find some other place for it." She didn't know where she herself would go—it might be in the Brixen region; it might be Paris; after that she might go to Ramooh or down to Capri.[13] Her primary concern now was to practice the violin and regain her figure so that she could return to the concert circuit.

It was in this way that the only daughter of Ezra Pound was left in a peasant's house high in the Dolomite Alps. It was midsummer; the wet nurse, Hanne Marcher, needed to return to her husband, farm, and the three-year-old-foster child whom she already tended. Olga Rudge went to Gais, a village in the Pustertal, inspected the house and thought the arrangement good enough. By mid-August, she was back in Paris, with Pound once again writing letters about her cover story ("When do you want him [George Antheil] to have your address?") and learning of his daughter's whereabouts only on 30 August. "So IT has arrived there [Gais]. Am sending it the money it want fer immediate."[14]

It never occurred to Mary de Rachewiltz that she had so lonely a beginning. In her autobiography, she represented the scene of her "homecoming" with her beloved father present, respectful and attentive to the peasants who were going to take charge of her for the foreseeable future. According to her, Pound looked at the "low, wood-paneled room, the black vaulted kitchen, the stable leading off from the entrance" and noted that the air was good and that one could hear the river and elm trees. He spoke rudimentary German, left a generous amount of Italian money, indicated that he wanted his daughter to grow big and strong—*gross, stark*—and left in a big, black car, promising to return in two months.[15]

But if other written documents are to be believed, nothing of the kind happened. Mary's memory was a conflation perhaps of other trips, perhaps of desire, perhaps of the kindness of adults creating stories for a child who hungered for legitimate origins and attention. Olga did return by herself at the end of October. She was at first furious with the Marchers, for she arrived during bread-making—a day of intense and focused labor in a Tyrolean household—and two-month-old Maria (as she was called) was not clean. She eventually regained her composure long enough to send Pound a postcard saying that "La mia leoncina sta benissima apparently—holds its head up for itself—needs bigger clothes, nearly bald—going to Brunnco to have its photo taken first time—country very fine up there with autumn coloring."[16] At the end of November Pound still did not even know that Gais was near Austria. He had to be told that one could pass it going to or coming from Vienna.[17]

II

What Ezra Pound said to his wife, Dorothy Shakespear, about the personal events unfolding in the Tyrol or what she surmised on her own is not recorded. A number of years later, Richard Aldington observed that Dorothy did not generally give the impression of "a woman who is hurt and offended by infidelity, but simply a pathetic *quelle morne soirée* feeling. Why should she object, merely because her husband had found the only trained musician in the world who would take his ridiculous vaporings and caperings seriously?"[18] But Mary remembered her mother saying that she would never have asked Pound to give her a child had she been the first woman to come between him and his wife. "It was Iseult [Gonne] that broke up the marriage, but Dorothy would have let herself die and Babbo then promised her mother, Olivia, always to take care of her. The story goes that Hope Shakespear would have also let himself die when Olivia wanted to leave him."[19] This account may get closer to the truth of Dorothy's real, if undisclosed desolation. In any event, she chose to leave her "capering" husband to his own devices. She spent the fall with her mother Olivia in Siena and then went to Egypt in December. On Christmas Eve Pound wrote to his father that "D[orothy] is in Cairo; sailed from Genoa Thursday December 17, arrived in Cairo Monday December 21."[20] She returned on 1 March. Pound summed up her trip by saying that she "has had about enough of Egypt." She was "somewhat worn

by trip; or at least desiccated with Egypt, and disliking sea travel." He did not
say that Olga had arrived in Rapallo on 11 December, nor did he report that
Dorothy's ultimate (vengeful, desperate, longing?) response to Olga's arrival,
Mary's birth, her husband's infidelity was not "hurt" or "pathos" but a life of
her own. She returned from Egypt pregnant.[21]

If Pound had waffled about the birth certificate of his daughter, offering
to sign papers but ultimately colluding with Olga's false declaration of Arthur Rudge as Mary's father, he did not do so with Dorothy's son. Or rather,
he colluded in a second declaration of paternity, this time with himself as the
falsely designated father.[22] Doubtless out of good motives, desiring to shield
Dorothy, perhaps with the same sangfroid that had led him to tell Olga that
a false piece of paper was not immoral unless it saddled someone with un-
just or unwanted responsibility, he claimed the boy as his own. On 11 September 1926, the day following this child's birth in the American Hospital in
Paris, he went to the Mairie at Neuilly where he wrote: "Omar, du sexe mas-
culine, de Ezra Pound . . . homme de lettres, et de Dorothy Shakespear . . .
Dressé le onze Septembre mil neuf cent vingt six, seize heures quinze, sur
déclaration du père . . . Ezra Pound."[23]

Rumors were rife in Paris, and no wonder. Pound was in the city, but it
was Ernest Hemingway who took Dorothy to the hospital in Neuilly. Pound
almost immediately returned to Rapallo alone. Dorothy remained in Paris
until she was well enough to travel; then she took the child to England where
her mother had arranged for it to have a nanny—a retired woman who lived
in Felpham in Sussex, a village near the sea to the east of Bognor Regis. Dorothy stayed away for a whole year, returning to Rapallo in September 1927.
T. S. Eliot watched at a distance and finally wrote to Ezra asking for "the main
facts regarding D. the child and yourself." W. B. Yeats, who continued to keep
in touch with Olivia Shakespear, first wrote to say that Dorothy would make
an excellent mother and then changed his tune on 24 September when he told
Olivia, "I divine that you have already adopted the grandchild."[24]

Pound had no interest in Dorothy's son—he did not even meet the boy
until he was twelve. They met only because Olivia Shakespear had died and
Pound went to England to dispose of her property. But one deception led
to another, as it would for the remainder of Mary and Omar's lives. One
can imagine a quid pro quo arrangement at the beginning: Pound trading his name for his wife's agreement that the boy would be raised by
someone else; Pound recognizing that one infidelity had provoked another.

But once uttered, these prevarications, which already had the force of law, acquired the force of fact, particularly with Pound's parents, Homer and Isabel Pound.

Pound offered them no outright lies in his letters to America, but neither did he level with them. Instead, he concocted a brew of insinuations, dissimulations, and omissions, which were impossible to decipher did one not already know the actual circumstances. Rather than say that his son had been born, he announced that the "next generation (male) arrived. Both D & it appear to be doing well."[25] Then, for several months, he distressed his parents by not mentioning Omar at all. At the end of November, in answer to their evident anxiety, he told them not to worry. "In any case no expected calamity ever arrives. Them that arrives is onexpected." And a few days later, he reassured them that Omar was not up for adoption. The baby had smiled, Pound wrote; he had cut a tooth . . . passing on news from Dorothy's letters from England as if she were sitting in the opposite chair with the infant at her breast. In response to a letter that seemed to indicate that they had surmised the truth, he merely responded, "If on the other hand your information is meant to indicate that the ancient neosaurian race that used to inhabit Wyncote about the years 1895 to 1900 is in the act of dying out, I can regard you as overly optimistic; much as I might like to accept the idea, I must insist on a wider survey."[26] He made no mention of Mary, whose existence he hid for years, while the elder Pounds continued in their mistaken belief that Omar was proof that their "ancient neosaurian race" continued to flourish.

Instead, on 7 January 1927 Pound wrote to Olga about other secret arrangements, saying, "His blood money is come! If she wants anything, she say SO." The next day he shared the money with her: "I enclose some of the fru-its of blackmail, in whopes that you won't get stranded."[27]

Before his daughter could take her first step, her life was hedged in complications that would have repercussions for generations. One Pound family group stood on legalities and relied upon the respectability of appearances; for them, paternity was what James Joyce called a "legal fiction."[28] The other had concocted its own legal fiction but insisted on a natural reality that preceded the requirements of law. This division between what is legal and what is true shaped Mary de Rachewiltz's sense of the structure of the world. It would take years for her to learn the facts about her origins. Once she did, she began to make the distinction between "'Babbo's' legal family and his moral family," but she did so with what Hugh Kenner would later call "impassioned reticence." In 1973 she admitted, "It will take generations to put an end to things started in feigning—to the despair of it."[29]

III

Coming to consciousness in Gais, Mary thought, simply, that she was Tyrolean. She called her foster parents Mamma and Tatte; their house was the only house she knew; their way of life was the first imprinted on memory. Olga later said that "the place seemed ideal for a small child . . . [except for] the dialect, [which] became an impossible barrier."[30]

She took a tourist's view of things. For centuries European travelers have seen the stunning side of the Tyrol. Johann Wolfgang von Goethe preceded Olga Rudge in appreciating the majesty of the mountains. In 1786, he wrote about his journey into the Alps from Innsbruck as entering a territory "more and more beautiful—no description can pay it justice."

> By well-prepared roads one climbs up a gorge which sends water down into the Inn, a gorge which offers the eye the most incredible variety. When the road passes right up close by a rock face or has even been carved out of it, one can see on the opposite side gentle slopes which are used for farming. Between fields and hedges on those high and broad plains stand villages, houses and huts, all painted white. But soon the picture changes: fields become meadows, until they in their turn merge into steep slopes. . . . Now it became darker and darker: the individual details lost themselves and the blocks became larger and more magnificent: finally, when everything before me seemed like a deep, mysterious picture, I suddenly caught sight of the snowcapped peaks, illuminated by the moon, and now I wait until the morning brightens that ridge which divides the North from the South.[31]

But no matter what beauty visitors experienced, the land was "ideal for a child" on its own terms: language is deep; children internalize landscapes, and the dialect was indicative of a distinctly Germanic worldview. Olga Rudge failed to see that she had committed her daughter not simply to a farm with good air, but to an array of values and attitudes, born of daily life in a harsh environment, peasant frugality, and more broadly from the South Tyrol's contested place in modern European politics.

Mary joined a household oriented to the movement of ice and sun and to the work of survival on a *Steilhang* or *Alm*—the high mountain inclines and meadows that give the Alps their name. "And I grew up like one of them and was ''s Sâma Moidile.'"[32] Hanne Marcher had already survived five stillbirths by the time Mary arrived to lie in the wicker baby carriage that had been prepared for their recently lost son. She was a devout woman, fond of reading—though her only books were *The Life of Christ* and *The Lives of the Saints*—and a prodigious storyteller. She had organized the life of her husband, restored a derelict house, seen to the installation of a new roof, and supplemented his meager income with good management and industry.

Over the years, perhaps as a way of coping with the loss of their own children, perhaps as a shrewd way to augment the family's income, the Marchers took in foster children, often illegitimate, for whom the state paid a small stipend. Eventually they raised seventeen abandoned infants, but at the time that Mary came, there was only one other, a three-year-old girl named Margherita. Margit saved her glass marbles; Mary lost them. From the beginning of consciousness, one child perceived her poverty and the other sensed a greater largesse from the monthly checks that arrived from her *Pessen Lait*—her wealthy people. That outsiders provided for her was clear; she didn't know who they were, and for a few years it was irrelevant. Her affections were for those who nurtured her and brought her into the life of high-mountain farming.

Jakob Marcher—Tatte—had fought as an Austrian against Italy in the Great War, had been wounded and finally dismissed with medals for valor. A straightforward, industrious man, pious, gregarious in the evenings, and apparently charismatic to children, he easily won the heart of his American charge. It was this father who gave her coins for sweets, carried her on his back, took her to the pub where she could fall asleep to village stories and brought her home again. For the early years of her life, she slept in the same bed with him, and, in later years, when she evaluated her heritage, it was not the absent *Pessen Lait* who made Mary feel rich, but Tatte, "because I could always count on [him]."[33]

He had a hard life with clear loyalties and deeply embedded values. As the sole inheritor of his family's farm, his existence was bound to an agricultural cycle, and at the heart of this cycle, measured by the farmer's almanac, were planting, sowing, cutting wood, and breeding animals. The steep terrain of the Alps dictated that all these activities entailed lifting and carrying. He carried hay, animals, manure, water, wood, cheeses, bread, children, and responsibility for the welfare of everyone in his household, and did so with a shattered hand, shrapnel in his back, and good grace.

Mary Rudge's earliest memories were bound to the basic things of Jakob and Hanne Marcher's existence. She grew up in a sturdy *Stube* with an enclosed tile fireplace built out into the room. She ate at a square corner table under a crucifix decorated with wheat. She was accustomed to oak or larch pine paneling and carved ceilings; she sat on wooden benches around the edges of the room or near the fire. The kitchen was dark and smoky, but it served for the preservation and storage of bacon or ham, fruit, potatoes, and rye bread. The attic lofts and barns were filled with farm implements, sleighs, baskets, plows, equipment for weaving wool or flax, equipment for making dairy products. From her mother she learned legends, superstitions, a deep spirituality, and respect for the observances of the Catholic Church. She came to understand the central importance of bread, butter, and smoked meats, and as she grew, she participated in making all of them. Her father raised her to understand gardening and the care of animals. Eventually, when Ezra Pound began to visit her, Tatte showed her off by letting her take the reins of the horses or balance heavy, manure-laden wheelbarrows across rutted fields, but behind each hard-won skill was something more general and deeply engrained: she grew into a child, who like the villagers she lived among, was attuned to the necessities of climate, movement on high slopes, and the dangers and beauties of living in the lee of glacial peaks.

In July 1927, Pound went to visit her, reporting to Olga that "Have now seen it under the WORST . . . circumstances."[34] The two-year-old was sick; he rushed her to a doctor, but remained only two hours—even by his own judgment too short a time to stay. He returned nine months later, in April 1928, bearing a small violin that was a gift from Olga. The violin was unwelcome— the little girl banged it around. At three she already preferred the simple tunes that her foster sister sang so beautifully. Olga went for several weeks in the summer of 1927, staying at the Hotel de la Poste; she returned to the hotel in January 1928, and in the interim they wrote letters discussing their child's character.

Mary was apparently a wayward ("quite contrary") girl, which Pound attributed to her genes. "Waal I 'spose someone'll have to smack it, but Lord knoze-oo. The kussink and swearink is, as you say, hereditary. If it adds your stubbornness to my kussedness, it will be a remarkable character."[35] Olga responded with an anecdote that she understood to be indicative of the girl's strong will. Hanne Marcher had told her about a day when no one knew where Mary was. They found her sitting on a nest in the hen house, oblivious to the people calling for her. "When scolded for not answering her call, Mary said, 'How can I? I am a hen—when I have laid my egg, I will cluck!'"[36] Olga interpreted this as a sign of her daughter's imperious nature: "the Leoncina makes F. Marcher do just what she wants—won't do anything if someone suggests it—*which is like Him*." With less of the feeling that had led her to want the child of an artist whom she lionized, she might have regarded this behavior as the sign of her daughter's imaginative entry into the natural life that surrounded her or as a way of expressing her knowledge that small creatures need mothers who stay with them or even as a displaced way of acting out her early sense of having been "hatched" in an alien world, but Olga Rudge remained oblivious to the consequences of her own absence. In her eyes, Mary was the daughter of an American poet and a violinist, temperamental because they were temperamental, high-handed because it was her due.

With all their cosmopolitan experience of the world, neither of them considered their daughter the product of her Tyrolean upbringing. But she could hardly have been anything else. By November 1929, when Mary was four, Rudge wrote that no one had even laid eyes on the girl for a year and a half. "I've got to do *something* about the Leoncina—either to go there or have her come. . . . I have been putting it off and putting it off . . . no reason why she should suffer for my complexes. . . . She is of [an] age to understand grown-up conversations, to get it into her head that she is abandoned, different—not healthy ideas to grow up on. *It's a year and a half since anyone has seen the child*, and I have been in Italy most of that time. . . . I only want to be sure in the most selfish manner that duty to offspring not going to lose the amante."[37]

While her parents struggled to define their relationship—the mother fearing that her child's very existence posed a threat to her uncertain bond with Pound—Mary trailed around fields oblivious to their turmoil. She helped in the stables, kept a black lamb, and grew to understand that wealth is measured in useful things rather than money. By the time she was twelve, she could explain exactly how to grow hay, dry it, turn it, and gather it in. She knew the dangers posed to ricks by untimely rain, how high the stakes should be that held them, the proper circumference of each sheaf. She understood how to bundle and bind wheat, separate the grain from the chaff, and how animals were fed with the residue. Her life was divided into the levels of alpine meadow that successively sheltered cattle, until, in late summer, young people ascended into the highest meadows to oversee hundreds of grazing beasts and make butter and cheese from their milk. Speaking of the life of an unkempt young man named Giovanni, she observed, "Can there be a life simpler than this? But he is always happy and healthy, sings and plays and amuses himself more with his cattle than a gentleman at his sport."[38] She had already internalized the reversed prejudices of her mountaineering class with its contempt for untested people of leisure.

In 1929, perhaps as a response to Olga Rudge's letter, perhaps because changed circumstances made it possible, Pound brought his father, Homer, to Gais to meet his four-year-old granddaughter. The elder Pounds had just moved from Philadelphia to Rapallo. Homer had retired from his job with the United States Mint, and his father, as Pound reported to Olga, was "duly and properly pleased at nooz of his granddaughter . . . said he hoped when he passed on he would be able to leave something."[39] The three generations had their photograph taken together in Bruneck, but otherwise the visit was kept a secret. At Christmas the two men had decided that Pound's mother Isabel was "not yet sufficiently Europeanized" to adjust to the news of an illegitimate grandchild. Indeed, Homer said that "she'd take the next boat back" if she were told.

As Mary was told the story, doubtless by Jakob Marcher, the adults talked about farming techniques, Homer drawing on his experiences in rural Wisconsin to indicate through elaborate gestures that American cattlemen clipped the horns of their livestock. Pound translated in rudimentary German and somehow the Tyrolese dialect *Puschtrerisch* was overcome enough for them to establish camaraderie. But though Marcher retold the tale with quiet good will—tinged with a peasant's skepticism about the theory that short horns helping to produce more milk—the visit caused consternation. It was clear to the Marchers that Pound wanted his father's advice about what to do about "the Leoncina" and that their home was not good enough for his daughter. They had grown to love Mary and sensed that her life with them was threatened. Homer, to their great relief, thought that the child was too young to be separated from Hanne. "It would kill her. The plant is too tender to be uprooted."[40]

To Mary, the visit conferred "a sense of stability." In her own words, "the Herr and the Frau were difficult to figure out, but a Grossvater you do not conjure up out of nowhere. It means there is a background."[41] She took comfort from it and cherished a porcelain doll that Homer brought as a gift. But if the visit was revelatory, it was also clandestine, pivotal both for what it established as well as for what remained hidden. Pound did not tell his father that Olga Rudge was Mary's mother, nor did he use this occasion to disclose that

Omar was not really his son. Homer returned to Rapallo with his secret, though as subsequent letters reveal, he had no idea that Pound was still not leveling with him. Ten years later on the eve of the United States' entry into World War II, when he finally learned the truth, he wrote:

Aug 3
My Dear Son
A clap of thunder out of a clear sky could not have been more startling than yours and D's letters.

For 10 years we have been here. D[orothy] has been giving us Omar's photos & it is hard to realize the truth. Why did you suggest our remaining? As matters have developed there is no pleasure in our continuing here. We shall arrange to depart-

Your Old Dad[42]

Isabel's response, coming from complete ignorance, put the emotional matter even more succinctly:

July 30/39
Dear Son
The situation is to me amazing—*one disloyalty provokes another but why continue the deception* so many years. *One can not transfer affection—*

Why be rude to your Mother, when we meet in Rapallo or elsesswhere?

y-v-t

Mother[43]

After fourteen years of mystification, the truth could not abridge affections already given nor restore relationships never established.

IV

When Mary was four, Johanna Marcher brought her down from the mountains for her first visit to Venice. The previous fall, in 1928, Olga had combined money given to her by her father, a prosperous businessman from Youngstown, Ohio, with a gift from her friend Renata Borgatti to buy a house in the Dorsodoro. The house was very, very small, located on the calle Querini—a cul-de-sac near the church of Santa Maria della Salute. It had once been a worker's house, more recently in the possession of an American expatriate, Dorothea Watts. It wasn't much to look at; the paint was peeling; it was in an out-of-the-way place, but Olga later remarked that the house changed her life. Although she had long had access to her mother's rue Chamfort apartment in Paris, she used it intermittently, especially since she often relied on income from leasing it to others. Venice was her first commitment to a place, to a settled life, and at first she hoped it would lure Pound away from Rapallo. It was not to be.

When she approached him about the subject—her idea was that Pound's friend Adrian Stokes could buy the adjacent house and offer Pound the use of a studio in it—he declined. "I could put [in] a chattière, and give you double entrance and exit, very convenient for comédie Venetienne,"[44] she suggested. But Pound didn't bite. "He thinks next step after pied-á-terre is really LARGE CAGE. . . . he ain't goin' to have his cage in a cellar, he don't care WOTT it is nex' to . . . however, he will endeavor to visit the Queen of the Adriatic."[45]

In the end the house next door didn't matter to her. She desperately wanted a place of her own that she would never have to rent out; she wanted to practice the violin; she wanted not to be a perpetual houseguest. She went ahead. Then, amid all the preparations for moving in, Pound wrote that he wasn't coming for a visit; indeed, he implied that he might never come: "I think you'd be happier if you'd get me out of your mind for awhile. . . . I should think there might be something brighter to think of . . . he wishes her a gran bel nuovo amante . . . it is a rotten idea her sitting round waiting for him to come."[46] Three days later he spelled out his view more fiercely, calling her a fool and a vampire. "You have a set of values I don't care a damn for. I do not care a damn about private affairs, private life, personal interests. You do. It is perfectly right that you should, but you can't drag me into it."[47]

Olga responded with defiance, defending her need to work in peace and reminding Pound of the cost of her peripatetic life: "She has tried to adapt herself to other people's situations and *failed*. . . . She is now trying to make circumstances suit *her* needs, but He is not interested."[48] Within two months, her self-assertion had turned to entreaty. She felt as if she were being thrown away. To her pleas for understanding, Pound responded with another brush-off—get a younger man; forget about me. And on they went, airing their resentments, the married man casting off responsibility, the mistress railing at her exclusion: "The *monde* of 'Mr. and Mrs. E.P.'—only people who can tell a good anecdote of the 1890s admitted. . . . You should have a nice crowd of Bolsheviks to break up all the smug people you have around, who talk about 'artistes.' . . . I shall bring the Leoncina up illiterate, let your damn Omar have the '90s."[49]

Ten months later, unaware of the explosive prelude to their journey, Mary and Johanna Marcher boarded a train, both excited and worried about the ten-hour trip ahead of them. The girl entertained the other first-class passengers by tying a curtain strap around their necks and calling them cows—*Kuh-Kui*. When she met Olga, she called her mother a *sella Fock*—a sow—because she thought her bare legs immodest. Frau Marcher tried to smooth things over, saying simply, *Nix Strumpf*—no stockings—but when Olga let her touch her legs, she thought the nylons were made of glass. Other of her mother's civilized customs struck her as equally mysterious. She saw no need to wear gloves if the weather was mild; she had contempt for vegetables—thought them fit food for the pigs. Restaurant water appalled her. "In Gais one was very fussy about water, always had to go to the main fountain for a pitcher of spring water before meals. But it seemed to be part of my education to drink foul water and wear gloves."[50]

The trip, of course, was intended to begin a kind of reclaiming, to wean Mary from Gais and introduce her to the world of her parents. What they had not anticipated was their young daughter's ambivalence about the new aspects of her identity. By this point she understood that Olga and Pound were *die richtigen Eltern*—the "right" parents, but beyond that she knew nothing about them except what she saw and what she heard in Hanne Marcher's voluble retelling of her impressions when she got home. To both, there was danger, foolishness, and enchantment to the city. They were homesick, afraid of falling into the ocean, worried about Olga's open, unprotected fires. Hanne Marcher spent countless hours crying and doing the rosary in the adjacent church instead of taking her charge walking on the Zattere.

Despite their anxieties, none of the animosity that had preceded their visit was apparent. Pound was there, conciliatory, gentle; Olga, whom Mary now called Mamile, seemed "majestic and beautiful like a queen." They placed the girl on a high blue armchair on cushions and a leopard skin. In her memoirs, Mary described the house in a way that no four-year-old could have perceived it, but it gives us an excellent sense of how Olga Rudge lived and the world she wanted her daughter to enter . . . a world of taste, correctness, and the modest elegance that poverty could manage. To the child, it was a place of veneration—from the yellow and ocher tones of the walls to the velvet couch on which her mother slept, to the exotic objects that adorned shelves and walls. There were mirrors, a kimono, and Japanese shoes; a jewel-studded silver bird; a bright glass star hung from the ceiling. "And on the studio bookcase the great Ovid bound in wooden boards and the marble bas-relief of Isotta da Rimini set in the wall by the desk." Later she recognized that Pound commemorated Olga's "care in contriving" in *The Cantos* (Canto LXXVI), but from the beginning it was to her a place of "learning, wisdom and harmony." It was also, of necessity, a house of "tense symbols."[51]

Two years later, Olga brought her there again, this time without Pound, but Adrian Stokes was visiting and thanked Olga for being able to meet the "Young Lioness." The high blue armchair was replaced by a new bed that Olga remembered had to be hauled up through the first-floor window; her daughter remembered being "pretty and pink on pink sheets, with golden hair on a pink pillow, gazing starry-eyed at the most beautiful young man she had ever seen before (or since?). But her dark infant soul held some grudge against the female parent."[52]

What was she to read from this setting? Its very existence made her life into a cipher. If this was her parents' world, what was her place in it?

She had no idea it was *not* their world, but a life stolen briefly from real time. It was a secret retreat from the forlorn solitude of the mother and the respectable and comfortable marital arrangements of the father. In the parlance of *die richtigen Eltern*, it was a "Hidden Nest," hidden until this point from the already hidden nest in which they had let their child grow up.

V

At home Mary spoke *Puschtrerisch*; at school she was forced to speak Italian, a fact that locates her childhood in the turbulence of modern European history. All the men whom Mary knew in Gais, with one exception, had fought for Austria in the Great War, unaware that their fate had been sealed in a London secret agreement in 1915. There, on 26 April, the Entente powers had promised the South Tyrol to Italy in return for entering the war on their side.[53] Thus, in 1919, when the mayors of all the South Tyrolean cities and villages presented U.S. President Woodrow Wilson with a petition asking for help, he turned a deaf ear. Although the Tyrol was already occupied and under a military administration that the German-speakers of the district experienced as draconian, Wilson ceded the South Tyrol to Italy "without provisions for autonomy or minority protection."[54] The Saint Germain treaty was ratified in the Viennese National Assembly on 6 September 1919, where Eduard Reut-Nicolussi gave an impassioned speech anticipating the violent consequences of this action:

> In the face of this treaty, we say with every fiber of our being, with rage and pain: No! An eternal, irrevocable No! . . . In South Tyrol, a desperate struggle will now begin for each farm, each townhouse, each vineyard. This will be a struggle utilizing all the weapons of the mind and all the means of politics. And it will be a desperate struggle because we—a quarter of a million Germans—are being pitted against 40 million Italians in what is truly not a battle of equals.[55]

He was right, although not in ways that he could anticipate. The Fascist struggle for control of Italy culminated in a March on Rome at the end of October 1922. Earlier that month Mussolini had delivered a speech in which he made clear that he would tolerate no resistance from the people who inhabited the Tyrolean farms, houses, and vineyards that Reut-Nicolussi held so dear. He said, as the *Piccolo Posto* reported: "A big job awaits us, one that must be done with tremendous energy. Germanism must be eradicated from the soul just as its physical manifestations have been obliterated. This region must become Italian, and its inhabitants must become Italians, so that everything here is Italian and brings to mind only Italy."[56]

There followed an elaborate plan for the eradication of German culture in South Tyrol, its features assembled by Ettore Tolomei, who, for some reason, had made this project his life's work. On 15 July 1923, he announced his thirty-two *Provvedimenti per l'Alto Adige*. He itemized the things to be Italianized: German place names, public signs, street signs, German family names. He listed the organizations that would be disbanded, including Tyrolean newspapers; he mandated that all German bureaucrats would be dismissed, that Italian would become the language of official government business and all civil and criminal court proceedings, that the Brenner border would be closed to all persons on whom Italian citizenship had not been conferred, even that the monument to Walther von der Vogelweide would be removed from Bozen. All German banks and German-held mortgages were to be eliminated, and for each institution that was dismantled, an Italian version would be constructed and subsidized. All these measures would be enforced by increasing the strength of the carabinieri and general military presence in the area. By 8 August, even the use of the name "Tyrol" was prohibited. In the last issue of *Der Tiroler* before the ban went into effect, one writer bade farewell to the world that he knew: "Now commences a new beginning; at the end those who are not especially well disposed to us expect us to be displaced as a people and uprooted from our homeland."[57] These measures were not all implemented at once, but by the time Mary was born, Italian was mandatory on all levels of federal, provincial, and local government, and it was the only permissible language in courts of law and in schools.

"Only permissible" were the operative words, for the Marcher family unhesitatingly lived the lives established by their language, their land, and their culture. It is not that they were openly rebellious, but they, along with almost everyone whom Mary knew, still longed vaguely for the return of a kaiser. Living under a government imposed by treaty, they came to distrust bureaucracy and to shield their real allegiances with silence. Mary remembered her father being beaten by Blackshirts for not saluting the Italian flag— it had never crossed his mind since it was not *his* flag. She remembered Tatte boxing her ears in front of a road sweeper simply because he was an employee of the Italian government—she had thrown stones at a signpost and Herr Marcher had to make a show of being a strict parent. But she, along with all the neighborhood children, was sent to a "catacomb school"—one of many clandestine schools that were set up by unemployed teachers and priests with the support of Canon Michael Gamper after the passage of the new school regulations that forbade teaching German. He recognized the Fascist goal of raising a young generation of Italians "in our land as quickly as possible." Now, he said "we have to imitate the early Christians. When they were no longer safe from persecution while holding religious services in public, they withdrew to the privacy of their own homes. . . . And when they were not safe from harassment even there, they found refuge among the dead in the underground burial chambers, in the catacombs."[58]

Mary's school was in an out-of-the-way house whose owners were "notoriously unfriendly to strangers." The girls took handwork with them; the boys carried carpentry tools, and all were instructed to wipe their slates clean and pretend they were working if anyone entered the room. Even to children, the political implications of learning the Gothic alphabet were clear, and those who participated were sworn to utter secrecy. The burden placed on these students was considerable. Claus Gatterer, a South Tyrolean journalist, later spoke about its effect on identity: "We were torn, and our cover-up was lies—at home, we lied about school; in school, we lied about home and about our-selves."[59]

Mary swore herself to another kind of secrecy, for she sensed that Olga would disapprove of what she was doing. In Venice, she had to speak Italian and Pound was chided for helping her out with his rudimentary German. Her parents spoke English to each other, even in her presence, and so unwittingly they became part of a larger cultural pattern, joining the schools, the gov-ernment, and the law courts in trying to Italianize a child whose enthusiasms were undividedly Tyrolean. In personal as well as national life, language had become the vehicle for claiming her loyalty, as if by forcing a new speech pat-tern one could overwrite identity, wiping out a mother and a mother tongue in one gesture. Denied the freedom even to call their country *Südtirol* (it was now officially known as *Alto Adige*), they internalized their loyalties. As a writer from the *Innsbrucker Nachrichten* wrote in 1923, "If those who rule the Tyrolean south believe that they can completely eradicate the name of our land by the stroke of a pen, then their power may perhaps succeed in obliterating the letters in writing and in print, but this will merely burn the name of Tyrol that much hotter and deeper into the hearts of the Tyroleans."[60]

The child's impulse to hide her secret schooling was not mistaken, for Olga Rudge's own loyalties were unmistakably with Mussolini, and she was quick to send her daughter a Fascist school uniform. For the Marcher family, it was *Tumma Tanz*—nonsense, but Mary welcomed the black-and-white out-fit as a new dress—part of the paraphernalia of an educational experience she did not take too seriously. Like all school children in the Tyrol, she was registered as a member of the Fascist Party, and she was made *Capo Piccole Italiane*—the leader of the girls' Fascist group. "It was not," she wrote, "a matter of choice or of merit."[61] She learned the *giuramento fascista* and Ital-ian songs on Saturdays, but she and the others who participated found ways to undermine the loyalties supposed by the instruction; indeed, their religion compelled them to undermine it, for their catechism had taught them that to swear falsely is a deadly sin. The kids recited the oath, but with a *non* slipped in under their breath: "In the name of God and Italy I swear *not* to serve my country faithfully." Dissembling had become a way of life necessitated by the Italian usurpation of public life. At home, school learning was dismissed as nonsense both because it was recognized as propaganda and because it lacked practical application.

She continued to take seriously what was practical and what was sacred. Indeed, these aspects of life were intertwined both in imagination and in

fact. Religious practice and religious instruction were the only exceptions
Mussolini made to the ubiquitous requirement of using the Italian language;
and as Mary had surmised by the time she was twelve, the celebrations of
the Church and the secular customs of the high mountains were all rituals of
renewal that preceded, surpassed, and evaded the temporary impositions of
political regimes.

In 1937, having impressed the idea of cultural relativism on his daughter,
Pound asked her to write down what she found distinctive about her upbringing in Gais. In a thirty-eight-page essay that Pound later translated and had
published, the girl revealed a psychology rooted in pragmatism, shrewdness,
and careful judgment of use value. She described Christian and pagan festi-
vals and superstitions—the *Kirchtamichl*—centered around an effigy "born
in great secrecy" through whose defense the village asserted its strength—
the Nigglas play, which enacted the expulsion of the Devil by Saint Nikolaus
and his angels on 7 December—the customs of Easter, and the Catholic li-
turgical year. Entitled "The Beauties of the Tirol," the essay is not about nature's grandeur, but an astute evaluation of peasant life. It contains no
description of Gais as a place; there is no encomium to the majesty of the Alps.
Beauty to her is human beauty as revealed in custom and work and the endurance of hardship. People are identified both by their function—one is a
priest, one a beekeeper, one is hired out to haul and saw wood, another is
the oldest son of a motherless family with special obligations usually accorded to a woman—and by the number of children living and dead in
their family unit. They are understood by their pragmatism or lack of it; they
are recognized to be almost uniformly poor and under the obligation to earn
their bread.

Although Pound may have encouraged this exercise to foster his child's
ability to see her life in perspective, it is unambiguously the writing of an insider, explaining her way of life to someone who would otherwise not see its
contours. She knows the adults in her world because they help her; she understands the effect of the dead children from the household she lives in. In
these years Hanne Marcher had another, her sixth, stillbirth. Mary wrote,
"But the loss of a soul was more unbearable than the loss of a life. To comfort
Mamme, a nun gave it emergency baptism before removing the little corpse to
a box of sawdust in the hospital morgue. . . . 'Don't cry,' [I kept repeating
to Mamme], 'You have a little angel in heaven.' . . . Yet, the tears that Tatte
surreptitiously wiped off with his crippled hand during the rapid funeral
next morning made me wonder about God's fairness."[62]

Into this world, and all that is implied by Mary's saying that "And I grew up like one of them and was 's Sâma Moidile'" came letters, injunctions, and visits that unsettled her sense of belonging. "To me," she wrote, "those letters were on the whole vaguely disturbing, for whenever I behaved like the rest of the village urchins, which was usual, I would hear: *sham de*—fie!— your people don't pay for you to grow up like a *Strousnraba!*"[63] But by the time she was seven, these interruptions had come often enough for her to have a sense of what she lacked as well as what she had. In 1932, she made her First Communion. She wore the dress that Olga herself had worn as a child, but Olga was not there. At Christmas of that year, no one visited her. Pound wrote only that "Her Xmas present had to be sent back cause it wuzzz wrong, & heaven knows if she will get it at all."[64] Hanne Marcher finally wrote to Olga, "The child cries so much she might even die if they don't come."[65]

Pound finally did come on 4 September 1933, bringing Homer with him again. Against the neglect implied by Mary's incessant crying, he offered her one day of company: "Leoncina and I had lovely walk in a porfik day." Olga visited with Renata Borgatti a few days later, on 10 September. They brought Mary to a hotel in Merano, where she was mercifully, and strategically, well-behaved. She had no idea of the importance of her decorum, for with no official papers, it was only her demeanor that persuaded the hotel owner to stop "asking embarrassing questions [and] let the matter be." After nine years, having done nothing to clarify the legal situation of her daughter, Olga finally began to worry about the consequences of the falsified documents that had recorded Mary's birth—a matter that would preoccupy her for the next several years as the political tensions in Italy and in Europe continued to rise.

The following year, spending her Christmas once again with her friends the Richardses at Hook Heath in England, Olga read in the papers that "some ten thousand desertions were reported in the Tyrol." In January 1935, she wrote to Pound asking him to see if Mary was safe. "Expect mostly lies, still she wishes He would write Leoncina and tactfully ascertain whether all quiet there, if not could just keep her at Sant' Ambrogio, or put her to the Ursulines [nuns' school]."[66] By 18 December, still brooding over Mary's legal status, she came up with another scheme, mercifully never carried out, to compound falsehood with falsehood by getting a "certificate at the consulate in Paris stating that she was the sister of Arthur Rudge, and thus Mary's *aunt* and legal guardian."[67]

At this point, the "desertions reported in the Tyrol" that set off these schemes had nothing to do with Italy's invasion of Abyssinia or other rumblings of war, but with the lingering unrest and real distress occasioned by the Fascists' tenaciously held plan to denationalize the northern mountains. Their efforts to reclaim the land had continued unabated through Mary's childhood until even primogeniture—the system of handing down family farms in undivided units through the eldest sons—was threatened. In 1929, the ERA (Ente di rinascita agraria per le Tre Venezie) became autonomous in its mission to take over operations from farmers who were forced to give up their land during the Depression. Mussolini's aim was to facilitate the migration of Italians to the region, to "conquer the soil" by breaking up parcels of land, and through this imposed division to make economic survival impossible for South Tyrolean farmers. In the 1930s these efforts were supplemented by massive importation of Italian laborers into the Bozen Industrial zone, by the complete dismantling of the Austrian Civil Law Code and even by the destruction of the Walther Monument, since the Italians considered Walther von der Vogelweide a symbol of Germanness. The "desertions" that Olga Rudge noted were undoubtedly the result of these attempts to break up a traditional way of life, but the Tyroleans who survived this onslaught responded with renewed resistance, until the entire region was awash in propaganda and counterpropaganda. Later in life, looking back on her difficult relations with her daughter, Olga Rudge wrote, "the differences between Mary and me grew out of the difference of race she absorbed with Frau Marcher's milk,"[68] but Mary's opposition to her mother's attempts to make her into an Italian "lady" had as much to do with the alignments of history as it had to do with the sad and kindly woman who had offered an ailing child her breast.

Eventually, with Hitler's assumption of power in Germany in 1933, this oppositional dynamic acquired more complicated and more sinister implications, for Germany no longer denoted a simple fatherland, although it continued to suggest custom and language to the South Tyroleans. Mary lived in one of the very few parts Europe where the German search for *Lebensraum* could possibly carry positive connotations and, indeed, hope. When the referendum in the Saarland on reunification with the German Reich was held in 1935, bonfires were lit in the mountains over Gais, and people began to say *Heute die Saar—wir übers Jahr* ("Today the Saar, next year it's our turn").

When "their turn" came, as it did in 1939, it was no liberation, but a radical, bitter choice, engineered primarily by Hermann Göring. Once again the Tyrol was to be sacrificed to European politics. According to an agreement made between Mussolini and Hitler, its inhabitants could choose either to opt for German citizenship, in which case they would have to resettle outside of the Tyrol, or they could retain Italian citizenship and continue to face the cultural, economic, and legal encroachments that had dogged them since 1919. Today we would call this drastic relocation plan "ethnic cleansing"; in 1939 the Nazis referred to it as "human resource deployment," and its implementation caused scars that were as deep as the choice was extreme. As Rolf Steininger put it, "The bitter alternative [the Option] was either to betray one's Germanness by staying or to betray one's homeland by going; to resettle to the German Reich or a territory that Germany had conquered, or to remain in the increasingly Italianized homeland under the constant threat of being resettled 'south of the Po.' The overwhelming majority of the South Tyroleans (approximately 86 percent) became 'goers'; the 'stayers' were simultaneously accused of treason."[69]

Jakob and Hanne Marcher chose to stay; but it is against this tumultuous background that the young Mary Rudge faced options that were much closer to the bone. As her yearly trips to Venice continued, she had to establish a relationship with the *Pessen Lait* who had given her the Tyrolean life that they seemed increasingly to undermine. They were all that separated her from being a *Schlumpe*, with its connotations of being "unwanted; outsider and charity"—in this sense she wanted her parents—but they were strangers.

VI

In a preface for a new edition of *Discretions* in 2004, Mary de Rachewiltz wrote that her memoir was "a dialogue with my country (USA) and with my parents, intended to honor their genius and their courage, as well as testifying to the good sense and devotion of the couple who raised me. Different qualities of affection formed my memory."[70] This discrimination and generosity undoubtedly characterize the seventy-nine-year-old woman who sought to put her life in perspective, but the process of sorting out these affections was far from smooth. The child was both pragmatic and perceptive and she picked up on emotional cues. In her first visits, before she learned Italian, she was forced to rely on facial expressions to understand anything about her experiences in Venice, which usually occurred in September of every year.

Intuitively she adored Pound and was afraid of Olga. "Perhaps I disliked her," was her judgment in her forties: "An incomprehensible entity with a grudge, a dark resentment as though I were permanently doing her wrong."[71]

She felt clumsy, inarticulate, and as if she was a permanent disappointment. Even reading stories together with her mother brought the tensions of an examination, as if she were expected to know the meaning of English words that were unintelligible. "I never felt safe," she recalled. She was simply around in the mornings—Pound went across to the other side of the Canal to write in a room rented from Signora Scarpa—and forced to take a siesta on the third floor in the afternoons. The room was austere; she felt trapped in it; the only books were in languages she couldn't read. She was punished for defacing a bas-relief of Ixotta. The prank was fostered by sheer boredom: she liked the effect, but Olga was furious, and her father regarded it as a "profound indication" (Canto X). He alone seemed to recognize the resentments that the young girl could not express—even a mild deracination from the "uprooting" that was implied by her presence. "The room downstairs where the sounds came from was on another planet of floating colors and sounds, a choking huge cloud. A wall as thick and impenetrable as the one facing my window—the long, high wall of the Dogana—separated me from Gais, from a ground to stand on."[72]

The lunchtime arrival of her father brought liberation, fresh air, compliments from strangers about her blond hair, and the pleasures of collecting foods in the shops and open-air markets. Pound treated her companionably, teaching her how to choose the best fruits, vegetables, chocolates, and coffees. Their walks gave Olga time to practice the violin, whose sound "precise, passionate" would greet them on their return along with a "Miao," which was their private welcome.

To discover the nature of her father's art was more difficult, for she had almost no idea what "writing" was. Gradually she sensed that it was not limited to a desk or a series of hours but was a vocation—to her a kind of companion who would call for her father's attention, even when walking. She remembered how he would grow pensive. "Inherent in his silence was suspense, a joyous sense of expectation, until he broke into a kind of chant that sometimes went on for hours." Pound would hum "as though some alien power were rumbling in the cave of his chest in a language other than human"; he would grab for some paper, tear out a newspaper clipping, write in the margins of a book. Eventually she would identify this interior world as "Le Paradis," recognizing that it was here that Pound lived most fully "For a flash, for an hour" (Canto XCII). She became familiar with her father's trance, understood that her role was to be quiet when he went into it, and later, much later, believed with bitter vehemence that the accidents of all their lives were as nothing to the order of this sacred place of creation. "It has taken his Herculean labors through *Rock-Drill* and *Thrones* to make it "cohere" according to The Law, even if our lives, on the surface, do not cohere."[73]

For the middle years of her childhood, there was certainly to be no coherence. She went back and forth to Gais, engrossed, busy, and alternately resentful of leaving and curious about what lay beyond the mountains. One slender thread of integration was provided by Pound's growing interest in her rural life, an interest that the Marchers encouraged. They prepared an *Öberstube*—a separate upstairs room for Pound and Olga. Pound used it; Olga did not. Pound decided he wanted to buy a field for his daughter, and though he, Homer Pound, and Jakob Marcher had tried to communicate in rudimentary ways about farming, he did not understand what he was asking. There was the difference between an *Acker*—a unit of measurement—and a *Weise*—a naturally occurring expanse—and in any case, the system of primogeniture ensured that both were likely to be entailed in ancient family holdings. That plan shifted to something more manageable: buying sheep for Mary to tend on the condition that she keep track of the economics of raising them; then helping his daughter become a beekeeper. Whatever the explosiveness of his character in other circumstances, he was a gentle, patient father who took the time to inquire about his daughter's world and to understand, without rancor, that her affections were dispersed, especially after the Marchers took in a small boy named Loisl, for whom Mary felt a particular attachment. When she expressed *Heimweh*—homesickness—during one of her visits to Venice—wanting Loisl, wanting to help with the heavy fall harvest, he arranged for her to return to Gais. The aloofness, the emotional detachment that distressed Olga, seemed more in tune with his child's natural temperament; he understood her pragmatism, and she, in turn, responded to this courtesy with adoration.

With her mother, relations never seemed to improve. Her father saw strength in his sturdy daughter; her mother saw stolid, rough manners and lack of breeding. "So, I was growing into a problem: a clumsy pigheaded peasant instead of a graceful bright sprig."[74] When Pound told her that Mary wanted to return home to Loisl, "the room filled with repulsion and hostility. A solid blackness. She started to cry." Neither then, nor later, did Mary empathize with, or even really understand, her mother's feelings. To her they were "a mere bundle of discriminations"; she associated tears with "real pain: losing a baby, physical suffering, cold and hunger. What were these deeper bruises from phantoms and feelings? *La machine infernale.*" She understood that she had misspoken in wanting to go back to Gais, but she also sensed that her father should somehow have smoothed over the rejection that Olga felt. "An uncomfortable inkling that my trust had been betrayed."[75]

In 1935, Mary met James Laughlin, then a tall recent Harvard graduate. He, Pound, Olga, and John Slocum stopped to pick her up on their return from a trip to Salzburg and the Tyrolean town of Wörgl. She had her picture taken in a dirndl, donned goggles for the ride to Venice in a rented car, and promptly got a crush on Jas, who spoke to her in German and Italian, carried her on his shoulders into the Lido, and sent her beautifully illustrated books from America. No one in Gais could read *Celtic Legends* or *The Arabian Nights*, but they appreciated the pictures, and Mary puzzled over the meaning of Laughlin's greeting to her, "Dear Princess" (*Cara principessa*), and "love from Jas." "I fancied," she wrote, "the letter and the books were a key to my future, perhaps to my origin." The following summer Olga set her straight— "love" was "affection" and "princess" a term of endearment for a young girl, but her response reveals the questions that hovered around her identity and her place in "that other planet, stationed in Venice" that undercut the firm ground of Gais.

Emissaries from that world continued to arrive. Pound brought her along when he and George Tinkham revisited Monte Grappa, where Tinkham had fought in the Great War. To the girl the whole visit was confusing, for she recognized the landscape through the "myth of Tatte's heroism" as a beloved place that was defended and then lost to the Allies. Tinkham was described to her as a great man, and yet he was also, in her mind, "the enemy." He belonged to the wrong side.

No one enlightened the child. Her father wrote "Laws for Maria"—a code of conduct that eventually replaced the catechism in her moral imagination, but neither he nor any other adult from "the world away" explained the foundations of their own moral choices. Mary was

1. Not to lie, cheat or steal.
2. If she asks inconvenient questions, to be told:
   All countries do not have the same customs. That her father was like that, or that such was HIS custom and that she can discuss it with him when she thinks she has arrived at suitable age.
3. That if she suffers, it is her own fault for not understanding the universe. That so far as her father knows suffering exists in order to make people think. That they do not usually think until they suffer.

4. That she is not to judge other people's actions save from two points of view: A. objectively as elements in a causal sequence i.e., as effects of causes (anterior) and causes of subsequent effects. B. as to whether such action or course of action is one she wd. LIKE for herself. A preference which has NOTHING whatever to do with its being suitable or likable for someone else.

In case of disliking things, to blame 'em either on the universe or on herself. The former course is in some religions considered presumptuous.[76]

Later, when she verged on adolescence, a time which Pound referred to as "passage from vegetable to animal life," more rules followed. She was to learn NOT to be a nuisance, to be able to do "everything you need for yourself," to be *Bauernfähig*. "The moment a family is separated from the land everyone must be able not only to DO something, or MAKE something, but to sell it. When the land is no longer there, nothing will WAIT. People not peasants must think QUICKER than peasants." He wanted her to learn typewriting, the Italian language, the art of translation, and inventive writing. "That is to say, I can only teach you the profession I know."[77] He already understood that his daughter had no inclination for the violin even though he had twice brought her instruments. The folk tunes of peasants and the clarity of Margit's voice appealed to her far more than Olga's classical repertoire.

From this attention, the gradual "uprooting" that Homer Pound had recommended was slowly accomplished. Mary met her mother's one living brother, Edgar Rudge, and his two children, John and Peter; he sent her a projector and Mickey Mouse films that intrigued the entire Gais neighborhood, adults and children alike. The world beyond the mountains came to seem "more of an asset than a hindrance," while more and more often she judged aspects of rural life to be parochial: Mary was caught doodling instead of paying attention to religious instruction. On another occasion she was suspended from school for two weeks for insubordination. She judged it to be unfair: Pound called it *Dummheit, nicht Bösheit*—stupidity not badness—but in any case, she had finished the fifth elementary level, which was the end of schooling for children in Gais.

For her this meant free time once again in the beloved fields, with little sense of what the next phase of life would entail, although somehow it would involve *die richtigen Eltern* whose powerful, elemental images hovered over her emotional landscape: "The image of my Tattile always presented itself as a huge glowing sun at the end of a white road, but I never dared look at it for too long because I knew that after a while a dark cloud of dust would enfold it. . . . The light and the dark never merged, casting a ring around me which made me feel powerless, deranged in feelings and reason."[78]

The inner divisions of her life had already been established. Idealization and antipathy existed side by side, divided cleanly, and probably inappropriately, between father and mother. What she could not see was the motivation of her own heart. She had conjured a father-sun god out of desire. Several years later, Olga summed up the real situation of her daughter: "In thirteen years the L'cna has had the benefit of His company for three weeks all told."[79]

CHAPTER 2

The Enigma of Identity

Italy, 1937–43

I

Olga Rudge decided on a convent education for her daughter. At the recommendation of Maria Favai, a Venetian friend, Mary was enrolled in the Regio Istituto della Nobili Signore Montalve alla Quiete outside of Florence. In the early fall of 1937, as was their custom, Olga, Pound, and Mary met in Venice, where, amid the reading of cantos in the evening, and regular expeditions to the Lido for swimming and boating, Mary's parents outfitted her for school. Pound agreed to shoulder the tuition and bought his daughter a leather suitcase; Olga arranged for the rest of her gear, carefully engraving Mary's initials on silverware that had once been her own and overseeing the linens that the sisters required for all their charges. In Olga's mind, the convent was to rectify the deficiencies of her own life—"She regrets a misspent youth and not knowing more"—and the defects of her daughter's character— "that miserable Leoncina growing up just as cocky and ignorant!"[1]

At the time, it was not clear to Mary that she was leaving Gais for good, and she conjured images of noble ladies cultivating the best of Italy's youth in order to anticipate her immediate future. Although treated with scrupulous kindness by the elaborately wimpled nuns, she was quickly confronted with the ramifications of her Tyrolean upbringing: she knew virtually no Italian, and she did not feel comfortable in her new environment. She had been transported from close, sturdy peasant rooms to chill, high-ceilinged parlors filled with Della Robbia ceramics and Carlo Dolci Madonnas, from open mountain fields to formal gardens with baroque statuary and fountains. Rules of conduct were similarly stringent. The sole student in her class, she applied

herself diligently to learning grammar—by the next year she was prepared
for the regular courses in Italian—but she also recognized, as she had when
she wrote "The Beauties of the Tirol," that "I had no language to express
myself in."[2]

Initially she was a pious, disciplined student, whose training was entirely
and vigorously classical. She studied Italian, French, Latin, Greek, history,
geography, algebra, and geometry, with high marks in all. When the Reverend Mother Clara Merheri Mousalva wrote to Pound to clarify some of her
school expenses, she said that "we have been well pleased with Mary's general behavior and her progress in her studies during the year."[3] The nuns
taught her solfeggio, began giving her piano lessons, and asked Pound about
buying a set of watercolors for the child. When Olga dropped her off at the
convent in mid-October, she reported to Pound that the "Leoncina . . . was
quite content and had been playing tennis." Frau Marcher had sent a parcel
containing Mary's Ballila (Fascist) cloak, a fountain pen, and her vaccina-
tion certificates, so she considered that all was well.[4] But behind the scenes,
there was an uprooted child who also understood that her parents brooked
no self-indulgence. She was to be transformed into an educated young lady;
she was not to complain or call attention to herself. In the words of her *richtigen Eltern*, she was to "consume her own smoke."

Her letters to *il Babbo* and *la Mamma* were correctly affectionate. Frau
Marcher, who received the real outpourings of the child's heart, learned that
she had "spent the first three months huddled up behind the grand piano,
crying."[5] Pound's response to his daughter's reported distress was to write to
Olga that "she can tell his darter that the way to GIT OUT is to learn English
and frog and that Ez having swatted to git her into the vest scuola in Italia
molto caro etc / she orter appreciate it and git edderkated."[6] She was obedi-
ent. Though she pined for Gais, she replied, "Yes dear Papa, I understand,
and I will do as you say. I do not study German, but I take one lesson a week
so as not to forget what I know. Do you approve?"[7] While the nuns incul-
cated the rules of deportment, while Olga sent the "cheeild" a book about
Giotto with illustrations and "some sweets to sweeten the pill of kulchur,"[8]
she persevered. In early December, she received what her parents called a
"Normos present"—a Kodak camera—but she was worried that she would
be left alone for the Christmas week.

Mary's fears were allayed when Frau Marcher reported that "the Frau has
written you can come to us for a week. But I must not let you know, only stop
crying immediately." Olga wrote that she would take her daughter skiing in

"Siag."[9] Once she sorted out the mirror word game, Mary was ecstatic. When Olga dropped her off in Gais, she heard the familiar greetings—*Schau, schau's Modile*—smelled the crisp air, listened to the river and in her excitement forgot to say goodbye to Olga, who was going on to the more comfortable Hotel Elefante in Taufers.

Each day she would travel to Olga, who chaperoned her while she skied. The mother found it burdensome—she was in the midst of transcribing the Vivaldi scores for which she would become renowned—and the daughter found it boring. Olga longed for Pound's company—"wishes Him here and liking it, which is unlikely"[10]—Mary would have preferred riding sledges with her friends and with Loisl. By the end of the week, she realized she belonged nowhere. When she was at la Quiete, she wished for the comfort of the mountain farm; when she got to the farm, she found the rooms stuffy and small; when she was with Olga, she wanted to return to Mamme; when she returned to Gais in the evenings, she would reach for napkins that weren't there as they had been in the convent. The others thought she put on airs; they teased her. She stayed home instead of making the customary New Year's rounds. "No longer one of them." The pain of leaving this time was the pain of a recognized displacement: "I felt I had not really been *home*."[11]

Her solace at the convent was religion, for, as Mary put it, she could talk to God in German. The nuns recognized very clearly that a mother tongue was appropriate for approaching the sacred, and at her request, bought her a Latin-German missal. Pound erupted at the extra cost, read his daughter's letter of explanation as a prevarication, warned the Reverend Mother that her character would be warped by associating "religion or the religious object" with dishonesty, but Clara Merheri Mousalva intervened on the girl's behalf. It was their fault, she explained; no one knew that the German edition would be more costly than the Italian; the school would pay for the added expense. Pound relented, but the Mother Superior had good reason to take the child's part. She recognized her as someone who might have a vocation.

Just a few months after her arrival, she had been selected as one of six "angels" in the Daughters of Mary. Quickly, as she put it, she "climbed the ladder of honors," and two years later, on 8 December 1939, was elected the president of the sodality. It was a remarkable achievement for one so young but supported by a real sense of mysticism and manifested to others by hours of prayer and meditation. She applied herself equally to her studies, and Pound and Olga saw fit to leave her at la Quiete over the summer of 1938 so that she could study more Italian. Neither could take responsibility for her care, and unrest in the Tyrol made them wary of sending her back to the Marchers.

Throughout the spring they wrote to each other about European politics: Olga noticed the preparations for Hitler's visit to Florence; she complained about the faith British people placed in Anthony Eden; Pound railed about munitions manufacturers and international bankers; but it is not clear how they evaluated the international scene's repercussions for their daughter. The Anschluss of Austria in March 1938 had reawakened boundless hopes in the South Tyroleans, though as time passed, their faith in the motivations and integrity of the negotiating parties wavered. At first they hoped, simply, that Mussolini would "give" the Alto Adige to Hitler as a "wedding present" in honor of their new alliance. As Rolf Steininger has written, "With German men at the Brenner Pass in March 1938, jubilation and elation . . . were boundless in South Tyrol. A new age seemed to have dawned; the years of persistent waiting appeared to have paid off. It seemed to be only a matter of time until the *Fuhrer* would also bring South Tyrol 'home into the Reich,' and the new border would be drawn in the vicinity of Salurn."[12]

This, of course, did not come to pass, for Hitler promised Mussolini that he would respect the Brenner as the clear border between the Reich and Italy. Later in a speech in Rome on 7 May 1938, he reiterated his "unshakeable will and his mandate to the German people to look upon the Alpine border established by nature as forever inviolable." His words aside, German expansion in Europe enflamed the conflicts that had destabilized the South Tyrol since the Great War. Mussolini's own skepticism can be measured by the military installations he continued to develop there; the response of people like the regional chief, Peter Hofer, was incredulous for different reasons. He believed that Hitler's stated policy was a camouflage, a temporizing measure designed to ensure an Italian military alliance, which would eventually fall to a German Reich stretching from the Alps to the Baltic. In his judgment, Tyroleans had, once again, to bide their time.

He was, of course, not party to the secret negotiations that would once again sacrifice the Tyrol to both Italy and Germany, solving the explosiveness of minority conflict by arguing the right of the nation over the right of domicile. Even as Mary learned her Italian verbs and read her German missal, Hermann Göring, for the Nazis, and Mussolini's son-in-law, Galeazzo Ciano, for the Fascists, negotiated the tangible division of the two ethnic identities that Pound and Rudge had, by their choices about child-rearing, brought together in their daughter. Ciano noted in his diary that if the Alto

Adige was geographically an Italian land, with mountains and rivers that could not be moved, it would be the people who must be transferred to German soil. His aim was "to resettle the German contaminants that dominate the region of Alto Adige today to the almost complete exclusion of others, and to kick them back beyond the Brenner where they belong. . . . The 200,000 Germans who are polluting South Tyrol must shoulder the biblical blame for the sins of their fathers."[13]

None of this would come to fruition until the following year, but then the Marchers were right in the center of this terrible ethnic cleansing, having to decide whether to give up their farm or their culture and sure of keeping neither one, since rumor had it that Mussolini would deport any of those remaining to Sicily or Abyssinia.

Amid the vigorous propaganda war that ensued, Pound wrote Mary a letter, dated 23 November 1939, which he asked her to translate for the Marchers. "The newspapers are saying that you must choose whether you want to remain [in the Tyrol] or leave," he began. He was modest, saying forthrightly that he couldn't advise them since he didn't know enough about their lives for the previous thirty years, but he did offer them some thoughts. If they stayed, he cautioned, they must become forthright and loyal Italians. "L' Impero Austriaco non essiste piu"—the Austrian Empire no longer exists, he reminded them, adding that he thought it unlikely that the war (Italy was not yet in the war) would ever come to Gais. They would be certain of food and basic survival. He then said that "il Governo di Mussolini è un governo ed un sistema magnifico, non ancora abbastanza conosciuto"—Mussolini's government is a magnificent government, a system that is not well enough understood. In his judgment, it was the best government in the world. He ended by saying again that since he knew very little of the local details of the situation, he was only offering a view from the distance.

It was a properly unassuming communication, but a revealing one, for Pound urged the Marchers to trust the very government that had, aside from its dogged, twenty-year denigration of their cultural lives, declared them "contaminants" and was in the midst of engineering their removal. And though the Marchers did stay, becoming part of a minority that remained, Pound's misprision gives some indication of the magnitude of the inner division that he unwittingly imposed upon his daughter by educating her "among strangers" at a genteel Florentine convent. For him, cultural identity was fluid: he was a cosmopolitan "modernist" who had lived comfortably in the United States, London, Paris, and Rapallo. His imagination was steeped in Confucius, the poetry of the French troubadours, eighteenth-century American culture; he was a poet, but he was interested in economics and in Mussolini's supposed openness to monetary reform. The Marchers lived by stoic German loyalties that had been passed down for generations. For the next several years, indeed for almost the rest of their lives, they would abide with the political ramifications of their choice. Bombarded by slogans like "German or Dago! Stand by one another and build a new homeland together," faced with flyers, inflammatory broadsides that ostracized those who planned to stay, called "wops" and the true "traitors," Mamme and Tatte understood that the psychological repercussions of adhering to the land were tremendous, even after the imposed time of decision had passed. Their life—what Mary called her "firm ground to stand on"—was no longer secure.

The Marchers' anxieties were clear to Mary. The past and current intricacies of her parents' lives were not. Her life of diligent study was transparent; their relationships in the world remained entirely, intentionally, and maybe appropriately for a child, obscure. They affected her nonetheless. In March 1938, Olga went briefly to the South of France where, at the home of Etta Glover, she found herself in the company of Richard Aldington and his young lover. For her, Aldington was simply a bad writer. She wrote to Pound that he had "written another awful novel . . . a sop to suburbia," but she had, by accident, walked into a net of personal, and personally relevant, relationships that made her own history with Pound look placid.[14]

Aldington was in France to avoid any and every person he had known in England. The immediate reason was his latest affair, which had torn apart the lives of those closest to him, for he had fallen in love with Netta McCulloch Patmore, the wife of Michael Patmore, the younger son of Bridget Patmore, with whom he had been living for eight years. To H.D., the Imagist poet and his not-yet-divorced wife, he wrote, "Dooley, we're madly in love with each other. And believe me, the marriage with Michael was not a real one." But the situation was messy, for he had caused injury to both a mother and a son simultaneously. More to the point, he told H.D., "We want to marry and have a child. As soon as the legal 'evidence' is ready for both sides we shall leave England and live abroad. If you will set me free to marry her, I shall bless you indeed."[15]

Even though H.D. and Aldington had not been together for almost twenty years, she was stunned. To George Plank, she confided, "I think the State of Denmark pretty rotten . . . [Bridget] is on the war path," but the real causes of anxiety were the complications of her own past and the even more complicated way of representing them to the British courts. She consulted experts about appropriate legal strategies, but the psychological repercussions of formally separating from Aldington remained. His request had stirred up a constellation of emotions not just about partnerships—of which there had been many in her life as well—but also about children. While Olga was making cutting remarks about Aldington's talents, while Aldington was complaining about the "idiotic and unreal" nature of court procedures, H.D. was undergoing a rigorous self-examination. As she put it, "I have lived with a subterranean terror, an octopus eating out my strength and vitality for almost eighteen years."[16] She reflected that her separation from Richard had frozen her emotional life, leaving her in the position of a distant "chorus" to her own experience, but her immediate concern was for her daughter, Perdita, who, like Mary, had been born with a false declaration of paternity.

All of this came rushing back in the wake of fear that Aldington might now try to interfere with the nineteen-year-old girl's life. On 24 February, just before meeting Olga in Le Lavandou, he reassured H.D. that he would never do such a thing, explaining that "I don't think I have mentioned the matter three times in the last fifteen years and then only in the strictest confidence. For many years by my silence or in so many words I tacitly admitted paternity in order to spare you in any way possible."[17] Perdita was really the daughter of Cecil Gray, a composer and music critic, whom H.D. had met while Aldington was on active duty in the Great War. As soon as the war was over and civilian travel was possible, Gray skipped town, leaving the shell-shocked Aldington to shield the woman who bore his name, but the marriage itself was beyond repair.

H.D. went on to establish other domestic arrangements that, by their singularity, attest to her extraordinary nature and probably her extraordinary need. She set up a partnership with Winifred Ellerman, the independently wealthy daughter of a British industrialist. Ellerman, otherwise known as Bryher, was a lesbian who fell in love with H.D. in the midst of her marital troubles. Since H.D. was then dangerously ill in a lodging house, Bryher arranged for the nursing home where Perdita was born, then for a nursery for the baby, and finally for her care and upbringing. The two women shielded their idiosyncratic privacy with various arranged marriages. That is, Bryher married—first Robert McAlmon—then Kenneth McPherson, who was also H.D.'s lover. Men came and went for the remainder of H.D.'s life, with various degrees of attachment; Bryher remained—even formally adopting Perdita with Kenneth McPherson—but the person she most associated with children was someone she never lived with. It was Ezra Pound.

And here things get psychologically complicated, for H.D. conflated a child with what she called "the Child" or the *Wunderkind*, the child imagined as the incarnation of affinity, of spiritual and erotic union, the supreme manifestation of *Eros* in the rare times when it visits, and for her that instant, which she called "the fiery moment," had occurred long ago in her American youth when the young Ezra had courted her. Her parents' disapproval, some kind of scandal at Wabash College, Ezra's leaving for Europe, had severed her from those feelings, buried them, and left them inaccessible to memory and understanding until late in life. In 1958, the year that Ezra was released from his imprisonment in St. Elizabeths Hospital, she revisited her lifelong relationship with him, recalling that he came to see her at the nursing home on the day before Perdita was born—at a time of "grave crisis in my life"—to say, "my only real criticism is that this is not my child." She remembered that he had displayed no "tenderness," only "passion and regret."[18]

She associated this strange, strangely moving, and hair-raising event (she wanted to scream but couldn't—Pound was already married to Dorothy Shakespear) with a similar one in which Pound had intervened. She had wanted to go off on the honeymoon of Frances Gregg, a woman whose affections had filled the vacuum left by Pound. Ezra had met her outside of her house before the journey, pulled her into a taxi and told her, "You are not going with them." H.D. described this scene as another time of "grave crisis" and remembered that Pound had established his right to intrude by saying, "I as your nearest male relation."

It was as if both recognized the prior claim established by the other, even though circumstances did not allow them to act on it. "You either catch fire or you don't catch fire" was one of the refrains in *End to Torment* . . . the fire is divine. She had shared that inner intensity with Pound and came to see that life had betrayed her or that she had betrayed her own life by not bearing Pound's child. Some result was missing.

These thoughts and associations did not become explicit until 1958—at which time H.D. could also see that living with Pound would have overwhelmed her—but clearly some sense of the connection between that powerful erotic initiation, creativity, and procreativity was at work in 1938, when H.D. finally picked up her pen and wrote to Pound about Mary Rudge.

She reproached him for keeping her in the dark. Why had she, one of his oldest friends, a constant correspondent, and "in the know" about Olga, been placed in the position of learning about the child's existence from a conversation during her trip to America (1937–39)? Why had she been dependent upon rumors? Was it true that Pound had wanted a son?

Pound dissembled—or rather, he told the exact truth about his feelings in the wrong context. "WOT wd / I have done with a male offspring / It wd / have indubitably been philistine of worst type or gone to the bowwows."[19] His answer fueled H.D.'s suspicions about Omar's parentage, for she knew of his existence, but Pound's answer did nothing to settle her preoccupation about Olga, Mary, and their position in Pound's life.

In March 1938, she did a remarkable thing: she suggested that she give the money in her Italian bank account to Olga, a woman she barely knew, to use for Mary, a child she had never met. When Pound questioned this gesture, she explained, "O. is as it were ME and twice-doubly, mathematically so is (more so) the Marienkind." She then reminded him of the scene of Perdita's birth, claiming that she was "'Ezra's oldest femaile [sic] relative' your phrase with a change of gender one day back in 1919."[20] In so many words, she admitted that she wished Mary were her child with Pound. When she finally received photos of the girl, she went even further and offered to become her legal guardian and to set up a bank account for her. To her, Mary was, or should have been the "fiery moment incarnate."[21]

This is not to say that years of speculation about Mary's existence had not preceded this curious offer. Even before the girl's birth, Bryher had written to Robert McAlmon, her former husband, asking if he knew who Pound's lover was. In April 1925 he had responded, "I don't at all know who the X lady might be. Nobody I know I guess, as Ezra's world and mine never crossed very much. . . . Really, I'd let the Ezra thing solve itself otherwise. You have complications enough and he knows that. It's not so awful as all that. In Italy, France, or elsewhere it's easy enough for her to go to a small town as a married woman, and he could be in the vicinity. Short of adoption what could you do? And being a nursemaid isn't your specialty."[22]

And it is likely that H.D. also knew of the work of her own former husband, Richard Aldington, who addressed the confused issue of paternity in the Pound household in his 1931 short story, "Nobody's Baby." Olga may have thought of Aldington's writing as "a sop to the bourgeoisie," but he had used speculations about her un-bourgeois personal life in a brief novella à clef, where Ezra was transposed into Charlemagne Cox, Dorothy into Mrs. Cox, and she herself into Maggie. In it, two male interlopers try to sort out "the mystery of the infant" and find their hypotheses becoming "more complicated and perturbing," finally deciding that "the whole business is such an extraordinary muddle that I can only think of the unfortunate Juliette Isolda as nobody's baby. On the evidence she can't have any parents at all."[23]

The story bears some relationship to fact, but it relies on constant transpositions and inversions—the child in question in the story is a girl, obviously like Mary (named, however, after Iseult Gonne), but the circumstances most closely resemble those of Omar's birth. "Was it possible that the child was really Ophelia's but not Charlemagne's, and that all the curious hanky-panky in Paris which had perplexed us so much was simply a clumsy but generous plot on the part of Charlemagne and Maggie to shield the erring but repentant wife? . . . Rendle maintained that the precipitate flight from Paris was because Cox had registered the child as his, and the French police had found out that it wasn't."[24] But, having "cribbed" the circumstances of Omar's birth, the story then alludes to the circumstances of Mary's: "The child wasn't Mr. and Mrs. Cox's, it wasn't Mrs. Cox's by another man, it was Maggie's and Charlemagne's! I remembered how Rendle had discovered Maggie had been away from Paris for some months previous to the nativity."[25]

Olga's desire for privacy in the matter of her daughter had obviously been violated by rumors that had circulated for years, but it is not certain if her 1938 visit to Etta Glover was marred by knowing Aldington's scurrilous interest in her past. She left Aldington behind to attend the first concert of the Vivaldi Society in Venice, went on to the Palazzo Capoquadri in Siena, and sent Mary books for her thirteenth birthday: *The Happy Prince* and an Italian translation of *Uncle Tom's Cabin*. Pound forgot to send anything, but they all expected to meet, as usual, in Venice in the early fall.

In September, Pound and Olga began planning for the visit. Olga picked Mary up in Florence on the eighteenth; the two of them traveled together as far as Bologna; Mary went on alone to Gais, which was now apparently considered safe enough for a thirteen-year-old's solitary travel. In a letter to Pound written on the twenty-ninth, amid news that "everyone is gibbering about war," Olga reported that "their strong-minded daughter has arrived alone at 252 . . . lugged heavy valises here herself!" Pound came on 2 October and wrote the same day to report to his wife, Dorothy, that "offspig has got rather large and hefty," and two days later to say that he was trying to teach Mary how to hold her tennis racket properly. By 5 October he was gone. He sent Olga a note about Dorothy's ill health, saying "I see no chance of getting back to Venezia now. Elfride says will take D/ two weeks to get right, with luck and longer without it. . . . Salute the egregious offspring wiff my regrets."

Then Dorothy's mother, Olivia Shakespear, died in England and Ezra was dispatched to dispose of her belongings. Olga was left to explain things to Mary, without explaining anything at all. Something about a "friend" dying was mumbled; something about England, and the elusive father disappeared again until the middle of December. Caught between outrage and disappointment, like a mother bear mindful of her cub, Olga wrote to defend the daughter, who Pound now called "the Hippopotamina."[26] Pound's idea of child-rearing was simply that children should be no trouble—the "consume your own smoke" philosophy—but Olga wrote fiercely that she hoped the Leoncina would "do no such thing. It may be . . . convenient . . . but as a steady diet it's depressing, and I should like that child to have a good time—if there is such a thing. . . . She i.e., Lcna thinks same to be had in America (she begs He will not undeceive it)."[27]

Left to her own devices with Mary, Olga fretted about the indignity of her position and felt pity for the unsuspecting girl, who had spent so little time in her father's company. She saw Pound's desertion as an indication of holding the wrong priorities, and in this case she was right. "She doesn't care two hoots if D loses L 100 worth of furniture. She has always considered that His time wuz worth more and she hopes He not getting thoroughly in-borghisito-ed—and loosing all sense of proportion."[28] While she struggled with the meaning of her life's unorthodox but serious commitments, Pound sorted ashtrays and silver forks, receiving literally hundreds of directives from Dorothy about the disposition of household items: "I want the large silver acorn buttons for my fur coat. Can you bring? Lead and green Russian buttons and clasp can go. Give some of the junk to the maids."[29] By November, Olga had had it: their arrangements were unfair, humiliating, one-sided— Ezra called all the shots, had all the keys. She was always discreet regarding his family "but still He doesn't trust her. And now I have got to explain all this to the Leoncina—without making a tragedy of it!"[30]

She did her best, taking Mary to the Uffizi Gallery in Florence and to the cinema and "to have an ice cream soda which she drinks patriotically as being American and she saw 'un American and Oxford' and would like to go to college—which please do not disillusion her about yet."[31]

Totally unaware of these scenes, Mary learned what was presented to her to learn. By now she understood that her parents were both Americans and she was attempting to master English as well as Italian. "Please please what does 'slither' mean? . . . It isn't there [in the dictionary], so be patient and ex-plain."[32] In due course, further rules from Pound arrived—this time entitled "Amenities or laws of conversation." Pound cautioned his daughter to listen before speaking; he said that polite conversation required one to find out if the other person was interested in a topic before introducing it, and that speaking with another person implied "well wishing toward the interlocutor or a desire to placate them or to arouse their interest or sympathy in a given degree." He then told her that he believed personally that no one had a right to demand anyone else's attention until he or she had produced a work of art.[33]

Beneath the quiet exterior that she continued to present at la Quiete, his daughter considered the full complexities of her heritage, at least as she un-derstood them. Under the calm tutelage of the sisters, she continued with her formal studies, but she had been told to impress upon them that her father, a poet, had tutored her and she harbored memories of their Venetian summers, where people like Manlio Dazzi, the director of the Quirini Stampalia Library, spoke to her about her father's genius: "Il tuo Babbo è un fenomeno"—your father is a phenomenon. "I did not understand the word . . . but I knew he meant something huge and beautiful, and I felt very proud. . . . I fancied that all the passersby applauded and bowed to the hero."[34]

In reality, a remarkable inner transformation was taking place that man-ifested itself in a growing independence of thought and small acts of out-ward rebellion. As she matured, Pound began to send her his articles from the *Meridiano di Roma*: "Something you can now understand, or time you learnt." The nuns debated about whether she could read them—newspapers were forbidden—and there was the added complication of the name "Ezra Pound" when the child's name was Mary Rudge. Mary invented: she said it was a *nom de plume* because she couldn't think of anything else to say, but she was not going to refuse her parentage: "Und überhaupt stamm ich aus. Pourquoi nier son père?" I come from him; why deny one's father?[35]

The sisters eventually noticed a more general change of demeanor. They thought she was too serious for a fourteen-year-old girl and told her that she acted as though she were carrying the weight of the world on her shoulders. She mocked them by hunching over her shoulders. Then they thought she was too ill-mannered for a fourteen-year-old and placed her in solitary con-finement for three days. By December 1940, the honor of being elected pres-ident of the Daughters of Mary was revoked. Mary had been caught reading Alexander Dumas with a flashlight in bed, and though, by this time, she read widely—Papini, Cronin, de Kruif, and Saint-Exupéry—Dumas was on the Index.

Some of this behavior was the result of genuine religious doubt; it was a young girl's struggle with questions of dogma. Some of it was a product of the uneasy politics of the time and with the convent's inability to shield its pupils from the German aggression that had unsettled all Europe. Mary now thought she wanted to be a nurse rather than a nun, but it also manifested her preoccupation with very specific injunctions from Pound himself. He wanted her to learn to think independently; he wanted her to learn to write.

CIAO CARA

To learn to write, as when you learn tennis. Can't always play a game, must practice strokes. Think; how was it different to go to the Lido to play tennis? I mean different from when one went to play in Siena? Write that. Not to make a story but to make it clear.

It will be very LONG. When one starts to write it is hard to fill a page. When one is older there is always so MUCH to write.

THINK: the house in Venice is not like ANY OTHER house. Venice like no other city. Suppose Kit Kat or even an American needed to be told HOW to find the Venice house? How to recognize you and me going out of the door to go to the Lido. He gets off train, how does he find 252 Calle Q?

Describe us or describe Luigino arriving at ferrovia? Has he money, have we, how do we go? A novelist could make a whole chapter getting protagonista from train to front door. Good writing would make it possible and even certain that Kit Kat could use the chapter to find the house.[36]

Mary finally judged the sisters of la Quiete to have provided her with a good, if anachronistic, education. But they did not really stand a chance. By the time she left their establishment, Pound, with his idiosyncratic and passionately held beliefs about what to learn and how to live, had entirely eclipsed their understated conservatism. He wrote to her about the need to think of what endures in life and asked her to consider the long-term consequences of her behavior—at her age, she was preparing for "una vita vera"—a true life—and that she needed to exercise patience; he wrote to her about the difference between being "a workman [and] an architect" of life[37] and sent her

Ta Hio—The Great Learning, which she studied along with Confucian ethics. "His opinion on any subject became dogma to me and no one was to question his opinion."[38]

II

Abruptly the world of structured, protected girlhood changed. The larger
world had been heralded by trips that had punctuated convent life. At Christmas of 1938, Pound had taken both Olga and Mary to Rome, where they had
combined cathedrals with cafés, zoos, and cinema. In the evenings she had
been taken to meet the Carlo Menotti family and then Filippo Tommaso Mari-
netti, the futurist painter. She remembered the honor of being introduced to
Monsignor Pisani and seeing Sant' Anselmo on the Aventino. He showed
her a sight that she remembered all of her life: looking through a keyhole, she
saw "the dome of Michelangelo in the pale gold mist of the setting sun."[39] He
also gave her a cornucopia of La Tour chocolates, which became for her the
manifestation of a more general gift economy: once her father had asked her
to give her Suchard chocolate roll to another, wistful child; now her generosity was repaid; she learned that good will circulated and returned. What she
did not learn was the psychological cost of this trip to her mother. Olga almost immediately became ill in Rome, but a year later, she revealed to Pound
what she had endured during that week: "I was glad when you took the child
out to see people in Rome because it gave her confidence with her school
friends . . . but and if I had not providentially been ill in bed with flu it would
have been very humiliating for me to explain that I did not know your
friends: she will soon see that you have every right in my house . . . and yet I
am absolutely locked out of nearly all your life and concerns."[40] It was the
repetition of a refrain—the insecurity of the mistress of a man who refuses to
leave his wife, but as war approached, those insecurities reflected the dangers
latent in the arrangements Pound had always imposed on those around him.
He mollified Olga and Mary with outings to see Walt Disney (at the same
time that he mollified Dorothy with postcards about architecture), while re-
fusing to address the serious issues of relationship that Olga raised.

A few months later, Olga attempted the tricky maneuver of bringing Mary
to Rapallo, where Dorothy, Isabel, and Homer Loomis Pound lived. In April
Pound decided to go to the United States, and Mary was granted a few days
away from school to see him off. This did not happen, for reasons the child

could not understand, but she at long last caught a glimpse of the bond that united her parents. She also began to amplify her view of her mother, seeing for the first time a woman whose artistry transported her beyond the realm of unexpressed resentment. Years later she recreated her first impressions of Olga's peasant cottage in the hill town of Sant' Ambrogio above Rapallo—its orange color with painted columns, its green front door swathed in honeysuckle and Virginia creepers, the narrow stone steps that led up to it through the hillside of olive, eucalyptus, and lemon trees, the view of the sea, the light, the austerity. Where Dorothy Shakespear's world was filled with lacquer boxes, brooches, and silver trays, Olga Rudge's was composed of a Zen-like emptiness. It had a few pieces of furniture that Pound had made; Mary's room contained "the Yeats furniture"—an iron bed, a marble-top night table, a chair. Otherwise "there was nothing else in the house. . . . No junk, no clutter. Only candlelight."[41]

It was in this place that Mary heard her mother play Bach's Chaconne and recognized for the first time the expressive integrity of music and her mother as the means of that integrity. To this point Olga's endless violin practicing had seemed an oppressive sound; the violin itself a vehicle of manipulation—it had been impressed upon her as a child in the Alps where she had no way of understanding what it meant, aside from the will of people she barely knew. Now she watched Olga as if through her father's eyes, appreciating what Pound later commemorated in *The Cantos* as "The birds answering fiddle and her between me and wisdom and view of the bay." Finally, she said, "I had a glimpse of their true world *nel terzo cielo*."[42]

This moment of veneration was fleeting. Pound took Mary walking to explain that she was not, after all, to see him off at Genoa. He made excuses for his parents: they were the ones who would drive him to the boat; there was not enough room in the car; it was too stressful for the grandmother to meet her just at the time when her son was leaving. Instead, she and Olga went alone to Genoa on 13 April, lunched at a hillside restaurant where one could see the harbor from a distance, watched the boat pull out and then walked around in the narrow streets near the waterfront. She enjoyed the Ligurian coastline, the shop windows, the adventure implied by her American father's return to his country of origin. She temporarily forgot her unmet grandparents in the happiness of celebrating Olga's birthday and in the fantasy that this event was the prelude to her "own great voyage." Increasingly America became a symbolic destination, a place that could answer what she sensed was unspoken in her own life, as if an unknown country could supply the candor that was lacking at home. Looking back, she asked, "Did I at four-teen or fifteen start to understand?"

Pound, with his busy political and literary agenda in the United States, did take time out to consider his daughter's future. In May, he consulted an attorney about adopting Mary.[43] In the event of war, American citizens might be forced to vacate Italy. How could he bring a girl to the U.S., whose papers bore the name of neither parent? He, too, was tiring of the charade. By the time he returned to Rapallo he and Olga had it out with each other. "Is the cheeiYld old enough to be told that I don't care a damn about repentances; but that causes have results."[44] For him it was a pragmatic matter, not an ethical one: Mary was the consequence of Olga's desire for a child. But in-creasingly Olga found it impossible to keep her side of the bargain. She had agreed to raise the girl herself; she had agreed not to burden Pound with her own upkeep and to work so that he would be free to pursue his art; but feel-ings are not immutable, circumstances had changed, and Europe was no longer the place that had drawn them to it in their youth. She was blunt:

> She knows He has put her off every time she tries to get Him to con-sider subject of present triangle. I see no reason for a "marital front" or façade. Kept up (as I was told, in 1924) out of respect for feelings of D's parents, to be kept up now *in same way* when circumstances have changed—He has told her He did not believe in marriage. He has im-plied that D. did not. Certainly, no church would consider a marriage entered as He told her his was—as sacred or binding. I don't know how a Confucian would view a woman who had not wanted children by her husband & who then introduced an other man's child into the family as her husbands, being given all the consideration owing to a wife—while the true child had not even legal status & any privileges given it or planned for it, were at expense of its mother—i.e. an adop-tion that would make it over to you and implicitly to D while I would lose every right. . . . There is never enough time for me to talk about even important things.[45]

A day later, she was repentant: "Sorry I trouble you with my concerns—will not do so again."[46] Pound tried to placate her by saying that he had considered staying in America and that his return was in itself a mark of his affection—but he was weary: "my idea of hell is a place where everything has to be written down . . . it is also a place where people try to live each other's lives instead of their own."[47] He nonetheless took Mary with him for a brief holiday in Viareggio, on the Tyrrhenian Sea in the north of Tuscany, where news of the child's small pleasures (she learned to roller skate there) provoked another of Olga's outbursts: "Yes she has to correct cheiild & mind the uninteresting details & other people enjoy its sassiety—and it has a nice time with them and at home sees me busy drudging—and it will soon get the idea that that is proper state of affairs—in fact everything combines to make it thoroughly self centered and selfish. . . . I have no intention of being poor devoted mother drudging in background so that 'daughter' may have advantages."[48]

Despite Olga's resentment of Pound's "leave me alone" attitude, despite her worry about being eclipsed by the daughter's obvious pleasure in her father's vacationing company, Olga did not forget what was serious and important. She had learned about a recent bill, passed into law on 3 May 1939 that affected Mary's legal status. H.R. 6127 denied children born abroad to U.S. parents the right to automatic citizenship and its wording made the law retroactive. Not knowing what else to do, Olga wrote to the Supreme Court of the United States. She stated the facts in her case, pointing out that "a child of 14 cannot during her vacation from school stay at any hotel or pension without documents. She wd. even in time of peace be unable to continue her schooling in Switzerland or in France, for simple reason that she cannot cross these frontiers without a passport. The penalty of the recent ruling therefore falls not only on me but on the child."[49] No answer was forthcoming, and a year later when Pound was in Rome, he was still trying to straighten out the problem with an unsuspecting child: "Babbo seemed harassed as though something was out of control. . . . He explained to me that it was necessary to have an identification document that was valid in Italy, but that my legal status and citizenship would be set right as soon as we were able to get to America. When it would be possible for the two of us to satisfy the legal residence requirements was hard to foresee. I had no clear idea what was wrong with my status, nor did I care."[50]

In the unknown world across the English Channel, Dorothy Pound was going through similar maneuvers to clarify the legal status of her own child. During Pound's trip to America in April, she had received a letter from the consulate in Paris inquiring if Omar was registered there. She went immediately to London, where she was shocked to find most of the city dug up for shelters and her son traveling routinely with a gas mask. Omar was to have no problem claiming his American passport.

In September, still living under the "please don't undeceive it" practices of her parents, Mary returned to la Quiete, where in late 1939 it was anything but quiet. Her parents received word on the first of September that the school would close in the event of war. Pound still thought that "mebbe still some chance of England or Italy keeping out of the shindy," for he had noticed "one phrase of his [Hitler's] speech seems to give a chance for localizing the show/ but no use pretending, it is a large one."[51] He was wrong. Two days later, on 3 September, England and France declared war on Germany; on 17 September, Russia invaded Poland, the Baltics, and Finland. Although Mussolini and Hitler had signed a nonaggression pact as early as 1936, and although President Franklin D. Roosevelt declared America's neutrality, the times were especially unsettled for foreigners living abroad. Pound wrote to Olga that he was "now think of going to America=how. Anyhow?? Submarine or via Japon??"[52] And for the first time, he began to speak about espionage. He told her that all his English letters up to 31 August had been opened by a censor, and a few months later said he thought he was right "in thking the Leoncina's wuz investergated at Firenze. Or mebbe they dunt bother wiff, biglets postale."[53]

On 9 September, Pound wrote another, seemingly unrelated letter to Olga about a young man who had asked to meet him the previous summer. "Young Angleton has turned up/haven't yet seen him/I spose his pa had some inside inf/as to not needing to hurry ome."[54] Why Pound would think that a Yale undergraduate had an inside track on U.S. policies, international intentions, and the conditions subsequently affecting its citizens living abroad is not clear; but the fact of this communication, arriving just when Pound was pondering a return to America that would have changed his fate and that of his family, leads to some interesting speculations.

James Jesus Angleton had initiated the contact the previous August. He was then on summer holidays, living with his father in Milan, and had just finished his sophomore year at Yale. Having researched Pound's address at the American consulate in Genoa, he wrote asking for an interview for the Yale literary magazine. Pound apparently did not reply, for Angleton's next letter, dated ten days later (23 August 1938), repeated the request, noting that he was already in Rapallo. "It is not my intention to bother you sir. I want only to get a few spirited ideas . . . together w/a photo or so." His brashness did not pay off, for Pound was in Siena with Olga, not in Rapallo, but he was anxious to impress the poet nonetheless: "Incidentally should you ever pass through Milan, my father, who spent 3 years of his youth in Idaho, would be pleased to make your acquaintance . . . he is President of the National Cash Register Co. for Italy & the President of the American Chamber of Commerce for Italy."[55]

What he neglected to say was that his father was, by the late 1930s, one of the best-known Americans in northern Italy, a prosperous, well-connected man who was an intimate friend of William Phillips, the American ambassador in Rome, and, through his numerous business contacts in France, Germany, Poland, Romania, and Hungary, a conduit for information about German arms manufacturing. He was also a member of the Masonic Order, whose "brothers" kept him informed about the Italian foreign minister Count Ciano and the inside workings of the Italian Fascist Party.[56] According to Robin W. Winks, Angleton was protected by his fellow Masons who, for example, warned him when his telephone was tapped. From this point, Angleton exchanged information with his contacts only when he appeared to be on outings with his children. In other words, protected by Italians and Americans alike, he served as an unofficial spy for the United States from 1939 to 1941.

A meeting with the son was finally arranged, the photos were duly taken, and young Angleton left Rapallo a convert to the *Ta Hio* and Cavalcanti, convinced that Pound was the greatest living poet. From this point until Angleton graduated from Yale in 1941, Pound would be bombarded with requests for contributions to undergraduate magazines and with Angleton's schemes for disseminating his work in America. On Pound's voyage to the U.S. in the spring of 1939, he persuaded Pound to interrupt his trip to James Laughlin's home in order to have dinner with himself and his roommate Reed Whittemore's family; he came up with a scheme for compiling a full bibliography of Pound's work, and for Yale Library to "get all of your manuscripts . . . I can put the exhibition off until you arrive in May."[57] He also served as a conduit of information about American student attitudes toward Roosevelt and the prospect of war. Knowing Pound's dread of a conflict between Italy and the United States, he emphasized student resistance, even claiming to be part of it,[58] but in fact he had voted with most of the students to come to the aid of Britain.[59] By an odd coincidence, Angleton, his sister Carmen, and Pound were all on the same ocean liner returning to Genoa in June 1939, where Hugh Angleton met the boat; and from this point, the Angletons, father and son, took an interest in Pound's fate in Italy. By

February 1940, Angleton was addressing Pound as "Ez old man" and offering his family's financial assistance: "I talked to Dad . . . and mentioned the little shekel which you might need, and he said O.K." A few months later, explaining that he himself could not return to Italy ("They wouldn't give me a passport to get back"), he again offered help: "I will try to explain everything to [my father]," but indicated that his father had inexplicably gone to Paris. "I don't know if anything happened other than that he had not intentions of leaving Italy."[60] From this point, Hugh Angleton wrote to Pound when he was on family outings, finally, in 1940, making some undisclosed proposition which Pound refused. In a letter to Olga on 23 August 1940, he said, "also wrut to Dr ang/ an thazzat."

Although Pound refused to accept any money, their letters during this period indicate first, that Pound did intend to return to the U.S. as early as May 1940 (this is also when the U.S. Embassy in Rome began to urge Americans in Italy to return home) and that he reconsidered returning in September 1940; second, that Hugh Angleton, with his international political connections, advised Pound that it wasn't necessary for his safety; and last, that he and his family were willing to support Pound while he remained in Italy. Given that Ambassador Phillips personally warned Hugh Angleton in the fall of 1941 that the U.S. intended to enter the war and given that Angleton chose to escape to Switzerland with his family, it is worth noting that he advised Pound that it was safe to remain. Far more was being engineered during Pound's trip abroad than the technicalities of Mary's passport, though all these activities show Pound mulling over how to position himself and the various members of his family well before Italy's official entrance into the war on 10 June 1940.

But the decision was not his alone to make. Dorothy got into the act by suggesting that "Japan will be the only other place to go to or to take the children to,"[61] and Olga was not planning to leave Italy in 1939 in any case. As late as October 1940, she continued to insist that "it doesn't feel like war here"—so she carried on with her position as secretary of the Accademia Musicale Chigiana in Siena. She wanted by the end of the school year to bring Mary there to introduce her to Count Chigi, to the opera, and to the wider world of music to which she belonged. But this could not happen until she considered her daughter *Salonfähig*. Amid air raid sirens and bomb scares, amid rationing and food shortages, she insisted that Mary continue with Italian and French, attend to her grooming, and learn to be graceful. Pound wrote that she should be made to practice fencing positions. At Christmas,

Mary agitated to return to Gais. Olga wrote to Pound that their daughter had a "Jeanne d'Arc" complex, that she wanted to "console" her friends and family for their wartime situations, and that she'd even got Mother Francesce Chiera on her side. Olga refused. "I have explained at length she cannot go to the Tirol until all foreigners are allowed to circulate through Italy—also that it isn't then freely."[62] In July, having acquiesced during the year, Mary asked to go there again. She wrote to Olga that she'd worked with her head all year and that she now wanted to work with her hands; then, once she'd been permitted to go, she asked to stay for sixty days rather than the fifteen that Olga had originally specified. She proposed to take cooking lessons and to help in the fields, and she pointed out that Frau Marcher needed her help with the younger children.

Olga was disconcerted: Mary would "revert" to the soil: she would get a swelled head being an educated person among peasants. Her letters, she complained to Pound, "have slumped into conventional Gais mentality. She is a perfect cameleon [sic] . . . I think rather hard she should always be exposed to other influences considering the trouble I took to get her decent parents."[63] The other "decent" parent was more reflective about the meaning of his daughter's proclivity for the farming life. Conflating American agrarians from the past with contemporary German ideologists, joining Jefferson and Madison with Hitler, he thought that his daughter might be "a decade or 20 years ahead. Anyhow Adolf doing his best to elevate the status of Bauer, return to the land etc/ possibly the only solid rock that will remain."[64]

In September 1940, Pound's little "natural family" had a temporary reprieve for private life in Siena. Mary was finally taken to the Music Festival and to the opening of Vivaldi's opera *Giuditta triumphans*. Count Chigi was generous and attentive, but, as Mary put it in her autobiography, "a threatening feeling of hunger seemed to be hanging over us."[65] Adjusting her "pace and aesthetic values" was no longer a sufficient coping mechanism for the encroaching displacements of war. Olga's job with the Count was in jeopardy, and Pound, once again, was considering going to the U.S. Consulting Charles U. Clark[66] in Rome, he had discovered that taking a plane to Portugal was the cheapest way to travel. Initially he considered going alone, but within a few days, he began writing urgently, urging Olga to get her papers in order, saying "he don't want' em to be on two sides of a blumin ocean fer indefinite"[67] and that American Express would not make a reservation for her without a proper, updated passport. He also reported that Avv. Nicoletti was seeing about getting her a *cassetta di sicurezza* and that he had just seen Carlo Camagna at the Agenzia Stefani, and that money for work he did for the agency could be deposited to an Italian account for her or for his father.[68] Mary remembers worrying at the time that her parents were going to abandon her, and it seems that this, in fact, is what they intended to do, at least temporarily, for on 12 October, Olga telegraphed Pound that she would join him on Sunday evening or at the latest on Monday morning. That their daughter did not spend the war alone in Italy is due, at least in part, to the scheduling problems of the clipper service, for Pound telegraphed abruptly that they couldn't leave until 14 November. Although Olga had already sent in a plane reservation for herself, she was relieved, thinking, incredibly, that American Express and the airlines were just trying to trump up business in a "dead season" and that the trip was akin to a holiday. "She of course wd enjoy to go along."[69] She urged him to wait until spring and soon was chatting about Mary's blue coat needing to be let down. Neither parent seemed to have considered that, had they traveled to the U.S., their passports, like Jim Angleton's, would have permitted them no return to Italy. What Dorothy Pound knew about these plans is not at all clear, for she was in England, writing alternately about London burning from constant Nazi bombardment and Omar's enjoyment of his holidays at Bognor. Mary knew only that her piano lessons were to be discontinued because there was no time in her convent schedule for sufficient practice.

It was to be her last season at la Quiete, and, though she did not know it, the end of her formal education altogether. Although she wanted to go to college, Pound was very clear, at least behind her back, that it was out of the question. In his judgment, universities "unfitted" people for productive living. In early April 1941 Olga arrived to take her once again to the consulate to address the lingering problem of identity papers; by the end of the month, she was instructed to cart her gear to Sant' Ambrogio, where her only security was that Pound had paid the rent until the autumn.

III

On 4 June 1941 the American Department of State received a dispatch from the American consulate in Genoa asserting that Ezra Pound was pro-Fascist and that he had refused to return home when other Americans had repatriated. On 12 June 1941 Pound wrote to Olga about his recently written radio scripts, saying, "Waal Ranieri [San Faustino] sez they are using me stuff/ so

I did another." On 1 July 1941 U.S. Attorney General Francis Biddle received a letter about Ezra Pound's "stuff" from something called the "Listening Post," which he forwarded to the Criminal Division for further investigation on 9 July 1941. 9 July was Mary Rudge's sixteenth birthday.

She had left the convent only to take up another life of retreat, this time in the company of her mother in the peasant cottage in the Rapallo foothills. As she put it in *Discretions*, "The only person I saw between 1941 and 1943 was Father Chute."[70] This memory is not completely accurate, for letters show her to have returned to Gais in the summer of 1942, but in general it captures the cloistered life of two women subsisting with few resources amid wartime conditions that even Olga could no longer ignore. Food was scarce; fuel even more so; candles nonexistent. Pound's plan was for Mary to read, write, and translate; Olga provided the structure of exercise, cold baths, and scheduled discipline that encouraged this life of the mind. A young girl came into puberty seeing herself as "a pathetically naked girl" in the mirror and chaffing at Olga's routines. She remembered loneliness and moments of feeling the sea's "suicidal attraction." But gradually the inner logic of her mother's sparse vigor revealed itself: while Olga practiced the violin, she warmed herself by a small iron stove and entered the Latin and French she was learning, the Italian translation she was undertaking (first Thomas Hardy's *Under the Greenwood Tree*, later Pound's *The Cantos*), and the course of English reading she had set herself: Jane Austen, Thackeray, Stevenson, Hardy, and Henry James. They ate chestnuts and potatoes boiled on burning pinecones; their lives, in memory, were understood to be a work of art: "nothing superfluous, nothing wasted, nothing sloppy."[71]

"Babbo" came and went, alternately instructing and declaiming. He was, obviously, a lifeline for his daughter, providing "magnitude, momentum" and a belief that art was at the center of life. But if he was a demigod, he was also a demagogue, for Pound rehearsed his Rome radio speeches in Sant' Ambrogio, revealing to an unworldly but perceptive child the "two voices" that would determine the circumstances and priorities of her future life: the one "voice" "calm, harmonious, heroic" when he recited lines from Homer's *Odyssey*; the other "angry, sardonic, sometimes shrill and violent" when he practiced for the radio. With the retrospective knowledge of 1972, understanding only too well the results of the United States' interest in Pound's "shrill and violent" side, she thought of the time between 1941 and 1943 as idyllic, crystallized in an image of herself and her father walking through the olive trees and near the tides of the Ligurian coast; but even at the time, she knew that such years were precious. "Nulla per me io desidero/che la vita continui cosí," she wrote. "I desire nothing for myself, but that life continue as it is."[72]

But, of course, it did not. During the summer and fall of 1941, as Pound continued writing and recording discs for the *American Hour* for Rome Radio (EIAR: Ente Italiano per le Audizione Radiofoniche), making his trips to and from Rapallo, he seems to have considered making serious changes in his living circumstances. Usually, he stayed at the Albergo d'Italia in Rome, visiting the Italian friends who, out of wartime necessity, served as his companions. But as his wartime options diminished (on 12 July 1941, the State Department instructed the American Embassy in Rome to limit Pound's passport to "return only to the U.S. status"; in 1943, it instructed the Swiss to confiscate his passport altogether), Pound began to explore the idea of moving to Rome with Olga and Mary, and to find work for Olga, possibly with the Ministry of Popular Culture in Rome.

Amid news about his recording sessions, his lunches and dinners, his initiation into the Sovereign Military of Malta[73] and his interest in "redeeming" (*redenzione*) the island of Malta, he paused to say "maybe it's fate that we should get an apartment here. . . . Roma wd be more amusing fer the kid than St Amb."[74] A few days later he reported that he had started house-hunting. "If I telegraph you to come/?? Might leave M/ for a few days."[75] This time, Pound and Olga did let Mary in on their plans, for she wrote to her father that she hoped "very much that we may be soon settled all together. I think it would be very nice to stay at Rome"; but once again their plans were complicated by the formalities of civilians moving around a nation at war. Pound quickly wrote again to say that it was premature for Olga to travel, but as the months passed, it was clear that he continued to pursue the idea of resettling in Rome: he had been talking to Adreano Ungaro at the Ministry of Popular Culture about formally including Olga in his broadcast work as a researcher and translator,[76] and he also reported that his friends the Santinis were willing to let them live in their apartment for several months in the spring. Amid reports of his social engagements, he told Olga that "there will be people fit fer the young 'un to speak with" and that Lydia San Faustino, the wife of his immediate superior at the Ministry of Popular Culture, was looking forward to introducing her daughter to Mary.[77]

All these plans were put on hold in December 1942, when Pound wrote a long, reflective letter to Adreano Ungaro about his understanding of changed circumstances. He distinguished between open and secret broadcasting—he had been writing material that San Faustino and others had been reading on the air—and reasoned that he could speak in his own voice, but not supply material to others. "I believe the effect of what I can say (in accord with my own conscience and the law of the U.S. as I understand it) would have more weight in the long run if it can be proved that I am not indulging in clandestine propaganda of any kind."[78] He had had time to think about his situation, since San Faustino had warned him a full year previously that the "Listening Post" in the U.S. was "annoyed" by his broadcasts.[79] He knew his talks were monitored, though by whom and to what purpose remained unclear.[80] Pound went back to Rapallo for about six weeks; then he began broadcasting again.

While her father was being monitored for signs of Fascist ideology that might give "aid and comfort to the enemy," Mary was translating *The Cantos*. While the world listened to the increasingly raucous voice of a poet turned propagandist, his daughter entered into the still majesty of his poetry. That he was a Fascist sympathizer was clear to her, but she, as an Italian born, Fascist-raised girl, saw nothing untoward in this. That he was a "conspiracy theorist"—though no such term then existed—might have been clear to a few people. To Jim Angleton, for example, Pound said forthrightly, "a foreign power TOOK over the US gov't in 1863 and the Americans are such . . . suckers they haven't yet found it out."[81] To Adreano Ungaro, for another example, Pound was accustomed to writing, "will they never learn that ALL American politics has two sides/ the public and published side, and the real side. . . . Does no one in the Dies committee know the life story of William Wiseman, British spy and director of the first firm of Kuhn, Loeb?"[82] But this view was certainly not clear to her. As an Italian, Mary understood the United States and England to be the enemies of her country; as a Tyrolean, she had ambivalent feelings about Italy; as the daughter of Americans who were expatriates and critical of Roosevelt's leadership of their homeland, she had no way to see other American points of view. As someone whose identity had had to shift with the tides of her parents' desires, she probably understood better than most how she, and in fact whole populations, could become victims of international geopolitics. In the midst of strife in so many untoward directions, she turned inward.

Pound took her translation of Hardy to his friend and fellow writer Enrico Pea, who was so pleased with it that he judged it worthy of publication. But she considered that tooth-cutting work, the prelude to her own father's poetry. Pound explained to her that the great epics of western literature echoed throughout *The Cantos*. Themes from Homer, Dante, Ovid, and Malatesta

formed a fugue, each an instrument of thought, whose presence, repeated
and varied, dropped and reintroduced, formed part of Pound's vast orches-
tration of modernity.

She began with Canto XXVII in the middle, proceeding according to
his instructions. No work was to be presented for his inspection until a full
page was completed and neatly typed. He was invariably critical, ripping
and shredding what had so carefully been assembled. According to Pound,
translation was an act of re-creation according to the idioms and rhythms of
the new language. He would taunt his daughter with *non si dice*—they don't
say it like that—and send her back until the phrasing and sound patterns
were true.[83]

The importance of this period of Mary's life cannot be overemphasized.
In it, she established the contrapuntal relationship with the world that would
characterize the remainder of her life. From these quiet years in Sant' Ambrogio would come the inner conviction of her father's greatness as an artist
and his fundamental sincerity as a man. While she worked, he continued with
his own translation of the *Great Digest* of Confucius into Italian. He did
not consider *The Cantos* his finest gift to his daughter, but the teachings of
Confucius, particularly about the origin of civic order within the psyche
of the self-disciplined person. He taught her to listen for "the tones given
off by the heart" (inarticulate thought).[84] Later, when he himself was vilified,
she continued to use this training to make judgments that ran contrary to legal
opinions and popular attitudes. It was an indispensable education, for, from
this moment in her life, her own efforts to understand her father's inner life
would unwittingly run in converse parallel to the efforts of several foreign
governments to understand and criminalize her father's political affiliations.

IV

For Christmas in 1942, Mary received 1,000 lire from Pound along with the
question of what she would do with it, since, according to him, a good economy depended upon the free circulation of money. Understanding that she
should never hoard resources, she asked to accompany him on one of his trips
to Rome. He was pleased with her answer, seeing the request as a step out-
ward toward a useful and self-sufficient life. Olga saw it as another phase of
Mary's entry into the world of polite society and set about preparing her to
meet genteel people: she must be suitably dressed—old school uniforms were

dyed and recast into more fashionable styles—and suitably mannered—once again the fencing exercises were trotted out to encourage grace. Table manners and even facial expressions were explained and practiced. Finally, in May, she was ready to go.

Pound prepared a "card for Moidile" for her week with him. She was staying at the home of her mother's friend Nora Naldi, but her days were occupied by lunches and dinners and punctuated by visits to the radio station EIAR. Pound had received a free ticket to the opera *Così fan tutti*, but since there was only one, he used it himself. The Francesco Menottis invited her, as did Signora Rosetti Agresti, the San Faustinos and various other people associated with the radio station and the Ministry of Popular Culture. She wore black at dinner; Pound reported to Olga that his friends appreciated her company and that she had been "getting romanized. I dunno as she will be wantin to git back."[85] In fact, she extended her stay beyond the originally planned week when the Princess Troubetzkoi, a fellow broadcaster for the *American Hour*, offered to chaperone her. Baedeker in hand, Mary spent mornings wandering the city, indulging in her translator's propensity to compare—though in this case she was not comparing sounds in Italian and English, but qualities of landscape to lines of poetry or scenes from novels. Thus, she saw Rome through the eyes of Henry James and Cori through the eyes of Goethe's Roman sonnets, just as later she would see scenes of her own life transcribed into *The Cantos*.

One of the most curious of her father's friends was her so-called chaperone, the Princess Troubetzkoi, a woman whose identity to this day remains elusive. J. J. Wilhelm, the author of *Ezra Pound: The Tragic Years*, assumed that she was the wife of Pierre Troubetzkoi, scion of Russian nobility living in exile, whose family seat, by the 1890s, was the Villa Ada on Lago Maggiore. The Troubetzkois were cousins to the Romanovs, and both Pierre and Paul were successful portrait painters and sculptors, who worked in Russia, America, England, and Italy with extraordinarily distinguished, and often royal clients. This princess was better known in the United States as the novelist, poet, and playwright Amelie Rives. Pound had first met her in London through Ford Madox Ford; in 1945 he commemorated her death in Canto LXXIV, and, indeed, it was her cousin George (Giorgio) Nelson Page who had created the *American Hour*, which aired from EIAR Rome before and during the war. But if Rives's biographer is to be believed, this Princess Troubetzkoi lived most of her married life (Pierre Troubetzkoi was her second husband) at her family home in Castle Hill, near Richmond, Virginia, and most

certainly remained there after her husband's death in 1937. By 1944 she was
ill, blind, and living in a nursing home in Charlottesville, Virginia.

The more likely chaperone was an entirely different princess whose name
was Natalie Troubetzkoi. Born in Lublin, Poland, in 1897, where her father was
governor of the province, she studied art and medicine in Moscow, served as
a registered nurse on the Russian front toward the end of World War I, and
then moved to England. For twenty years she was a member of the British
Imperial Nursing Service, and she described herself during those years as
"busy . . . with welfare work, lecturing and broadcasting." Before the start of
World War II, she moved to Rome. Pound knew her through EAIR (her letters to him are written on the stationery of the *ministero della cultura popolare*
and signed "Natalie") and through her broadcasts on conditions at the Russian front. She also wrote reports of (poor) working conditions for the Russian
people under Communist leadership. Pound had lunched with her for years
in Rome, was so taken by her transmission on "Russian Dumping" that he
arranged for another of his close friends, Signora Olivia Rosetti Agresti, to
translate it into Italian. He apparently knew her family, for he mentions knowing Goleniewski, who was a "friend of your mothers."[86]

Rumor had it that she was a spy, and there might have been some truth
to this supposition, since other Troubetzkois worked in espionage for the National Security League during World War I. Her family friend Michal Goleniewski was indeed a Russian spy who, after the end of World War II, worked
in the Polish intelligence and security service (SB), establishing a liaison/in-
formant relationship with the KGB before he defected to the West in 1961.
She was, in any case, like almost all of the Troubetzkois for generation after
generation, a Freemason (the Pichel Order), a member of the White Russian
community in Italy, and for these reasons able to assist the Allies both during and after the war in their fight against the Axis and later against communism. Or, conversely, she could have assisted the Russians in their struggle
against capitalism, though this, given her royal lineage, is more unlikely. After
the war was over, Boris de Rachewiltz told Mary that he had seen her in a
British army uniform and that she refused to recognize him. And it is worth
noting that her pro-Fascist broadcasts, though paid for by the Ministry of
Popular Culture, broadcast on the same frequencies and expressing many
of the same opinions that Pound articulated on the *American Hour*, aroused
no charges of treason.

Her interest in Mary was immediate and intense. She invited the girl to
tea, to lunch, and then arranged a Sunday expedition with another young

couple. Boris Baratti turned up at the train station without his Czechoslo-vakian fiancée, so the three of them went on to Cori, where, apparently, the princess wove her young charges into what Mary later recognized as a fictionalized scenario for one of her broadcasts: here were two young people, one with an Italian father and a Russian mother, the other with two American parents, both raised in Italy. They liked each other. Why were Italy and the United States at war? The afternoon closed at a peasant's cottage, where the three were offered homemade bread, olive oil, and onions, but in a sense, the afternoon never ended, since Boris was to spend the next two years courting Mary and eventually marry her.

Mary returned to Rapallo, taking the Princess Troubetzkoi's name, ad-dress, and phone number with her. She was someone to whom Mary could, and did, write about the displacements of her life, and especially about the longing for Gais that haunted her when she was in her parents' "other world." Then, in July, Olga allowed Mary to travel back to the mountains.[87] Her trip to Rome had occurred on the verge of a great transformation, heralded, even before she departed, by sirens and propaganda leaflets dropped by the Al-lies, who had just succeeded in taking Northern Africa.

In July their leaflets were replaced by bombs. A few days later, King Vic-tor Emmanuel II arrested Mussolini and named Marshal Pietro Badoglio as head of a new military government. These events, visible to everyone in It-aly, heralded the end of the public world as the Pounds and the Rudges knew it. Their private world was soon to suffer a similar upheaval. On 26 July 1943, unknown to any of them, Pound was indicted for treason in the United States, and Frank R. Amprim was dispatched to Italy in search of evidence of his guilt. He arrived in August and very quickly set to work interviewing the San Faustinos and the Ungaros and the Carlo Camagnas, using against Pound the very Italians who had just befriended his daughter, offering to her, through their hospitality, conversation and knowledge of culture, a glimpse of the larger civilized world.

While this stealthy individual drama unfolded, new political alignments were being made on the national level. Badoglio tried secretly to extricate Italy from the war; but Hitler continued to pour troops into Italy, and the Allies persisted in strafing Rome in anticipation of their arrival in the capi-tal. Badoglio then declared Rome an "open city" (a demilitarized zone), but to no avail. No one was willing to honor such status. By the third of Sep-tember he was ready to sign an unconditional surrender to be kept secret until the planned Allied invasion of the mainland. On 8 September General

Eisenhower made the announcement of Italy's capitulation, timing it to co-incide with General Mark Clark's amphibious landing of the Fifth Army at Salerno, just south of Naples. German Supreme Commander in Italy Kes-selring continued to move south; Badoglio, caught in the invasion of Rome, responded by fleeing with King Emmanuel, leaving no one in charge of the city. It was a cataclysmic cowardice and caused displacements on every level. Ordinary Roman citizens rose up against the German occupation, and they would continue their resistance for the 270 days that it took the Allies to liberate the city, but there is no doubt that Kesselring was in charge.[88] Ran-ieri San Faustino, not wanting to work for a German-controlled broadcast-ing system, left the Ministry of Popular Culture in September, so that when Pound returned to Rome, there was no professional world for him to return to. But by then he had other things on his mind.

V

Although Mary had come back to Gais for a wedding and to help with the harvest, she returned to a political and military situation colored by the Ty-rol's long history of unstable frontiers. The events in Rome—Mussolini's arrest, the Italian surrender—elicited different responses in the northern mountains, due largely to Fascism's long repressions and its collaboration in the forced resettlement program. Many Tyroleans welcomed the end of Fas-cist rule and hoped for liberation, the reunification of the Tyrol, and, indeed, outright annexation to the German Reich. This did not happen in 1943, for German paratroopers rescued Mussolini a few days after his imprisonment and Hitler did not want to insult his ally by such blatant aggression. Techni-cally the Tyrol belonged to Mussolini's new Republic of Salò, though it re-mained, in practice, subject to German administration. By November of that year, everyone who lived in this now ambiguous "operations zone" was sub-ject to conscription in the German army. As troops poured south, many mountain regiments, trained in Bozen, were among them.

During the last half of September Mary observed "mysterious meetings" between the German commission in Bruneck and one of her neighbors in Gais. Herr Bacher, who had been "a most zealous advocate of freedom," began to affect an extremely Prussian manner and one day was seen on the stairway of the building that had housed the despised Italian carabi-nieri. He, along with another prosperous farmer named Moar, arrested the

Italian police and walked them into Bruneck with some German soldiers. That night there was great joy in the village, for it was the symbolic end of twenty years of Italian subjugation—the end of taxes, mandatory Italian, the repression of custom, of native language, of ethnic identity—or so it was thought.[89] It was an action that paralleled in miniature the arrest of Ettore Tolomei, the extreme Italian nationalist first responsible for engineering this Italianization, who was sent through Innsbruck and Dachau concentration camps to be interned in Thüringen until the end of the war.[90]

The arrest of the Italian police was one of many local incidents that signaled the strategic importance of the Dolomites, in both official and unofficial ways, for mountaineers could offer safe passage in and out of the country through locally known routes, and they could smuggle goods and messages with equal facility. Although Pound and Olga invariably reasoned that Gais was a place of safety and abundance for their daughter, it was in fact almost impossible for local life to evade international implications. A simple trip to a mountain *Alm* (like the one Mary and Frau Marcher took that summer) could occasion one's arrest; a girl and her mother hiking up to rest in a dairy hut had to worry about identity papers and alibis and explanations lest they be considered spies or messengers heading into Austria or Switzerland.

In mid-September, shortly after she had returned from her mountain outing, Mary approached her Gais home to find Frau Marcher waiting anxiously for her arrival. Pound, tired and almost unrecognizably disheveled, had appeared unannounced and was waiting for her upstairs. He had refused food but was now resting on Mary's bed. He embraced his daughter silently and allowed concern for his blistered feet and patter about his travels momentarily to eclipse the reason for his hazardous journey. He had walked out of Rome, traveling almost 400 miles on foot and by train to tell Mary the truth of her life circumstances. After participating in years of dissimulation and evasion with Olga, Dorothy, and Homer and Isabel Pound, he understood that she deserved to know the arrangements that had produced and sustained her. Asking her to turn out the light, he began to talk.

Incipit vita nuova. Here begins the New Life. Along with this discarded line from Canto LXXXIV, Pound described the details of his travels—the degli Ubertis' offer of boots, hat, and knapsack; Nora Naldi's provision of eggs and tea and bread; the nights on benches. He considered the tenth of September his symbolic entry into "the Republic of Utopia, a quiet country lying eighty years east of Fara Sabina."[91] If, through this language, he meant to indicate his new commitment to honesty and a Confucian order governing his life, he meant also to extend the possibility of such order to his daughter: a young life could not be constructed on falsehood. What he had to say was merciless.

He explained that he was married to Dorothy Shakespear and that her mother was not his wife. He told her that Dorothy had had a child, not his own but bearing his name, who lived in England. He told her that his arrangement with Olga had never and presumably would never include marriage, and that both of them understood this. He admitted that Olga had wanted a son and that this "fact now named" explained why it had been impossible for her to win her mother's affection. He regretted the falsification of history that surrounded her birth and understood that he would have to correct formal records when the war was over. She was old enough to understand such things now.

She listened in the same stark way that he spoke. It was as if the two of them had entered into a utopian world, where honesty, even belated honesty, served as its own bond and where human beings could live according to rules of their own devising. He impressed upon her that art demanded and occasioned its own set of inner laws, that ethics could have a dimension beyond and different from the human laws that governed the lives of ordinary people like the Marchers. Nonetheless, he said, after the war, Dorothy would go to England to live with Omar, who would take the name of Shakespear. Mary would take the name of Pound.[92] In 1971, when she published her memoir, Mary represented this scene of disclosure as something that was "all plain and simple. I felt no resentment, only a vague sense of pity."[93] She said *buona notte* and went to bed.

Sleep could not have come easily. To learn that you have lived eighteen years without knowing the foundations of your own identity cannot be a casual event. It cannot be an experience whose ramifications become immediately apparent. At the time, neither Pound nor Mary could measure the futility of his intentions, given that he was shortly to be arrested by the United States government and no record would ever be set right, but throughout her life Mary remained convinced of the "extraordinary sense of responsibility, sincerity and affection"[94] that prompted her father's journey.

In later years, she was not so sanguine, for dissimulation, whether it involves the law or human affections, cannot simply be undone. Four years earlier, when Homer and Isabel Pound had finally been told the truth about Omar and Mary in 1939, they had been shocked, and not simply because of a violation of conventional morality. Isabel had written, "Dear Son, the situation is to me amazing—one disloyalty provokes another but why continue the deception so many years? One cannot transfer affection." Homer had been even more expansive: "A clap of thunder out of a clear sky could not have been more startling than yours and D's letters. For 10 years we have been here. D. has been giving us Omar's photos and it is hard to realize the truth. Why did you suggest our remaining? As matters have developed there is no pleasure in our continuing here. We shall arrange to depart."[95] During the next several months, the senior Pounds apparently reconsidered moving back to the States, but the matter of readjusting emotions remained. On 5 October 1939, Dorothy wrote to Pound that she was going to tea with them "this for Old Man's sake only. I appear to be forgiven for my iniquities—which isn't the point." But Homer was still railing against "that *awful* letter Ezra wrote his mother." There were several issues for the older generation: they had been deceived; they had been affronted for their more conventional understanding of marriage; and they found that, after fourteen years, they couldn't forsake one barely known boy for a totally unknown girl raised in the mountains.

Why Pound waited four more years to share this knowledge with Mary is not clear. One can imagine eighteen as a symbolic entry into adulthood; one can imagine the extremities of war pressing against the discretions of day-to-day practices. But from this day in September 1943, Mary considered that she knew the truth: she understood the facts; and she began to contemplate the emotional valences that generated and sustained the distinctive relationships among Pound, Dorothy, and Olga.

Her father stayed in Gais for a short time while he considered what to do next. His arrival had aroused the suspicion of the same local officials who had deposed the Italian carabinieri. Several of them, including Herr Bacher, came to make inquiries. Pound fit no category that they could understand. As Mary put it in *Discretions*, he was "not Italian, not a spy, not a Fascist, not a Jew."[96] The Marchers' answer, *Inso Moidile's Tatte*—he's our daughter's father—made no sense on the surface, and his papers were equally puzzling. Pound's American passport had been confiscated, but he had an Italian Radio and Press membership card, and, had they looked further, an Italian military map given him by Admiral degli Uberti when he left Rome. Finally local loyalties prevailed. Mary had grown up among them; they eventually believed that he was her American father, whom the Marchers had housed many times, and he was also personable and interested in their views. Pound soon had them conversing about economics and international relations, soon had them admiring both his ideas and his profile, and by the next day was mulling over apprenticing at the Bachers' sawmill. The family, for several generations, had been gifted, traditional woodworkers. Even Mary had never before seen the great hall where they kept their carvings.

Although he was perceived as both an employer and a well-educated gentleman, Pound insisted upon an equal status with the Marchers while he was under their roof. He ate at table with them; he made himself useful around the house; he listened to their anti-Italian sentiments enough to understand the symbolic meaning of the suitcase left at the base of the Alpini monument in Bruneck: it was time for the Italians to pack their bags and leave. These experiences were stored in memory and eventually made their way into *The Cantos*, even though Pound did not then know, beyond the immediate need for rest, the direction of his own future. Villagers variously suggested escaping to Switzerland over the mountains, making his way north to Germany for further radio work, and remaining with them to do manual labor.

When Olga wrote to say that things were quiet in Rapallo, Pound decided to return there. He and Mary went to Bruneck for the required travel permit. Mary accompanied him to Bozen, where resentment of Italian domination was similarly present in the renamed Piazza della Vittoria. It was now Walter Platz. But with this sign of reaffirmed cultural pride came all the trappings of German militarism. Mary saw her father onto a train carrying cannons to the south. Never, amid this period of high altitude revelation did Pound mention that he had been indicted for treason—"adher[ing] to the enemies of the United States, to wit, the Kingdom of Italy, its counselors, armies, navies, secret agents, representatives, and subjects . . . with which the United States at all times since December 11, 1941, have been at war." Nor did he share the contents of his letter to U.S. Attorney General Biddle, where his defense was that he had spoken only according to conscience and to his duties as an American citizen. He believed that freedom of speech had to include free speech over the radio, and he summarized the hysteria and vitriol of his transmissions as the attempt to convey "some of the facts which are an essential part of the total which should be known to the people."[97]

Although she had wanted to go to Rapallo with Pound, Mary Rudge, who was presumably one of the enemies her father had adhered to, returned to Gais.

CHAPTER 3

Transmission, Interception

Italy, 1944–46

I

Even as Mary and Pound stood waiting for the train in Bozen, indeed, from 10 September 1943, the day that Pound trekked out of Rome on foot, Hitler had ordered changes in the military and civil administration of Italy. He had used German paratroopers to free Mussolini on 12 September, and would appear, as once before, to honor the supposed autonomy of his "ally"; but in fact he had divided the country, establishing two German operations zones in the Adriatic coastal region and the Alpine foothills region where Mary lived. By 6 November he had mandated universal conscription in these places, with the order that those who avoided enlistment were subject to the death penalty and those who tried to escape could expect their families to be taken hostage. According to Rolf Steininger, it didn't matter whether one had opted for Germany or decided to stay in Italy. Members of both groups were assigned to German units, even though this was a "clear contravention of international law."[1] No one paid attention to it.

No one paid attention to Mary's irregular status as the child of Americans either. As someone who could speak and write in both German and Italian, she was needed for local work and later for the German war effort. She was raised in Gais, on cheeses, rye, potatoes, and *Knödel*, but she was educated in ways that other local students had resisted, so she was called into service.

Soon after Pound returned to Rapallo, the Marchers' celebration of the *Kirchta*—the Tyrolean harvest festival—was abruptly and unexpectedly interrupted by the arrival of Herr Bacher. He was the same person who had

ousted the carabinieri and he told her that their neighbor, Herr Moar, had
been elected *Bürgermeister*. Since the corollary of booting out Italian officials
was the necessity for local administration, Mary had been chosen to be his
secretary. Whatever interior journeys she took as she came to terms with her
father's revelations were, from this point in time, accompanied by the duties
of a municipal job. As she sorted out cantos and Confucian philosophy, as
she considered wives and mistresses and the requirements of her father's interior life, she also kept track of ration cards, the distribution of petrol, and
the records of ordinary people and property in a mountain village.

She was strong; she was strong-willed, and she possessed the idealism of
youth. Once informed of her ancestry, she followed the signs of her father's
inner life, the life glimpsed in and through the poetry. She dismissed the
implications of illegitimacy; thinking, wrongly, perversely, rightly, that the
social markings of identity could be subsumed by spiritual kinship. "I had
come to enjoy and be eager to participate in Babbo's work through translation, and to understand some of his ideas and theories through study. This
meant more to me than being legitimate or illegitimate. . . . What carried
weight in my life then was Babbo's inner order; everything would forever
depend on that."[2]

In the meantime, she struggled with proper conduct toward Herr Moar
and with wording documents properly. She had plenty of experience with
one—Herr Moar was a prosperous farmer, whose corn she had helped harvest, with whom she had shared meals and said the rosary. She knew his
mother, the intimacies of the family's *Stube* with its mighty statue of the
Christian God looking like Jupiter—and knew nothing whatsoever about
the other. The office and the typewriter seemed to alter everything.

But they also gave her access to papers that she would otherwise not have
seen. Amid sorting out tax forms and keeping track of horses and cows, she
realized that she was also in charge of birth records. This was brought to her
attention by the arrival of one of the herdsmen of the *Jagdhaus* dairy whose
sister had had an illegitimate child; and once involved in figuring out how to
certify the birth and provide for the baby, she decided to investigate her
own documents. There she discovered that she was legally the daughter of a
dead man: "figlia di Arturo." So she changed the records from "di" to "fu"
("of" to "was"), symbolically killing her mother's lie about paternity, at least
in the village where she had grown up. The issue of her own illegitimacy and
the falsification of documents could not have been as uncomplicated as she at
first insisted.

When a formally trained secretary arrived in Gais, Mary was reassigned to Bruneck, where she continued to do similar work through December. Now that the Tyrol was free to reclaim its cultural heritage, she had been keeping records in the German language; she went comfortably to Christmas parties where German carols were sung along with *Deutschland über Alles*, but when she heard gossip that even young women were to be recruited into the German army, she became alarmed. She imagined work in a hospital to be a possible alternative to a fighting unit or a munitions factory, but such a transfer was difficult to arrange. Even when she'd passed a typing test and had qualified as secretary to a doctor in Pocol, the Bruneck *Bürgermeister* told her it was impossible to shift anywhere except into the army—the population was already mobilized.

Her only contact, a Dr. Waldner, whom she had met at the 1943 Christmas party, intervened on her behalf, and consequently Mary spent the remainder of the war working at the Bellevue hospital in Cortina. She lived among Austrian and German nurses, was greeted by *Heil Hitler* when she went to the office, and began keeping track of the patients' case histories. She worked among sick and dying soldiers, and it was immediately and inescapably clear to her that, on the human level of war, suffering has no nationality. Knowing nothing of concentration camps or the policies of Jewish extermination that were integral to the cause for which they fought, she saw boys like the ones with whom she had been raised who were in hospital. She hoped, like they did, for victory.

By November 1944, there were changes in personnel and in workloads. More nurses and doctors, previously stationed farther to the south, arrived as Kesselring evacuated troops from central Italy. Mary herself was sick with angina for a while, but was told, only half-jokingly, that she had better speed her recovery since more wounded soldiers were arriving. The hospitals in Verona were overflowing; houses and embassies were quickly turned into temporary surgeries. "Men that had escaped from the disaster at the Po River . . . had to lie on straw in their dirty clothes and shoes. They had no papers or luggage; they were all fighting men, defeated soldiers."[3]

As the retreat of German forces became general, the hospital employees were instructed to remain indoors. Everywhere they looked they saw desperately fleeing soldiers, all hungry, exhausted, and searching for shelter. Wearing her Red Cross armband, Mary passed among trucks, confused animals, armed Germans, and similarly armed partisans, continuing the increasingly chaotic efforts of the hospital to care for injured men. She persevered in notating their passbooks, even as she recognized that "in those days very few gave any importance to a written paper and signature."[4]

This service reflected choice—insofar as Mary's deepest loyalties were to her village and the people who had raised her—and necessity—in that some service to the Germans would have been demanded in any case. Despite his intimate revelations, her father did not understand this. His own idea was that she should work for the Salò Republic. In December 1943, he wrote to her saying that he was going to put her in touch with Prefetto Nicoletti in Salò. "If you arrive here," he said, "your stuff will be in a package in the care of Dott. Politi at the Albergo Benaco" [*my translation*]. He would not see her personally since he was leaving for Milan "under orders" on the following day. He would be staying at the Ambassciatori guesthouse—or if not there, he would leave word where he could be found.[5]

She was not interested; she did not go. On 29 December 1943, Nino Sammartano, Inspector of Radio, wrote to Pound saying that she had not yet arrived in Salò to take up service. Where Pound maintained an active hope that Italian Fascism might still embrace his policies for economic reform, Mary was both more pragmatic and more idealistic. "I shared [Pound's] faith in the Republic—primarily as luminous *idea*—though basically I had the Tyrolean mistrust of Italians."[6]

In fact, it was difficult even to stay in contact by mail during this time. By the following spring, Pound wrote that Olga lamented her absence, but that he, personally, was glad that the war might soon be over and that she was well nourished, "strong, obstinate, good and tough" [*my translation*].[7] He sent his blessings. In October 1944, after months without communication, he asked Sammartano, now stationed in Venice, to help him contact Mary and to send her a copy of his "Introduction to the Economic Nature of the United States." By this time, he knew that she was in Cortina d'Ampezzo but "it seems that she remains without any news of me for a long time, and I would like her to know that I am still alive. Perhaps the mail will still work from Venice" [*my translation*].[8] Had she wanted to follow her father's politics, it would have been difficult for Mary to learn what he was doing or writing, much less what guided him, either internally, as he continued to support Mussolini, or externally, as the Germans forced him to evacuate the apartment that he and Dorothy occupied in Rapallo. The coastline was needed for German defense, and they were considered "aliens in a prohibited area."

As she worked with doctors and nurses in the mountains, Pound reestablished contact with many of the same colleagues who had worked with him in Rome. To him, the Republic was not simply an idea, but a goal, and his efforts in these years were, in retrospect, discordant. On the one hand, his correspondence with people like Giacchino Nicoletti and Fernando Mezzasoma, who worked in the new Ministry of Popular Culture, were filled with explicit propaganda and plans for public broadcasting in support of Salò. "I am anxious to help," he wrote to Mezzasoma, "Nothing will be done until I or someone who understands the meaning of this war has been granted the use of a printing press. . . . The Fascist regime is only as good as its propaganda."[9] He submitted articles to *Il Popolo di Alessandria* and to Admiral degli Uberti's *Marina Nationale Repubblicana*, published by the Ministry of the Armed Forces; he issued pamphlets on the causes of the present war and on the "nature of economics in the U.S.A." In late November 1943, on a trip to Salò, he wrote to Olga that he had met with Conte Filippani who, interestingly, had asked him to write about the Illuminati for a new publication called *Volonta Repubblicana*. A few days later, he reported that he had decided to write about Babeuf and the Illuminati, and that he'd invited Agresti, Vicari, and Barilli to contribute to the publication as well.[10] He proposed a series of books to be translated into Italian and he put himself forward as an appropriate adviser to *il Duce*. "My duty, as I see it, is to stop certain things from being believed or done because of ignorance of historic facts."[11]

His hatred of Roosevelt continued unabated (he said his books would "demonstrate how Roosevelt is a scoundrel, based on historical facts") as well as his conviction that this war, like other wars in modern history, was carried out for the covert benefit of bankers. His conclusions were always based on two premises: that social profit went into the hands of private, corporate bankers; that corporate bankers were by and large Jewish people like the Rothschilds, the Kuhns, and the Loebs. With the theme of usury came, often, a virulent anti-Semitic rhetoric. "It's time to make an analysis. Hebrewism isn't race, it's illness. When a nation dies, Jews multiply."[12] According to this logic, anyone who played into this profiteering scheme was a Jew; it was not a matter of racial identity but of poor social priorities, greed, and secretiveness, so that Roosevelt, Churchill, and Eden were also "Hebrews." It was a horrible choice of rhetoric, compounded by ignorance of unspeakable mass slaughter that, by this point in the war, extended into Italy. In 1943 Fascist Italians rounded up between 7,000 and 8,000 Jews and participated directly in the Final Solution. The person who offered himself to Mussolini as an educated adviser was himself "ignoran[t] of historic facts." The person who insisted on precision in using language had become someone whose words were out of control. Even his forgiving daughter—"acquit of evil intention"—recognized "his excessive use of vituperative terms."[13]

Pound coupled this anxious, aggressive participation in the cultural programs of Salò with a return to Confucius. Eventually he tried to integrate this study with a publishing program for the new republic, where he argued that a series based on Chinese classics would instruct in philosophy and in contemporary international relationships. He proposed the collected works of Confucius, *The Unwobbling Pivot*, the *Book of Mencius*, other documents and odes collected by Confucius, and, somewhat incongruously, various Japanese Noh plays.[14] By April, he learned that Mezzasoma had approved the publication of the *Odes*.

And so encouraged, he persisted in metaphysical reflection and translation amid destruction that by September of 1944 was local. Rapallo had been bombed, the railroad bridges destroyed, and the Allies and Royalist Italian forces had moved into Pisa, Lucca, and Pistoia. Whether he knew it or not, Liguria, the area around Genoa, was almost entirely isolated from the rest of Italy. He paused in his translation, to ask the Minister of Popular Culture if he could "halt the destruction" and if he could also arrange for someone to bring cement to Rapallo for making cisterns so that people "can go on a bit longer."[15]

It is not clear how these various programs fit into a vision of the future . . . whether Pound continued to believe in an Axis victory, the endurance of Mussolini beyond an Allied victory, or whether, thinking the war lost, his vision had shifted to a millennial mode . . . doing something, anything, for an undefined and indefinitely long future. Or if the discordance of these activities shows the confused desperation of a person who no longer knew what to anticipate amid general military and civilian collapse. On 12 April 1945, Franklin Roosevelt died. There was no longer any central figure to bear Pound's animus. On 28 April 1945, Mussolini and Claretta Petacci were shot at Mezzegra, their bodies carted to the Piazzale Loreto in Milan, and hung in degraded display. There was no longer any figure to bear Pound's projected image of an Italian republic.

In the meanwhile, he had been living in his own personal dystopia for over a year. In May 1944, he and Dorothy had accepted Olga's offer of shelter when they had been forced to evacuate their via Marsala flat. The reason he had asked Mezzasoma for cisterns was thirst. As he knew from experience, "the main problem in these hills is the lack of water; the evacuees (myself included) drink up what little there is left."[16] Mary did not learn until much later that Dorothy Pound had been living in her room in Sant' Ambrogio, supplementing the Yeats's furniture with a rug she had brought up from the town. She also learned of the emotional cost to her mother, who always thought of appearances and propriety but who suffered nonetheless. The triangle was a private hell endured silently while it continued, but finally expressed with all the hostile improvidence that the circumstances had elicited: "One solid year, Dorothy made use of me to the fullest, shared my house [while] I worked like a slave—cooking, cleaning, finding food—which I only undertook owing to her incapacity, so that E. should not suffer."[17] Dorothy's version was similarly strident. She hated living with Pound's mother, Isabel, but she considered that "this life is a mild purgatorio compared to the HELL of No. 60."[18]

Mary, while understanding the "hatred and tension [that] permeated the house," characteristically mythologized the circumstances: Pound "was pent up with two women who loved him, whom he loved, and who coldly hated each other. . . . I had a glimpse of the madness and the vision: Zeus-Hera-Dione, the two different consorts of one god, one a sky goddess and one an earth goddess . . . many shades of emotion remain hidden, embedded in *The Cantos* as mythology."[19] But she did this retrospectively. In January 1944, even before undertaking this fraught living situation, Olga had written to Count Chigi that it had been eight months since she had seen Mary—and she would not see her again until May 1945. She admitted to the count that "eighteen is a bit young to have to be on one's own,"[20] but she did nothing to alter the situation, and, indeed, there was little she could do. In February 1945, Mary wrote that the Allies had bombed the train lines through the Dolomites; in March she heard that the Hotel Post, where she had stayed with her parents as a child, had also been bombed.[21]

On 30 April, seemingly out of the blue, Mary received a letter from Olga. It began by saying "I am writing in haste just to give you a few addresses you may need in case anything should happen to me." She listed, among others, her brother, Teddy Rudge, in England; Mabel and Ethel Duncan, "our dearest friends" but whose address Mary would have to look up in a Paris telephone directory; Don Arturo Brown, who was in Buenos Ayres somewhere, but whose address Mary might be able to get through a Paris hotel; Adrian Stokes, who had not seen Mary since she was an infant; a Mrs. Ernest Harold Baynes, "if she is still alive" in North Carolina; Reverend Desmond Chute, who by this time had been deported from Rapallo and was being held prisoner; and T. S. Eliot, care of his publishing house, "to give you advice about your writing." She explained "these are all very dear friends of mine"—appending that many of them were in fact Pound's friends—and hoped that her daughter would meet them some day. She spoke about a few pieces of furniture that might remain in Paris; some jewelry that she valued and her Japanese kimono ("most important!"). She told Mary that she would have a lot of papers to sort, and on the edge of the letter, written sideways she added, "Dear child take care of yourself and try to forget the war and read E.P.'s works and study them well."[22]

The letter was enigmatic, for Olga offered no reasons for her haste or sense of impending danger; 30 April was, in fact, the day that Adolf Hitler shot himself in his bunker—but this news had been purposefully kept from the public until the evening of 1 May. And although Rudolf Rahn, the German ambassador to Mussolini's government, S.S. Col. Eugen Dollmann, Gen. Karl Wolff, Supreme Commander of SS and General of the German Wehrmacht in Italy, and even Franz Hofer, the Gauleiter of the Tyrol, had been secretly negotiating for a surrender of German troops for months, she had no way to know this either. The announced ceasefire occurred three days later on 2 May. The letter was, then, a response to a more nebulous sense of anxiety; it was also a testament to the paucity of Olga's resources, in that it offered a sorry list of people half forgotten, not visited, and to the girl, certainly not known, as possible protectors. Who among them could have offered an eighteen-year-old Tyrolean any tangible help?

In response, Mary rushed to get to Rapallo. Whatever anxieties she had about her parents were compounded by feelings of identification with the Women Auxiliaries whose heads were being shaved by partisans to further the shame of their defeat. When she asked for a few days leave from the hospital, a staff officer recommended that she ask one of the patients, "Dr. E.," how to travel through a ravaged country. She was preoccupied and worried, so she did not pause to ask how "Dr. E." would know about such logistics, but later she suspected that "he had in effect been negotiating and probably helping partisans and Americans before the war was over."[23] If this was so, he was one of many, for informants were everywhere. By 1945, the suffering of German troops, the hopelessness of their battles in Italy without any supporting air force (the striking power of the Luftwaffe had been largely destroyed by the end of 1943), the complete fantasy of Hitler's new super weapon—something that would exceed the destructive power of his V-1s and V-2s—were facts that were widely known in the German high command. By the end of April, various Germans had been using Allen W. Dulles and the American OSS in Switzerland as a conduit to the American command center in Caserta.

Despite Mary's having only an expired Italian identity card, "Dr. E." arranged American transport for her as far as Milan on the condition that she deliver some letters to a private residence there. American and British courier jeeps carried her as far as Belluno and Verona; then she hitchhiked to the outskirts of Milan, took a tram, and was greeted by "Ludmilla's mother"—a White Russian who fed her borsch and gave her a spare bed before sending her out to find Dr. E.'s friend "Willi." Willi took the letters and the gold cigarette case that supposedly proved that she was a trustworthy messenger, and then she was free to figure out the remainder of the journey. A train to Genoa, a motorboat from Pegli to Santa Margherita and then a two-hour hike brought her face to face with a mother in tears.

II

She learned the story gradually, and it took even longer to absorb its meaning. Olga told her how two partisans, whom the peasants on the hills of Sant' Ambrogio regarded as common "ex-Fascist convicts," or *due brutti ceffi*—two ugly snouts—had taken her father away at gunpoint on 3 May. Dorothy had been visiting Isabel Pound at the time; she herself had been shopping below in Rapallo and had to reconstruct the story from Anita Pellagrini, the woman who lived on the ground floor of Casa 60. Pound had thrown her the key, picked up a eucalyptus pip, and made the sign of a noose with his hands around his neck. He was being taken to Zoagli.

Olga followed, worried at this point not about Americans but about partisan vendettas, nebulous grudges, and the general lawlessness of people in quickly shifting political situations. And, indeed, she was right, for Pound's arrest initially had nothing to do with the FBI or with American criminal investigations, but with greed: these men had heard that there was a ransom on Pound's head.

She found Pound in custody, looking at ideograms in a Confucian text and listened while he insisted on being taken to the American Command. Instead, the partisans drove them to a Chiavari prison, where the walls were covered in blood. In 1962 Pound remembered that "they had been shooting [people], and I thought I was finished then and there. Then finally a guy came in and said he was damned if he would hand me over to the Americans unless I wanted to be handed over to them."[24]

But Pound did want to be "handed over." He thought the treason charge was a mistake and that it would be dropped as soon as the authorities understood his motivations. He was also afraid of being murdered by the partisans. So at Pound's own insistence, he and Olga were driven to Lavagna, and from there to U.S. Counter Intelligence Corps headquarters in Genoa, where the CIC detachment of the 92nd Division shared the sixth floor of 6 via Fieschi with a branch of the Office of Strategic Services (OSS).

It's not clear how much detail she gave to Mary, but years later Olga recalled the days of camping in waiting rooms and offices as "among *the happiest of my life.*" For her it was a limbo, a time-out-of-time, a private *paradiso* constructed out of K rations and isolation. She remembered it in terms of coffee and sandwiches and hot bouillon. She remembered it in terms of intimacy.

Frank Amprim, who arrived the next day, on 4 May, seemed to respect her feelings, but he played on her naïveté. He had in fact been in Italy collecting evidence against Pound since 1943, tracing his connections with Fascist officials, collecting files from the Ente Italiano per le Audizioni Radiofoniche (EIAR), and getting Pound's radio scripts from the Ministry of Popular Culture. While Olga noticed friendliness and patience, while Pound welcomed the chance to explain his opinions to someone who took careful notes, Amprim did his duty, working closely with Ramon Arrizabalaga, to elicit evidence for the U.S. government's case against Pound. He was dressed in the uniform of a U.S. Army major; neither Pound nor Olga had any way of knowing initially that he was an FBI agent, and one can only imagine his responses to Pound's request to send a cable to President Truman, to engineer a "Confucian" peace with Japan, and to send one last radio broadcast to the United States urging justice for the defeated Axis nations. The two labored at complete cross-purposes.[25]

On the morning of 6 May, while Pound was in the interrogation room, Olga finally realized what it was all about. She read in the *Tribuna del popolo* that Pound had been condemned as a traitor *in contumacia* (by default). From this point she advised caution. "It was your mother," Pound wrote to Mary, "who saved me from stupidities . . . she was blessed with more sense of reality than I. It was her intelligence in making me see that I should not babble and joke about being 'the American Lord Haw-Haw.'"[26]

Olga didn't learn much more. On 7 May, Amprim and Arrizabalaga drove her back to Sant' Ambrogio where he (lawfully? unlawfully?) collected Pound's books, letters and, reportedly, 7,000 pages of papers. Once again he was courteous, and when he returned to Casa 60 the next week, he was apologetic as well, for Olga was poor and had only bread to offer him for lunch. This time he took Pound's Remington typewriter. Amprim had no search warrant. He simply instructed Olga to remain available as a witness, should there be a trial, but he wouldn't tell her where Pound was, nor would he let her communicate with him.

Mary stood at the door of a ruined world. Casa 60 was cluttered with Dorothy and Pound's possessions; Dorothy was gone, but the spare, light-filled artist's retreat that she had known as a child was now haven only to fear. Olga had traveled back to Genoa hoping to get news but had been rebuffed. During the two days that Mary stayed there, the two women engaged in worried speculation. The irregularities of their position haunted them: where once they had measured values according to an inner emotional logic, they now began to imagine how the legal world would judge them or how "public opinion" would see things: Mary was illegitimate; she had been working in an enemy hospital. Olga's thoughts veered in contradictory and desperate directions: maybe her daughter should disappear into the Tyrol and seem not to exist; maybe she should get a highly visible job with the Americans. "We must stand ready. We must be prepared. There will be a trial. His life is in danger."[27] She eventually entrusted Mary with Pound's seal ring and an expired American passport and sent her to Genoa in the hope that a young girl could elicit more information than a distraught adult. Mary went to the CIC headquarters but learned nothing. She thought the officer with whom she spoke to be "impassible" and dismissive, but Ramon Arrizabalaga was neither. He was simply a military man following orders. He had, in fact, been courteous to her father while he was in his protective custody, and in 1956 remembered talking to her, knowing exactly who she was and that she lived in northern Italy.[28] But he was enjoined not to reveal information, and Mary left in ignorance. She had given Olga her money, and she had, in effect, no life other than what she could make for herself.

On the way back to Cortina an inner transformation began. No longer protected by her parents, she began to protect them. In Olga, she recognized a particular helplessness in practical matters; in her father "the hero, the victim, the righteous man who had tried to save the world and had fallen prey to evil powers." Years later she recognized the insecurity that had brought her conviction into being, but from this moment, she became a sort of vessel, enacting and embodying a moral position contrary to the highly visible and notorious judgments of the United States Department of Justice. Whatever Pound's fate in the world, she would adhere to his "ideas and ideals, as far as I could grasp them."[29]

At this time, "ideas and ideals" were all she had. For six months she did not know where her father was or even if he was alive. From Cortina, she returned to Gais, where, in August, she was still writing anxiously to Olga, speaking about John Drummond, a young lance corporal in the British army stationed in Rome, whom she and her mother had come to rely on for news from military sources. "I asked him to write to you as it might be quicker that way. Wasn't he even able to find out where E. is? Well, war is over now, but I have never been in such an agitated state of mind as in these last months. I hoped to get some rest here in Gais, but there is always enough news coming to make one worry. . . . If I get no further news from you I shall come down by the first of September."[30]

III

Pound had, in fact, been housed at the CIC in Genoa for several weeks while Arrizabalaga sought further instructions about his disposition. Mary didn't know this, but she was aware of the intricacies and continued dangers of Tyrolean politics. Indeed, she was living with Hawaiian soldiers who were billeting with the Marchers and writing letters about her neighbors' fear of the Italians, their perceived need of protection by the British and American forces, and the "tense, extremely interesting" political situation that surrounded her.[31] She saw through the eyes of her life experience, with no way to judge the continued strategic importance of northern Italy to the Americans, who already measured the end of one war in anticipation of zones of postwar influence or even occupation. To them the Tyrolean "problem" was no longer the continued animosity between German or Italian peasants, but the possible occupation of these lands by Communist forces. Where the zones of Allied or Soviet occupation in Germany and Austria had been fixed by prior agreements, this was not the case with Italy, which, since the fall of Mussolini, had been treated as an ally. While Mary resumed mountain farm work, while she worried about the fate of one person, the Allies considered the implications of intercepted communications in which Stalin instructed

Tito to shift his military across northern Italy as far as the French border, establishing, through the conjunction of these forces with French Communists, a Soviet-controlled belt across southern and western Europe.[32]

Amid these overarching concerns about the political and the military fate of Europe, the commanding general of the Mediterranean Theater of Operations took time to order that "Ezra Pound, War Criminal," be transferred under guard to the Disciplinary Training Center at Metato, near Pisa, to await further investigations.[33] At the end of August, Dorothy Pound finally was the first in Pound's extended family to learn where he was.[34] She was informed that she could write to him and arrange a personal visit. A month later, on 20 September, Lt. Col. John L. Steele, commanding officer of the DTC, told Pound he was authorized to write to his wife—only to his wife—and on the same day Pound asked Dorothy to notify Olga.

By this time Mary had rejoined her mother in Sant' Ambrogio. Olga had spent the intervening months thinking that Pound was already in the United States and that she and Mary must be prepared to join him there. She wanted her daughter with her at the same time that she fretted about the dangers of traveling through a country whose infrastructure had been destroyed.

The only civilian transport Mary could arrange was on a truck that came once a week from Genoa to Sankt Georgen to collect cardboard. She packed carefully, collecting everything she valued in a large trunk. When it was lost in transit—whether through design or mishap she never knew—she had her first taste of the fate that was inescapably hers as the bearer of relics, the purveyor of materials whose value extended far beyond her personal delight in them. The trunk had contained her father's seal ring, an emerald ring and gold brooch from Homer Pound, some of her father's books, and the map he had used to guide himself from Rome to Gais. It had contained her accumulated war savings, photographs, and food. In Milan, left only with pocket money and cigarettes, she returned to the home of "Ludmilla's mother"—the house to which she had delivered Dr. E.'s mysterious letters; when no one was home, she went on to "Willi's." There, to her surprise, she discovered Dr. E. in civilian clothes. Whoever he was, the British had since extricated him from his situation in Meran, and in his new prosperity and "radiance," he was generous with advice and money. Implying that Mary's delivered letters had been instrumental in securing his freedom, he gave her 10,000 lire, and on learning that she was an American, he told her that the American military were more likely than Italian police to help her recover the trunk.

But the trunk was irretrievably lost. The officials offered her a ride back to Gais to collect more food and clothing, but the privilege they accorded her as an American was cancelled by their response to seeing Pound's photograph on the wall of the Marchers' house. One of the drivers called him a "swine" and dropped into silence when Mary identified herself as his daughter. They carried her back to Milan, unaware that they transported a child into despair. It was not only a suitcase that had vanished. With this journey died Mary's dreams of the cultivated world that might open to her through her father. Pound could no longer guide her to America, as he had guided her through Venice, Rome, and Siena; Homer was dead, and all she could imagine before her was "a dreary crossing with Mamile to see Babbo imprisoned and the great specter: to watch him led to the electric chair."[35]

Olga's welcome was hardly less difficult. On the train journey from Milan to Genoa and from Genoa to Rapallo, Mary had been accompanied by an intrusive stranger who insisted on carrying her luggage up the hill to Sant' Ambrogio. He talked incessantly about Compton Mackenzie's *West Wind, South Wind, North Wind*, disconcerting first Mary and then Olga, who, though offering him tea, noticed that he paid undue attention to their books—perhaps he was a spy.

Whether he was or not—Mary noticed that he had quickly located Olga's copy of *West Wind, South Wind, North Wind* in the bookcase—the two women had, in a very brief time, entered into the mistrust of the hunted. The world could no longer be taken at face value; its potential for betrayal was to become a constant neighbor who threatened reliable boundaries. Olga had, perhaps, this suspicious penchant already—she was a student of the occult who gave credence to the predictions of the *I Ching*—but for Mary it was a new territory.

Soon her own value seemed as dubious as that of the stranger. When she finally admitted that she had lost Pound's seal ring, Olga's greeting shifted to wrath: she could not trust her own daughter; it was not only a loss but a "sign" of Pound's misfortune. It was, more profoundly, a sign of the strained relationship between two dissimilar and barely acquainted adults. The six months that followed, unmediated by the adored father/lover, were, in Mary's words, "strained" and "painful."

The barbs flew in all directions, and Pound, in his cage and later in his tent in the detention center, heard most of them: Dorothy was "terrified of meeting Olga" in town, for she had made "an appalling scene"[36]; Olga reminded Dorothy that it was essential to safeguard Pound's reputation and that it couldn't be done by "bickering among ourselves or showing anything but a united front to strangers."[37] Dorothy knew that Mary was in Rapallo— indeed by 10 October she was sending "3 lots" of cantos up to Sant' Ambrogio for Mary to type for her father—but complained, "I daren't write direct to Mary: unless you specify—I wish you would: it might be convenient but I am afraid of contaminating her."[38] Mary, having walked into all of this tension, added to it by telling her mother to be a "good loser."[39] Nonetheless, she carefully typed the poems and returned them in duplicate to Dorothy.

In early October she received word that she, as a "minor child," would be permitted to visit Pound at Metato for thirty minutes once a month in the presence of two guards. She and Olga arranged to travel there with South African soldiers stationed in Rapallo on 17 October. By this time, Pound had survived what he summarized for his old friend Viola Baxter Jordan as "one month death cells, four month solitary" and considered that he had "recovered mentally and physically."[40] Olga saw a man who was "being well-treated and is in better health than before"; she saw someone "very calm and cheerful."[41] Mary, who had last seen him in dusty exhaustion after his trip from Rome to Gais, recognized underlying distress when she saw it; she noticed that his eyes were inflamed and that he had aged in the short time since their last meeting. She had no way to visualize the cage he had been kept in previously—Pound used the Italian word "gabbia" and did not elaborate on the iron spikes that had surrounded him, the lack of sanitation, the exposure to sun, floodlights, and cold. He was glad to see them; he spared them. At the end of the allotted half hour, they said goodbye. There was nothing Mary could do for her father; there was nothing that he could do for her. They parted in mutual impotence.

A young prison officer at the detention center, Homer Somers, took credit for helping get Pound out of the cages—Pound reminded him of his father back in Tinmouth, Vermont. Both were literate men "of the old school" and the young man appreciated Pound's quick retorts. He also liked Mary, whom he described as "a beautiful thing . . . a nice looking honey blond."[42] But the real reason Pound had been moved to an officer's tent in the Medical Compound was that he had collapsed from the strain of isolation, exposure, and anxiety. While he waited to learn his fate, he wrote. By the end of October, he had by and large finished the *Pisan Cantos*; between 5 October and 5 November, he worked on translating the Ta S'eu [*Ta Hio*] and the Chung Yung [Pound's name for it was *The Unwobbling Pivot*], plus abridged editions of the analects and Mencius. Whether he knew of Lt. Col. John Steele's increasing unease at holding a civilian prisoner is not clear. A few days after Mary and Olga's visit, Steele sent a message to the War Department saying that the DTC would release him unless they received further instructions. He noted in his memo that "all FBI Agents [in Italy] will have departed for the UNITED STATES by end of October."[43] He had already written once before asking for clarification. In fact, he had telephoned Frank Amprim in Rome, asking what to do with Pound on 4 August and had been told that returning Pound to the U.S. would in no way prejudice the FBI's investigation. Steele urged the Department of Justice to authorize Pound's return in August, but it wasn't until 5 November that he learned that 14 November was the probable target date for Pound's transport.

In the interim, Mary continued receiving cantos to type. They still had to come through Dorothy and through the base censor with an explanation that they were neither subversive nor a kind of cipher, even though they contained local references to the life of the DTC. The responsibility for typing them correctly weighed heavily on her, but through the details, she began to understand her father's profound suffering and his equally profound capacity to transform suffering into chilling clarity. Through his language, she traveled with him: "'We who have passed over Lethe.' For me he had by then entered into the dimension of the Beyond. This feeling had nothing to do with hero worship or morbid attachment. It was respect. Transcendental . . . *The Cantos* slowly became the one book I could not do without."[44]

This growing inner life, its compulsions and commitments, its vision of depths, its sorrow, occurred amid similar struggles within Olga and Dorothy. Although Mary had by now learned that both women in the older generation lived by a code of self-containment ("feelings are things other people have. One never spoke of them or showed them"),[45] she saw her mother break down when she read Canto LXXXI with its cry of "AOI." She understood through this outburst that, though her father was now imprisoned, Olga's "captivity" had been ongoing, an emotional restriction forced upon her by her position in relation to Dorothy—a position that had, of course, been exacerbated by cohabiting during the war. She also began to see that although *The Cantos* contained no wartime ciphers that an army officer might censor, they were replete with personal codes recognizable to those most intimate with her father. Dorothy was included in this private circle, but her responses were ones Mary was forced to imagine.

In retrospect, judging by her letters, we can see that Dorothy coped by continued restraint. She missed Pound, but once she was permitted to write and visit, she communicated with calm and even pedestrian understatement. Amid chatty news of visitors and daily activities, she kept Pound informed about Omar, who had enlisted in the U.S. Army stationed in Bremen, and she finally admitted—in fact it is a theme in her letters during this time—that she wanted to make a home for the three of them once Pound's political troubles were resolved. She seems never to have doubted that they would be resolved. The problems, in her mind, were pragmatic ones like finding the appropriate legal representation for her husband, and her views were reinforced by Pound's reiteration of his belief that he had abided by the United States Constitution. He also thanked her for her steady, British good sense: "You have given me thirty years of peace clear as blue feldspar and I am grateful."[46]

Pound never responded to Dorothy's vision of a postwar, post-trial "home," and he never interrupted her flow of mundanities with the fears he expressed to those around him that he might be condemned to death. She seems to have survived by a continual denial of complexity. This veneer was punctured, interestingly, by her continued curiosity about Mary's presence in Rapallo. She first noticed the girl on the street—"recognized her by likeness round the nose & mouth to Isabel & her legs resembling Olga's. She had her hair all loose on her shoulders—no puritan-peasant 'braids' anymore! I do hope the child can think, & not only imitate others."[47] Pound knew that she could "think," and he assumed that his wife and daughter would continue to collaborate in preparing his work for publication. In January 1946, Dorothy finally reported that she had met the girl at "Ma" Riess's, but by this time everyone's life circumstances had changed.

Just before Mary's next scheduled vision to the DTC on 23 November, Pound was taken away. Hoover's orders had finally come through, and with Pound's extradition to the U.S. on 16 November, a set of circumstances far too complex for any individual family member to comprehend, much less to combat, was set in motion. On 18 November his plane landed at Bolling Field; on the next morning he went to a preliminary arraignment before Bolitha J. Laws, chief justice of the District of Columbia District Court, and was sent back to jail. On 26 November, the attorney general announced a new indictment charging Pound with nineteen overt acts of treasonous broadcasting between 11 September 1942 and 15 May 1943. The next day he was formally arraigned and then put in the Gallinger Hospital in Washington because Julien Cornell, his lawyer, had argued that Pound might lose his sanity if he were to remain in jail. He continued to base his defense on the issue of Pound's sanity. As the machinery of state moved forward, Cornell, considering the hostile political climate in general, and Hoover's animosity in particular, had Pound examined by four psychiatrists (three provided by the government) who all judged him to be insane and unable to aid in his own defense. On 21 December, Judge Laws ordered Pound to St. Elizabeths Hospital for the Insane, where he was placed in a small cell with an iron door. By 27 December, having spent years at the "hunt" and untold resources of the military and civilian government, having radically disrupted the lives of Pound's family, Hoover lost interest in his prey. He issued a memo to the FBI Communications Section: "Department has authorized discontinuance of investigation. Pending further court action as to Pound's sanity, you will be advised if investigation desired at later date."[48]

For Mary, the drama occurred offstage, and she discovered what little she did know through newspapers and then, indirectly, through Dorothy who had the news from Omar Pound, and still later from Homer Somers. No one from the U.S. government had thought to contact the family. Omar, who had tried to visit Pound in Pisa, arrived at the DTC shortly after Pound had been taken to the military airport near Rome. He took the news immediately to Rapallo, where he spent ten days with Dorothy, but apparently neither of them sent word up to Sant' Ambrogio, for Mary and Olga were in town trying to find a jeep to take them to Pisa when a woman in a news shop asked them if they had seen the papers. And that was that. They climbed the hill again to wait.

Sometime during this visit, between 20 November and 30 November, Mary saw Omar Pound for the first time. She and Olga had gone to meet John Drummond at a local bar when he walked in. Drummond offered embarrassed introductions, but Omar showed no signs of recognition. Mary wondered why he was so cold—"No ice was broken. We evidently had nothing in common"[49]—but, in fact, Omar had no idea who she was. He too had been raised in ignorance, which, in his case, had not been broken by confession. On 22 December, Dorothy wrote to Ezra, perhaps in response to Omar's inquiry about the girl in the bar, "I told Omar all about Mary. . . . I thought it better, as so many now know & I found him quite capable of understanding it—That was, I felt, enough for one visit" and without pausing went on to say that her son had seen *Tosca* in Paris and hated it.[50]

Omar left, and then she and Mary returned to their tasks—Mary typing cantos and putting in Greek; Dorothy inserting Chinese characters and then sending them on to T. S. Eliot and James Laughlin. For Dorothy life resumed its pattern of small enjoyments—she chatted on about her favorite foods and expressed the hope that Pound was getting enough "rest and relaxation"; for Olga, the poorly paid English lessons by which she supported herself continued. To Mary, none of this mattered. Around Christmas she received what Pound called a *vers de noel*. From St. Elizabeths he wrote, "Dearest Child, tell your mother I bless the day I first saw her and thank her for all the happiness she has brought me. A gleam of hope now the sun is reborn. Love to both of you . . . 'First must now go the road to hell and to the bower of Circe's daughter Proserpine.'" And in early February, she received some more lines of verse expressing the reality that underlay an otherwise mundane exchange of news: "The soft wind from the south/ Draws safe to the bough/ Mother, mother, my pain!"[51]

While she thought about what she should do with her life, Mary worked. Father Desmond Chute was editing a book of Eric Gill's letters and needed a typist; another elderly member of the English colony, Mrs. Riess, needed a companion. Her tasks were minimal, and she often had time to write for long hours, even before the severity of her father's fate had time to register: "My dearest Father . . . Two days ago I received another letter from Menotti saying your trial has been put off. I think all the prayers that are being said for you are having their good effect. I do hope that they'll soon acknowledge their mistake and review months of suffering."[52] She described this period in her life as a time of self-hatred, overeating, and writing bad poetry.

In January 1946, Dorothy Pound returned a book to Mrs. Riess and came face to face with Mary for the first time. Olga thought the visit had been arranged out of malicious curiosity, and there may have been some truth to Dorothy's impulse to snoop, but it was not spiteful. "Had the good luck to meet Mary on Sunday: chez Ma Riess: She is helping look after the old lady. . . . I was so thankful for the encounter, senz l'altra. Also, I had a message for Olga, wh. was useful. She's a large healthy object! Ma. R. says so competent & likes her so much—I expect there's some charm; but we only had ten minutes."[53] A few days later she wrote: "I am hoping to get into friendly relations with Mary—via Ma Riess: but must go very carefully."[54] The proprietary impulse, manifest in 1939 when she wanted to adopt Mary and in 1940 when she wrote to Pound about taking "the children" to Japan, evidently continued. "I met Mary again last Sunday," she informed Pound at the end of the month: she poured out tea for us chez Ma Riess: they get on 1st rate together. M. very happy there. I shan't be able to see her again, as she has to go back to No. 60. I like her: she has an awful prim *jeune fille bien élevée* manner that is unpleasant: but I think it melts. I am reading & correcting her m.s.s. re Gais &

the hospital etc: mostly interesting. She was apparently asked whether she wished to meet me!—& (wisely!) said yes. I believe she wants to go back to Gais: feeling she has nothing to do here: also, Ma. Riess says some people look askance at her here. . . . 'instead of being *more* kind to her.' She has put her hair up: & looks charming: she's looking very business & nice and neat. Her face will always be a little wide: but anyway, that's a good fault so to say."[55] She continued by saying that she was "really hoping I can help Mary . . . but it all depends on how free or independent she is from No. 60."

She need not have worried. Mary was independent in every sense. She formed her own judgment of Dorothy ("I met D. here. I like her.")[56] But liking did not imply needing a surrogate parent. She didn't care what other people thought of her, nor did she want to be engulfed in what Pound, a continent away, could sense and express as "the multitude of my family's calamaties" [sic].[57] The rancor between her mother and Dorothy had already poisoned the everyday world. Whatever glimpses she had been given of cultivated life in Venice, Siena, and Rome were empty of promise; Rapallo she described as "devious and treacherous"; America, once the locus of longing and hope, now frightened her. She formed a plan that included neither Dorothy nor Olga, based on an unspoken bond with her father. Its two pillars were books: Confucian ethics and Ronald Duncan's memoir about communal farming in the west of England, *Journal of a Husbandman*.

She shared her inner life, to the extent that she shared it at all, with a young, unexpected correspondent—the second lieutenant who had guarded Pound in Pisa. Several weeks after Pound left the DTC, Homer Somers wrote, ostensibly to ask her for a copy of Pound's one-page treatise on economics and history. He explained that it had been his duty to censor her father's mail and to look in on him at the camp. "At first I found him too deep," he said, but eventually the two had formed a bond and Pound had taken on a professorial role. "I shall never forget him . . . E.P. wrote a thank you note to our section. Needless to say, we were pleased to hear from him and honored that he should think of us. He impressed everyone here favorably—soldiers and prisoners."[58] He rightly surmised that she would have trouble getting news and included press clippings about him. As he continued to send clippings, he added details about himself and his own opinions—he couldn't wait to get out of the army; he wanted to study more and then retreat to his home in Tinmouth, Vermont. When Pound was pronounced "insane" by the psychiatrists, he said that he didn't agree with them "but the people have been heated up by publicity plus the success of the British Courts . . . and some plausible excuse must be given."[59] Finally there was no news to share—Pound had retreated into the silence of St. Elizabeths—but Somers continued to write, eventually asking for Mary's photograph and expressing the desire to visit her in the Tyrol. He was not ambitious—he liked the hills and lakes around his home—he liked to garden; he had a fine library; he enjoyed solitude. He was inclined to lead exactly the kind of quiet, industrious, and literate life Mary anticipated for herself in the face of her family's collapse. "Your conflict is exactly like mine," he told her, thinking about the tensions between the agrarian life and the life of the mind, "only you have started."[60] Years later he thought that his letters had probably been "pretty conservative. I couldn't let her know how much I ached for her."[61]

It is not clear if Mary discussed Ronald Duncan with Homer Somers, but she was deeply influenced by his recently published *Journal of a Husbandman*, evidently recommended to her by Pound, even though he himself didn't like it. ("Ronnie's rather terrible Husbandman book has come.")[62] Duncan was as distinctive as her father in his choice of lifestyles and in his independent political thought. An Englishman born in Rhodesia, he had met Pound in 1938 on his way back from a long visit to Gandhi in India. He took from Gandhi a commitment to peace (he was registered as a conscientious objector in World War II); he took from Pound the impetus to found and edit the magazine *Townsman*. On his own, he had decided to retreat to a farmstead on the border of Devon and Cornwall to experiment with communal farming. The experiment failed, but Duncan continued to dwell in a small, dilapidated millhouse in Welcombe with his wife, Rosemary. As a matter of principle, they lived in a primitive style, "collecting their timber and firewood on the beach and carrying their milk and groceries down the steep hill from the village."[63] He combined the arduous tasks of growing food and animal husbandry with writing and publishing from a printing press in his kitchen.

The book offered Mary a bridge between two worlds that had, until she read it, remained without any imaginable means of integration. "Surely to grow one's own bread is the minimum base for political morality," she read. And she continued reading about Duncan's satisfaction in providing the tangible means of his own existence: "To take a loaf from the oven, a cheese from the press or even finding a nest of eggs, these are real pleasures . . . more reliable and satisfying than most of the abstract fiddling most of us had toyed with. . . . Somehow or other we have fallen into the rot of thinking that pigs and poetry are incompatible. It is not so."[64] "You are very much here in Rapallo," she wrote to Pound in response. "Duncan's journal has helped me.

I'm convinced now that it's best for me to becoming a good farmer first of all—that would not interfere with my lettering interest and will put me in a position to have something to say."[65]

While Duncan's book helped her to imagine a practical path for herself—a return to Gais, an independent cottage, self-reliance in all things and all things arranged according to William Morris—have nothing in your home that is not both beautiful and useful—she returned to Confucius as a guide for her interior life. This is not to say that she became a philosopher, but rather to see that she undertook to live a life of sincerity and self-discipline. Lacking a foundation in formal education, lacking a family—she could see that her presence in Rapallo did nothing to increase Olga's happiness—lacking money, she decided that she must build on character, that is, by "looking straight into the heart and then acting on the results."[66] She would combine cultivation of the land with self-cultivation.

Her plans had to be made privately and they were, perforce, modest. Herr Bacher in Gais was at the heart of it, for she anticipated returning to the Tyrol with its patrilineal transfer of land. She had no Tyrolean father from whom to inherit and she was the "wrong" gender in any case, so she would need to rent and borrow, but Herr Bacher had a suitable cottage and she anticipated that his long affection for her and respect for her father would stand her in good stead. She wanted to learn woodworking and sculpture from him; she wanted to become an artist with a medium of expression not dependent upon language, for there was no language in which she felt at home. With wood sculpture, she would not have to "rent and borrow" words but could work directly with her hands.

As idealistic as these intentions were, they give us a way to imagine the depth of the interior dilemma of this young "Confucian" woman: at the very moment when Pound was declared "insane," she staked her life on the "inner order" of her father's emotional landscape. During the time when the fraught relationships of Pound's extended family exposed a lack of order or prudent self-government, she decided to carry forward what she perceived to be both his values and his virtues, as if he somehow existed above or outside of the hatreds and rivalries remaining in Rapallo. "I thought I was rejecting all the lies and pretensions and compromises," she wrote, "Mamile's dark resentment, grandmother's stubbornness, Dorothy and Omar, whatever, whoever they were. . . . All I wanted to keep was something to believe in— the freedom to live the kind of life I thought Babbo had meant me to live— simple and laborious."[67] By early February, she confided her plans to Ma Riess, who thought she should devote more time to education before returning to the mountains and handed her some volumes of Shakespeare to read.

It was Olga who delayed Mary's departure by pulling out the will Pound had written in 1940: I, Ezra Pound, "being sound of mind and body. . . . The said Mary I declare to be my daughter. . . . My wife . . . has approved it. . . . In no sense to be taken as injurious. . . . She and her son are otherwise provided for."[68] "All that I possess"—money and securities, books and artworks—were left to Mary.[69] She was the sole beneficiary of his estate and its executor. So she spent months sorting the papers that Frank Amprim had not taken as evidence for Pound's trial, papers that were presumably guiltless, tying her heritage into bundles, stowing it in boxes and making lists before she could depart from the life that she had never really had in the first place. She found the work unbearable. "Embalmed. Deadweight. . . . Light and lightness had fled from the house, hovering, shrouded, and sighing among the gray olive branches outside."[70]

During these months, she ran into Father Chute, who concurred with Mrs. Riess's opinion that she should remain in Rapallo. "Remember," he told her, "that in the eyes of God, according to our Catholic faith, your mother is your father's true wife."[71] She listened, unmoved. She had resolved to leave. Olga was miffed. Dorothy considered that she had "fled." From across the ocean, Pound wrote, "Cheeild a comfort."[72] Mary quoted bitter Shakespeare to sum it all up. After she was gone, Olga discovered lines from *The Merchant of Venice:*

"Farewell, and if my fortune be not crossed
I have a father, you a daughter lost."[73]

CHAPTER 4

Secret Agents

The OSS and FBI in Rome and London, 1944–46

I

At the end of February 1946, Mary returned to Gais. While she had been away, preoccupied by the fate of her father, the village, and indeed the entire South Tyrol, had become the object of international negotiation. Reiterating history, the Allied powers once again treated the region as if it were the spoils of war, ignoring the Tyrolean desire for autonomy and calculating its fate according to entirely extraneous political requirements. "The political situation here is very tense, extremely interesting," Mary wrote to Olga as soon as she arrived.[1] Even Homer Somers, who was still on duty in Pisa, could see the area's strategic importance and understand the issues that were rekindled with the defeat of the Axis. Amid a wistful, understated courtship-by-mail, he paused in his reflections to observe to Mary, "I wouldn't be a bit surprised if the Tyrol reverts back to Austrian control. Of course, the hydroelectric plants and a few minerals will be missed by the Italians," he continued, "but they are a Germanic people and should be under their own political leaders."[2]

Surrounded by vociferous local opinions that by 1945 had been institutionalized in the South Tyrolean People's Party (*Südtiroler Volkspartei*), Mary reassembled her life. There were, once again, the necessities of everyday existence in a peasant economy. In March the plowing began. She made wool; she did the spinning. She helped Frau Marcher care for her foster sister Margherita's child. Although she had spoken to Herr Bacher about the little cottage on his land and about becoming an apprentice wood sculptor, she had to wait for the current occupant's lease to expire. Until that time of anticipated independence, she had to compromise with a private garden plot between the Marchers' house and the road, and a single sheep.

Discordant communications arrived in the post: Olga, pointedly, sent her a poem quoting Pound's definition of a lie. From Dorothy came offers of money with their implicit but clearly understood claims of kinship and influence. In early April Dorothy reported to Pound, "I sent the money (5,000) lire) as you wished to her. Have had an answer, thanking me—no land for sale & she wouldn't . . . dream of . . . spending yr. money for anything else - & has sent it back to her Mother. So, I am awaiting some kind of explosion."[3] It is not clear if Dorothy also forwarded Julien Cornell's letters from the United States explaining the implications of Pound's incarceration. Cornell was careful to keep in touch with her, and to put the "insanity" judgment in some kind of perspective: "I am sorry that you may have been startled and alarmed by reports of your husband's condition," he wrote, continuing with the reassurance that "I feel quite sure that you will find that he is his usual self, and the mental aberrations which the doctors have found are not anything new or unusual, but . . . would pass entirely unnoticed by one like yourself who has lived close to him for a number of years. In fact I think it may be fairly said that any man of his genius would be regarded by a psychiatrist as abnormal."[4] But it seems unlikely that this information was shared, for in April, having to some extent mended the breach with her mother, Mary was prattling on about where Olga and her father might live in the near future: "I think it [London] wd really be quite nice—much better than the States, for I dare say you would feel more at home. I think I personally wd. prefer it."[5] In her judgment, Pound cared more about his "moral family" than his "legal family," and she wrote to her father as if he were simply having a rest, and asked him to visit her in Gais; "I would like to spend a few weeks just with you alone to make up for all the time I missed you."[6] Only when James Laughlin wrote in June to say that it would be dangerous to try to secure Pound's release "too soon," did she revise her sense of imminent reunion. No letter from anyone conveyed the fragments Pound scribbled on 1 January when he found himself in a ward for the criminally insane: "Mental Torture. Constitution a religion. A world lost. Grey mist barrier impassible. Ignorance absolute. . . . Coherent areas constantly invaded. Aiuto [help]."[7]

She saw what was at hand: "demonstrations and processions everywhere. Last week we had a rather serious row in Brunneck—a German farmer was killed by an Italian carabinieri—an allied commission had to come and put things in order again." In May it was the same thing: "The whole population is excited about politics. I never saw anything like this."[8] She was reading Reut-Nicolussi's book about the Tyrol, augmenting common knowledge with historical perspective, watching as 150,000 signatures were gathered and as Austrian Chancellor Leopold Figl appealed for the return of South Tyrol. Later in the month, there was a general strike.

Neither the Italians nor the Austrians knew that Washington, London, and the Council of Foreign Ministers had already decided "by default" that they would not redraw borders to accord with the desires of the local population; they would be guided by expediency rather than social justice. To hand over the Bozen area to Austria might, they argued, "assist Russian designs in Central Europe and operate against the establishment of a Western democratic regime in Italy."[9] In September Italy's Prime Minister Alcide De Gasperi and Austria's Foreign Minister Karl Gruber signed an agreement in Paris that "envisioned" special measures to preserve the ethnic identity of the South Tyrolese. While this did nothing to settle the unrest that surrounded Mary or to calm the demands for an immediate "Break with Rome!" that peppered local headlines, the accord, sometimes referred to as the Magna Carta of the Tyrol, laid a foundation for a more open future; at the least, it established that the area was an international problem and no longer simply the internal affair of Italy.

But none of this was visible to ordinary people in 1946, and intentionally so. As Noël Charles, the British ambassador in Rome, observed in a "Top Secret" memo, "we must be prepared to use the same methods for keeping communism down in Italy as the Russians are using in order to have their views prevail in this country, i.e., supporting clandestinely one particular party with weapons of propaganda, finance and steel."[10] And so local protest in Gais continued, as did Mary's farming and her earliest attempts at writing poetry.

II

Shortly before Mary returned to Gais, Frank Amprim returned to Rome to continue his clandestine work. Where Mary counted wealth by the ownership of a single animal ("I was sure Tatte or one of Mamme's brothers would lend me a cow. My existence seemed to depend on a cow"),[11] Amprim had the resources of the United States government at his command. He had arrived in Italy in August 1943, with an extensive mandate from the FBI but, paradoxically, with no authority to operate outside the United States. His first move was to initiate a meeting with Vincent Scamporino and to request help.[12] Scamporino was then chief of the Italian Division, Secret Intelligence (SI), Rome, and his primary duty at the time was "to obtain information, documents, and intelligence" about the relations of the Italian government with Germany, Spain, Portugal, England, Russia, Japan, and South America.[13] He was also to identify enemy agents operating in the German-occupied part of northern Italy where Mary lived and to infiltrate subversive movements or political organizations of security interest.[14] He, in turn, had no authority to assist the FBI, so he wrote directly to William Donovan, head of the Office of Strategic Services, to ask for approval. Because both Scamporino and Donovan hoped, in turn, to "milk" the FBI for information about Italians in South America, this authorization was granted; Amprim was given a military uniform as "cover," and he proceeded with his long list of tasks. J. Edgar Hoover wanted the OSS's help not only with arresting Pound, but also in providing information about members of OVRA (Organizzazione Vigilanze Repressione dell' Antifascista); documentary evidence of communications between ex-combatants in the U.S. and the Italian Fascist government and/or the Dante Alighieri Society; information about the Italian Tourist Company, which it suspected of providing cover for espionage activities of OVRA agents; the Nazi Party in Italy; the Italian Chamber of Commerce; the photographic office of the Ministry of Popular Culture; the names of correspondents for the Agenzia Stefani; and various kinds of information about Italian businessmen and industrialists with contacts in Argentina.[15]

By the time Pound was apprehended in Genoa, Amprim had been working under military cover, and with the cooperation of the OSS, for almost two years. His reports to the Army Liaison Section indicate that he was initially at sea regarding Pound. In one, for example, he reported (as was not the case) that Pound was enrolled in the National Fascist Party; in another he falsely claimed that Pound had acquired Italian citizenship. In a still later memo, he reported that Pound was "a writer and also a dentist."[16] But he continued to work on a profile, going to the EIAR on 5 June 1944, where he found employees who remembered seeing Pound reading into a microphone from a manuscript; a few days later he rummaged through the EIAR's storeroom and found two of the discs, which he numbered and labeled and photographed. By 1944, most of the people Pound had worked with had left the station—first it had been handed over to the Germans when they occupied the city; then in September 1943, it had been claimed by the Allies. Ranieri de San Faustino had resigned voluntarily when the Germans took over;[17] others, like Adreano Ungaro at the Ministry of Popular Culture, had been dismissed. Amprim tracked them down, along with Salvatore Aponte, Cornelio di Marzio, G. B. Vicari, Luigi Villari, Odon Por, Admiral Ubaldo degli Uberti, Camillo Pelizzi, Natalie Troubetzkoi, Olivia Rossetti Agresti, Nora Naldi and her husband, until the people who had befriended Pound's daughter in her brief introduction to Roman culture became, as he put it, "confidential foreign sources" who could "give information regarding the subject's treasonable acts." Ranieri de San Faustino had told Amprim that he thought Pound's personnel file had been destroyed, but in October Amprim succeeded in locating it, not at the radio station but at the Ministry of Popular Culture. He sent it to the Psychological Warfare Branch of the army in Rome.[18]

Amprim was relentless. He assembled a list of all the newspaper reporters who had been in Rome at the onset of the war and got statements from Reynolds and Eleanor Packard of the United Press, Herbert Macken from the *New York Times*, and Bill Stoneman from the *Chicago Daily News*. He scrutinized a list provided by the Roman Questura of all Americans currently living in Rome. He went to Milan in search of possible files. And he read 7,000 pages of Pound's confiscated papers and manuscripts, forwarding some of them to Washington, including "letters to Pound from his daughter MARY RUDGE."[19] He also sent a scrapbook of clippings covering Pound's visit to the U.S. in 1939, which had been handed over to him by the partisans who arrested Pound in his home—a fact that suggests that Amprim knew the partisans and, perhaps though certainly not verifiably, had secretly arranged their raid.[20] In August he went out to the MTOUSA Discipline Center to reinterview Pound to ask him if anyone had ever seen him type the original manuscripts. The answer was "no" but that he sometimes had shown the finished typescripts to Olga.[21] He then returned twice to see Olga, the second time taking her photograph and forwarding it to Washington. These two visits were the basis of Olga's belief that she had to remain ready to go to the U.S. for Pound's trial. While she anticipated the ways that she could help explain his ideas and motivations, clearly picturing herself as a witness for the defense, Amprim wrote to Hoover that Olga Rudge was one of the best witnesses for the prosecution, since she could come closest to linking Pound's writing manuscripts (her part) to his actually broadcasting them and receiving money from the Italian government for their production. Later in the same month, he received an unexpected gold mine, for Sidney L. Henderson from Military Counter Intelligence (G-2) sent him a file on Pound that had been found among the dead Mussolini's papers.[22]

But as he was preparing to go to "northern Italy" to interview people like the Marchers and Bachers and presumably Mary herself, Amprim received word that he was to suspend work on the "general case" and to focus his efforts on finding two witnesses to each act of overt treason. Looking through the voluminous materials Amprim had provided, the adjutant general of the War Department simply and pointedly observed that the witnesses who saw Pound read could not say that Pound had prepared the manuscripts that they observed in his hands. "Thus these witnesses would not fulfill the statutory requirement: two witnesses to same overt act."[23] Amprim was at a loss, for as he clearly admitted, once he had formed a picture of how things worked at Radio EIAR, first, that the only witnesses who had seen Pound at a microphone had observed him before Pearl Harbor—their testimony would be worthless since Italy was not then an enemy nation;[24] and second, that Pound and an informant from the Ministry of Popular Culture had both explained, and he himself had corroborated, that the later recordings were made in a basement studio with no windows connecting the sound rooms with the adjoining rooms, so it was impossible to actually see Pound doing anything at all.[25] Thus, even as he prepared his final report, joining his findings with those of the numerous American-based agents who had worked the case in the States, he explained to Hoover that no evidentiary chain had been or could be established, no matter how many Italian radio technicians the FBI might want to round up as possible witnesses. "The weakness of this chain of proof is that only one witness is available."[26]

He did not mention in his summary report the other problems with the Pound case, namely that he knew Pound was wrongfully imprisoned. In September, John Drummond, writing again on behalf of Pound, "authorized by his wife and mother," asked the assistant judge advocate general at MTOUSA if and how Pound's solicitors, Messrs. Shakespear and Parkyn, could visit Mr. Pound to discuss "engaging counsel for the defense at the coming trial in America." He observed that the solicitors could not approach an American law firm unless and until they knew Pound's preferences and had his authority to proceed.[27] A few days later, Lt. Col. M. R. Irion, writing on behalf of the military, forwarded Drummond's letter to the FBI, saying, "Mr. Pound is not under the jurisdiction of this office or BOJAG."[28] Amprim received Drummond's letter, forwarded a copy of it to Hoover, and told him that he had advised Drummond that "Ezra Pound is not a prisoner of the Federal

Bureau of Investigation and that, therefore, the writer cannot advise him."[29] But if Pound was not under the jurisdiction of either the American military or the Federal Bureau of Investigation, by whose authority was he locked in a cage? Those who had assumed (specious?) responsibility for his confinement could, at the least, see the human consequences of their actions: "Now confined at Disciplinary Training Center is EZRA POUND. Psychiatrist reports that due to age and loss of personality resilience, premonitory symptoms are discernible of mental breakdown. Return to UNITED STATES recommended without delay."[30] Aside from his disclaimer of responsibility, which effectively denied Pound legal counsel, Amprim did nothing.

III

Sometime between November 1944 and September 1945, again while assembling his profile on the case, Amprim re-interviewed James Jesus Angleton. The years since he had graduated from Yale, with his youthful fervor for Pound and undergraduate magazines, had changed Jim Angleton from a modern literature enthusiast to a very different kind of person. In 1939 he had been writing to Pound about his poetic genius and his role as a political visionary: "There is no doubt about it that people are going to wake up to the fact that (and e. e. [cummings] told me this) that Pound is right after all. The whole country is hot after war. We had a peace petition anti-credit to the Allies etc. which got over 1000 names."[31] He was routinely referring to Pound as "the sage" and "the world's unappreciated genius," beseeching him for cantos to print, asking his advice on books to read about economics, agreeing that "what must go to Hell is the foreign bank influence in the U.S.,"[32] and complaining to Pound that the Roosevelt administration was trying to pass "laws against the fifth column [as a] way to stop anti-war believers."[33] Amid his continued pleas for Pound's contributions to *Furioso* and *Vif*, he bragged about the photographs he had taken of Pound in the summer of 1938 in Rapallo: "I have your pictures which have been ogled at by every Yale English Professor . . . my instructor . . . almost wept with joy when I gave him a small picture of you staring full faced at the camera. . . . Here at school, I have been incorporating myself into a sort of Ezra Pound Information Bureau."[34] In May 1940, just before he graduated, he offered Pound a place to stay, should he need shelter in the U.S. and said with apparent sincerity, "I want to do something for you. . . . Please let me know as I have the summer and I would be willing to give all the time to this. Everything is up to you, my dear Ezra."[35]

By 1943 he had become an informant against Pound for the FBI.[36] Angleton was, of course, one of many people the FBI tracked down in the United States as it began to build its case against Pound. But after following scores of leads, the FBI considered his testimony the most useful—it survived dozens of Bureau analyses and remained, almost in its entirety, in Amprim's final report to J. Edgar Hoover in 1945. Angleton provided them with details of Pound's life that they had not gleaned from other sources, a full view of Pound's movements and contacts during his 1939 trip to the States, an analysis of his social credit theory, a summary judgment of his status as a poet and an explanation of Pound's political theories. He took (false) credit for Pound's coming to America ("it was largely due to his suggestion that Dr. Pound made this trip to the United States"), and he told the FBI about Pound's anti-Semitism ("subsequent to the war POUND went to Paris where he developed a tremendously strong anti-Jewish attitude") while neglecting to mention that he routinely expressed a virulent anti-Semitism in his own letters to Pound.[37] According to Angleton, "when Pound gets into the field of economics or politics he proceeds to become irrational and he believes that he has even noted a strain of insanity in these particular fields."[38] He told the Boston agent that he would be willing to testify against Pound in any prosecution for treason. Then he handed over photographs of Pound. These images, once the joy of the literary circle at Yale, became the means by which Pound was identified to FBI agents in the field and the secret service of the United States military.[39]

Amprim's second interview of Angleton occurred in Rome, and it was apparently occasioned by his need to verify a few facts—another of his informants had mistakenly remembered the date of Pound's trip to America as 1938—and Angleton was able to reconfirm 1939 as the correct year. There was nothing remarkable about the meeting except that it occurred at all. A strange circuitry of events had brought Angleton back to Italy in August 1944; and though he was in a position of authority, he found himself, through a series of covert circumstances, in unexpected rivalry with Vincent Scamporino, Frank Amprim's "protector" in the military secret services.

Angleton had left Harvard Law School to enlist in the U.S. Army in 1943.[40] Within a matter of months, he had been pulled from his original assignment with the 711th MP Battalion by a special request for his transfer to the Office

of Strategic Services in Washington, D.C. It is possible that his father engineered the reassignment—Hugh Angleton had himself joined the American
war effort and was working at OSS headquarters in July—but it is more likely
that his former literature professor at Yale, Norman Holmes Pearson, was responsible. Despite his patriotic fervor (spurred perhaps in part by seizure of
his business assets in Italy), Hugh Angleton was not a conventionally talented
soldier. His knowledge of Europe and his numerous business and political
contacts at first made him seem an ideal candidate for "strategic" assistance
to the Americans as they planned their attack on Italy and struggled north
toward German strongholds, but records indicate that he repeatedly failed
military examinations including Italian language training, and that his su-
periors refused to consider him for positions of responsibility. He had very
little authority, and by the end of July he was in any case en route to Algiers,
assigned to assist James Murphy, later leader of X-2, in the field.[41]

Jim Angleton was immediately forwarded from Washington to London
where, Norman Holmes Pearson, a founding member of the newly formed
"X-2" or counter-espionage team, eagerly awaited him. On 14 September 1943,
Pearson was told to expect the imminent arrival of his former student, who,
in James Murphy's opinion, was "especially well equipped for his assignment
and should prove most helpful to EF-001 as regards Italy."[42] The Yale literati
who had swooned over Pound's writing, had anthologized it, tried to collect
it for the Sterling Library, and delighted in owning his photographs were
reassembling for work in counterespionage in London. And Jim Angleton in
particular was heading for the desk that would follow the FBI's progress in making its case against his erstwhile hero. He had fashioned himself into a very
different kind of "Ezra Pound information bureau."

IV

Angleton was as anxious in London to make an impression as he had been
at Yale to enter the avant-garde scene and to be perceived as a leader of it.
(He wrote to Ezra Pound, "You would kill me if you knew what I have been
saying about my visit. I exaggerated the five days into months and have supplemented the time element with extracts from "Culture." . . . I told [William
Lyons Phelps] that you were a very good friend . . . the old boy almost passed
out when he heard that I knew you").[43] He strode into action as if he had an
instant expertise. Other writers have attributed this confidence in spy craft

to his undergraduate interest in modernism, as if "decoding" ciphers were somehow the fruit of interpreting innovative texts, but Angleton's interest in modern writers, from all available evidence, was entrepreneurial rather than interpretive. His imagination was spurred by the intrigue of literary politics, and, if his undergraduate writing is any indication, by intrigue in and of itself.

At Yale he had turned a difficult and unrewarding relationship with the conservative professor William Lyon Phelps (he tried unsuccessfully to get Phelps to extend an invitation to Pound to give the Bergen Lectures) into a full-blown detective story in which the main character is a great friend of "Billy Phelps." But if he is a "friend" of Phelps in the story, where in life he had been foiled by him, he portrays himself as similarly befriending others whom he means to betray. One is a "friend" for covert reasons: "It cannot be stressed how cleverly he worms himself completely into the heart of his employer." The central conceit of Angleton's undergraduate fantasy is an FBI agent (Crush) who, under the name of Humphrey Beagle, infiltrates the home of his subject (a White Russian gun smuggler) by posing as his gardener: "The identity of Beagle is never revealed until those last few minutes when he informs his employer with a gun in his own hand that he himself is Crush. Crush being none other than the long waited for Beagle. This relationship, in short, to his employer is that of Iago to Othello. . . . At the end his mask of cruelty and incongruous straightforwardness falls off to reveal him the Angel of Justice."[44]

It is not possible to know what Angleton felt when the FBI intelligence that was routinely forwarded to London began to cross his desk, but by then the imagined "mask" of Humphrey Beagle had become a daily enacted routine.[45] By February 1944, he had become chief of the Italian desk for the European Theater of Operations, routinely reading all Italian espionage and counter-espionage "traffic"; by August 1944 he was in Rome as commander of SCI-Unit Z, the only American cleared to read Top Secret Ultra information. By March 1945 he had become the commanding officer of X-2 for all of Italy. It was a meteoric rise from an initial status of Technical Grade Five, and by 1944–45, when Frank Amprim approached him in Rome, he must have felt that he had much more important things on his mind than a writer whose advice in literature, economics, and general life principles ("After I left Rapallo I was very excited about the Ta Hio and have read it often")[46] he had once cherished. By then he was at the center of an ever-expanding network of information, enmeshed in the world of purposeful deception and its

mirrored recognition of the deception of others. He was specifically reread-
ing the military intelligence Vincent Scamporino had assembled from a
Vatican source referred to as "source Z" or "Vessel," and undermining what
Scamporino considered to be a cache of reliable information about the Far
East. The fact that Angleton was eventually proved right did nothing to diminish the immediate and intense animosity between the two divisions.[47]
But regardless of other preoccupations, he dutifully initialed everything he
read "JA," so we know that some lingering interest compelled him to read
the FBI files on Pound.[48]

It was not as if he had forsaken the world of literature for the world of
espionage; he had simply forsaken Pound. London was, after all, one of the
centers of literary modernism, a place once shaken by Pound's welling enthusiasms, still the home of Pound's friends T. S. Eliot (about whom Angleton had written his Yale undergraduate thesis), H.D., and Bryher. He arrived
with a door that was opened to him by his friendship with Norman Holmes
Pearson, who, in turn, had been welcomed to London by H.D. In short order, Pearson took Jim Angleton in hand, installed him in the office next to
his at 23-B Ryder Street, arranged to share his secretary, Perdita MacPherson, and guided him into the company of artists for whom the moral issues
surrounding Ezra Pound were much more complicated than handing over
photographs and turning state's witness.[49]

V

"Would one help Ezra?" H.D. wrote to Pearson on 6 August 1944.[50] There is
no record of Pearson's reply, but the question bears witness to a shared burden of complexity—or at least to one person's burden and another person's
willing role as confidant. For H.D. the question grew out of a tidal surge of
damage and liberation that Pound seemed always to provoke. To her he was
poet, lover, mentor, traitor—representative of the path she had taken as an
artist; representative of the life she had been denied as a woman, historically
a current undoubtedly joined with her own, and now seemingly flowing in a
dangerously divergent direction. Did his support of Italian Fascism obliter-
ate the obligations of that joint history?

In 1944 she had been in London for almost five years, living in a cramped
flat in Lowndes Square with Bryher, enduring the Blitz and the sounds of
anti-aircraft guns, and worrying as her daughter, Perdita, drove a volunteer

food canteen through various bombsites.[51] In 1941 Perdita left that work to become a typist at Bletchley Park, working for the British secret service, "doing," as she said, "Italian, which is rather a joke seeing I don't know a word of the language, except just one word, 'perdita' which keeps on occurring."[52]

Pearson's arrival in April 1943 was a godsend for all of them. Remembering the war years in 1986, Perdita recognized that he triangulated between her mother and Bryher, who felt trapped together with only occasional respites from each other. And his practical influence in her life was also immediate, for within months, the OSS in London had created a separate unit to work in tandem with the British XX Committee in detecting German agents operating in the United Kingdom and in penetrating German ciphers about troop movements, flight plans, and so forth. Pearson got her a job as his secretary; when Jim Angleton arrived, she worked for him as well. In August Pearson wrote to H.D. that her daughter was "working in splendidly. . . . I admired the ease with which she has stepped into a new situation and caught up a new kind of work."[53] No longer billeted at Bletchley Park, Perdita moved into a flat across the street from her two "mothers" and gradually learned that H.D. had met Pearson in New York in 1937 when William Rose Benét sent him to New York to interview her for *The Oxford Anthology of American Literature*, which the two men were editing together.[54]

Now, six years later, war had brought them together again. H.D. could invite Pearson, and later Angleton, to various soirées that continued to be held in London and to readings to benefit the war effort. She included them in the circle of people who shared "dull yellow cake" with them on Sundays: Edith and Osbert Sitwell, Silvia Dobson, the Hendersons, Robert Herring, and George Plank. As cosmopolitan, well-traveled men with Yale literary backgrounds, Pearson and Angleton could comfortably enter into their ardent, meager world. But as civilians, H.D. and Bryher were not privy to any of the work that their OSS guests did. Perdita could write, as she occasionally did, about the effects of the summer heat on their work: "We just sit and pant over our Most Secret documents,"[55] but nothing substantive could be shared. A wall of secrecy surrounded work on enemy espionage networks. In fact, Robin Winks has identified Ultra (the code name for the project of "cracking" German military ciphers) as "the most closely held intelligence coup of the war. Not one word of it escaped to the general public until nearly three decades after the war when, in 1974, the publication of the first book on the subject opened the door to a dozen more."[56] So whatever H.D. shared with Pearson as she struggled with the moral issues at stake in Pound's Rome

Radio broadcasts were, perforce, shared in one direction only. He would have
been enjoined from letting her know the military and FBI intelligence that
arrived in Ryder Street.

Thus, the Pearson whom H.D. invited to tea, entrusted with her daughter,
confided in, and came increasingly to depend upon for criticism and advice, appeared to be "a strange mixture of superhuman courage and . . .
well, what?" She couldn't find the right word, although "pathos" came to
mind.[57] She was thinking about his having had his bones re-broken and re-
set in response to a childhood accident; she was thinking about his carrying
on in the face of fragility, about his OSS work "of very real importance."
H.D. saw his gentlemanly concern, his love of literature; she responded to
his steadiness. In their private parlance, he became her "Chevalier"—not a
lover, certainly, but a kind of literary attendant, who encouraged her, read
her drafts, arranged publications, and eventually recommended her for the
American Academy of Arts and Letters. Donna Hollenberg claims Pearson
helped her "to engage in a process of literary consolidation that complemented
the psychological integration she had sought earlier in her analysis with
Freud."[58] What can be said unquestionably is that he encouraged her to
write during the trauma of the war, indeed, to deal with trauma through
naming it. Between 1941 and 1945, H.D. worked on a war trilogy: *The Walls
Do Not Fall*, *Tribute to the Angels*, and *Flowering of the Rod*, as well as *The
Gift*, *Tribute to Freud*, *Writing on the Wall*, and *H.D. by Delia Alton*. Whenever Pearson could get away, he joined H.D. and Bryher, sometimes in their
guest room in Lowndes Square, sometimes simply for dinner; he celebrated
one of H.D.'s birthdays with a meal whose centerpiece was American corn
on the cob; Susan Silliman Bennett, his wife, sent gifts of other foods from
the U.S. Within a short time, Perdita was referring to him as "Uncle Norman," and later in life, when she married in the U.S., Pearson stood in the
place of her father during the ceremony. On 12 July 1943, H.D. wrote to Pearson, "I wonder if Ezra knows how near 'we' are?"[59] She was referring to their
geographical proximity but using that proximity as a trope for another
emerging closeness.

H.D. accepted the "hush-hush" nature of Pearson's work without inquiring into its implications. For her it was the simple concomitant of a war
they both believed in. But retrospection tells us that espionage work divided
people who continued to live straightforward lives from those for whom fur-
tiveness, manipulation, and participation in a covert world had come to seem

ordinary. Pearson had entered a realm where people were known only by code names (his was "Puritan," Angleton's was "Artifice") or initials like "C"; where buildings, if their locations were known at all, had false entrances and labyrinthine back connections; where betrayal was considered craftsmanship.

Like James Jesus Angleton, Norman Holmes Pearson's war experience had not only given him secrets, but the frame of mind to protect that secrecy. There was another side to his character visible only to those who worked with him at X-2. Hubert Will, the first head of the unit, called Pearson a "Machiavellian, outspoken Anglophile."[60] Edward Weismiller, a young poet who joined the London group after his first book of poetry, *The Deer Come Down*, had been published in the Yale Series of Younger Poets (1936), understood Pearson to be a man of extraordinary calculation, who loved the exercise of power and who "did tortuous things with gusto."[61] Angleton, who became Pearson's confidant, saw his superior as "very energetic" and "very devious."[62]

These kinds of judgments were apparently passed in all directions, for Hubert Will valued Angleton for similar qualities, praising him as a man who could "remember his lies and never forget the ends in view." Edward Weismiller, who continued to write poetry amid training to be an agent in the field, valued Angleton because he read his manuscripts and because they could reflect together about the meaning of intelligence work. These two came closest to articulating the dynamic that now guided their lives, understanding that X-2 trained them to lie about the extent of their knowledge. They contrasted their hidden purposes, their lurking secrecies with the work of the poet whose vocation was to reveal, to show forth, and to expose previously undetected relationships.[63]

Though H.D. drew strength from Pearson's attention, their alliance contained all the implicit dissonance of their divergent purposes. For one, categories and political allegiances were unambiguous but called forth and justified both personal and national dissimulation. For the other, stealth was anathema, and the categories of the imagination more diffuse than the allegiances of nationalism, its hatreds, and its covert means of supporting policy. Pearson, like James Jesus Angleton, cradled his clandestine knowledge of the massive case that the FBI was mounting against Pound; H.D. struggled overtly with its meaning. For one, personal identity was chameleon, assumed according to the demands of espionage, and Ezra Pound was primarily a subject to be penetrated by secret means; for the other, he was a multitude

of complexities to confront with all the resources of mythology, contemplation, and dream.

VI

It all came flooding back to her. As she put it, a barrier had been broken. "The
debris that cluttered the streets of London, sometimes left a half-house
open. . . . One looked into rooms in another dimension. So, I think this ex-
ternalization of peoples' private lives, somehow, in the end, sliced open one's
own house. One looked into one's own interior private life, a life shut off until
now, even to oneself."[64] In *A Sword Went Out to Sea*, her account of wartime
London, H.D. cast Pound as the character Allen Flint, whom she recognized
as someone like herself whose "obsession with lost beauty led him back to
Italy." She spoke of her shock when she learned that he began to be known as
a follower of Mussolini and his abuse of "non-Aryan races." And she reported
that she had heard that he had been taken prisoner trying to escape to Switzerland. "He was found," she continued, "half-starved on a mountain-trail.
He was challenged by the sentry and wounded. I have heard various versions
of this tale. One written to me from my friend in Delaware, is that Allen was
returned to Italy, chained to African deserters and sent to Rome."[65]

This was largely invented, for H.D. had no way of knowing exactly what
had happened to Pound at this point in time. Her novel served a psychological function, to put to rest what she called a "psychic wound." And though
the writing did not accomplish this (H.D. would think and write about Ezra
Pound for the remainder of her life), it did show the complexity of her regard
for the man who had been her lover, her initiator into the ecstasies of sexual
awareness, her mentor, her guide in writing, the first manifestation of the way
two people could complete each other psychically. He was, as he had said to
her long ago, her "twin." Losing him to Dorothy Shakespear had sent her on
a lifelong quest for another person who could fill this void, as if Pound had
opened a door of human and artistic possibility, and then, with the new room
open, had left the building empty. If Pound was a "traitor" to H.D., it was
personal—he had inflicted "the first blow," but she did not stop loving him
because of it.

In the dream sequences that follow in the novel, Pound's stand-in haunts
the writer. She remembers him as "tawny like a young lion. There was all of
the sun in him." She remembers that her first husband, Richard Aldington

(Geoffrey in the novel), had recognized that she didn't love him, and in fact couldn't love him because she was preoccupied with another "a ghost, a spectre; *chère belle fantôme.*"[66] "I was sixteen years old when I laid the foundation-stone of my life,"[67] she recognized, and because of this inalienable connection, she experienced Pound's distress as her own personal disaster as well. Until she knew for certain that he was alive, she imagined "a street of gibbets. . . . I thought my friends were dead and the city struck down with plague."[68]

Her different political allegiances did nothing to alter this, for she considered that "[w]e are or we become what we love." She and Pound were inseparable and so, incidentally, were she and London. The city had fostered her talent and her return there in 1939 had been spurred largely by feelings of loyalty to a place that had believed in her when America seemingly did not. Pound, she could imagine, held a similar allegiance to Italy. There were artistic reasons that both continued to live as expatriates. She had found what she needed in England; Pound had gone on to a new country, but their searches were always for that "lost beauty," which transcended national boundaries and single historical epochs.[69]

Several years later in 1948, knowing that Pound was incarcerated in "the Tower" of St. Elizabeths, H.D. returned to this inquiry without the displacements and reconfigurations of fiction. "I wonder so much what DID HAPPEN," she wrote to Bryher. "It may have been confusion about the last war, being there and not being in it, and E[zra] was made much of by many people; I know how they changed in tempo during the first war, and he may have felt they were no longer interested in the same way. He appears to me now, to have BEGUN the down-curve at the end of or just after World War I. . . . Anyway, I feel there was some definite break or repercussion or even percussion in or at the end of War I, that sent him back to the old shock of being asked to leave Hamilton College." After several days, she continued, "I have been going over the old American scene and 1914 pre-war Paris and a number of things now crop up, sign-posts that relate various phases of Ezra to certain things . . . and certainly the main factor was . . . his father being in Mint; E[zra] saw shelves of gold which to a child anyway, were in his father's hands, and he had no use of it; all so very, very obvious—his 'usury' (whatever that is) complex that crops up again and again in *The Cantos*."[70]

When Rebecca West's book *The Meaning of Treason* came out the following year, H.D. read that too, remarking to Norman Holmes Pearson that she found it "very good," but she could not see Pound in the same light that West

cast William Joyce (Lord Haw-Haw), who had broadcast during the war from
Berlin. To West, William Joyce was "not only alarming, he was ugly. He
opened a vista into a mean life." He was "pinched and misshapen . . . flimsy
and coarse," with a "mincing immobility to his small mouth."[71] Her weasel-
ing description was clearly created to arouse moral repugnance as well physical revulsion. Though Pound was most frequently, and for obvious reasons,
compared to Joyce, H.D. did not agree. She merely went on to tell Pearson
that she had not heard from Ezra since she had sent him *By Avon River.*[72]

By then her habit of writing to Pearson was well established, but she was
perhaps mindful that, during the war, he had warned her not to include references to Pound in her correspondence. "I have deleted the whole line-
reference to E[zra]. Just left "my first live poet, E.—this was thanks to your
suggestion."[73] Whether she knew Pearson's reasons for this advice (he was
in a position to know that her mail was routinely opened by MI5) is not certain, nor is it clear that she understood the mental strategy by which he
avoided looking at Pound as a complex human being capable of error. To her
face, Pearson spoke of Pound in glowing terms, even making the claim that
there was a triangle comprised of himself, Pound, and H.D. which was a
"magic," a "cabalistic" mystery.[74] But with others he was more forthright about
the mental habits that denied Pound his humanity while letting him retain
his position as an interesting cipher to decode. "I belittle him [Pound]," he
admitted to William Carlos Williams, "on his own terms by still admiring
much of what he did as a poet while distinguishing his poetics from his ideology and from him as a man. He started . . . as the Longfellow *de nos jours*;
he ended up something much nastier."[75] Pearson left the Second World War
with the U.S. Medal of Freedom, the Médaille de la Reconnaissance Fran-
çaise, the Knight's Cross first-class of the Norwegian Order of Saint Olav and
with a mastery of the XX (double-cross) system. If poets reveal the world,
Pearson was clearly no poet. His talent was for subterfuge.

CHAPTER 5

Waiting for Signals

The Tyrol, 1946–58

I

The plans Mary had made for herself—Herr Bacher's cottage, an apprenticeship in wood sculpture, economic self-sufficiency through agriculture—were interrupted by letters from Boris Baratti, the young man she had met in Rome through the Princess Troubetzkoi, and then, in late spring, by his arrival in Gais. While Pound and Olga corresponded about their daughter's character—Olga complaining that Mary didn't confide in her and Pound responding that her closed nature ("Child chiusa as io chiuso. Made that way") was inherited from him, while they shared opinions about her first efforts at poetry ("a vurry nice selection. Am telling the cheeild that a cow's 'claw' is a hoof"),[1] and while Olga returned to her position as secretary at the Chigi Foundation in Siena, Mary continued to work in the Marchers' fields, read books at night, and write. She was hungry for intellectual stimulation.

To her father, she wrote open and clear letters about how she lived and what she wanted. He was worried about Olga being alone, but aside from that, he took an avid interest in what the girl was doing. In fact, Mary's life in the Tyrol, with its pragmatic cycle of activity, probably gave Pound the first respite from depression, for she was the only one of the women in his life who seemed capable of going forward in the wake of his incarceration. Though he repeatedly entreated Olga to get on with life, she just as repeatedly bemoaned her loneliness, and though he continually enjoined her not to focus on the actions of others, it is clear that "the actions" of his child preoccupied him. In imagining her circumstances, he breached the walls that confined him, or as he put it, "the only way to make prison after cataclysm bearable is to have a world outside with individuals in it."[2] He came upon the idea of growing maple trees as a long-term source of income for Mary, and for years devoted himself to the project of finding seeds, sending her articles from farming almanacs, and singing the praises of maple syrup. In the short term, he arranged for the Red Cross to send blankets to her; in the long term he imagined, with a telling, displaced obsession, a grove of trees with running sap and the means of tapping the sugar and converting it into a cash crop. If Mary couldn't buy farmland because of primogeniture, she could, he reasoned, buy a deforested hillside and circumvent the laws of inheritance by intelligence and industry.

But the Red Cross did more than distribute blankets. At the end of the war, it delivered telegrams that allowed people in the south of Italy to communicate with loved ones in the north. Mary had received a simple "Happy New Year" from Boris and soon found him as willing to listen to her home-grown plans as Homer Somers. One correspondent was a stolid, unambitious farmer/gentleman in the making; the other was learned and reckless, determined and filled with grandiose schemes. She fell for the dreamer.

One day she returned from the fields, still unwashed and dirty, and found that Boris had come to see her. Something in him responded to solid, good sense wedded to intellectual acumen. Where else could he find a young woman who knew that durum wheat yielded twenty-five bushels to the acre and had translated Thomas Hardy into Italian? His ostensible reason for traveling to Gais, aside from seeing Mary, was to buy a cow; once there his imagination refused the pragmatism that had originally propelled him. Mary showed him Herr Bacher's cottage. Situated at the foot of a mountain and at the edge of a forest, it was called *Schoutna*—in the shade—and its name expressed Mary's sense of her symbolic position in life as someone who lived, and who wanted to live, in the protected shadow of history and art.[3]

This was not Boris Baratti's idea of a future. He looked up and saw a castle, which apparently served as the material counterpart of a submerged yet potent romance of personal identity. He was, he told a tired, unscrubbed girl, descended from the crusader Raimondo, founder of the Order of Canossa—and the list of ancient credentials poured forth. He needed to locate a seat for reestablishing the Order. To Mary, the farming pragmatist, the thought of living in a castle was initially ridiculous. She saw Neuhaus through village eyes as the site of legend and history, as the destination of religious processions, as the site of a pub that offered refreshment on Sunday afternoon walks. But she also knew that the property had no ostensible owner as a result of the Option of 1938. To Mary, the daughter of Ezra Pound, the idea reso-nated with the symbolic landscape of *The Cantos*. "I had not heard such topics mentioned since the days I walked on the *salita* with Babbo." In her memoir, Mary remembered the appeal of Boris's intelligence, his physical resemblance to Gaudier-Brzeska, his empathetic conversation. She listened to an idea that had not occurred to her: that a castle could become a private retreat for artists, writers, and scholars. To her father she wrote, "We have mated."[4]

Clamor arose immediately from all sides. Frau Marcher considered Mary too young, Boris too Italian, too urban, too un-German, too incapable; and she had, in any case, harbored the secret hope that her foster daughter would marry a rich farmer. Olga was outraged; her idea of an appropriate husband for her child was a person of stature, good breeding and, if not achieve-ment, at least potential for it. In her judgment, Boris had none of these qualifications. Letters were immediately fired off across the Atlantic to a rather nonplussed Pound, who pointed out that men were in short supply after the war, and inquired if the young man, whose full name had not yet been given to him, were healthy.

In subsequent months, he was bombarded with opinions, judgments, re-ports of action that show how deeply, and seemingly irrationally Olga was affected by Mary's decision to marry. She could not see, or refused to see, the hidden logic of her daughter's choice, would not face that Boris bridged, rather than exacerbated, the seemingly irreconcilable oppositions of her child's up-bringing. By conceiving of a "refunctioned" place of habitation, he suggested to Mary that one could live in the mountains without forsaking the world of letters. Even if the desire to buy Neuhaus was fed by pretentious hopes, it had a pragmatic side to it, for it was an actual place to live in a landscape more usually governed by the exclusions of family ownership. As to his person, his education, his murky background, he spoke, more honestly than adults were willing to admit, to the shaky antecedents, the poverty, the unconventional but passionately engendered life of the mind that characterized a real, as opposed to a desired, daughter.

Though she assured Pound and Count Chigi, to whom she had also spo-ken, that she would not interfere or criticize Boris to his face, Olga immedi-ately set out to find out who had snared her daughter. She also wrote to Frau Marcher to enlist her tacit support. On the one hand, she stood on ceremony ("I will certainly wait to be approached by the *famiglia* before speaking of any official engagement"); on the other she admitted that it sounded like a "complete fairy story," and couldn't imagine the other family's consent. But almost immediately, Mary presented her with a "bombshell of possible consequences." By May, she thought she might be pregnant; by early June, she considered herself engaged; later in the month she worried that Olga had abandoned her and left for the United States without even a word ("I felt rather 'shut out' on hearing that you intended to go to the States on 16.6—later of course I convinced myself that if you had left without telling me sometime before it was only my own fault").[5] When she learned that her mother was still in Siena, she wrote and told her that Boris's father had indeed come to Gais and had begun inquiries about the purchase of the castle for the young couple, which, to his credit, he seems to have taken as a serious proposition. But since it was an extensive property, with a dwelling, a farm, and a chapel on the grounds, negotiations would have to be pursued with the owner, Count Strassoldo, who lived in Venice. Assuming that an agreement could be reached, she and Boris would marry in the chapel on the grounds and then, after Christmas, would go to San Marino "so that the child would not be an Italian citizen and also to avoid local gossip."[6]

That was as far into the future as Mary could see. She was practical about the issue of divorce, should love not last, but she could read her mother's silence like a book. "I have hardened my heart once because I felt your doubt and your suspicions. . . . I did not expect you to applaud me, I expected you to reproach me, but I did *not* expect you to say that I have acted like this only for vanity." She assured her mother that Boris's titles had nothing to do with her decision, that, if anything, it was his desire to pursue a diplomatic career that worried her, since she had no experience in such a world. She had also learned that Olga had tried to drive a wedge between Frau Marcher and herself. "I do not think it's fair on your side to arouse her suspicion by your post card. We have been living very harmoniously till now. . . . Please, whatever you do, never try to put yourself between me and anyone else. . . . Your act seems to say: I don't believe a word of all you tell me—a fairy tale. Well, if it is so you ought to have told me from the beginning, not be nice at first and then try to find out something at my back."[7] It was a futile request. By September, Mary knew that she wasn't expecting a child, but she now understood that she wanted one. She dropped all pretense of farming; she dropped all attempts to communicate with her mother and followed Boris back to Rome.

Once the prospect of a shotgun wedding was behind her, Olga reconsidered what to do. She enlisted the help of Father Chute, Count Chigi, and John Drummond, now stationed in Rome, who all made inquiries on her behalf.

Count Chigi's friends ("high up in monarchist and Vatican circles") discovered only that the family was "not known." Desmond Chute's informant apparently discovered that the Baratti family had shares in a brothel. From this, Olga jumped to the conclusion that their interest in Mary was to enlist her in "white slavery"—a fear that she confided in John Drummond, who had himself been consulting the carabinieri to see if the father had a criminal record. Then Olga received an anonymous letter warning her that the family was debt-ridden and interested in Mary's money. She followed her daughter to Rome; met the father, saw the son's studio, which she dismissed as retro-kitsch, and tried forcibly to impede any possible marriage by taking Mary back to Rapallo with her.

Nothing worked. She wrote to Pound about Mary's "present imbecility," called Boris a liar and the father a "confidence trickster," allowing, however, that she had "heard nothing definite against them in a penal sense."[8] She complained that the young couple had cut themselves off from the Princess Troubetzkoi, who, having introduced them to each other, might have been able to give Mary an honest appraisal of Boris, and continued by saying that "Mary wrote me last May that the Princess was a 'wac going round in uniform apparently more *avventuriera* than princess!!'" Olga used this as evidence that neither young person would heed the truth—but it is equally likely that the information was true—Boris did, in fact, see Natalie Troubetzkoi in British uniform at the end of the war[9]—and equally likely that she did work for the British military. It is certain that she knew Frank Amprim, that she had volunteered to testify against Pound should it be necessary,[10] and that she sent Amprim her address and best greetings after she returned to London, where she complained about the delay in her next posting to the Middle East.[11]

Even the friends most interested in Olga's well-being began to sense that the real danger was not the marriage, but the estrangement between mother and daughter disclosed by its prospect. After John Drummond and his wife, Fifi, met with Mary in Rome, they cautioned Olga that there was nothing she could do: one couldn't "bring an action against the family on the grounds that they are unpleasant people, and one can't think of blackmailing them."[12] He advised her to accept the situation with as much good grace as she could.

But the good grace had to be achieved at a distance, for Mary and Boris married in private. Olga had to learn about it from John Drummond, who had been going secretly to the Ufficio Matrimoni to see if any marriage had taken place and suggested "we might put the *avvocato* on their tracks."

Instead of a lawyer, there was a priest. The young couple married, or at least registered their civil marriage, at the Church of S. Saturnino on 17 October. Drummond learned that Mary married in her capacity as an Italian citizen, and, still plagued by her uncertain international status, didn't know if she should reveal her new situation to the passport authorities. He tried to soothe feelings by telling Olga that Mary was thoughtless rather than malicious ("brutal" is the word Olga used) but suggested all the same that the marriage was ill-fated. "I feel she is perhaps a little disillusioned already with married life. They get most of their meals either out or at via Agri [the home of Boris' father] . . . the time may come when she will need you to fall back on after all, so the sooner you start preparing the ground the better."[13]

Olga was not to be so easily assuaged. "Well, caro," she wrote to Pound, "frankly I'm not fond of her enough to put up with that kind of thing. . . . I feel if she is left to her Barattis she may have her eyes opened in time, but I refuse to do anything more for the pleasure of two selfish children."[14] She would not "be made use of." In less than a month she was cautioning Pound not to worry about "cheeild. Its doon what it wanted!" and urging him instead to concentrate on returning to her in Siena.[15]

Even in seclusion on another continent, Pound could see what was happening. He sent Mary a prayer: "Let me not be engulphed in the/multitude of my family's afflictions/ nor tern make nest/on a sand-storm."[16] Finally he received a letter directly from Mary. She and Boris had survived the turmoil. They were back in Gais, living at Neuhaus, even though no terms for actually buying it had been reached. Since the political situation between Italy and Austria had not been settled, property in the Pustertal could neither be bought nor sold. For the time being, they had permission to live in the castle without paying rent. They had no money; conditions were Spartan, simple, solitary. The tenant in the farmhouse continued there; they themselves occupied a large, wood paneled room in the castle itself with a big stove and high window. They had dry wood and the Marchers provided them with milk and bread and eggs.[17] They occupied themselves by reading Russian classics, and Mary, by sewing cloth diapers. Boris had no job; he knew he would have to return to Rome to find work and the education to prepare him for it. But for this winter, blanketed in Alpine snow, the two were happy.

Mary found Boris to be surprising and agile: "dreaming things into being, creating with ease, forever flowing, never rigid, unattached, non-possessive, ingenious."[18] Small things sufficed: ringing the castle bells; sitting in the *Burgbewohner* pew in the parish church; a good lunch on Sundays with the Marchers.

Frau Marcher, somewhat pacified, began to think of the practical aspects of having a relative living nearby; she imagined her other foster daughter, Margherita, serving as a cook or some of the adopted boys working the land. From St. Elizabeths, Pound wrote, "You give me plenty to rejoice about," and sent the young couple a wedding blessing from the Odes of Chêng: "such beauty hath thy house."[19]

On Easter Monday, 8 April, Siegfried Walter Igor Raimondo was born, his name a testament to the imaginative allegiances of those who most welcomed him into the world: Walter, from Pound, who considered that Walter von der Vogelweide was an apt precursor for his first, Tyrolean-born grandchild; Siegfried, from Mary, who loved reading the *Niebelungen Lied*, and Igor Raimondo for Boris's ancestors. The child had blue eyes and blond hair; she thought his mouth seemed like Pound's, the nose like his father's, conceded that most people thought he looked like her and reported that "since his birth, I am in a continuous state of bliss."[20] She wanted Olga to come to see him. She also wanted Isabel Pound to come stay with her at Neuhaus.

Olga refused; Isabel came. At eighty-seven she was recovering from a broken arm and needed to be transported by chauffeured car—a two-day journey, which the old lady found full of "wonderful beauty." She also derived great pleasure from her great-grandson, who elicited stories of Pound's childhood. Mary took photographs of Isabel's entrance into the castle for her father and sent news of a Christmas celebrated in American style with turkey, cranberry sauce, and mashed potatoes.

But the symbolic importance of these events—the responsibility toward home and family asserted in implicit rebuke to both Olga and Dorothy—turned into the realities of housekeeping with no money. The castle was ill-furnished; Isabel was uncomfortable, and soon she was ill. In July 1948, a fire started on their farmland; then lightning struck the electric wires, and the whole village was without electricity for two weeks. Mary spent her time in front of smoking stoves and wet wood. In January 1948, when Isabel had a stroke, she tended her grandmother herself; at night, she engaged a nurse, using what money Isabel had to cover expenses. Finally, when she sent Olga a telegram, "*nonna gravissima*,"[21] Olga wired 20,000 lire and traveled to Brunneck. She refused the hospitality of her children but arrived at Isabel's deathbed in time to hear her ask when she could "stop having to be a person."[22]

Olga credited herself for whatever decency there was to Isabel Pound's funeral. She dressed the body in a pale pink satin jacket and lace scarf, as if she were a "*très grande dame*,"[23] but it was her own sense of decorum that was satisfied. No priest would come, nor, as a Protestant, could Isabel be buried in sacred ground. At the last minute, Mary's cousin, Peter Rudge, said the Lord's Prayer over the grave, which was dug on Neuhaus land, near the chapel that belonged to the *Schloss*.

It was Father Chute, back in Rapallo, who had the largeness of heart to say a Requiem Mass in Isabel's honor. He also had the breadth of understanding to try to hold the remainder of the family together in whatever way he could. He assuaged Olga's feelings, telling her that "without you, [the burial] . . . might . . . have been sordid [but] was turned into beauty"; but he also refused to buy into Olga's version of her daughter's marriage. He approved of the couple, thought them to be in love and devoted to their child. He tried to point out the difference between youthful inexperience and deceit.[24]

Like John Drummond's earlier admonitions, Father Chute's counsel fell on deaf ears. After Isabel's death, Olga went through the elderly woman's banking records and papers, outraged over what she considered misspent money. Boris had been researching his family's history; Mary had been covering domestic expenses connected with Isabel's illness with checks that were apparently uncovered, doing her best, at twenty-two, to run an establishment that, aside from her grandmother, now included Boris; his brother, Igor; her cousin Peter Rudge; and a baby.

Back in Siena, Olga wrote to Pound, "You were right in not wanting a child. I was wrong. I have been wrong from the start, and no way to clean up the mess."[25]

II

The "mess" was actually a small group of young people starting their intellectual lives with whatever guidance Ezra Pound could provide from the confines of another continent. Pooling resources, working abilities, and ideas, Mary, Boris, Igor, and Peter Rudge settled into collective life at Neuhaus. By early March 1948, Mary had translated the first ten cantos into Italian; Igor was learning to type, studying Mongolian, and (too slowly for Pound who waited impatiently for installments) translating Mencius; Boris was reading Guicciardini in preparation for the Vatican diplomacy school and working on the genealogy of the Baratti family. Both brothers absorbed esoteric knowledge as naturally as they breathed mountain air; soon heraldry, hieroglyphics, and ancient symbols vied with bread and butter as ordinary family fare. Initially Mary surveyed the scene with satisfaction. "Thank goodness I have a husband and a son and the company of other two men and am able to get on with all of them," she wrote to her father. She began to understand her mother's harping as the pastime for an "idle ladie [sic] without a man,"[26] and to some extent, she was right, although it would take Olga several years tinged with unacknowledged jealousy to admit that her daughter was "much more sensible than I ever was, in many ways, older, but she has wot she wanted with a minimum of waiting."[27]

What she wanted most at this point was simply a break from caring for everyone. Her cousin Peter helped with chopping wood and tending the fire, but the Baratti brothers were "city boys more interested in Egyptian hieroglyphs and in Chinese radicals than in pioneering."[28] While Pound suggested reading Greek tragedy, Ovid, Fenollosa, Antoninus Pius, and Ford Madox Ford, she had kept a baby in diapers, tended a sick old woman, and fed three sedentary men with water that had to be fetched from a river on a sledge with an axe to chop the ice from the surface. By the middle of March, she decided to go to England with Peter and to accept the hospitality of her uncle Teddy.

Olga's brother, Edgar Marie Rudge, who had lost an eye during the First World War, had become a country doctor in Spondon, near Derby. A disappointment to his ambitious sister, who thought he should have become an artist, his home on Dale Road nonetheless became Mary's refuge for two months while she rested and made her first visits to Ronald Duncan and T. S. Eliot. Years later she remembered being shocked at how ill-kempt Duncan's farm was.[29] The agrarian/intellectual ideology that had inspired Duncan and had, to some extent, directed her own course in life was pulled whole cloth out of sloppy, jerry-rigged enclosures, thistles, and mud. Olga, who visited Duncan in 1950, was able to see Welcombe with romantic eyes as "most beautiful and unspoiled, not even a petrol station, [with] soft air, drizzle of fine rain on one's face,"[30] but Mary contrasted its makeshift, amateur construction to the firm infrastructure of Tyrolean mountain farms and wondered who and what she had let inspire her.

She had similar doubts about T. S. Eliot. Olga's visit with Eliot led to a letter to Pound which asserted that "the Possum . . . does love Him, she feels it."[31] Mary's time with him was more distant and more frustrating, since she went to him in hopes of eliciting support for her father's immediate release, and instead discovered an emblematic chilliness. The fireplace was blocked up; the biscuits were thin and dry: she remembered wanting to stoke up a blaze and feed him wholesome bread and butter, but mostly she remembered his words: "I fear your father does not want to accept freedom on any terms that are possible. The idea that you should be sent over to persuade him to sign a statement that he is mad is a travesty."[32]

John Drummond, who was in touch with Duncan, reported on the trip to Olga, "About Mary he [Duncan] confines himself to saying, 'She is a nice girl, and we both [he and Eliot] liked her.' No mention of Boris, so let us hope that he will not be taken in by the Barattis. . . . I don't think Ronnie's such a fool as not to see through the pair of them—or at any rate Boris—as soon as he knows the situation better."[33] But, of course, Boris had not been there for anyone to see through or not. In June he came to England to ask Mary to go back to him.[34]

III

Going back was not to anything familiar, but to Boris's new dream, the place he spoke of when he said, "*Il mio cuneo batte su Brunnenburg*" . . . an odd way of saying that his heart was bent on living in Brunnenburg castle, since it was in the territory once owned by his ancestors the Longobards.[35] He and Mary had first seen the castle when Mary had gone to Martinsbrunn Clinic in Merano for Walter's birth. Boris's rationale for the move was an imaginative reclamation of the extended lands of his ancestral family, but the real reason was that Neuhaus had to be let go. The young couple had no money to buy a place with lands and farms and tenants. And so, with reckless, infectious optimism, they moved into a haunted ruin, discounting its ghosts and seeing only the gladness of the villagers who were willing enough to welcome young people with a real child in arms to replace the haunts that had filled their imaginations and populated their stories for generations.

Years later, Hugh Kenner described the landscape by saying that "the massive land is restless."

> Subterranean water jets and pours down hillsides. Springs gave a name to one castle built in 1244 on Roman foundations above a sheer drop where the valley widens: the Castle at the Well, Castel Fontana, Schloss Brunnenburg. A land bridge and, legend says, a tunnel, once joined it to another castle still higher, but the bridge collapsed, tradition says by earthquake, leaving a boulder-strewn saddle. Castle Brunnenburg was

to lapse slowly too, uninhabited, neglected for centuries. Fire brought down wooden beams, and walls fell with them. *"Estrema decadenza,"* says a regional history of its state at the opening of our century, when a certain Herr Schwickert acquired it. Herr Schwickert had noble ambitions, and a bride, less alluring, tradition hints, than his young niece. . . . In 1904 . . . stone masons from the village of Tyrolo were making it new once more atop its spur: a warren of serene rooms at many levels; a square central tower, square room above square room; an adjacent round tower up which coils a dizzying stone stair; a dark enclosed court; a minute garden with pines. The site is high, the surrounding peaks are higher; on a misty day they whelm it with menace. Tradition has Frau Schwickert plunging—pushed?—from a balcony outside one long sunlit room, down past sheer walls, down past sheer cliffs, down to the lesser spurs that slope into Merano.[36]

Originally built on a military site that had existed in the thirteenth century, the castle had once been an essential platform for the defense of the Tyrol; it had been badly damaged while under siege from Karl of Böhmen; then, in 1457 it had been bought by Hans von Kripp whose family retained it until the early nineteenth century. Farmers neglected it until Herr Schwickert's strange family relationships plunged it once again into murky rumor.

When she recorded this period in her autobiography, Mary gave little credence to folklore; she remembered being preoccupied with building a shelter for herself and her family. "And the spirit moving us was *dos moi pou sto kai kosmon kineso*—give me a place to stand and I will move the universe."[37] They stayed in a local inn for several weeks until the highest room in the tower was habitable. A carpenter and his son moved in and did repairs; they got architectural advice in exchange for "good mountain air" from a man, who was "expert in propping up, mending, shifting, making do."[38] Rumor had it that they slept on straw, that the shadow of Margaretha Maultasch (the Ugly Duchess) of past ages had reawakened and roamed the halls, but they trumped gossip with joy, making happiness out of paint and scrap iron.

They also went into debt—populating their imaginations with the verses of Pietro Metastasio, thinking of their castle as an Age of Gold bid come to the earth, while owing the plumber and electrician for the water and electricity that heralded their noble intensions. Mary smoothed things over with her mountain dialect; the villagers associated her with the Pustertal and with wood and potatoes that contrasted with their vineyards and pears and apples. They hardly knew what to make of Boris, who spoke no German and who cultivated exotic rumors of his connection to czars and kings.

Both imbued the castle with meanings that eclipsed centuries of legend. For Boris, the place was filled with ancestral dreams. Olga complained that he spent meager family resources on genealogy, but for him it was serious business, both a matter of primary identity and an orientation in life. In 1955 he asked Monsignor Prof. Gustavo Tulli, the archivist emeritus of the Vatican, to create a formal history of the Barattis' royal lineage. Beginning with Thor, son of Odin, the principal divinity of Scandinavia, he traced the Barattis back to Rotari, who married Gundemberga, daughter of Queen Teolinda of Bavaria . . . who was from "the most ancient dynasty of the Kings of Lombard" . . . and so on through the ages. When he came to Matilde of Canossa, Tulli was brief: "The life, the works, and the merits of this lady toward the Roman Church are so well known and so fully documented . . . that it would be superfluous . . . to expound on them in this . . . history." But Matilde was the ancestor who most preoccupied Boris; for he understood that another of his relatives, Raimondo, had founded the Sacred Military Order of the Noble Cavalry of Canossa in 1289 and had died at its head "in the struggle against the Infidels."[39] It was, according to Tulli, a patrimonial dynasty by virtue of a document notarized in Parma in 1290. Raimondo's son Roberto had become the first grand master of the Order; Raimondo's brother Giacomo had acted as its first regent; and Boris intended to reestablish the Order with Brunnenburg as its seat.

"Haven't you ever heard of the Order of Malta?" Boris had asked Mary when they first met in Gais. She had replied that, yes, of course, she knew about them, about the Templars and the Aligenses, from reading her father's cantos, and in this exchange we can glimpse the attraction between two intellects, both schooled in unorthodox ways, both steeped in esoteric histories, both aware of the activities of the present world as the manifestation of a lively, usable past.[40]

In October 1948 Boris obtained a decree from the Corte d' Apello to legalize the Order of Canossa and Corona di Ferro and title of Principe de Rachewiltz. From this point in time, he would identify himself as Principe L. Boris Baratti de Rachewiltz, Conte di Lucca, Fossano, Bestagno, and St. Agnes, Signore de Carvere. In August 1949 he asked the same court to grant him independent diplomatic rights and immunity.

Pound approved. He thought it "a show of spirit, and last line of defense against rising tide of imbecility, demi-Xtens, etc."[41] He looked at the heraldry Boris sent him with interest and proceeded to recommend the kind of education his aristocratic grandson should have: the two-year-old Walter should sleep on a hard board instead of a bed; he should grow trees; he should learn "OBedience so he can have some self-control later,"[42] and he should definitely not bite the dog.

In September Mary learned that she was expecting her second child. Patrizia Barbara Cinzia Flavia was born on 22 February 1950. That November Olga was finally persuaded to stay at the castle, where she recognized classic domesticity when she saw it: "His daughter a bit on [the] thin side but looks better for it." The kitchen had a large basket of red apples from Walter's orchard on top of the white-wood dresser; the baby was in a still larger wicker basket "sitting up and taking notice of boy-blue brother, the kind of picture wot would make some poor painter's fortune as a cover for *Home* magazine—so American!"[43]

For the moment, quietness filled the house. But it was not, as Olga supposed, a thoughtless idyll. Under the conventional surface, and despite Mary's protests to the contrary (to Olga she wrote, "I like a simple and quiet home. . . . I hope Walter and the rest will do all the things I should have done and that they'll inherit not only their grandfather's tendencies, but also his genius. I could wish for nothing better in the way of a child and husband and home"),[44] her imagination was filled with intellectual and imaginative leanings that rivaled Boris's dreams of reclaimed chivalry. What she wanted to salvage was not an imagined countess but the honor of a politically disgraced father and the standing of a real family.

For her, Brunnenburg's meaning was as long as her memory of *The Cantos* and as deep as her love for her father and her children. From St. Elizabeths Pound wrote that he wanted an apartment in the castle with a room for his Gaudier-Brzeska drawings. She wanted not only to provide that room, but, in effect, a whole country for Pound—a principality governed by values that owed allegiance neither to specific governments nor to their leaders' punitive wrath. Boris's desire for diplomatic immunity served more than one purpose. "Our dreams soared high: we would achieve extraterritoriality, we would fight for his extradition from the U.S.A., and he could rule over a domain populated with artists."[45]

Gradually, as room was added to habitable room, Brunnenburg was elevated not simply into a place of safety for Pound's return to Italy, but into an incredible accommodation, as if a material transposition of *The Cantos* could be wrought from stone, wood, mortar, and the bones of growing children.

Its goal, even if not explicitly formulated, was to become "a house of good stone, each block cut smooth and well fitting,"[46] a place "where the spirit is clear in the stone."[47] Even Olga could see that something simple but profound motivated her daughter's life choices: "Them children are living in Paradiso all right," she wrote to Pound. "Walter [is] a very charming child, great sensitivity to the sound of words."[48]

By 1949 the castle was fit enough to welcome its first international guest—a young woman named Mary Barnard, an aspiring poet, translator of Sappho, and a friend and correspondent of Pound, William Carlos Williams, and Marianne Moore. It was Barnard's first trip abroad (Pound called it "Miss Barnard's invasion of Europe") and it was informed by his letters of introduction, his recommendation of cities that had inspired *The Cantos*—Rimini, Mantua, Sirmione, and Ferrara—as well as lists of hotels, pensions, foods, and wines. On her visit to him at St. Elizabeths, he had shown her a photograph of Brunnenburg, warning that he could not guarantee that it had a roof, but one look was enough to draw her through Verona on the Brenner Pass train to Bolzano and then on up the Adige into the mountains of the South Tyrol. "I thought I knew mountains," she wrote, "but I was staggered by the view from every window in every direction. . . . The stillness of the night, as I emptied my washbasin out of the window in the top of the tower, is one of the things I remember best, the immense hush that continued unbroken for a long, long moment, before I heard the faint splash of water on the stones far below."

"Still more impressive than either the castle or the setting," she continued, "was the twenty-four-year-old girl who was living there with her three-year-old son. Boris was in Rome, and I did not meet him. I had no need to say, 'Patience and fortitude,' to Mary. She had both."[49] Barnard was the first to bring personal news of Pound since he had been taken to America; she told Mary about *her* mountains and formed the basis of a friendship that brought her back to Brunnenburg for over thirty years.

It was, despite Barnard's fond memories, a rough construction job. In 1950 the dining room ceiling fell in, breaking furniture, china, clocks, and hard-won optimism. Pound and Teddy Rudge both contributed to the repairs; as usual, Pound insisted upon a precise reckoning of the costs: "NO reason to do without roof, or ceiling or land or furniture OR typewriter—please write clearly how much you need and whether you need it all @ once."[50] Mary also used the money for completing two small flats, for it was now clear to her that paying guests would be essential to their economic survival. From the U.S., Pound sent one suggestion after another for suitable possibilities. H.D. might come down from Switzerland; Pound's German translator, Eva Hesse, might want a vacation; Olga's old friend Renata Borgatti might want an alternative to her own castle. . . . But by February 1951, it was clear that none of these schemes were bearing fruit: there were no paying guests and no prospects of work for Boris. Pound discreetly advised Mary to put the castle in Walter's name, and in July 1950, when the family acquired an orchard below the castle, that property was transcribed in Walter's name as well.[51]

In February 1951 Mary chalked it all up and went to England with Peter Rudge again. She motored around the country helping her cousins look for a farm and lingered on. There was no point returning to "live [at Brunnenburg] all alone and not knowing where the next money is going to come from." She reported to Olga that she had spoken to Ronald Duncan again about Pound's situation and passed on the news that Duncan had met Omar in a train, had broached the subject of Pound's release and heard Omar say, "He is all right where he is."[52] Olga knew as much and was preparing to go the States to "get things moving." To Pound she confided, "I think she [Mary] is (quite unconsciously) making a refuge for herself and infants—and could do worse."[53]

Life was now distant from the "Paradiso" Olga had briefly glimpsed the previous autumn. Small things irritated even if they did not add up to a pattern. Mary could not understand how Boris, with his Russian-Italian lineage, could have been, as he told her, in the British Marines during the war; she grappled with his monarchist leanings; she was with him when he was stopped at the Swiss border for suspected espionage. Even Pound, who had never met Boris, sensed the difficulty and wrote, "I am probably more pro-Boris than either of you have suspected but I don't think he's going to have an easy time being understood."[54] He asked Mary if Olga had ever told her about the anonymous letter she had once received warning her against the Baratti family and asked if she could write about her in-laws in "Jamesian or Tchekovian DETAIL."[55] Finally in July Pound learned from Olivia Rosetti Agresti that Boris had landed a job (which was continually postponed) with the FAO— Federal Agricultural Organization—and would be stationed in Egypt. "If you visit him [there]," Pound advised, "for heaven's sake park the brats at Gais. Cairo no climate for growing kids . . . and told Mary that Omar had received a scholarship to study literature in Teheran."[56]

It was a short-lived relief. In 1952 Boris was still in Rome intensely searching for work. Mary wrote to her father asking if James Laughlin of New Directions might have a position for an Egyptologist. Pound naturally sent her
back in search of contacts in Rome, suggesting that even the Princess Troubetzkoi would be more useful than Jas.

By December 1952, Mary was also caring for a foster child, named Graziella, taken from an orphanage in Rome. There was, of course, precedent for
such an undertaking—Mary had been raised by a "nurse" in Gais; she had
been a foundling of sorts—but rumor had it that the girl was actually Boris's
daughter. No word was spoken, but life was now a matter of tending three
growing children: the unfinished castle became a place for hide-and-seek
games; daily routines were established. In retrospect Mary admitted doubts
about the way she educated the children—with "schedules, no indulgence,
rations, no toys except the discarded things that James Laughlin sent"[57]—but
it was a solid foundation for life, based on a peasant sensibility that emphasized good health and good tradition. Walter soon expressed the desire to go
to school with the local kids, so Brunnenburg became the locus of ordinary
life, its dailiness eclipsing whatever dreams had brought it into existence. For
the mother, it was lacking in intellectual stimulation, and Pound renewed his
efforts to find interesting guests for her. "With 3 minorenni/e easier for you
to get your society on the spot," he wrote.[58] Later, sensing the strain his
daughter might be feeling, he cautioned, "PazienZaaaa & let me know if the
knot gets too strangulatory."[59]

For Mary, getting her house in order was as much about setting records straight as constructing sturdy walls. The desire for honesty about her
origins was long-standing, exacerbated by the birth of children and made
even more pressing when she began to plan her trip to see Pound in the U.S.
at the end of 1952. She had tried to name herself "Mary Pound" on Patrizia's
birth certificate—to the consternation of officials who insisted on the
"Rudge"—but she did not let the matter rest with their "correction." On her
1951 trip to England, she had gotten a sworn statement that Lt. Arthur Rudge
had been killed in 1918 and thus could not possibly be her father—an act
that irritated Olga, who wrote to Pound that Mary had acted "without consulting me or worrying what consequences it might have." She then complained that she'd gotten a passport in San Marino as the daughter of Ezra
Pound and Olga Rudge and would "have to produce proof, which there ain't
and can't be."[60]

IV

In the end, Olga succeeded in getting Mary an American passport and she raised the money for the journey. Her own three-week trip to the United States in 1952, representing, as she put it, "the interests of Ezra Pound's daughter," had been brief and without results. Whatever friction existed between mother and daughter, they were united in their determination to free Pound from St. Elizabeths.

Thus, on 1 March 1953, Mary set sail on the SS *Independence* and began the next phase of what she later called her "dialog with America."[61] "What was I heading for?" she asked herself. "A junk shop and then a madhouse?"[62]

New York was neither: it was elegant, comfortable, astonishing from the smallest detail—a flower in a Japanese soup bowl—to the overarching splendor of the lights on Broadway. But Mary had not come for impressions or culture, but to rescue Pound and return him to Italy. So great was her instinct and desire that she kept her father waiting several days while she consulted with lawyers in the city. James Laughlin apparently urged her to persuade Pound to sign papers declaring that he was insane—though how an insane person could claim the self-possession necessary to make a judgment of his own incompetence seems not to have occurred to him. Nor had the travesty of a fake declaration worried him. One could, he reasoned, renounce the declaration once safely in Italy. But this was not the kind of vindication that a fiercely loyal child could accept, especially a child who had, for the previous seven years, been conducting a perfectly intelligible correspondence with her father. Laughlin did not persist, but introduced her to Julien Cornell, the Quaker lawyer who had carried on Pound's initial defense. He, in turn, brought her to lunch with counsel from the American Civil Liberties Union, Arthur Garfield Hays and Osmond K. Fraenkel. Later she would also speak to Rufus King, a lawyer whom Caresse Crosby had contacted on her behalf.

With these men she reiterated the story of Pound's intentions, actions, and rationale for action—the story that she had come firmly to believe was the truth. It was based on the right of free speech ("free speech without free radio speech is as zero"); on Pound's status as a public intellectual ("his long sojourn in Europe . . . made him 'qualified' to express an opinion"), and upon his good intentions ("He tried to stop the war. . . . Why should he be punished because his insight and courage were greater than those of most citizens in the United States?"). She told them about things they probably already knew—the letter to then Secretary of State Biddle, which had explained that he had spoken as a matter of conscience and not as the instrument of an enemy nation—and things they may not have known—that he had been denied counsel and the right of habeas corpus.[63]

This perspective was so self-evident to her—it had been the narrative that had sustained her for years and it accorded with Pound's own self-understanding—that she did not want to listen to other views—what she called "legal reasonings and professional codes." In her correspondence with Olga over the years of Pound's imprisonment, the real culprits had seemed to be ignorance (if people understood Pound's motives, they would acquit him) and a reticent but nonetheless real selfishness on the part of Dorothy Pound, who preferred her husband in the arms of the law rather than those of his "moral" family. From the distant perspective of postwar Europe, from the encircling concern of filial relationship, perhaps no other viewpoint was achievable. Certainly in 1953 it was not possible to measure the magnitude of the FBI's investigation of her father or to discern the colossal use of national resources that had secretly drawn Pound into discredited silence. That is, she could measure current attitudes without knowing the processes of state that had led to them.

Years later in April 1975, when she finally did go to the FBI archives, she wrote to Olga, "The papers at the FBI are not 'news'; just radio material of which there is plenty . . . and letters from various people, including mine."[64] But regardless of its "news" value, there were thousands of pages of dossier material scattered among the radio transcripts that represented the resources and will of a nation.

Long before it had sent Frank Amprim to Italy in 1943, the FBI had dispatched agents in search of Pound's perfidy to Birmingham, Alabama; Salt Lake City, Utah; Reno, Nevada; Butte, Montana; St. Paul, Minnesota; Hailey, Idaho; New Haven, Connecticut; Denver, Colorado; San Francisco, California; Springfield, Illinois; Chicago, Illinois; Boston, Massachusetts; New Orleans, Louisiana; Newark, New Jersey; Philadelphia, Pennsylvania; Baltimore, Maryland; New York City; and Washington, D.C.

Once Wendell Berge, assistant to Francis Biddle, had labeled Pound's radio broadcasts "enemy propaganda" on 30 November 1942, there was no turning back. On American soil, the FBI had involved the Department of State, the Naval Investigative Service, the Foreign Broadcast Intelligence Service, the Office of War Information, and the Criminal Division of the Justice

Department. They had asked assistance from the embassies in Genoa, Rome, Vienna, and Berlin; investigated the Philadelphia Police Department's criminal records on Pound (they had none); had lab reports made verifying Pound's handwriting, and had his letters examined for the presence of secret ink (negative results).[65]

Why this was necessary is not clear. The case against Pound, as set forth by the Baltimore office of the FBI, was "giving aid and comfort to the enemy," and that case could only be made in Italy. Its steps were set out in a document dated 3 July 1945:

A. Proof that Italian Radio is Operated by the Italian Government.
B. Proof that Broadcasts were Made by POUND.
C. Admissions that he was Paid for Broadcasts and Made Them.
D. Witnesses who Saw POUND in Italy and Heard Broadcasts and can Recognize his Voice.
E. Witnesses who Saw POUND in Italy and can Recognize his Voice.
F. Witnesses who Heard Broadcasts and can Recognize his Voice.
G. Witnesses who can Recognize his Voice.
H. Witnesses who saw POUND in Italy.
I. Books, Writings and Statements showing POUND'S Fascist Sympathies.
J. Other Potential Sources of Information.[66]

None of these steps involved Pound's American friends; nonetheless, over a four-year period, the FBI contacted not only James Angleton and his father, but also drew into the investigation James Laughlin, John Slocum, Reed Whittemore, Nancy Cunard, Caresse Crosby, Richard Aldington, George Antheil and his wife, Ernest Hemingway, William Carlos Williams, Francis S. Bacon, Theodore Spencer, John Slocum, Archibald MacLeish, e.e. cummings and his wife, Marion Morehouse, Viola Baxter Jordan, Irving Fisher, Max Eastman and his wife, Eliena Krylenko, Karl Shapiro, F. O. Matthiessen, Saxe Commins, Louis Untermeyer, Conrad Aiken, Reynolds Packard and his wife of the United Press, Bill Stoneman of the *Chicago Daily News*, Herbert Macken of the *New York Times*, and others.[67] Though she could not know it, the people to whom Mary turned for help were sometimes the very people who had expressed willingness to testify against her father.[68]

Thus, Mary's later, impassioned assault on officials in Washington, D.C., was met with an equally determined rudeness and silence. She came gradually to understand that her efforts were entirely futile. From Francis Biddle, who cut her at a party, to bureaucrats at the Department of Justice, who advised her that it would be a mistake to reopen the case, she was dismissed with barely disguised annoyance. In retrospect, we see that these responses were based on sexism, contemptuous attitudes toward youth, toward foreigners (how could an Italian princess be a "real" American citizen?), the assumption that identity is stigmatized by association, and an unwillingness to challenge guilt that had been assumed from the start. "At social occasions," Mary later wrote, "as long as I was the charming young princess with a fairytale castle in Italy, everything was fine." But any serious attempt to address Pound's situation was stonewalled. "So, it was true," she finally recognized. "They hated him."[69]

When she finally went out to St. Elizabeths, she saw, as she put it, "a man hit by history full blast."[70] She used this phrase to describe the diminished man she saw in the halls of a psychiatric ward—but the "full blast" had initially been the secret services of the United States government more than the current inmates who provided his sorry and intrusive company.

Several years later, Archibald MacLeish offered an impression of the scene: "Not everyone has seen Pound in the long, dim corridor inhabited by the ghosts of men who cannot be still, or who can be still too long. . . . When a conscious mind capable of the most complete human awareness is incarcerated among minds, which are not conscious and cannot be aware, the enforced association produces a horror which is not relieved either by the intelligence of doctors or by the tact of administrators or even by the patience and kindliness of the man who suffers it. You carry the horror away with you like the smell of the ward in your clothes, and whenever afterward you think of Pound or read his lines a stale sorrow afflicts you."[71] Mary's description was similarly grim. Her father lived among "empty husks rocking . . . in front of blaring televisions . . . leering younger shades," and keys and chains.[72] It was the "first must go the road to Hell" he had predicted in his 1945 letters to her.

As long as they were alone together, the visit went well. On 12 March Mary wrote to Olga, "I have spent the whole afternoon with Babbo, and I too seem to be appointed as guardian and can stay from 1 to 4. He is wonderful—in fact . . . exactly like in Rapallo. Only to tell you the truth I am discouraged, but perhaps I will be able to talk to him tomorrow. He talked all the time. Just for my education like 10 years ago. He says there is no question of my leaving on the Andrea Doria He wants me to stay till May. Apparently he is arranging for a place for me to stay and wants me to write! At this moment this thought seems even repulsive as I only want to 'move things' and get him out and back to Italy."[73]

Her eagerness turned to frustration and then to depression. Pound was at first delighted to hear stories about Boris, the children, and the castle, but very quickly their privacy was interrupted by the return of Dorothy and Omar. After a week of it, Mary admitted to Olga that she had come to the end of her patience. Omar dropped in "three minutes after [she] had been there and [sat] absorbing all the conversation." And it was impossible not to notice that Pound had lost interest in hearing about her life. "But then I suppose it is just my fault for not having a more interesting life or more ideas."[74] Her role shifted quickly to a passive one in every sense. Not only did she witness the apathy of others, but she came to see that her father's deep weariness ("There is fatigue deep as the grave")[75] somehow guided and informed everyone's lethargy.

He was intransigent about not securing his own immediate release, thinking that any challenge or defense that Arthur Garfield Hays might attempt would ruin the family financially.[76] Better, he reasoned, to continue working; never, he argued, should he falsely declare guilt or mental incompetence. Four years later, writing to Harry Meacham he admitted, "I would naturally prefer to go live with my daughter to staying in the bughouse."[77] But with the live, present daughter he counseled patience that she could barely tolerate. "I agree," she told Olga, that "his reasoning is perfectly logical and sound, but I still think things can be speeded up a little."[78]

On the personal front, there was little she could do. One consequence of Pound's failure to stand trial was that he had forfeited his own legal identity. His wife now made all civic transactions on his behalf. The technical term for Dorothy's position was "committeé" and its sign, in Mary's eyes, was the pitiable woman's purse with which Pound doled out small coins for her lunch at the hospital canteen.

She was reduced to disapproving spectator on other fronts as well. Knowing nothing of American culture and even less of American counterculture, having no way to "read" the style of the Beat generation, seeing ill-kempt hair and poor manners, she judged her father's visitors to be "third rate" people. She settled for Pound's assessment of them as useful . . . as if companionship were a stratagem . . . but there was much more to the guests who came to sit with Pound on the lawns of the hospital, more raw emotion, more need, and attachment on all sides.

Some of the "regulars" would become politically dangerous when the climate for Pound's release finally did emerge in 1958—people like John Kasper, whose racism was undeniable and extreme. Some of them were collaborators in writing projects—people like Eustace Mullins, who concurred with Pound's economic theories and extended his research into the Federal Reserve System. Others still were extremely distinguished—as were, for example, the novelist Katherine Anne Porter, Huntington Cairns of the National Gallery of Art, and the art historian Kenneth Clark. A very few were young artists whose work Pound genuinely valued and who, in turn, longed for his support and encouragement.

One of these was a young woman named Sheri Martinelli.[79] H.D., looking on from distant Küsnacht, Switzerland, her views informed by letters from Norman Holmes Pearson, and her memory prompted by her analyst Erich Heydt, wrote that "Undine [Sheri] seems myself *then*."[80] "The Maelids/in the close garden of Venus/asleep amid serried lynxes."[81] She understood, as Mary did, that much of Pound's teaching at St. Elizabeths was futile. She imagined his audience as ants: "the *Ameisen* (ants), he seated on the grass, clutch eagerly for the scattered grains. . . . Bushel baskets of inseminating beauty fell upon barren ground."[82] But she also understood, as Mary did not, that Martinelli was different . . . somehow both creatively and erotically entwined and, as events would have it, about to be "dumped."

She was a visual artist, and Pound was instrumental in having her work published by Vanni Scheiwiller, claiming, in the introduction to the little book that "Undine [was] the first to show a capacity to manifest in paint, or in *la ceramica* what is most to be prized in my writing."[83] She experienced herself as loved. "Grandpa loves me. It's because I symbolize the spirit of Love to him, I guess," Martinelli told one reporter,[84] and she was, consequently, shattered when, at the prospect of Pound's release, he told her to leave. "He killed me," she wrote to H.D. "The male just can't go about like that, ditching a spirit love. I have known Ezra for 6 years. The last 4 years I took a vow in St. Anthony's Church in NYC not to leave the Maestro until he was freed. A month before he was freed he made me break that vow."[85]

H.D. recognized the situation, for it had once been her own. She called the girl "swallow—my sister." "Poor Undine! They don't want you, they really don't. How shall we reconcile ourselves to this?" For her that sundering from Pound had been disintegration that opened toward rebirth. Severed psychically from friends and family by her youthful love for Pound in Philadelphia, severed, ultimately from Pound himself, she recognized that he was the kind of person who aroused emotion only to destroy domestic serenity and security—and that only those with the strength for creative reintegration could endure that terrible break.

The analogies that H.D. retrieved from memory tell us a great deal about her relationship with Pound, but to some extent they, too, were a misprision. The attraction between Pound and Martinelli was doubtlessly there; it was erotically charged, but it was (ostensibly) transformed into a filial relationship. When she approached, Pound would leap up, run his hands through her hair, and give her an energetic bear hug. He paid the rent on her apartment and gave her a dollar a day to live on. Dorothy chose to read the situation as that of a father and daughter and extended her own affection to the young woman, whom she often escorted around town. "Here comes family," she would say, when she saw her walking across the lawn.[86]

Mary, the real family, too ignorant of the deep history that played itself out even in the deplorable surroundings of a mental hospital, saw only the hedonism of beatniks—and maybe she saw the dope they smoked. Their self-indulgence soon merged with the contrary extravagances of McCarthyism to create an impression of America that left her "indignant, then depressed, then amorphous."[87] She could not join in, so she turned away. Poetry, history, economics—abstractions of her father—took the place of the stagnation of his actual life and all that surrounded it.

Eventually she met Craig La Drière and Giovanni Giovannini at the Catholic University. They seem to have provided a still center of sanity for her: they were patient and intelligent men; they were well-informed, could sort out information, attend to facts, and, as she put it, they had an *éducation du coeur*—educated hearts. In May they invited her to the university to read Pound's Canto I and her own Italian translation of it. It was to be "quite an affair" and she was miffed that neither Dorothy nor Omar had accepted Giovannini's invitation to attend. She made it a policy to appear in harmony with all members of Pound's extended family, but increasingly she understood that she could not rely on them. "I am convinced that he [Pound] has a very good idea about people's characters. And I do think that he knows what he is up against. He also realizes that he has made mistakes. But he has such a marvelous character and I think it is his inner conviction that one pays, in one way or another, for the mistakes one makes," was her final assessment of the whole scene—she saw a man of integrity surrounded by unfathomable indifference.[88]

In June she turned her back on the United States and headed to Italy, convinced that nothing could be done for Pound on American soil.[89]

V

Domestic problems waited for her: sulking children who had stayed with Olga under eyes constantly watching for "formal politeness";[90] a dining-room roof that had caved in once again, and an unidentified rash that turned out to be poison ivy imported along with Pound's maple trees.[91] She dealt with these issues pragmatically, if not serenely, for she had returned with renewed purpose: Pound had appointed her his official publishing representative in Italy,[92] and his letters to her from this point bristled with ideas and plans. In early December, Mary met Giovanni Scheiwiller for the first time—a man who would play an extraordinary role both in Pound's rehabilitation in Italy and in Mary's own emerging life as a poet in her own right.

She returned to her work of translating *The Cantos* and Confucius into Italian and to fitting out the castle for receiving long term guests. By the end of the year, twenty rooms were finished, and she was once again writing to Pound about purchasing more land, discussing down payments, the legal expenses of transfer, taxes, yearly payments, and anticipated income. By the fall of 1954, Pound was satisfied that the investment was sound and sent money for the first installment, saying that he was relieved the money was out of the country.[93] In response to Mary's excitement about finally owning more than the walls of Brunnenburg, Olga sent a rebuff—too much; too soon—which floored her daughter. "I can't understand," she responded. "If there is one thing Boris and I have done for the past eight years it is just struggling FOR THIS PLACE—FOR THE LOVE OF THIS PLACE AS OUR HOME."[94]

As she struggled with homesteading in the Alps, she also confronted other mountains. She turned to the issue of Pound's anti-Semitism. In mid-December she wrote a letter to the *Fiera Letteraria*, saying that "it might be useful if for once people did not look only at the *forma* but also at the *contenuto* of Pound's writing and they would find that in Cantos XX and XXIV (to cite only a few) he talks sympathetically about the Jews, which proves that he has not feelings against the race, only against usurers." She wanted to know "according to what standards ideas are defined *giuste* [just] or *sbagliate* [mistaken]."[95] But she was "climbing" in the face of evidence to the contrary, for she had recently received, amid recommendations of contemporary writers to read—Jaime de Angulo, Juan Ramon Jimenez, Felix Zielinsky—the added advice that she might read "Adolf's 'Secret Conversations,'" which Pound considered "very entertaining . . . quite nuts on world domination, but VERY sound on race and cash."[96] The issue was not to be so easily dealt with, as she was to discover between May and September 1954, when the Robert Fitzgerald family came to stay in one of the Brunnenburg apartments.

Fitzgerald, who was to become the Boylston Professor of Rhetoric and Oratory Emeritus at Harvard, chancellor of the Academy of American Poets, and consultant in poetry to the Library of Congress, had moved his young family to Italy in 1953. In 1947 he had married Sarah Morgan and had spent several years as a fellow at Princeton and then at Indiana University in Bloomington. In the '30s and '40s he had made a name for himself translating Greek classics (Euripides' *Alcestis*, Sophocles' *Antigone* and *Oedipus Rex*) with Dudley Fitts, but in Italy he was working on his own poetry.[97] Sally was engrossed in raising their five children, who ranged from three months to five years old. The elder Fitzgeralds were deeply religious Catholics—and one might have predicted harmony at the castle based on a common faith and the love of poetry, classical languages, the art of translation, and the value of family life.

But in August Mary received an extraordinary "memorandum" from Robert Fitzgerald, which he prepared with exquisite care after having Pound's radio speeches microfilmed and sent to him from the Library of Congress. After telling Mary that he respected her feelings about her father and her fidelity to him, he said that he felt "the best immediate thing I could do would be to help you read" the broadcasts. "You would then see what the people at home in the United States had to go on in your father's case. They couldn't just hear or read what he said about Joyce's writing and Lewis's and cummings' or Celine's. They had all the broadcasts, two years of them. Taking them into account, how could they help thinking that he had joined the military enemies of the United States?" "It seems to me important for you to see this," he continued. "It would be a pity for you to go any further in developing a general resentment and dislike of the United States and its people. And it would be a worse pity for you to think that your father's indictment was in any sense Jewish vengefulness."[98]

In a seven-part document, he laid out the Pound Case, as he saw it. He began with a textbook explanation of the Constitution of the United States. He made the distinction between thinking and acting, claiming that "[t]he

Constitution says that when the United States is at war it is a crime for a citizen to join the other side . . . you may adhere to them in your opinions, but you are not free as a United States citizen to adhere to them to the extent of *doing* anything for them." For him, speech was a form of doing. He then went through each point of the indictment, which a former student of Norman Holmes Pearson named John Edwards had managed to get from the Department of Justice, concluding, simply and as if self-evidently, that the radio broadcasts were a form of doing and that their existence alone constituted proof of treason. "Could any honest juror fail to conclude that their contents bear out the indictment?"

Having made the equation "radio broadcast=treason"—assuming as true what remained to be proved in a court of law—he then went on to address the issue of free speech, claiming that it was not an unlimited or unqualified freedom, but existed only insofar as it was not used to injure others. He conceded that "many of the things Ezra Pound was saying in his radio talks were being said aloud and printed in the United States during the war by opponents of the administration—for example that Roosevelt had exceeded his powers, broken his promises, and violated his oath of office." It was not the content of Pound's thought, Fitzgerald claimed, but the spectacle of a noted American citizen publicly criticizing the United States that had "aided and comforted" the enemy. It was a tricky argument—for one could use its logic to claim that a person expressing Pound's ideas on Chicago radio or in a Milwaukee journal was within his rights—an argument that implicitly demonstrated Pound's point—that he was denied the coverage of the Constitution and the rights implied by his own passport—because he continued to live and to speak on foreign soil. Fitzgerald argued that he was "in the pay of the castle"—that his speeches had been vetted and paid for by the Ministry of Popular Culture and thus implied Pound's complicity with "the enemy." Pound continued to assert that his disclaimer at the beginning of each broadcast—that he spoke according to conscience—effected a legal separation between himself and his employer—the obverse of what is the case when we hear on public radio and elsewhere the phrase, "the opinions expressed by this commentator are solely his/her own and not the responsibility of the broadcasting system."

But it was a disingenuous argument in any case—Fitzgerald didn't seem really to care where Pound spoke or whether freedom of speech entitled him to express aberrant opinions—it was clearly the content of Pound's radio speech that offended him. It was his belief that Pound had been in collusion with the Nazis or Fascists or both, that his thought was indistinguishable from foreign propaganda and that it was blatantly, abhorrently, and undeniably anti-Semitic. "What [the broadcasts] say as to the war then in progress may have been, in Ezra Pound's mind, only his private propaganda, but it coincided so well with Axis propaganda at many points as to be indistinguishable from Axis propaganda. But there is more to be said than this. The broadcasts contain evidence that they were considered to be Axis propaganda by Ezra Pound when he wrote them: that he was speaking consciously as an Axis propandist combating anti-Axis propaganda. . . . He spoke as an adherent not only of Italy but of Germany and Japan, not only of Mussolini and Fascism but of Hitler and Nazism."

Fitzgerald continued "reading" the broadcasts for Mary. "On April 16, '42 he speaks of. . . . on April 30. . . . on April 6, '43 . . . on March 25, '43," and then he addressed the question of the Jews directly. "It's a big and puzzling matter, this anti-Semitism. The broadcasts are pervaded by it in all aspects, not only economic and political but religious and racial. . . . Why?" He quickly dismissed one of the premises of Pound's thinking, *The Protocols of the Elders of Zion,* by saying that had *he,* Robert Fitzgerald, believed them to be true, he would have "state[d] [his] belief openly, day in and day out." Since, to his knowledge, Pound didn't do this, he concluded that Pound didn't really believe in a Jewish plot that involved banking, that he only suspected it, and that, lacking proof, he spoke irresponsibly.

He continued with his speculation. Could Pound have used the subject of Jewry as "a way of catching attention, making people listen, appealing to the lower orders?" Were the broadcasts "a distorted reflection of what he thought?" He dismissed this idea by saying "if a writer like Ezra Pound can't make clear exactly what he means, nobody else can." But it was only speculation; he had no answer. "It would stand to reason that in these broadcasts he meant what he said, no more and no less." By the end of his "memorandum," Fitzgerald made it clear to Mary that, in his judgment, what she, as a Christian woman, had to face was that her father had been purely, vehemently, and in undeniably "vicious practice," a collaborator in the destruction of the Jews. "You can't interpret this anti-Semitism as something else." He brooked no argument to the contrary. "If [Giovanni] Scheiwiller had read these broadcasts he could never have written of the 'cruel legend of his [Ezra Pound's] anti-Semitism for horrible and absurd racial motives.' The anti-Semitism is not a cruel legend . . . but a fact, cruel or not. 'The very logic of the broad humanistic culture of a poet and thinker like Ezra Pound makes racialism or

anti-Semitism impossible,' said Duarte de Montalegre. That is arguing without data. The broad humanistic culture in this case did not prevent racialism
or anti-Semitism. 'The essence of Ezra Pound's teaching,' said Duarte de Montalegre, 'may be summed up in these words . . . *He inveighed against usury.*
This is why many people believed him to be an anti-Semite, erroneously identifying a vicious practice with a whole race. Once this misunderstanding
has been removed no serious grounds for the accusation remain.' But the
misunderstanding has been the other way round. A lot of people have had the
idea, as Montalegre apparently did, that Ezra Pound was mainly against usury
and not seriously against the Jews. If the radio talks mean anything, this aint
so. He was as seriously against Jews as you can be."

He added, as if the United States were not the home of Civil War, the
KKK, and continued segregation of races, "They aren't American, these
attitudes," and as if the Catholic Church had not participated in its own
extended collaboration with the Nazis, "neither are these attitudes . . .
Christian. . . . the Catholic position on anti-Semitism was stated by Pope
Pius X, now a saint of the Church . . . 'Spiritually, we are Semites.'"

In light of these purported horrors, he told Mary what he thought Pound
should do. "If it goes too much against the grain for him to plead guilty, he
can, as John Edwards brought out, make a plea of *nolo contendere*: 'I don't care
to dispute the charges.'" Fitzgerald considered that he had all the facts and
that the facts condemned Pound. Sooner or later, he reasoned, the doctors at
St. Elizabeths would pronounce Pound fit for trial and he would lose. Better
face a judge's penalty immediately. "You tell me that Laughlin, Cornell, and
Eliot all gave advice to this effect in the past; now Edwards, Drummond,
Lowell and myself agree in advising it."

Fitzgerald concluded by reminding Mary that her deepest loyalties had
to be not to her father but to "one's central sense of what is true and right."
"We who are Catholics," he continued, "have the standards Christ gave us."
Admitting that his counsel might be unwelcome, he nonetheless repeated "it
isn't possible . . . to say that Ezra Pound was not *filonazista* in 1942. His recorded words prove that he was. Well, all right, he was. You can still maintain that there were some good things about Fascism in Italy. . . . You can
maintain with conviction that Ezra Pound was neither dishonest nor
treacherous, that he sincerely supported men and policies that seem to him
to promise a better life, and that his vision of a better life was in some ways
a piercing one. . . . But speaking both practically and morally, what you cannot do, as I see it, is conceal or deny or shove under the rug the fact that he

did speak for the enemies of the United States during the war and the fact that he did, with fervor, embrace racial anti-Semitism."

It was a straightforward analysis, its logic laid out in terms that many other American intellectuals believed, including, as Fitzgerald maintained, John Edwards, John Drummond, and Robert Lowell, with whom he claimed to have discussed this. He was afraid that Mary lived in ignorance or that she would falsify facts or that her resentment of his treatment at Pisa would blind her to the full perfidy of her parent. He worried that she would "mind" if her father were labeled a traitor, which, in his judgment, trial or no trial, he was. Although he insisted that everything he said was "fact," he told her that he hoped she would write an answer to him. "Will you, busy as you are, give it some thought and let me know?"

There is no evidence that she responded to him directly. "Acquit of evil intention," was what she wrote in *Discretions*. No one could deny *what* Pound said. But Fitzgerald could not know Pound's motives. On 4 August she wrote to Olga about the scholars staying at the castle: "As for Edwards: I do not like him. Definitely. Don't think he is at all well intentioned towards Babbo. We were naturally very nice to him, and I think he enjoyed himself very much but his attitude towards Babbo when the Fitzgeralds were present did really worry me. Mrs. Fitzgerald is really *venenosa* [poisonous] whenever the subject of Babbo crops up, and she gives the tone in the house . . . [She says] 'The only thing one can be sorry for is that he ever talked over radio.' It is just too distressing," she added, "to see how all the Americans I have met so far, as soon as they are no longer alone with me change tone; they try simply to pull poor Babbo to pieces. . . . They would all like to *pacificare le lor coscienze*, but they do not feel sorry for Babbo a bit, and what is most important, they do not realize what he has been trying to do. Fitzgerald went to all the trouble to have the microfilm of the radio speeches sent to him, which might be looked upon as deep interest in the case, but I am sure will serve nothing else except point out further things Babbo ought not to have done and said." She assured her mother that the Fitzgeralds would only be tenants and that there would be no intermixing except on Sunday at tea. Years later, in one of her own poems she wrote:

Failure can be judged by him alone who
Knows the fathoms deep he reached the peaks
He climbed tallied with his aims
    And no hair split.[99]

Fitzgerald might have argued that she was evading the truth—but it was the truth only as he saw it. He was speaking to a Catholic; he was speaking to a Tyrolean; he was speaking to a woman whose father who had been held captive in a private prison for ten years and to whom, as she understood it, mercy was due. "I said that a bit of sincere sympathy for his present condition might help," she had told Sally Fitzgerald. While they were in her home, the Fitzgeralds stood on ground that had been conceived as extraterritorial space for people caught between territorial loyalties. It was intended to abrogate the very distinctions that Robert Fitzgerald relied upon for his argument against her father. Mary refused to concede that Pound was an anti-Semite or that he did not have the right to speak on the radio, given her understanding of his intentions.

Both she and Robert Fitzgerald were close readers looking for evidence. One looked for anti-Semitism, the other for pro-Jewish sentiment—both found in Pound's texts what they hoped or feared to find, and both were right. Fitzgerald, in trying to persuade Mary that Pound was "un-American," argued that "no member of the Adams family would write or talk or think like this, Jefferson would not, Lincoln would not." But Walt Whitman might have: "Do I contradict myself? Very well. I contract myself." Pound's writing contained outrage and sublimity in piercing juxtaposition. It was maddeningly inconsistent. As Norman Holmes Pearson wrote of *The Cantos*, "They are an ambitious poem and a great poem, and the problems he presents (even when I don't agree with the solutions) are the problems of our age."[100]

Mary confronted these problems with the mind of a person for whom the issue of nationalism was fraught in ways that Fitzgerald, with his roots on American soil and his unwavering service at Pearl Harbor and Guam, could not fathom. In her lifetime, Italy had been neutral; Italy had been America's enemy; Italy had become America's ally; the Tyrol had been Austrian; it had been arbitrarily handed to Italy as spoils after the Great War; when another war brought German occupation, Italy became its enemy. She had been forced to wear an Italian Fascist school uniform; she had given blood to German soldiers. Boundaries and allegiances had been drawn and redrawn according to political expedience until Mary questioned the very the foundations of nationalism. "Whose World?" she asked. "Who makes the rules about what is just and what is mistaken?"

The Fitzgeralds left in September. Numerous guests came and went,[101] but the life of the mind continued. Between 1951 and 1955 Boris worked at the Pontificio Instituto Biblico in Rome, pursuing his love of Egyptology. In 1953 he attended the Vatican Diplomacy school—Accademia Vaticana. He continued his practice of going back and forth between Rome and Brunnenburg, his mind as curious and as credulous as ever. In 1952, he joined the Fortean Society and published a transcription of the "Tulli Papyrus" in the group's magazine, *Doubt*. Professor Albert Tulli, director of the Egyptian Museum of the Vatican, of the same family that had drawn up the Rachewiltz genealogy, had apparently directed his attention to a papyrus that described "circles of fire" in the ancient skies—a description Boris took to be an affirmation of extraterrestrial life. He was apparently drawn to secrets, to the occult, to anything that countered the mundanity of ordinary life in postwar Europe. The "show of spirit" that Pound had admired from afar seems to have been at work founding a new Order of Canossa, for in October 1954, Pound wrote to suggest that the Comte de Gramont "might do" for the order, and then, on hearing of the numerous guests who were becoming a common feature of Brunnenburg life, advised "Probably time for order of chivalry to go SECRET."[102]

Mary stayed at the castle, more interested in good society than secret society. During these years, she formed and deepened the working relationships of her life. Giovanni Scheiwiller, who was publishing Confucius, *Lavoro ed usura*, and Pound's *Rock-Drill*, would settle into Brunnenburg to correct proofs and "do ideograms." In May he and Mary met Giovanni Martersteig in Verona to discuss a new edition of the *Pisan Cantos*. In Munich, Eva Hesse continued her project of translating Pound's work into German. Signora M. L. Molinari in Lisbon was engaged in another translation project. In publishing Pound's work, Mary hoped gradually to push his image away from that of rabid, duped instrument of governments toward a more consistent memory of his greatness as a poet. Aside from translating, which continued with varied responses from Pound ("COMPlimenti, translations in wop—Prospetti, best yu have done";[103] "Now that I've sent him final version of Cathay he utterly dismissed it as <u>no</u> good . . . so I don't know where I stand,")[104] she was organizing a *Festschrift* for his seventieth birthday. She had invited Luigi Villari and many others to contribute.

The renewed energy of Pound's letters to Mary reveals the healing power of this arrangement. He began to discuss qualities of paper, vellum, margins, and layout for the new cantos. "Morgan is howling for more cantos/but til I know WHEN Vanni is gittin the fire built under the mule, I cant tell when he will incinerate the wagon. Also, Stock yowling in orstralia."[105] It was as if his daughter existed as an extension of himself, an agent of desire, able to accomplish what he, in his imprisonment, was denied. Instructions poured forth year after year: "tell Vanni . . . ; send Villari . . . ; I think it would be better if you wrote to La Pira." He involved Mary in getting Sheri Martinelli's work published by Scheiwiller. He told her what to read, to whom to write, and what to say, until, after years of this instruction, apparently in response to some urgent inquiry, he wrote, "I thot paternal affection wuz UNDERSTOOD, however if reiteration is good for morale, let us REiterate."[106] This said, he continued, "IF you want to be useful, might be good thing to contrast E.P.—Confucio vs. Marx-Hegel, especially the clarity of *Lavoro ed usura* with the confuscionism of *Das Kapital.* . . ."[107]

Amid instructions, he reiterated the central ideas that had formed him as a "citizen" as well as a poet. "Note that Dante brought MORE matter into poetry than perhaps any other writer. And grampaw is also bringing in stuff that didn't use to be thaaar in poetry . . . not that there are only 2 people who expanded frontiers."[108] He told her had enjoyed rereading Alexander Del Mar's "marrrvelous account of rascality" in *The History of Monetary Systems*; he spoke of the importance of Brook Adams's *The Law of Civilization and Decay* in his mental development and asked, "E.P. refrain on air: This is what B. Adams said in 1903. Can this be Axis propaganda?" He remarked "the aim of law is to prevent coercion either by force or by fraud."[109] And he told her "E.P. opposed falsification of history, i.e. false news ABOUT Italy."[110] He had felt, he told her, that the real enemy of western civilization had been the Russians and that Germany was the only nation that "would BOTHER to keep 'em in order and that the only balance to keep Germany from getting too big for her boots is a STRONG ITALY which existed in 1934."[111]

It was as if Pound had implicitly positioned his daughter as the judge of his interior life and, in laying his life choices before her, asked for the fair judgment that history, as he saw it, had denied him. This singular, epistolary education coexisted with rants against "the kikes," the supposed repressions of the English and American press, and "the American system of turning every border skirmish into a world war."[112] Pound told her repeatedly that there had been no "gas ovens in Italy." For years Mary winnowed wheat and chaff, sorting genius, originality, and thankfully renewed vigor from unabated prejudice and illusion, forced to read her father's vituperative language and to see his continued belief in an Italy that had never existed outside of his desire for it.

In July 1955, Olga returned to the United States. She traveled in the wake of a frail optimism emerging from expanded support for Pound's release. Ernest

Hemingway, after winning the Nobel Prize for Literature in 1954, suggested that it would be a good year for releasing poets. In Italy, Duarte de Montalegre (pseudonym for José Vitorino de Pina Martins, a Portuguese writer teaching at the University of Rome) spoke on Vatican Radio. In *Prometheus Bound* he emphasized the difference between Pound's hatred of usury and anti-Semitism and pleaded for his release. Giovanni Scheiwiller made a public statement saying, "Non ha mai potuto supportare la stupidità e la malafede: per questo egli è ancora in manicomio criminale." (It's no longer possible to support the stupidity and bad faith: it's criminal that he's still in a mental hospital.). In Switzerland, the *Weltwoche* published an essay naming Pound the greatest living lyricist and identifying *The Cantos* as a magnificent synthesis of European and American cultures, embodying "*Die One World der Poesie*."[113]

Pound anticipated Olga's arrival with ambivalence, for he understood that she would push him toward action. He told his daughter frankly that "Olga is NOT a help toward a quiet life and can always develop six or seven resentments at any moment. . . . and as for arranging my life, I am about FED up with attempts to do THAT."[114] He was right on both counts. She walked onto the St. Elizabeths grounds, lifted her lavender parasol over Sheri Martinelli's head and, with this shaded glance, surmised her erotic replacement. She argued, cut relations with Pound, and stopped writing to him.

This situation turned Mary into not only the judge/advocate of her father but also the arbiter of her own parents' travail. Pound understood the trauma of it. To Mary he wrote, "Waal, she'za nice gal/and she wuz lookin beeyewteeful, not only elegant . . . but the WRONG time and the WRONG place/ and no use mentioning history . . . about which she can do NOTHING. . . . The ironies of the GODS/ she wd/ probably explode if she knew her ally in the anti-Martinelli campaign wuz young Omar/so for garzache don't MENTION that."[115] Mary found herself listening to both sides—Olga's lament and Pound's justifications "No, S, can't be said to complicate my life," Pound explained to her. "After all I can't leave the 'location', and when she drifts across the scene here it is . . . in serenity . . . and the spectacle of the Cosmos, a volcano chucking up hell and heaven." "Having had the whole of Europe fall on one's head does in a ceratin [*sic*] way simplify things/ I mean calamities do not seem so large in comparison."[116]

Mary tried to mitigate the damage to Olga, but it affected her as well. "I really don't know what to make of the whole situation," she admitted. "Babbo seems to be so hard to please, but it would all have been all right had I still the feeling that we are all collaborating." Nothing worked. Mary could say, "I understand that he has hurt you very much, but he still needs you more than ever," but her admonition fell on deaf ears. Pound made one more attempt to use his daughter to intervene, "AND to soften the shock to O/, can you suggest that in the Middle Ages, after crashes men wore out and retired to monasteries. My case VERY involuntary."[117] But words cannot assuage rejection, and from this moment, Pound ceased to mention Olga Rudge in his correspondence with Mary, warning only that the relations of any two people are always unfathomable to any other. He repositioned his faith, and in so doing, repositioned the location of his writing archive as well. He asked Mary to go to Rapallo and "take ALL E.P. archivio to Brun/." "Thank gawd," he added, "there is a civilized spot left."[118]

VI

Mary understood the timing of this move in relation to other shifts in the constellation of her father's extended circle. In May 1955, she learned that Omar Pound had married Elizabeth Stevenson Parkin. Despite Pound's distrust of educational institutions, Omar had been attending Hamilton College on the GI Bill of Rights and studying Persian and Islamic history at the London School of Oriental and African Studies. Mary had little formal education, but the archive was her heritage, so she engaged a *camion* to bring Isabel Pound's things and Pound's papers and furniture to the castle. It was generally a time of change: Boris's brother, Igor, had also finished his education, moved to Australia, and married. Eva Hesse married and in September 1956 finally visited Brunnenburg with her new husband. By December 1955, Boris was en route to Egypt (Pound called it "EGG/ wiped") on the *Esperia*.[119] The following June, when he returned to Italy, Mary met the Italian ambassador to Cairo at a party and reported that "it looks as if we might all go to Egypt for the winter—would be a relief in many ways."[120] In September she was still preparing for the journey—Boris's scholarship had been renewed and he had been proposed by Professor Selim Hassan for a position with UNESCO.[121] But when political unrest broke out, they decided that the situation was too risky for the children. Boris returned alone, writing reports of life in Cairo to Pound, who alternately told him "to stay OUT of politics for another ten years" and suggested that his son-in-law use the pseudonym Selim Essain when making political commentary.[122] Despite

his preoccupation with his writing life, Pound seemed to register these activities and approve. "Your generation," he admitted to Mary, "looks to me
rather better than my own, maybe merely that I know OF more individuals
with some sort of horse sense at tender age."[123]

That was all she had at the moment. "We *must* go on living some sort of
life of our own," she wrote to Olga, "I feel it's in the long run the only way to
help Babbo." She reported that Professor Hassan was keeping Boris busy in
Egypt, that Boris sent consistently good news and that neither of them had
"illusions about UNESCO as such—merely another step."[124] In March 1957,
Patrizia celebrated her first communion, and then Mary was to go to Sirmione
to meet Archibald MacLeish and his wife to discuss her father. When
Mrs. MacLeish reminded her that her husband was an excellent lawyer, Mary
was brought up short. "I hadn't thought of it—I saw only the poet. And the
man who had been challenged while holding an important position in government during the war, who had brushed politics aside and stood by his old
friend in trouble."[125] What could come of MacLeish's talent and good will she
didn't know. Boris returned to the castle in May, where he settled in to work
on his writing; Eva invited Mary to visit Munich in September, a respite from
work on an exhibition of the work of Gaudier-Brzeska to be held in Milan
and Merano. During the fall, Mary also began to formulate a plan to return
to the United States. She wanted to work more actively with her father on *The
Cantos*, this time taking Boris and the children to Washington with her—
and it looked as though Norman Holmes Pearson had access to funds from
Yale that could finance the trip.

But suddenly the momentum changed; their efforts to shift public opinion about Pound began to bear fruit. Giovanni Scheiwiller had submitted a
petition to Clare Booth Luce, the American ambassador to Italy, signed by
Salvatore Quasimodo, Eugenio Montale, and Alberto Moravia. Diego Valeri
presented her with another petition signed by Giuseppe Ungaretti, Enrico
Pea, Mario Praz, and Ignazio Silone. All of them urged her to support a "be-
nevolent re-examination of Pound's case and the withdrawal of the charges
against this illustrious poet [so that he could] return to his Italy so loved by
him, here to conclude his days in work-filled peace."[126] Although no government officials paid direct attention to her inquiries on Pound's behalf,
Mrs. Luce persuaded her husband Henry, the publisher of *Life* magazine, to
run an editorial calling Pound's room at St. Elizabeths "a closet which contains a national skeleton."[127] *The New Republic* followed suit (1 April 1957); so
did *The Nation* (19 April 1958). Archibald MacLeish wrote a review of *Section:*

Rock-Drill in the *New York Times* (16 November 1956). Dag Hammarskjold, the secretary-general of the United Nations, to whom Mary had sent a copy of *Rock-Drill*, began quietly to work on Pound's behalf, saying that the measure of a civilization is the way it treats its poets. He wrote to MacLeish; MacLeish reenergized T. S. Eliot, Ernest Hemingway, and ultimately Robert Frost, saying now that Ezra Pound was a matter for the State Department since his treatment affected the United States' image in the eyes of the entire world community.

In March 1957 Mary received a letter from MacLeish saying that Attorney General Herbert Brownell Jr. had ordered a review of the case. She didn't know what to make of this news either. "This may be nothing more than an official brush-off, but it may also be the prelude to action."[128] In January 1958, she still wasn't sure. The success of the Gaudier-Brzeska show had pleased her father so much that he had begun to imagine a room for himself in the castle surrounded by the drawings,[129] so she focused her attention on the garden flat as an appropriate place for them and on completing a room for the archive. Reasoning that Brunnenburg was a national monument they had saved from decay, Boris had applied for a *sovvenzione*, a government grant, to help with the work—and by April construction was underway.

Then, on 18 April, she heard on American-Italian radio that the indictment against her father had been dropped. "It certainly has been long," she wrote to Olga, "but it's just too wonderful even to speak about it."[130]

Wonder turned into a spate of arrangements, inquiries about boats, passports, dates, and letters of congratulation. Norman Holmes Pearson wrote to suggest that she use the stipend intended for her trip to America for her father's comfort at the castle. Amid preparations, a flap arose about the Barattis. "Poor Boris had to rush to Rome to save the family from *sfratto* (eviction) . . . I must say they have always been most decent to me, but they won't ever change, so Boris will have to keep at least the mother." She herself was preoccupied with planning rooms for Pound, for Dorothy, and for someone named Marcella Spann, "who seems a friend of Dorothy's and is coming with them."[131]

She was very focused. Brunnenburg was to provide "all the beauty and space and comfort" that St. Elizabeths had denied her father.[132] But it was more than that. In anticipation of this moment, Pound had written to her. "Yes. I am all for a SOLID base in Tyrolo/ sacred enclosure. TEMNOS."[133] A TEMPLE.

CHAPTER 6

Betrayal

Brunnenburg, 1958–62

I

The temple was ready, but the homecoming was fraught. Even before Pound set foot on Italian soil, Olga's fury erupted. Pound had written to Mary asking her to arrange passage to Italy for three people on the *Christoforo Columbo*, wanting to celebrate his release with a first-class cabin. She had negotiated a reduced rate for the travelers, but Olga was miffed nonetheless. She ostensibly cared about whose money would finance the trip, but her concern cloaked the disaster of her position in Pound's life. Having worked for years for his return to Italy, she was now excluded from its realization. "You seem to forget," Mary wrote in May, "that Babbo *is released into the custody of his wife*, which means he can't leave the country alone or ever be alone, for that matter. And if your daughter wants her father to stay with her she has to accept the wife as well and whoever the said wife sees fit to bring along. I am sorry, but in our case there are no limits or else they should have been set 30 years ago."[1]

She counseled a quiet, united front, saying that they could neither change the law nor afford to provoke notice. But having practiced patience and fortitude, and being a pragmatic person by nature, Mary had no idea what "no limits" meant. She thought of Dorothy Pound as a "calculating lady, with the law on her side,"[2] but nothing prepared her for Marcella Spann.

There was initially a time of great joy. How could there not have been? Mary met the travelers in Verona, lunched with them in Bolzano, and took them all to the gates of Brunnenburg castle, where photographers recorded a world renewed and for a brief moment made whole. Pound, relaxed, smiling, dressed comfortably with hat and walking stick in hand, met a handsome, articulate son-in-law and two well-reared and equally smiling grandchildren. They walked on land that Pound had taken a keen interest in; he entered, so to speak, the space of his own imagination, where fruit-bearing trees and bright-eyed children and solidly built walls measured wealth. It was, of course, the space of Mary's imagination as well, the result of her efforts, and the measure of her love. But she is in the background of the photographs, the unacknowledged, and as it turned out, the hungry author of the scene.

For a while, everyone played their imagined roles. In August Mary described their lives to Olga. "Babbo likes the place and seems very eager to have some building done and to start with has made us two little stools for the garden." He read *The Cantos* aloud before tea to children who were puzzled by the Greek passages; he wrote when he was not too tired. He enjoyed, in his daughter's judgment, "the feeling of 'home' and . . . to find familiar objects." The downside was his weariness, but Mary read this as inevitable and passing: "he still is very tired and hates seeing people and does not want to move at all."[3] By December she had changed to saying, "life is not easy."[4]

After years of simple, spinster-like living in Washington, D.C., Dorothy's autocratic mannerisms returned: she was consistently correct and polite, but she expected Mary to provide breakfast in bed, and lunch, tea, and dinner served at punctual times. Pound took it for granted that he would be agreeably and quietly provided for, that Mary would organize the house as well as continue to translate his writing; he assumed that his collaboration with Marcella Spann would continue without interruption. In fact, he had prevailed upon Dorothy to provide the young Texan woman with a salary of $1,200 a year and upon James Laughlin to direct royalties to her. In theory, Mary had agreed to all of this. After years of suffering, her father had, she told Archibald MacLeish, a right to happiness. "Whomever he wants to bring is welcome. He makes his own laws and I accept them."[5]

But with Marcella Spann, she had to face, as she had somehow evaded with Sheri Martinelli, the erotic dimension of her father's longing. Spann was not merely a "secretary," as she had originally been described. Pound may have discussed translation with Mary, but he was more invested in working on the *Confucius to Cummings* anthology with Spann, dependent upon her company, her optimism, her youth and probably her malleability. He was possibly playing with the idea of divorcing Dorothy to marry the girl. What he had written to Mary about Olga—that she was "beeyewteeful . . . but [in] the

WRONG time and the WRONG place"[6] was, it turned out, equally true for his daughter, whom he continued to regard as an unexpectedly stubborn extension of himself. She was to provide the selfless ground for everyone else's recuperation. Cloaking her desire to be appreciated in comments about the unworthy nature of the company Pound kept, Mary came gradually to see that she, too, was peripheral to the drama playing itself out in Brunnenburg, even though it was she who had created the stage—the "sacred enclosure"?—that allowed the drama to unfold.

Unlike Olga, who sulked behind the scenes, Mary spoke out. However much her father was a "demigod," he was a demigod whose genius was stoked by her cooking and clean sheets. He was there to fulfill his destiny as a poet, not to dally with a woman who was, after all, no older than herself. She had been loyal to her father through Olga, Dorothy, the Pisan camp, St. Elizabeths and, subconsciously at least, it was her turn for attention. It didn't happen.

By the end of February, the trio was gone. The story that Pound put out from Rapallo was that he could not breathe properly at high altitudes and that he was cold. To Dr. Overholser, the superintendent of St. Elizabeths, he wrote, "One needed more STOVES and repairs at Brunnenburg." A week later he told Harry Meacham, "Sad fer Mary . . . that the mountain air didn't inflate my poumons. I gasped like a whale out of water."[7] But both Mary and Boris regarded these explanations as nonsense.

In letters to Olga, another story gradually emerged. Uncharacteristically, Boris was the first to write, telling her that everyone had left in a taxi on the morning of 25 February, "loaded as for a North Pole expedition." He knew for certain that all of them were going to Sant' Ambrogio and he thought it probable that Pound and Marcella Spann would continue on to Rome alone. He then said that Pound had demonstrated a total lack of comprehension of Mary's suffering, that his excuse for leaving Brunnenburg was "puerile" since the weather had been exceptionally mild (most of them had had their windows thrown open), and that any difficulty in breathing Pound had brought on himself by incessant typing behind closed doors. He claimed that "the secretary" had demanded so much heat that the air became polluted, and that emotions were equally tainted by Spann's incessant efforts to alienate Pound's affections from his daughter. He said that the idea that Mary had been possessive was "absurd." The inverse had been true; Spann had carried on "propaganda" behind closed doors and that gradually "paradise" had been transformed into an "inferno" for everyone. According to Pound himself,

Boris said, Mary had come to possess a "morbid jealousy" and "the terrible erudition of Olga." Since Mary had assimilated many of the Marchers' religious and moral qualities, she had taken these reprimands to heart, had come to regard the entire visit as a *fallimento* (failure, bankruptcy). He assured Olga that all the family had behaved "according to conscience," that they had done everything possible to provide Pound with a dignified home, with descendants of whom he could be proud, and an ambience suitable for repose and work. Mary could not be blamed for excessive emotion in confronting her father. She had made mistakes, certainly, but there was no culpability that made it appropriate for her to be repaid in this manner.[8]

For once Olga relented. She responded by inviting the young family to Sant' Ambrogio for Easter. But Mary refused. "I know father does not feel like seeing me. . . . We would only hurt each other (I take it that I too have hurt him) and yet I could not bear coming to Rapallo and not see him." Olga then took offense, and Mary had to tell her that she could "only get over things by forgetting them" and letting time do the rest.[9] And indeed, her initial response to the abrupt departure of her father's entourage had been to go with Boris to a conference in Bolzano and then on to Milan to spend time with Giovanni Scheiwiller and some of their common friends.

But she was far from forgetting. In the following months, glimpses of her perspective on the Brunnenburg dynamic slipped out. She faulted herself for having lost her temper: "father is evidently not accustomed to have things said to his face." She defended herself from Olga's charge of "interfering" with Pound's life, saying that all she had done was write to a friend who had a house in Fregene when she learned that he wanted to spend time at the sea. "As for my being like grandmother, I'd be rather proud of it and if at the age of 80 I am as lucid and straight as she was, I'd be glad and even if at the time it was very painful to be considered 'merely a Rudge' and Omar *the* Pound." She claimed that she would rather not talk about Miss Spann, but the few observations she let slip, even though uttered in heat, probably get at the manipulations that she found so damaging. She reiterated to Olga that Pound had "'a right to do what he likes.' And Miss Spann will always give in and say yes and be utterly helpless and so unhappy because she makes other people suffer and she ain't accustomed to make people suffer and poor father will go round and tell everybody so." She ended this letter to her mother by repeating what she had said through all the years of Pound's incarceration; indeed, she spoke as if he were still incarcerated: "there is NOTHING I can do for father, except try to lead a decent life."[10] In the ensuing months, she admitted, "I am no longer sure of what's right and what's wrong"[11] and told her mother, "It's not courage I have lost, but . . . something much more vital."[12]

Before these events could be fully sorted out, Mary had to put on a good face for television crews. In mid-April D. G. Bridson of the BBC arranged to make a film about Pound at Brunnenburg. He and Dorothy arrived a few days before the crew, Pound, as Mary reported to Olga, "terribly rude and grumpy although I had pulled myself together and smiled." A few days later he softened and remembered that it was Olga's birthday. He told his daughter that he was grateful that he and Olga had resumed a civil correspondence, but in general he avoided private talk. Instead, he played the Poet for an imaginary public. "If ever I had doubted that Pound was a natural born actor, watching him before the cameras would certainly have convinced me," Bridson remembered. Brunnenburg, if not a home for Pound, was an appropriate setting for a Great Man. Bridson's film shows him "silhouetted upon the battlements, confronting Gaudier's bust of him that dominated the garden, pacing the stone corridors and climbing the spiral staircases."[13] Pound trotted out his "grampaw" role and read *Brer Rabbit* to Walter and Patrizia before rolling cameras. Mary remained unconvinced. "No, I am afraid I cannot see him in a new light," she told Olga, "His behavior is there as painful as ever." In a week he was gone, saying that he would not return. A month later, Mary admitted, "I suppose I am about the only person who doesn't know Babbo's address."[14]

In May Eva Hesse invited Mary, Pound, and his companions to Munich and Berlin to see the first German performance of Pound's version of *Women of Trachis*. The situation was not uncomplicated for Mary. After years of struggling to find a father in the wreck of history, she now recognized that he did not want her on any terms that she understood. Olga, equally exiled, listened to this turbulent readjustment: Pound had told their daughter that she was too preoccupied with his "glory" and that whatever she tried to do for him was "useless." He wanted Mary to concentrate on Boris; he had invited Arthur Moore, Dorothy Shakespear's solicitor, to Rapallo—Mary didn't know why—but it aroused anxieties about Omar, and she told her mother that she felt that she was always "in the position of the illegitimate trying to grab something." During her trip to Washington, D.C., she had asked her father if Omar "knew." "He merely said, 'I can't spring it on him after 3 days'—which leaves *me* in the wrong position. Of course, *we* can't speak of his 'legitimacy.'"[15]

In the end, she did not have to face her father in Munich. He cancelled his trip, choosing instead to take Marcella and Dorothy touring in Italy. While Pound revisited Pisa, Sirmione, and Lake Garde with a loyal wife and a new lover, Mary watched the symbolic equivalent of this journey on the German stage, where Daianeira (The Day's Air), the wife of Herakles Zeuson (Solar Vitality), struggles against her jealousy of the young woman Iole (Tomorrow) with whom her husband has fallen in love. Forced to share her palace with the girl who has been captured in battle, Day's Air says, "Let's figure out how we are to manage this cohabitation/ with this virgin who isn't one any longer/ 'cause she's been yoked. / Too much cargo, contraband, but keep my mind afloat somehow. / 'Double yoke / Under one cloak', / and I said he was so kind and dependable."[16]

No greater irony than this juxtaposition can be imagined. "The performance was magnificent. I am glad I saw it," Mary reported. To her, the father had disappeared into a symbolic recreation of his own situation. He had translated the words that represented his own erotic entanglement, and while she, as a daughter of "Day's Air," watched a dramatic mother lament her own "bitter ache of separation," from a father who "never gets sight of his children," Dorothy, another wife altogether, was forced to confront the possibility that Pound had asked Marcella Spann to marry him at Lake Garde. Mary did not yet know of this development, but she did understand the essence of the situation. "I am afraid I really was not strong enough yet to bear [*Trachis*]," she told Olga, "It has brought Babbo's tragedy to such focus."[17]

The full life tragedy had yet to play itself out with Dorothy Pound now assuming the role of Day's Air. Having endured Olga for thirty years, this was one "Double yoke / Under one cloak" too many. In the play, Day's Air kills her husband in the act of trying to rekindle his affection. It is an unwitting result—she sends him a cape laced with an aphrodisiac that turns out to be poison—and Dorothy's parallel strategy—to send Marcella Spann straight back to Texas—essentially ended her relationship with Pound as well. He lived, and for a while he continued to live with Dorothy, but from this moment, he was a broken man and Dorothy's role in his life broken as well. In the little writing he did during this period, he attributed to her (as he had earlier to Mary) "pride, jealousy and possessiveness/3 pains of hell."[18] We do not know what Dorothy Pound felt as she considered what to do with the consequences of her behavior, but Mary was articulate. "Slowly the vision withered, all the high norms and the poetry turned into dead letter. The letter kills . . . and kills the worth of every action performed by it. I felt as though my skin were a bag full of stones. Dead weary. And Babbo said: 'I thought you were solid rock I could build on.' I had thought so too, but all the *acque chéte* have corroded the foundations. *Stille Wasser graben tief.*"[19] Still waters run deep.

II

Mary was nonetheless left to pick up the pieces. In September, Pound described himself as "collapsed," and Arthur Moore informed James Laughlin that "it looks as if EP will make Brunnenburg his home."[20] By October he and Dorothy were both back at the castle. Instead of grasping "a lost shimmer of sunlight, the pale hair of the goddess,"[21] he took to his bed, where Mary held his hand or stroked his hair when she could spare time from housework. She reported that he was changeable, depressed, full of self-recrimination, and generally irritable. Archibald MacLeish sent $500 from the American Academy of Arts; Mary had learned from Jas that Pound's income from royalties was around $2,000, but money was not the issue. Laughlin suggested that Dorothy might absent herself—which she refused to do, saying that it would be impossible to stay in a hotel in Zurich when she spoke no German—and even renewed goodwill on the daughter's part could not prevent her from seeing that she faced "a fearful mess" that only the "greatest sincerity" could address. But she added, "the terrible doubt [is] that Babbo is *not* sincere."[22] Pound's crisis led him, briefly, to return to T. S. Eliot's *After Strange Gods*— the three lectures Eliot had delivered at the University of Virginia in the 1930s—so the household went around reading about "Personality and Demonic Possession" until Christmas when Mary, very simply, broke through the heaviness by saying that she had been praying that Pound would agree to meet Olga soon. She was willing, she told her mother, to go anywhere that would make Pound better, but under the current circumstances, she was at her wits' end.

Boris, too, was struggling. His book, *An Introduction to Egyptian Art*, had just come out (the first copy arrived on Christmas day 1959), and though he had hoped with its publication to receive a *premio* (literary prize), one of his rivals, Sergio Donadoni, had savaged it in the press. He had also, apparently, "sabotaged Boris in UNESCO." Mary understood these attacks to be politically motivated. Egyptology was an emergent field; Donadoni belonged to a cooperative for popular books, which she considered a communist propaganda series supported by the French, and when the French had been ousted from Egypt, Boris had been given a key position.[23] He had, in fact, become the protégé of Selim Hassan (1893–1961), one of the greatest Egyptian national Egyptologists, a former curator of the Cairo Museum, whose immense achievement was a sixteen-volume encyclopedia of ancient Egypt written in Arabic. Whatever discouragement Donadoni's attacks had occasioned, Boris had just learned that he was invited to return to Egypt with another noted researcher, Professor Elmar Edel, from the University of Bonn. He was to leave on 23 January 1960, and Mary hoped to go to Germany with him and possibly join the expedition in Egypt as well. Edel was continuing his work on the second volume of *Altägyptishe Grammatik* (1955–1964) (Late Egyptian Grammar) and was going again to Aswan, where he hoped to uncover more middle Egyptian grave inscriptions. Boris needed the academic credentials; Mary needed the rest. She presented the elder Pounds with a *fait accompli*: Pound was to go to Rome as the guest of Ugo Dadone, one of Boris's elderly friends, and Dorothy was to return to the Albergo Italia in Rapallo. "He did not want to go," she reported, but we (Dadone and Vanni) just pushed. Something had to be tried to get him out of the state of mind he was in." She thought it would be good for him to be away from Dorothy; she hoped her mother would try to see him while he was in Rome. She personally was trying to move away from the spell Pound seemed to cast around him. "Well, I wish he hadn't for so long posed as a Confucian patriarch or whatever. The mold evidently just was not for him. I should have realized sooner and saved myself and others a lot of misery."[24]

John Drummond wrote to Olga saying that he thought the trip to Egypt would be a great thing for Mary, since it might "shake her out of the past and disillusionment over her father's homecoming." His idea was for her to have a "future as her husband's wife rather than her father's daughter."[25] But the trip could hardly have served that purpose. For her it lasted only three weeks— from mid-April to 4 May—enough time to get an impression of a new country, the seriously demanding nature of archeological excavation, and a glimpse of her husband in a new setting. She liked both Edels very much, took a keen interest in the fundamentals of Egyptian life, in boat building, stone cutting, the rituals of washing and carting water, the water buffaloes and donkeys. She spent time in Cairo, in a country house near the Pyramids, in Luxor, and in Aswan. It was a colorful and leisurely several weeks filled with club lunches, museums, and botanical gardens. To her amazement, Boris seemed more at home in Egypt than he did in the Tyrol, and her summary of the trip was that she had been in a "real paradise" rather than the constructed ones of the intellect.[26]

In the next several months, she would be saddled once again with the senior Pounds and with her father's thrashing attempts to cope with what remained of his life. Pound could write, "Let the Gods forgive what I have made / Let those I love try to forgive what I have made," but he apparently did very little to foster that forgiveness. He refused to eat; he started burning papers; he spoke about various plots against him and then admitted that the plots were imaginary.[27] In August, Mary learned that Pound had shown young Walter "a letter of malediction" that he had received, and she reported that he spoke continuously about a "curse." A few months later, he upset the boy by telling him that he must change his name because "Rache" means vendetta and "wiltz" was a Jewish name.[28] By March 1961, Mary admitted, "I am convinced Babbo is incapable of feeling human feelings."[29]

In addition, the castle had now had guests who were "official" modernist scholars—Noel Stock was beginning work on his biography of her father and Daniel Cory, erstwhile friend, assistant, and editor of George Santayana, was assembling the book that would become *Santayana, the Later Years: A Portrait with Letters* (1963).

It was Stock whose presence was most difficult, and his arrival led Mary to read *The Aspern Papers*, by Henry James. Although the situation in the book did not mirror hers exactly, it had enough resonance to put her on guard against the possible rapacity of scholars at a time when responsibility for her father's papers already weighed heavily. "Can't you understand that I feel stranded with a lot of DROSS,"[30] she wrote to Olga. James, as she learned, wrote from the perspective of a man of letters who regards literary spoils as far more compelling than human life itself, and who insinuates himself into the Venetian home of a great poet's lover so that he can live under the same roof with the "sacred relics" she is imagined to possess. He assumes a false name, makes spurious love to Miss Bordereau's niece, and admits to an acquaintance, "I can arrive at my spoils only by putting her off her guard, and I can put her off her guard only by ingratiating diplomatic arts. Hypocrisy, duplicity are my only chance."[31] Once lodging in the house, he imagines Miss Bordereau's death—"she would die next week, she would die tomorrow—then I could pounce on her possessions and ransack her drawers"—and because he stalks, he envisions the two women to be "hunted creatures feigning death."[32] The extremity of the chase startles his acquaintance. "'One would think you expected from it the answer to the riddle of the universe,' she said;

and I denied the impeachment only by replying that if I had to choose between that precious solution and a bundle of Jeffrey Aspern's letters I knew indeed which would appear to me the greater boon. She pretended to make light of his genius and I took no pains to defend him. One doesn't defend one's god: one's god is in himself a defense. Besides, today, after his long comparative obscuration, he hangs high in the heaven of our literature for all the world to see; he's a part of the light by which we walk."[33]

Noel Stock was at Brunnenburg by invitation, of course, but he served as the precursor to many others, who like Mary herself, had been led to think that Pound was "part of the light by which we walk" through modernity. With Stock she was first confronted with being the child of a poet who was increasingly regarded as "the property of the human race," and initially the position was difficult. "If I think of the SEALS I was made to put on all his letterboxes," she wrote, "and how everything has now been defiled and profaned . . . now any [one] who turns up is told to go in his room and look at them."[34] James's narrator left the house in Venice after three months; Noel Stock eventually finished his work; Mary's task was just beginning.

III

Long before she knew anything about other scholars, who wanted, like Stock, to break the seals on Pound's letterboxes, Norman Holmes Pearson, following in James Jesus Angleton's footsteps, had been angling to get Pound's papers to Yale. Since the war, Pearson had ostensibly returned to campus life in New Haven, trading cryptanalysis and spy craft for deciphering undergraduate papers in the American Studies program. He and Angleton had parted ways—Angleton had, in fact, remained in Italy under the auspices of the War Department, which reassigned him to the Strategic Services Unit (2677 Regiment). This title was simply another way of identifying, while failing fully to identify, the United States' continued support for covert operations in postwar Italy, and its continued emphasis on liaison work with foreign intelligence services. Like Pearson, Angleton had been honored for his war work. He had received the order of the Crown of Italy, the Italian War Cross for Merit, and in January 1947, he had been inducted into the Masonic Lodge in Rome and awarded its Order of the Cross of Malta. Occasionally Pearson and Angleton had met in Paris, even after Angleton had been reassigned to the Rome office, as H.D.'s daughter, Perdita, recorded in a letter to her mother and Bryher:

> My pets,
> Just in haste—Norman is lurking behind the paneling waiting to carry this off to you . . . We're still terribly busy and working very hard . . . Things have been quite gay, because all the Chiefs gathered over the week-end for one of those jamborees when they hold endless meetings and drink and smoke and talk incessantly and achieve nothing whatsoever—however, they think they do, and it seems to raise their morale. Norman of course was here, and *my friend Ezra from Italy* [emphasis added], who went back after lunch and said he would ring you up tonight, though he is so erratic, I doubt whether he'll get himself organized before next week. But if a strange voice did ring up saying it was Lt. Angleton and had seen me—that was him.[35]

What pleasure the three got out of Angleton using Ezra Pound's name as a code while the poet languished in captivity is hard to imagine, but Perdita's letter bears witness to Angleton's continued, perverse identification with the poet he had secretly helped to imprison.

After the war it was Pearson who maintained that interest, and it grew, if simply because he lived stateside after his demobilization. It was buttressed, of course, by his continued friendship with H.D.; it was an outgrowth of a very real respect for Pound's genius as a poet, but the warmth he showed to the poet and to the poet's family stood in marked contrast to the contempt he expressed to people when they were not present. And like Angleton's earlier correspondence, his letters to Pound soon took on the protective coloring of Pound's distinctive, idiosyncratic wordplay, as if he were feeding back to the man not only what he thought he wanted to hear, but also the idiom that would make his sentiments most comfortable. By 1956 he was speaking of "Nude Erections" and "Knew Yok" and "Billums Willums." or saying that he "doughnut think NHP ought to make keyrections of keruptions wiffout EP's OK."[36] Having politicked to get his student John Edwards invited to Brunnenburg to work on a checklist of Pound's periodical contributions, he then denounced the young man when Pound complained of the inaccuracy of his work: "Don't think that I ever tried to teach Edwards anything. I don't think he' teachable! . . . He sent [the list] on to me, and—Keeerist!—it stunk." Having worked with immense personal satisfaction for Roosevelt during the war, he told Pound, when the Yalta papers were published, that they indicated that "FDR was no great improvement on Parsifal."[37]

"I work most effectively within my own limited powers. That is, a quiet finger poking here, a knife there. No shrieks, just surprise," Pearson told Pound in the mid-'50s. He was ostensibly explaining his reasons for not signing petitions for Pound's release and justifying his preference for quiet, behind-the-scenes diplomacy, but his rhetoric betrays the continued tendency for covert action that Pearson carried from espionage to academia. It is true that he did some fine things for Pound's reputation as a poet—he included Pound in a graduate seminar at Yale, arranged for talks about his poetry at the English Institute and at a meeting of the College English Association—but these activities cloaked another motive, which was to plant the idea that Yale was the only appropriate place for Pound's archive.

It was an ingratiating charade of personal concern, which extended to Dorothy, to Omar, to Olga, and to Mary without distinction.

IV

At Brunnenburg it became clear to Mary that her father was very ill. He was not physically sick; he was not "even (delightfully) off his head."[38] But he was filled with remorse, identified *The Cantos* as having "something rotten behind it all,"[39] and continued to burn papers. He would not eat; he rarely spoke. Eventually Mary took him to the Martinsbrunn clinic. Observing him there, she got the impression that he wanted to be shut up and that his behavior aimed consistently at self-destruction. When he did communicate, he spoke increasingly of Olga Rudge, whom he now believed he had mistreated. Eveline Bates Doob, who visited him both at the castle and in the clinic, remembered his resistance to general conversation and his "deep, *deepening* depression."[40]

She had met Pound through Mary and Boris, and she had met them almost by accident. She and her husband, the Yale professor Leonard W. Doob, were in Italy for the year while Leonard did research on the project that would eventually be published as *Patriotism and Nationalism: Their Psychological Foundations* (1964). They had planned originally to live in Bolzano but had been charmed by an apartment in Merano. It was nestled in the Passeier Valley, and when they stood on their geranium-decked balcony, they could see a small Roman chapel in one direction and snow-capped mountains that extended to Switzerland to the west. They had central heating, plenty of room for their children, and it was their son, Nick, who had first alerted them that a family with an American mother lived in the mountain village above them. Armed with a university identity card and the fact that they had known Norman Holmes Pearson at Yale, they braved the castle where Leonard asked the "lovely young woman" who leaned from the casement window above them if he could speak with Frau de Rachewiltz. "She said *she* was Fraud de R . . . [and] that she'd be right down and let us in. A bit informal as a way of entering a castle."[41]

For Eveline Doob, this was the beginning of a small, interesting social network. The de Rachewiltzes became cocktail and luncheon companions, with Pound occasionally joining them as a difficult, silent presence at the table. "Blinking, staring, SILENCE. Every question—that is, every effort to bring him into the conversation, NO RESPONSE." She was a well-read woman, an eager student of literature, an accomplished hostess, and she was taken aback by his refusal to enter into literary small talk (Pound called it her "beautiful performance"). She was also witness to untempered rudeness and equally untempered remorse. He tried to block Mary from loaning her a book of Noh plays—"This is the final outrage!" Just as unexpectedly, he asked her to "do what you can to save innocence!" Pound observed none of Yale's social niceties and so kept her constantly off guard, reaching for explanations of emotions that were beyond her range of experience. She thought he might be "the prototype of the hero at the moment of tragic perception"—but she was simply trying to classify what was outside of her understanding. Like Sally Fitzgerald, she was contemptuous of his politics and more comfortable with Mary's pragmatism and simple kindnesses, which she recorded in her diary, along with Pound's extremity. "'Here,'" she recalled Mary saying, "handing [the book of Noh plays] to me, 'It's no outrage at all. It's very beautiful. Besides, it's my book and I have the right to give it to her if I want to.'"[42]

For Leonard Doob (1909–2000), the meeting with the de Rachewiltz family had more far-reaching consequences. By the 1960s, he was amid a robust career in social psychology. In addition to serving on the Yale faculty, he was a participant in the Yale Program in Communication and Attitude Change, in its Institute for Social and Policy Studies, its Institute of Human Relations, and one of the founders of its Institute of Psychology. He was equally active off the campus as a member of many professional organizations and publications.[43]

His work had been interrupted, or perhaps simply redirected by the Second World War, when he had served as director of policy coordination in the Overseas Branch of the Office of War Information. He had a rigorous mind, a predilection for clearly defined categories, and his war service had frustrated his penchant for systematic procedures. "This was a hit-and-miss approach in a situation in which no one except an omniscient deity will ever know in detail what hit and what missed,"[44] he remembered, blaming his frustrations on wartime conditions that had been impossible to circumvent. With no way to collect appropriate data abroad, his agency had rarely been able to suggest policies, but had, indeed, usually "propagandized" decisions already made, using radio broadcasts, posters, newsreels, lectures, leaflets, and even soap wrappers to affect the morale of enemy populations. Within the OWI, he had often circumvented tricky situations—carefully protected institutional territories, personal jealousies, and prejudices toward academics—with personal diplomacy. He was a man of immense charm and discretion, talented at the human relations he studied professionally, someone who targeted conflict as a subject but conducted negotiations with a commanding ease. He recalled that organizational charts had been often ignored in favor of "information agreements and constant contact between people who liked and trusted each other"[45]—an assessment confirmed by various declassified documents from the OSS Morale Operations branch of the military, which reported on the ease of cooperating with him: "You will be interested to know that we have struck a deal with Doob of OWI whereby he now is able to plant selected rumor items in OWI newscasts. . . . We are continuing to supply Doob with a considerable amount of material and are greatly encouraged by the use of it. . . . Naturally this arrangement with Doob is on a purely informal and unofficial level and should be kept within the family."[46]

He left the war with a fully developed network of friends and colleagues. The "people who liked and trusted each other" went on to direct social science programs in many of the elite universities of the United States, to become the publishers of *Time*, *Look*, and *Fortune*; editors of magazines like *Holiday, Coronet, Parade*, and the *Saturday Review*; editors of the *Denver Post*, *New Orleans Times-Picayune*, and so forth.[47] That is, Leonard Doob was "linked in"; he was part of a powerful network of academicians, government officials, and directors of funding agencies. They routinely worked together, reviewed one another's work, and routed funds toward projects that were mutually beneficial.

Doob left the Office of War Information with an equally developed belief in the importance of the role his academic skills could play in the service of national interests, a sense of what had gone wrong ("Far too many risky and dogmatic inferences concerning the state of morale in enemy countries, for example, were made on the basis of radio transcripts and newspapers simply because these data were at hand") and a renewed commitment to "getting it right"—in his words, gathering "data and information of all experts in order to determine systematically—in terms of social-science principles—how people might respond to propaganda" in future.[48] Immediately after the war, he devoted time to analyzing the propaganda techniques that the Germans had used against their enemies,[49] and just as quickly he understood that the principal enemy of the United States was no longer fascism but communism.

In other words, Doob understood himself to live in a world with an urgent, continuing need for social scientists to analyze redefined opposition, to be able to recommend techniques of psychological warfare to policymakers and to tell them how to "to weaken [an enemy's] will either to fight or to cooperate with his own authorities so that immediately or eventually he will surrender." He wrote about how to conduct a war of nerves, to divide and conquer, to raise false hopes, to deceive, and to contribute to a target population's sense of futility. He devised ways to achieve these aims ("routes") and other ways to measure their success. In his imagination, the propagandist was always in control, and he was the creator of tactics designed for carefully identified populations.[50] His field was the psychological manipulation of large groups of human beings, and his work, before this European trip in the 1960s, had centered on sub-Saharan Africa.

Of course, none of this was visible to Mary de Rachewiltz when she leaned out of her window on that January afternoon. She saw a handsome American man in his prime with an articulate and well-meaning wife. The Doobs were welcome company to a young woman often left to her own devices; it pleased her that she had been identified to them as an "American mother," and, although she did not yet know it, she was a godsend to Doob, who, once again, wanted to work with "people who liked and trusted each other." He needed help in gaining entry to schools and seminaries to administer the questionnaires he had prepared about local attitudes toward *Heimat* (homeland).

Mary helped open doors for him, but almost immediately he could see that his research plan wouldn't work. Where he had originally thought he would study how populations are affected by outside cultures, making an analogy between Arab-European contact and Tyrolean-Italian contact, he discovered that the better analogy was the Zulu experience in Natal: "we were here first; not they." Instead of finding a place where questions about acculturation could profitably be asked, he encountered a German-speaking people whose patriotism and sense of belonging to Austria far outweighed any openness to Italian influence; if anything, the Italians had inadvertently heightened Tyrolean patriotism—and thus demands and actions that hopefully would lead toward reunification.

Doob cast his study in academic language, using clear categories like "predisposition," "demand," and "action," as if his inquiry were timeless and universal; but in fact he had arrived in the Tyrol when there was considerable urgency to understanding the psychology of Tyroleans, who in 1960 had ceased "demanding" and had started "acting" by throwing bombs. Fifteen years after a negotiated peace, which had traded their cultural identity for international expedience, "predispositions" had turned to violence.

While Pound sat in silence at the castle, while Mary struggled to maintain his physical well-being, while Doob refined his questionnaires, the world around them exploded. Olga Rudge wrote to Mary, asking if she thought Pound's frame of mind had anything to do with the political situation. Mary said "no," but there was every reason to be alarmed. Tyroleans had had enough of being a "minority question" discussed, and then dismissed, by superpowers. In this they were aided by Austria, which was finally able to act on its own in foreign affairs and had decided to bring the issue of Tyrolean autonomy before the United Nations.[51]

This move was entirely understandable—a nagging, unresolved ethnic issue finally coming to a head—but it came to international attention under new circumstances. Where the western powers had always placed the Tyrol in an international equation that pitted Italy against Austria and asked, "Which nation will be the stronger ally against communism?" now there was the added dimension of nuclear defense to consider. In 1959 Italy had agreed that the U.S.—as fellow member of NATO—could deploy nuclear missiles in Italy and had strategically chosen the South Tyrol as the site.[52] Where local people of German descent understood themselves to be demonstrating for cultural integrity—for, indeed, the Italians had spent the postwar years carrying on the Fascists' previous policy of construction, immigration, and denationalization—clandestine military negotiations between Italy and the U.S. insured that the U.S. would offer no support for Tyrolean autonomy.

President Dwight Eisenhower refused to come to Austria when invited; John F. Kennedy equivocated. Negotiations in 1961 between Austrians and Italians in Milan, Klagenfurt, and Zurich were futile.[53]

Tyroleans took things into their own hands. "Was Mary involved?" Olga asked with some urgency. "No," she assured her mother; they were all careful to keep out of politics, even Walter steered clear of controversy in his local school. But the controversy was there; a South Tyrolean Liberation Committee (*Befreiungsausschuss SüdTyrol*, or BAS) had been formed; demonstrations took place; propaganda was produced. Leaflets declared, "We want to remain German and not become slaves of a people that used treason and fraud to occupy our land without a fight and for forty years has been carrying on a system of exploitation and colonization that is worse than the methods the colonialists once used in Central Africa."[54] The "patriots" whom Leonard Doob studied in school settings emerged to bomb symbols of Fascist repression: the "Aluminum Duce" in Waidbruck was blown to bits; the house where Ettore Tolomei had lived near Neumarkt was destroyed.

In the spring of 1961, Mary decided that it would be good for her father to visit Ugo Dadone in Rome once again. Eveline Doob visited him there in March with apprehension—she had heard that Pound had given the Fascist salute at a reading by the Italian Nobel Prize winner Salvatore Quasimodo—but found nothing but quietness. "Here were two frail old men, both of them ailing, forlorn, and neither of them capable, even if they had wanted, to excite anyone about the hanged demon."[55]

Eventually quietness turned inward and descended again into depression and a vague sense of malaise. It is not clear who made the decision to move Pound to a clinic. Dorothy described it as a "rest cure"; Olga, who finally visited him, understood it as a sequel to St. Elizabeths—a beautifully manicured villa where the doors were locked. He had to be moved, but she, given her irregular status in Pound's life, could not authorize it. She telephoned Mary who spoke to Dorothy. All were agreed that the better place would be Martinsbrunn. In mid-April Mary went down to Rome to fetch him in a hired car. By now he was looking forward to Brunnenburg as a home of sorts—he wanted to make himself some toast when he arrived—but he was too weak and dehydrated for even a temporary return. He greeted Martinsbrunn with a tantrum, but illness trumped temper and he was assigned a room that harbored him for months. When James Laughlin had seen Pound in Rome, he had left with more questions than answers. "I was never able to determine exactly what the diagnosis was . . . those Italian doctors sound terribly sketchy to me. They had the poor man almost dying but couldn't seem to come up with a name for it."[56] But at Martinsbrunn Pound's doctors discovered the cause of his suffering to be urinary retention because of an enlarged prostate. While he recuperated, Mary and Dorothy alternated days of visiting. In May Olga came again, and by the end of the month she had conceived the plan of caring for Pound after he recovered more fully. "Yes," Mary wrote to her, "you certainly have earned the right to look after Babbo and it certainly would be the most logical and natural solution. . . . Casa 131 would certainly be a beautiful spot. And even economically it should be easy to arrange."[57]

By the end of June, Mary thought Pound was doing much better. "Babbo," she reported, "is greatly improving physically and considering that he has written you a long letter, I should say also psychically."[58] But it was a premature optimism. Pound lingered there through the fall and the following spring, with everyone afraid to tell him the news.

A nurse inadvertently let slip that Ernest Hemingway had committed suicide. Pound raged, saying that American writers were doomed, that America destroyed the best of them.[59] He met the news of H.D.'s death on 27 September with more sober contemplation. Norman Holmes Pearson, who had become her literary executor, wrote Pound a sentimental letter, "Remembering the yellow rose which Hilda sent to you and D.P. when you left on the *Columbo*, I took with me to Bethlehem for the interment a second golden rose to lay by her ashes from you, to speed her with love on her last trip of all."[60] Pound was unmoved.[61] But he was genuinely touched by a visit from H.D.'s daughter, Perdita, in the spring of 1962. "He gazed back at me. He didn't smile. But there was a fond look of recognition. . . . He was inspecting me from top to toe and back again, very grave and yet—no doubt about it—glad too. 'Well, well . . . well, well.'"[62]

He had no response at all to the political violence that raged around him, for it was not a heartening subject of conversation nor did it seem relevant to the subjective drama playing itself out in the heart of the Pound family. But Martinsbrunn shielded Pound from *Feuernacht*—the Night of Fire. During the Sacred Heart of Jesus Festival, protest escalated, moving from single acts of violence to a coordinated program of destruction. On the night between 11 and 12 June 1961, thirty-seven high-tension pylons were knocked over, cutting off power transmission to northern Italian industries. The aim to bring a cooldown to the Bolzano blast furnaces failed, but the major power plants in Lana near Merano, St. Anton, and Sarntal were brought offline.[63] The bombings were accompanied by flyers calling for the right of self-determination for South Tyroleans who, without any academic training, understood the usefulness of propaganda.

Mary, Dorothy, and the castle guests went without electricity. Mario Scelba, the Minister of the Interior, turned the South Tyrol into an armed camp—requisitioning inns and hotels to quarter soldiers and police; he searched private homes daily; he arrested members of the BAS and interrogated them with techniques that eventually aroused international demands for a board of inquiry.

Leonard Doob mentions some of these circumstances in *Patriotism and Nationalism*; he spelled them out more clearly in an essay he completed in 1962 for *Public Opinion Quarterly* called "South Tyrol: An Introduction to the Psychological Syndrome of Nationalism." And these remarks let us see that his presence in the Bolzano/Merano area at this time was not fortuitous but served United States policy issues. In his book he explained that the strategic goal of his work was internationalism: how can people with a strong sense of national identity be urged to work together? Quite apart from international agreements, treaties, or organizations, what psychological climates can promote international cooperation in general? "Lastly," he admitted, "the wording of the question suggests that internationalism is a desirable goal, a bias herewith admitted."[64] He was not interested, of course, in global cooperation but in cooperation in the face of a common enemy. "Just as members of local groups within a country tend to forget their own personal rivalries when faced with a common threat, so nationals may overlook their differences when confronted with a common enemy. But do they?"[65] What he really wanted to know was what to expect from Tyroleans and Italians regarding the cold war and with the perceived potential of World War III. While Eveline Doob appreciated glorious mountain scenery and picturesque window boxes, her husband understood that they were in the Bolzano/Merano area because it stood near the Brenner Pass and at the border of Communist Yugoslavia.

What he did not bargain for was Mary de Rachewiltz. When *Patriotism and Nationalism* was published in 1964, he dedicated the book to her (and Professor Josef Schwarz): "Two friends in South Tyrol. Each in a unique and different way embodies the deeper virtues and perplexities of patriotism and evokes envy and respect. They have been witting and unwitting mentors in this venture—Let them hear an expression of profound gratitude and affection." What might have remained a formal study with carefully tabulated results had, through Mary, gained a human face, a perspective on

national identity obtained through a personal history like no other, a reflection on life that was acquired by international conflict that had riven bone.
Where Doob went to various places to study the psychological consequences
of international struggle, Mary lived them every day. And the source of that
complexity lay silent and ill as Doob's work wound to a close.

In mid-August, Eveline Doob called Mary to ask if she could go to Martinsbrunn to bid Pound goodbye. To her surprise, she was refused. Then at
10 in the evening Mary appeared at her door. "He's just *dying*. . . . I can't understand how it could be so fast." Mrs. Doob took the distraught and disheveled younger woman in hand; they went out for a walk. Mary had called for
Olga to come; she was sorry, but she would have to cancel the farewell party
she had planned for the Doobs at the castle. It was a sad departure for Eveline
Doob. She thought she was witnessing the loss of a hard-won perspective. "It
seemed to be coming back, the whole horror, his arrest, incarceration, Saint
Elizabeths." She asked if there were anything she could do. Mary thought.
There in a strife-ridden Tyrolean town, she sent a message to unknown American compatriots. "'Ask them to be decent. . . . Tell all those people'—those
who'd accused her father—'to read *The Cantos* and then go on from there.'"[66]

And so the Doobs left Merano just as Olga Rudge arrived. She was still
working at the Chigi Foundation in Siena, so her visits had to be sporadic.
But they had a salutary effect. Pound's progress was slow . . . he accepted a
piece of ginger, a sandwich; he got up and walked around the room. Ronald
Duncan, who visited in October, looked beyond everyone's focus on Pound's
immediate health and considered Mary's position. He spoke to Olga about
Pound making another will. She refused to intervene. "Even if I would risk a
misunderstanding with E. (and I won't), a will would have no legal value now
that he has a 'guardian.'"[67] She left it at that, saying that the previous 1940
will "may or may not have legal value."

But the issue was an important one. Pound, amid his remorse and depression, either was confused or negligent, and Mary had known that since
1958. "I did not tell Babbo that I am NOT legitimized, in fact after what has
happened I no longer care, or at least I don't care for *myself*," she had told
Olga . . . but she did care about her children. Faced with Olga's rebuff, Duncan took up the matter directly with Pound. He wrote to him bluntly, saying
that he thought Pound's remorse excessive and self-indulgent ("trivial" was
his word). Then he told Pound to think about "Mary's loyalty. You are lucky
to have somebody who loves you as much as this and has your work so much
at heart . . . make certain that it is Mary who has the power to say 'yes' or 'no'

about your work."[68] He had, perhaps, seen the dynamics at the castle. Staying there during visits from Mary Barnard, Donald Gallup from Yale, and Giovanni Scheiwiller, who brought a first copy of the *Thirty Cantos* that Mary had just translated into Italian, he could see that Mary did not even control Pound's manuscripts in her own home. Dorothy sat "on everything like a hen," telling Mary, "You need not worry, I am responsible; he has been released in MY custody."[69] But it was not as simple as that, for Dorothy had "smuggled" all of Wyndham Lewis's paintings out of the house to give to Omar. It was the secrecy that had upset Mary. "She could have openly said that she had paid for those paintings or that they had been given to her and that she wanted to give them to Omar and that would have been fair," but the surreptitious quality of these dealings began to grate, leaving a sense of "things going on behind one's back" with unknown lawyers in Boston.[70]

For herself, she wanted transparency. She wanted to publish Pound's Rome radio broadcasts but found herself having to ask Dorothy's permission for it; she wanted to meet Archibald MacLeish, who was traveling in Europe, to ask him about the "committeé" situation. He, as a lawyer, might give her a professional perspective; she wanted Olga to write her memoirs. In November she got the idea of making a book for Pound's eightieth birthday. "All those lovely family photographs commented by *The Cantos* and anyway his *own* writings—after all he says of *The Cantos* 'Tale of the Tribe.' . . . I could then put in the photo of me with Nonno and Babbo—as a counterpart of Babbo with his grandfather."[71]

In the spring, no legalities had been attended to, but Pound was well enough to leave Martinsbrunn. Mary took him to Sant' Ambrogio on 25 April, right after the Easter holidays. He would live with Olga Rudge for the remainder of his life, alternating time between the Ligurian coast and Olga's house in Venice. For the time being, Dorothy continued to live at the castle with Mary. When Omar visited her in July, she put him up in a small hotel in Merano, claiming that it was too tiring for him to travel up and down the mountain in a bus. Instead, she went up and down the mountain in a bus, trying to prohibit a meeting between her son and the de Rachewiltzes. Boris finally put a stop to it by saying that he wanted to meet Omar. He invited him to tea, saying that it was better to talk things over instead of behaving as if there had been a quarrel. Omar listened and left; in October Dorothy decided to live in Rapallo.

The older generation was gone. Mary learned that Pound was thriving. Olga lavished care on him. He, in turn, read cantos aloud in the evening; she congratulated her mother on arranging her household beautifully. But Pound's return to Olga had not restored a family unit. Their correspondence was edged with recrimination, and Mary's with bitterness. "*Please*," she begged her parents, "let me concentrate on my work. . . . God knows that I would have liked nothing better than 'play' the daughter with house and grandchildren and all—but as that has been my one *great* failure in life so far, I don't like to go on 'pretending' in front of friends and strangers."[72]

"We who have profited by his inspiration."[73] H.D. was no longer alive to comment on this sundering, but it bore a resemblance to her own experience and to Sheri Martinelli's. H.D. had remembered Pound's desertion as a "two edged-humiliation, from the friends and family, from Ezra." She remembered that she had camouflaged it with "the weeds and bracken of daily duties and necessities," and that finally the chasm created by loss had been crossed by "a forceful effort toward artistic achievement."[74] She compared her situation to building life around the crater of an extinct volcano; she understood that it was instinctive to feel wrath: "If having been severed, painfully reintegrated, we want only to gorge the whirlwind or the forked lightning that destroyed our human, domestic serenity and security, that is natural."[75] And she might have been speaking to Mary when she had commiserated with Martinelli just a few years previously: "Swallow—my sister. . . . They don't want you, they really don't. How shall we reconcile ourselves to this?"[76]

1. Mary de Rachewiltz and Ezra Pound, Venice, circa 1930. Photographer unknown. Courtesy of the Beinecke Rare Book and Manuscript Library, Yale University.

2. Ezra Pound, passport photograph, 1922. Photographer unknown. Courtesy of the Beinecke Rare Book and Manuscript Library, Yale University.

3. Olga Rudge, undated. Photographer unknown. Courtesy of the Beinecke Rare Book and Manuscript Library, Yale University.

4. Mary de Rachewiltz with Hanne Marcher, Gais, circa 1926. Photographer unknown. Courtesy of the Beinecke Rare Book and Manuscript Library, Yale University.

5. Farmhouse, Tyrol, 1948. Photograph © Dr. Erika Hubatschek. Courtesy of Irmtraud Hubatschek.

6. Mountain hay carriers, Tyrol, 1939. Photograph © Dr. Erika Hubatschek. Courtesy of Irmtraud Hubatschek.

7. Dairymaid on the Kaserstattalm, Tyrol, 1951. Photograph © Dr. Erika Hubatschek. Courtesy of Irmtraud Hubatschek.

8. Hoeing, Tyrol, 1943. Photograph © Dr. Erika Hubatschek. Courtesy of Irmtraud Hubatschek.

9. Mary de Rachewiltz's foster sister, Margit, haying, Gais, circa 1929. Photographer unknown. Courtesy of the Beinecke Rare Book and Manuscript Library, Yale University.

10. Mary de Rachewiltz and Ezra Pound, Post Hotel, Bruneck, circa 1927. Photographer unknown. Courtesy of Beinecke Rare Book and Manuscript Library, Yale University.

11. Mary de Rachewiltz with violin, Gais, circa 1928. Photographer unknown. Courtesy of Beinecke Rare Book and Manuscript Library, Yale University.

12. Mary de Rachewiltz and Olga Rudge, Bolzano, undated. Photographer un-known. Courtesy of Beinecke Rare Book and Manuscript Library, Yale University.

13. Hilda Doolittle (H.D.) with daughter, Perdita, undated. Photographer unknown. Courtesy of Beinecke Rare Book and Manuscript Library, Yale University.

14. Dorothy Shakespear.

15. Omar Shakespear Pound in U.S. Army uniform, 1945. Photographer unknown.
Courtesy of Elizabeth Pound.

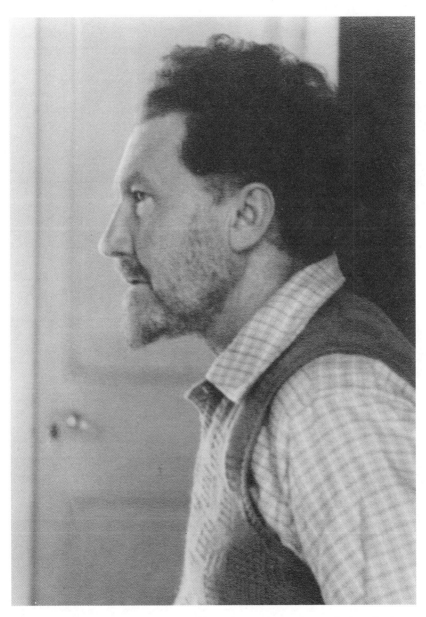

16. Ezra Pound in profile, 1939. Arnold Genthe. Courtesy of Beinecke Rare Book and Manuscript Library, Yale University.

17. Olga Rudge seated in chair, circa 1935. Photographer unknown. Courtesy of Beinecke Rare Book and Manuscript Library, Yale University.

18. Mary de Rachewiltz, studio portrait, Bruneck, 1949. Photographer unknown. Courtesy of Beinecke Rare Book and Manuscript Library, Yale University.

19. Mary de Rachewiltz with Feldwebel Lindle, Schwester Irmgard, and other German army officers, near Cortina, circa 1944. Photographer unknown. Courtesy of Beinecke Rare Book and Manuscript Library, Yale University, and Mary de Rachewiltz.

20. Boris de Rachewiltz in military uniform, circa 1943. Photographer unknown. Courtesy of the Brunnenburg Archives.

21. Norman Holmes Pearson, undated. Photographer unknown. Courtesy of Beinecke Rare Book and Manuscript Library, Yale University.

22. Norman Holmes Pearson at Bletchley Park with colleagues, circa 1944. Photographer unknown. Courtesy of Beinecke Rare Book and Manuscript Library, Yale University.

23. James Jesus Angleton.

24. Cages at Disciplinary Training Center at Metato, near Pisa, during World War II. U.S. Army photograph. Courtesy of National Archives and Records Administration.

25. Mary de Rachewiltz, Brunnenburg Castle, Dorf Tirol, undated. Photographer unknown. Courtesy of Beinecke Rare Book and Manuscript Library, Yale University.

26. Mary de Rachewiltz, Brunnenburg Castle, Dorf Tirol, circa 1951. Photograph by Mary Barnard. Courtesy of Beinecke Rare Book and Manuscript Library, Yale University.

27. Mary de Rachewiltz, Brunnenburg Castle, Dorf Tirol, circa 1951. Photograph by Mary Barnard. Courtesy of Beinecke Rare Book and Manuscript Library, Yale University.

28. Siegfried Walter de Rachewiltz, Brunnenburg Castle, Dorf Tirol, circa 1951. Photograph by Mary Barnard. Courtesy of Beinecke Rare Book and Manuscript Library, Yale University.

29. Patrizia de Rachewiltz, Brunnenburg Castle, Dorf Tirol, circa 1953. Photograph by Mary Barnard. Courtesy of Beinecke Rare Book and Manuscript Library, Yale University.

30. Leonard Doob, undated. Photographer unknown. Courtesy of Penelope Doob.

31. Mary de Rachewiltz. Photograph by Carol Loeb Shloss.

32. Olga Rudge with Carol Loeb Shloss, Brunnenburg Castle, circa 1995. Photograph by Mary de Rachewiltz.

33. Brunnenburg Castle, Dorf Tirol, circa 1995. Photograph by Carol Loeb Shloss.

CHAPTER 7

The Yale Network and the Archive, 1958–76

I

Mary dealt with "the chasm created by loss"[1] through translation and immersion in an inner world. "It is precisely Babbo's ideas that live on and are great and one's heritage." The academic world turned Pound into his papers. The tension between words and paper, moral vision and property, informed Mary's life from the moment of Pound's departure from Brunnenburg until well after his death in 1972. For her, Pound, the parent fantasized and longed for, was gone; the voice of the poet remained. Translation became both claim and reclamation. If she could not have a formal college education, if she could not benefit from an active filial relationship, she could enter what James Laughlin called the "Ezuversity," following the mind of her father and his instruction, creating a trade and an imaginative journey at the same time. When Olga told her not to think she could "take over," she defended herself forcefully. "My work," she said, is "a form of survival. I had hoped you and Babbo would understand. I cannot 'suppress the feel of it.'"[2]

In June 1964, Mary received a letter from Herbert P. Gleason of Hill, Barlow, Goodale & Adams in Boston saying that he had for some time been "concerned" about the "'papers' belonging to your father, which are at the Castle." He wanted to know if she was making an inventory of them, "so that we might at least know the dimension of the matter and the possible value of the collection."[3]

The seeming directness of this inquiry exposed another chasm created by forty years of domestic dissimulation. Who was the "we" who needed the information? Until this point, the papers—Pound's notebooks, drafts, first editions, letters, books, and artwork—had been Mary's inheritance, left to her in the will that Pound had executed in 1940.

She had had little occasion to worry about the legal standing of these treasures. They had been a burden, in the sense that she was, and had been for years, their keeper and guardian, but their status as a gift from her father was ratified by his expressed desire, by the will that her mother had shown her during the war and, as it turned out, reaffirmed by a notarized document prepared in 1949 when Pound was still incarcerated in St. Elizabeths.

Dorothy and Omar had evidently been thinking about the disposition of property for quite a long time, prompted perhaps by Norman Holmes Pearson's inquiries to Dorothy in 1947. Knowing nothing about the dynamics and unvoiced divisions that had governed the lives of the collective Pounds since the birth of Olga's child and Dorothy's child, he assumed that Pound's wife would be Pound's immediate heir.

After the war, Pearson had returned to Yale as an assistant professor in American literature. It is impossible (for a civilian) to determine if he continued his intelligence work for the government with this role as a cover. His papers at Yale carefully preserve a letter from Lt. Col. Paul M. Hart, G2, Intelligence, Department of the Army, who asked if Pearson would be willing serve the government again.[4] Pearson declined the immediate request but expressed a willingness to talk further. Pearson's letter of response (I won't serve) could be a piece of information or a piece of disinformation. Whether he accepted foreign assignments or not, he made no secret of his status as a "scout" for promising undergraduates who might join the CIA. And he never lost his taste for subterfuge.[5]

When, in 1971, Sir John Masterman wrote *The Double Cross System*, the book that finally made public the intelligence system that had contributed to the Allies' success in World War II, he turned to Norman Holmes Pearson to write the introduction. In it, Pearson revealed his passion for reading about espionage, the nature of working with agents, and the psychology of "turning" agents against their own countries and urging them to operate behind enemy lines. Masterman's book was, he claimed, the best account of espionage he had ever read.[6] Masterman, he explained, "gives us a world of strategems, inhabited by characters like SNOW, like MUTT and JEFF, like TATE and ZIGZAG and TRICYCLE. They were known only by these cover-names and in them they lived and operated. But each life was shared. It cannot be too strongly insisted," Masterman, out of experience, asserts, "that the most profitable cases were those in which the case officer had introduced himself most completely into the skin of the agent." "Nuance became all." For him what counted was "the system itself. In a philosophical sense it is the 'game,' which counts."[7] That the "game" was a procedure for systematically compelling the citizens of other countries to commit treason at the expense of their lives did not matter, because it produced useful information. "In the end," he observed, "there was an enemy to be induced down the wrong path, wrong for him but right for us. Fortunately, he went."[8]

In 1947 Pearson was invited to serve as the faculty adviser to the Yale Library, where Donald Gallup had been appointed curator of the Collection of American Literature. The two men had met as undergraduates; both had served in "secret" posts in the European Theater during the war, Pearson stationed in London and Gallup in Cheltenham; and both had used the time during and immediately after the war to strengthen ties to American expatriate writers. Pearson, of course, had maintained his relationship with H.D., Bryher, and Bryher's first husband, Robert McAlmon; Gallup had pursued his interest in Gertrude Stein and Alice B. Toklas. Reunited at Yale, they determined to shift the university's collection away from its focus on illuminated manuscripts and incunabula toward the talent of the present time. With this in mind, they approached other contemporary artists like William Carlos Williams, Carl Van Vechten, T. S. Eliot, Marsden Hartley, Thornton Wilder . . . and Ezra Pound.

Pearson wrote to Dorothy out of the blue. "I am wondering," he said, "if you will forgive me for the presumption—whether you are considering a place for Mr. Pound's manuscripts, of selling some or all, now or from time to time, and if so whether we could see whether we might not be able to raise the money to purchase them." He then told her that the library had previously supported poetry journals like *Furioso*, "Mr. Angleton's journal," and the current *Yale Poetry Review*.[9]

Dorothy prevaricated. She told Pearson that she was not yet accustomed to her role as "committeé," that she had to consider Pound's future needs, like the cost of getting him back to Italy "if your quite curious government administration ever decides to let him recover," and Pound's wish to provide for his grandson, Walter. She told him that three other libraries had been discussed as possible repositories for the archive and that she would also have to weigh the proper time to sell, given the instabilities of national currencies at the moment.[10] That is, she acted as if she owned Pound's letters even though she knew that Pound had bequeathed all of his papers to Mary, that she had left all of her possessions to Omar, and that this had been a mutually decided agreement.

Two years later, as a result of discussions with Julien Cornell, the lawyer who had prepared Pound's legal defense in 1945, Dorothy wrote not to the Yale Library but to Mary, enclosing a notarized document. She told Mary that Cornell had "cast some doubt" on whether Pound's will "made in your favor in Italy," would be valid in either the United States or England. Nonetheless, she continued, since Omar "would never violate Pound's wishes," he had put the matter (legally) "beyond question," to avoid any conflicts among heirs of the succeeding generation "who might not understand the circumstances."[11]

> FOR VALUE RECEIVED, I, Omar S. Pound hereby renounce all rights and claims to proceeds (royalties or whatever) from Ezra Pound's work in favour of Mary Baratti, of Schloss Brunnenberg, Merano, Italy, and of her son Walter or subsequent issue, provided however that should the said proceeds at any time exceed twice my own income from all sources, then in this event the said excess shall become payable to me or to my issue, and should Mary Baratti's line become extinct, the whole proceeds shall be payable to me, my line or assigns. Omar Pound
>   Washington, District of Columbia
>   Subscribed and sworn to before me this 22nd day of June 1949
>   Adam S. Wood
>   Notary Public

Put this in some safe place, Dorothy cautioned.

Here the matter rested, its urgency, from the library's point of view, somewhat mitigated by the mediation of Douglass D. Paige, a young teacher from Wellesley College, who had become extremely interested in Ezra Pound and proposed to work on several books about him. The first was a selection of letters that was eventually published by Faber and Faber as *Selected Letters of Ezra Pound, 1907–1941*; the second was a volume that he referred to as "an Ezra Pound evidence in the case book" to be assembled with the help of Mary Barnard. Even with elaborate planning (to Olga Rudge he mentioned including the United States treason law, the Rome broadcasts, the Bill of Indictment, Pound's letter to Attorney General Biddle, the reports of Pound's seizure versus "the actual narrative," conditions in Pisa, the preliminary hearing, and the reports from psychiatrists), the book never came to fruition.[12]

But since Paige had met Norman Holmes Pearson while he was at Yale doing preliminary research, and since he had gotten permission to read

Pound's letters, which were then still in Rapallo (actually Sant' Ambrogio), he could keep the library informed about what was there to be had. At first someone suggested that all the papers be transported to Hamilton College. Donald Gallup does not identify who it was, but it must certainly have been either Dorothy or Omar. Many years later, in writing about Yale's acquisition of the Ezra Pound Archive, Donald Gallup said simply that Hamilton couldn't "raise the funds necessary to defray the substantial shipping costs,"[13] to explain why Pound and Omar's alma mater did not get the papers, but this can only be a partial explanation, for in 1947, most of the papers were in Olga Rudge's possession, no one was certain who *owned* the papers, much less who could have authorized their disposition. In December, Pearson wrote to Dorothy Pound, thanking her for her "kind note" but no longer needing to deal with her since Paige was serving as an "intermediary." That is, he was going to go to Sant' Ambrogio (not Pound's flat, as Gallup asserted) to transcribe whatever he could of Pound's correspondence.

Apparently the library wanted photocopies of the stash as well as transcriptions. Someone wrote to Pound about the issue, who, as it turned out, was not averse to the idea. Gallup reports that Pound replied on 26 October 1947, suggesting that Yale provide Olga Rudge with a "proper camera."[14] This letter to Pound is itself a curious document, for its existence implies that Ezra Pound's authorization mattered, whereas Gallup's *Pigeons on the Granite: Memories of a Yale Librarian* announces in the first paragraph about this acquisition that, for legal purposes, Pound was a "non-person." "A majority of the principals negotiating with Yale could agree at least on one point: that Pound's own wishes concerning his papers were simply to be ignored."[15] On the one hand, Yale lauded Pound as one of the greatest epic poets of the modern era; his papers would contribute to the library's "glory"; on the other, it lured the cooperation of a person it considered not to be a person. Ezra Pound was not worthy of making a judgment about the disposition of his own life's accomplishment. This is surely the material equivalent of New Criticism, for the negotiating strategy that Donald Gallup describes is founded on the principle that only the text matters, as if the words on the page came to be there of their own accord. The creator need no longer be taken into account.

Olga was never sent a camera. D. D. Paige and his wife went to Rapallo in March 1948 after "it had been decided . . . that [he] would do the photographing" (who decided?) and that Yale would buy the images. Gallup makes a point of reporting "Pound's 'approval'" and then his "enthusiastic endorsement" of this arrangement. But a letter in the archive contradicts these statements,

for in January 1949, Norman Holmes Pearson wrote a letter to Pound saying, "I gathered from what [Warren] Ramsey said that Paige hadn't told you
that the library had in fact bought from Paige his transcripts of the letters
he's gathering at Rapallo." And then he repeated that should Pound want
the library to house the originals, "we'd do our damndest to get the money
for them."[16] The family had no idea that duplicates were already available for
scholars to use.

In any case, the purchase of Pound's archive was at checkmate. What
move could next be made? Olga had physical possession of the manuscripts
and many of the letters; Dorothy had guardianship of Pound's affairs; and
Mary was the intended owner of the Pound estate. At some point, Yale lost
touch with D. D. Paige, for in 1953, Norman Holmes Pearson wrote to Olga,
whom he had never met, saying he didn't know where the young man was,
and could she ask him to "drop me a note" should she run across him. He
also explained that "we" are bringing out a checklist of Ezra Pound's writing. Could she contribute to it? The checklist would eventually grow into
Donald Gallup's monumental, 550-page *Ezra Pound: A Bibliography*,[17] but
Pearson described the project as something he was "anxious to have . . . available for my graduate students."[18]

He was also anxious to keep diplomatic channels open. On a trip back from
Istanbul, he met, through introductions by Pound, John Drummond, Signora
Olivia Rossetti Agresti, and Boris.[19] In Italy once again in December 1954, he
told Pound that he had enjoyed an evening with Boris and Signora Agresti in
her home and expressed amazement that he found support for Pound and
concern for his "predicament" widespread in the American expatriate community in Rome and as well as the provinces.[20] His amiable reports to Pound
did not gain him trust. Pound simply replied, "I don't get the feel that NPH
DOES companionate or talk to any INDIVIDUALS." He also questioned
the "ORDER and precedence in his agenda???"[21]

Donald Gallup eventually followed in the footsteps of both Paige and
Pearson. In 1957 Olga finally gave him permission to examine the manuscripts at Sant' Ambrogio. Four years later, still working on his bibliography,
he learned that Pound had asked Mary to retrieve his possessions from Olga's
house and bring them to the castle.[22] By this time he was beginning to discern the complexity of the letters' provenance. He arrived in Brunnenburg to
find Dorothy installed there, Ezra himself ill in the Martinsbrunn clinic,
and Mary overseeing the entire ménage. On this trip he told Mary rather than
Dorothy that Yale would like to buy the collection, and then tried to oblige

Dorothy, who told him that, according to Ezra's will (the very will whose authenticity she had challenged in 1949), Mary would inherit the Gaudier-Brzeska drawings and sculptures and that Omar would inherit the artwork by Wyndham Lewis. It was Gallup who "smuggled" the *Red Duet* painting out of the castle to give to Omar, unwittingly fueling Mary's mistrust of the library's motives and apparently foreclosing any further negotiations.

For several years Donald Gallup listened to gossip about other maneuverings for the Pound archive, uncertain how to make amends, until Ted Hilles of the Yale English Department intervened in 1962. Hilles, who was a respected colleague, a friend of both Gallup and Leonard Doob, and a man of great integrity and diplomacy, was able to break the stalemate by inviting Mary to come to New Haven. It would be beneficial, he suggested to her, to see how research libraries organized their holdings and to learn how to catalog according to the formal conventions customarily used by archivists. The Doobs did their part: Eveline invited Mary to stay at their home and offered travel advice.

The trip loomed—an affirmation, a question, a blank. Mary didn't know what to expect from it. The archive was tangible proof of an origin she had never been able fully to claim; through it she could envision a bridge, not just to a particular American university but also to a nation; through it she could imagine a legitimate lineage, a place where she belonged. She was also canny enough to understand that she wasn't invited for herself.

She began working at the library on 13 January. Her task was to learn formal classification techniques, using H.D.'s letters to George Plank as practice examples. But she admitted to Olga that she had hardly been in her office because life at Yale had been a social whirl. Donald Gallup had taken her to lunch with Thornton Wilder's sister; the Doobs were going to throw a big party "with all the Eminent Professors, Deans, etc. on Saturday and probably Robert Lowell will be there."[23] She had an invitation from Tom Hefferman's parents to go to New York City, a letter from e. e. cummings's wife, Marion, whom she eventually met at the New York Harvard Club. James Laughlin came in from his country place for a lunch before setting off for Grenada. Through the Hilleses she met a Mrs. Parsons, who claimed that she had played tennis with Pound in Rapallo. Mrs. Parsons was a name-dropper who impressed Marion by mentioning Sylvia Beach and Caresse Crosby, now a New Yorker who continued to throw big parties.

It was heady stuff. Aside from the Doobs, who had already established a genuine affection for her, and probably the Hilleses, who also developed real fondness and respect, Yale put on a show for a convent-educated woman who had no way to give perspective to the seeming glamour of it all.

The whirl lasted two weeks. She spent a weekend in Boston, where she was given a tour of Harvard; H.D.'s daughter, Perdita, now married to John Schaffner, whom she had met while serving in the secret service in Britain, offered hospitality in New York. She was taken to Philadelphia so that she could see the landscape of Pound's youth; then she went back to New York to stay in Jas's flat so she could visit William Carlos Williams.

By mid-February she was back in Brunnenburg, with its routine of translation (she was working on *The Pisan Cantos*) and hosting an increasing array of guests from abroad. Hugh Kenner arrived from Johns Hopkins on 19 February, working on the groundbreaking book called *The Pound Era*. She liked him at the same time that he made her uneasy; it was *The Aspern Papers* all over again: "he was so *greedy* for seeing things."[24] Eva Hesse came from Munich; Peter Whigham, English poet and translator, and his wife were installed in the Gaudier garden flat; the Corys continued on in the flat with the balcony. At the end of March, to her surprise, Leonard Doob came for a week on his way to Lagos.[25] Ted Hilles wrote to say that he would visit in mid-July.

Then the Gleason letter arrived; a few days after that the first of a series of letters came from the Harry Ransom Humanities Research Center at the University of Texas at Austin, then correspondence from Bertram Rota, the foremost English dealer in twentieth-century writers—all of this prelude to years of international maneuvering to get the full Pound archive. A hornets' nest had been released.

Despite or perhaps because of Mary's visit to Yale, the University of Texas was the first to make an offer that indicated to Mary that she was playing in the major leagues. Almost a month to the day from Gleason's " I have been concerned about the papers" letter, Rota, who had been hired by Texas to give a formal appraisal, set out the terms of Texas's offer, explaining that without Pound's archive, Texas's current holdings were "like *Hamlet* without the Prince." Texas would immediately set up an Ezra Pound Modern Poetry Library to serve a world-class clientele; it would mount a major exhibition of Pound's work (hopefully in time for Pound's birthday in 1965). Depending on the final appraisal, they would offer $150,000–$200,000, and they anticipated the need for a curator of the archive. Would Mary consider an initial five-year appointment at an annual salary of $5,000? She need only be in residence two to six months per year, and she would, of course, retain all copyrights.[26]

By this time Mary had consulted her father and they had decided that the papers should go to America. She had also responded to Herbert Gleason's inquiry, but she sensed that Gleason was trouble. "Whose lawyer are you?" she asked. In the past he had represented Omar in buying a house and in making a will. But she should not be concerned about this, he claimed, for Omar now lived in England and had his own solicitor. He did not represent Dorothy in her personal affairs; she, too, had an English solicitor. "You are right," he admitted, "that I am Ezra Pound's lawyer in the sense that I represent his guardian who acts for him legally. . . . I don't think it creates a conflict."[27] But of course it did.

As he went on and on about possible tax consequences, providing for Pound's "comfortable support now," where the archive should go, he let drop that "Omar has communicated to me that he is very much concerned with what papers are made available to the public and he also feels that his children should derive a benefit from Ezra Pound's assets."[28] In other words, Dorothy and Omar were asserting rights not only with regard to the content of the possible bequest, but also to financial profit from it—all in the name of looking out for Ezra Pound's welfare. Gleason then told Mary that he had sent copies of his letter to both Dorothy and Omar (not to Pound) and advised her to get an independent attorney.

To James Laughlin, Mary confided that she was tired of "blind man's bluff." She wanted to enter into full possession of the archive "NOW." She could see all the benefits of selling the papers—they would be in one place; their sale price could be put into a trust fund for Walter and Patrizia's education; she could provide for both of her parents while they were alive. But Omar had apparently contested the validity of Pound's will on technical grounds, claiming that it had not been filed correctly and that, since it was typewritten, it would not hold up even in an Italian court of law. Mary wanted to talk more to Laughlin about another strategy that he had apparently suggested earlier: that Pound *give* the archive to her as a gift to avoid death taxes.[29] In Italy Pound was "legally a person" and could do anything he wanted. If not that, she wrote to Olga, could Pound rewrite his 1940 will by hand and file it properly?

Dorothy then took Mary aside and told her how things were going to be: Omar was to have all of her "things"; Mary was to have Pound's "things"; Omar would also own part of the archive. On the third and fourth of August, Mary made a hasty and urgent trip to Munich, where Leonard Doob was pausing on his way on back to New Haven. She had come increasingly to

confide in him, and whatever advice he gave, she returned from Munich re-
freshed, with a renewed sense of humor, and she now felt that she had "a
chance." Walter, she also told her mother, had been accepted at the Cate
School in southern California.[30] There was a brief respite from a problem that,
as it turned out, was not going to go away.

She wanted above all else to avoid throwing the archive into the "committeé tangle." James Laughlin was passing through Brunnenburg later in the
month. She knew that he could not take sides; nonetheless she hoped for his
advice, too. She didn't understand how the "committeé" functioned; she
didn't understand why Dorothy should *be* the "committeé"; nor did she know
why it was necessary on Italian soil at all. She showed him all the letters from
Texas, Gleason, and also one that Leonard Doob had written to Yale on her
behalf. After their meeting, she came away convinced that Laughlin understood all the legal points—but that he did not "understand my point." Jas had
apparently proposed that Dorothy provide an allowance for Walter and Patrizia
in lieu of a trust fund from their grandfather. "This hurts," Mary said. In her
mind, the "committeé" stood for "one of the facets of the Nessus shirt."[31]

By 15 February 1965, Mary understood there to be *four* lawyers "med-
dling" with Pound's work and still others working on his estate. She handled
the complications by sticking to her work. Walter was now in the United
States; she was working on the Jefferson and Adams Cantos. Each canto was
the guide to her own education, for she read what Pound had read; tried to
look at the images Pound had seen and steeped herself in the culture that had
constellated her father's creative imagination when he wrote. "The more I
learn about American history," she admitted, "the happier I am that Walter
is there and the more I hope he'll continue with college."

In the interim, Yale had become more focused on the means of acquir-
ing the archive. It was also trying, with increasing perplexity, to discover what
"the archive" was. Pound's correspondence and production had been voluminous to begin with; the library had acquired some of Pound's original letters with a William Carlos Williams bequest; it had bought still other letters
from Olivia Rossetti Agresti. Now Donald Gallup discovered through "a
snoop" that Dorothy had secretly sent all of Pound's St. Elizabeths correspondence to the Hamilton College librarian, Walter Pilkington, who was keeping everything locked in a file cabinet in his office.[32] Bruce Nichols, who was
then a student at Hamilton, remembers seeing "two sealed collections being
stored here: one consists of five sealed foot trunks, belonging to Omar, who
told me that no one but he knows the contents . . . as well as about twelve or

fourteen boxes, tied up by Dorothy Pound, containing all of the correspondence EP received while he was in Saint Elizabeths."[33] Next Gallup learned what Mary herself did not know: that James Laughlin had acquired a stash of letters, as well as Pound's notebooks for the *Pisan Cantos*, from Julien Cornell after the 1945 trial that had never happened. No one besides Laughlin knew what was contained in this hidden store; he revealed only that it was in a safety deposit box in New York and that he called it the de Rachewiltz Trust because he intended the sale to finance Walter and Patrizia's university educations. The "what" question was immensely complicated; the "how" question remained to be confronted.

Finally, Gallup located an " anonymous donor" (it was Sue Hilles), who could match the offer made by the University of Texas, with an additional $50,000 set aside for Mary. At this moment he ran face forward into the simmering legal complexities that were unfolding on several continents. He ran into Omar's legal birth certificate and into Pound's purportedly illegal will.

II

By the following year, there were *five* sets of lawyers, the Yale provost and treasurer, the Yale librarian, Leonard Doob, and Donald Gallup involved in trying to sort out the acquisition.[34] In March 1965, when Donald Gallup wrote to Dorothy Pound to thank her for her help in assembling his Pound bibliography, he added, "We are all hoping of course that all the complications in connection with the papers can be solved to everyone's satisfaction and in time so that we can have a big EP show for October. But Hamlet was quite right to lament 'the law's delay'!"[35] Three years later he unwittingly repeated the same phrase to her, saying that the acquisition of the archive seemed to be progressing "pretty well" . . . but alluding once again to "the law's delay." He hoped, eternally, probably wanly, that there might be an exhibition for another of Pound's birthdays.[36]

Mary initially proceeded by believing that sincerity, inner order, and patience would succeed. She urged Olga to be patient and invoked *The Cantos* to explain that Boris and Walter were building "The City of Dioce in the heart indestructible."[37] Hidden resentments surfaced when she had a conversation with Dorothy, who had mistakenly understood her reference to a trust fund for "the children" to mean Omar's children. Mary understood once again that she was confronted with the difference between "right" and "law," and acknowledged that she was not equipped to understand legal distinctions. She considered that she was right, and that until she knew irrevocably who formally owned them, the papers would "NOT" go to America.[38]

Eventually the library persuaded her that only legal counsel could protect her interests and resolve the impasse that bound them all. In 1966 Yale advanced her $15,000 in exchange for depositing Pound's letters to her and the notebook in which he had corrected her 1945 Italian translations. She hired Judge Thurman Arnold of Arnold and Porter in Washington, D.C.

Their first task, he convinced her, was to transport the papers to the United States. She wrote to Olga asking if there were any special items her father would like kept for him at Brunnenburg and what she wanted done with her personal letters from Pound, saying that Arnold had told her that she had "dithered" too long in giving Yale custody of everything else. She had sealed all family letters in separate boxes and planned to accompany the crates first by truck to Genoa, then by sea. The *Raffaello* was departing on 11 May, and Arnold had also advised total discretion about her movements.[39]

Even the terms upon which the library would accept custody were complicated. Yale's attorney John Ecklund gave her a letter stating what these conditions were; she submitted all the documents to Pound upon her return to Italy, and there the matter rested for nine months until Arnold wrote Mary that she must reassert her claim or else face the possibility of having waived her rights. "A doctrine in American law called 'laches.' It is a new twist which I did not know of."

"The difficulty," he told her, "has been that you had no lawyer to protect your interest either at the time Mrs. Pound was appointed as the 'committee' or at the time you received the papers from your father. The failure to define your rights has made the matter enormously complicated. It involves questions of Italian law and American law. The theory of Omar's that the will is not valid is based upon extremely complicated legal interpretation of Italian law."[40]

In the course of several years, she also learned, she had gone from being the recognized and rightful owner of her birthright, to being considered someone "who has been trying to STEAL AND CHEAT." It was a galling judgment, since her own principles had been something she had actively struggled to articulate. To Thurman Arnold she had written at length saying not only what her goals were with the archive, but the moral values that underlay those desired outcomes.

Basically, she wanted to follow Pound's wishes that the papers be kept as a single "cultural unit." Her reasoning was akin to those who fought against dispersing the archives for the modernist magazine *The Dial*. Pat Willis at Yale had argued that "to break up this irreplaceable archive is like taking a national monument and slicing it up in little pieces." Lawrence Dowler, director of the Houghton Library at Harvard, recognized a similar principle when he remarked, "We have laws that protect architectural landmarks, that protect buildings from being torn down, yet we have no laws to prevent the dispersal of this major cultural landmark."[41] She wanted the sale of the archive to be recognized as a "joint venture" undertaken with her father in which each would benefit equally. She insisted that Pound himself be included in every aspect of negotiation. And she reiterated the papers now at Yale "contain nothing personal about [Dorothy] and Omar—her personal letters etc." Should good faith negotiations break down, she said that she would reclaim custody of the papers, forgo the curatorial position, and simply wait for as long as she needed to wait. Arnold had apparently suggested a lawsuit on her behalf in New Haven. She understood the value of threatening legal action, but she wanted to avoid it.[42]

Pound, for his part, had indeed rewritten his 1940 will in handwriting. He identified it, also in handwriting, as "a copy of a type-written will which I made in Rapallo in 1940 and which I intend as my will this day 15 of August 1964. Ezra Pound." He had added a codicil, not dated, that reiterated and made more specific what should be done in the current circumstances: "The proceeds from any sale of archives must be placed in some form of trust to be applied to paying my expenses during lifetime & such gifts as I choose to make, Omar to have the W. Lewis work if he renounce claim to other material and future rights for self & descendants for sums accruing to me from author's rights or other sources. Ezra Pound." Mary knew that she was carrying out her father's wishes.

This was not how things worked out. The papers sat in the library basement for six and a half years while "the law delayed." To Mary Barnard, who had become an increasingly dear friend, Mary confided in 1965 that she was still supposed to be working on the archive, but it seemed "pointless." In 1967 she told Mary Barnard that she was still tied to Yale, but that her dream of founding an Ezra Pound Center there grew increasingly faint. In 1968, she wrote to Sister Mary Bernetta Quinn that "Yale, for all I know might have been swept off the earth."[43] She had been invited to a conference on translation at the University of Texas at Austin; as part of the trip, she planned to see Thurman Arnold because he still wanted to discuss a possible lawsuit. During these years, both Mary and Omar wrote to scholars that none of the papers could be viewed until they were "untangled."

In the interim, the ties Mary relied upon at Yale, indeed the very people who had brought her into affiliation with the Beinecke Library rather than the Harry Ransom Humanities Research Center, abruptly dissolved. In November 1975, whiles staying at Sue Hilles's apartment in New Haven, Mary learned that Norman Holmes Pearson had died. To Sister Mary Bernetta Quinn she wrote, "Poor Norman . . . it came to me as a great shock. . . . All Poundians are greatly indebted to him and I most of all. I shall miss him here at Yale. In fact, he was my oldest friend here."[44] Shortly later, "so soon after Norman," Ted Hilles had a heart attack.[45]

Now it was Dorothy who hesitated about scholars being able to use the papers. When she learned that Mary had taken the archive to Yale, she had made herself an unavoidable part of further negotiations by threatening to sue the university in her capacity as "committeé." Mary had, according to her, "stolen" her own heritage. As the library understood, Dorothy spoke for Pound as his guardian; even though she had not lived with him for almost a dozen years; even though her interests were now (and for understandable reasons) completely at odds with her "husband's," she had to be reckoned with. In 1968 Donald Gallup wrote to quiet her fears; in 1973 he was still writing the same reassuring words. "We are most anxious that the scholarly use of the Pound Archive by the Center for the Study of Ezra Pound and His Contemporaries shall not cause concern to you in regard to personal matters. The elaborate and carefully considered safeguards included in the old Lease-Option Agreement as last negotiated in July 1971 were contained in substantially the same form in the Family Settlement Agreement of 18 January 1973. Yale certainly intends to see that the Archive is used with due and diligent sensitivity to the personal privacy of Ezra Pound and the parties to the Family Settlement Agreement."[46] His view was that the manuscripts could be studied "with profit" even while personal materials remained sealed. Not until later in 1973 did he convince her.

III

There are some people for whom the law works as a form of personal betrayal. In the negotiations over the archive, from Mary de Rachewiltz's perspective, this seemed to be the case. In retrospect, it is difficult to see how it could have been otherwise. She lacked the necessary documentation of her parentage. (Remember Olga's letter to Pound in 1952 when Mary had tried to get a passport in San Marino as the daughter of Ezra Pound and Olga Rudge: there would "have to [be] proof, which there ain't and can't be.")[47] Omar had those credentials and a right to them. Pound had shielded Dorothy at his birth because he knew he was reciprocating for similar infidelity. And, since Dorothy had not told her son the truth until he was a grown man, affection, loyalty, and action were involved as well. He bore no responsibility for the initiating lie; he had already experienced a lifetime of affiliation.

One can imagine various outcomes for these circumstances. Omar could, for example, have abided by the notarized document Dorothy sent to Mary in 1949. Her son "would never," Dorothy had explained, "violate Pound's wishes." In 1949, Omar was young, single, and idealistic. By the 1970s he was shrewd, and, like Mary, he had two children whose welfare he now held in mind. But even in 1949, the Shakespear-Pounds had hedged their bets, for the document of "release to Mary" was predicated on the assumption that Omar *had* something to release, and it contained a monetary loophole: Omar would forego his claim to Pound's estate "provided however that should the said proceeds at any time exceed twice my own income from all sources, then in this event the said excess shall become payable to me or to my issue." When it became clear that the archive was extremely valuable, he chose to exercise a legal option and to negate a moral intention. No one doubted what Ezra Pound wanted; it could not have been clearer. It was written lucidly, typed, and then reiterated in handwriting, dated, and signed. But another "law" of release, the terms of Pound's extrication from St. Elizabeths, gave Omar's mother the right to claim that she was the sole interpreter of Pound's "wishes," and he chose to follow her lead.

Two institutions were finally established in the 1970s. One, the Ezra Pound Literary Trust, oversaw the distribution of royalties and made decisions about scholarly publications, artistic productions, and exhibitions. Another legal group took responsibility for sorting out Ezra Pound's estate aside from his papers. Both of these were commonplace organizations, but both were predicated upon a Family Settlement Agreement—the document Mary signed to avoid litigation in the 1960s and '70s. She had to swear in writing never to speak of Omar's parentage and she had to agree not to use the name "Pound." That is, she had to vow never to reveal the origin of her own displacement. In one of his trips to Egypt, Boris had discovered through independent sources who Omar's real father was. He had confronted Omar with the truth and with the de Rachewiltzes' knowledge of it.[48] But silence was to reign, and with it, an unequal distribution of profits from the Literary Trust. It would be split 60/40 in Omar's favor, with the implication that Mary had somehow transgressed to achieve this division of shares. The law had not only delayed but also hurt her.

The further consequence of the Family Settlement Agreement was that the Pound Archive was also arranged to disguise the origin of its own acquisition. Family privacy is, of course, a fraught subject. Relatives of prominent people, whose works are important enough to be deemed the heritage of all humanity, frequently want both the shelter and the reticence of the law. The distinctive circumstance in the Pound Archive was that Mary wanted openness, for only with full documentation and unrestricted access to it could her relationship to Pound be discovered and understood. From her perspective, the documents that revealed Pound's evolution as a poet now concealed "the tale of the tribe." It was a partial disclosure of his as well as her own life circumstances and thus, in her judgment, it participated in a "legal fiction." In other words, the archive perpetuated the deceptions that Olga, Pound, and Dorothy had set in place in the 1920s.[49]

The truth of this backstory could not come to light until Olga Rudge bequeathed her papers to the Beinecke Library in 1990. In them, along with Pound's will and the many years of correspondence that Olga, Pound, and Mary carried on throughout their lives, as they dealt with Pound's indictment for treason, his imprisonment, and the establishment of the "committeé," one finds Pound's stark, handwritten admission: "I, Ezra Pound, declare that Omar is not my son save in the legal sense. I am cuckold. That I have violated about every bit of Confucian good sense ever emitted."[50]

But that is a later part of the story.

IV

John B. Jones initially administered the estate of Ezra Pound. The Ezra Pound Literary Property Trust was overseen by a set of trustees. Eventually the group consisted of John B. Jones, again; Walter Pilkington, representing Omar; and Leonard Doob, representing Mary. The first record of its meeting is 1974, and the minutes record that James Laughlin, Mary de Rachewiltz, Olga Rudge, Louis B. Martz, Donald Gallup, and Doris D. Blazek were "invitees."[51] Even arriving at this simple structure had been contentious, and from the start the Literary Trust perpetuated the concerns that had led to its institution. That is, it too became a vehicle for manipulating the public's view of the extended Pound family.

By 1974, Pound himself had been dead for two years and Dorothy for one. But these circumstances did nothing to moderate Olga's vociferous judgments. From her imperious sidelines, she even tried to impede her daughter's choice of representative. To John Jones, she wrote that she refused to approve Leonard Doob because he did not know Pound well enough, he was not a Pound scholar, and he was "among other things, a well known psychologist, which would <u>not</u> have endeared him to Mr. Pound."[52] Mary was nonplussed. She agreed with her mother that he did not yet know enough about Pound, but she pointed out that Doob had twenty years' experience on the publication committee of Yale University Press and that this in itself was more useful than a trustee who only knew how to interpret a text. And, she added, "He is the only person who tried to be of practical help . . . without double or triple loyalties." She considered than he was only filling in a gap as a temporary trustee, and that her long-term hopes were for Walter, who would soon be able to manage his responsibilities. "I am sorry you feel you can't trust him [Walter] and not surprised he won't allow anyone to put him down."[53] In the end, it was John Jones's decision, and he found Leonard Doob a committed, sensible, and knowledgeable colleague.

For his part, Doob tried quietly and unflaggingly to placate Olga. His professional life continued to center around international conflict resolution. On his way to Cyprus, he had stopped off in Venice to talk to her face-to-face, listening as well as explaining. On his way home, he described the horrors of his trip—"hell broke out: first the coup with a gangster coming to power on the Greek side; and then the invasion by the Turks. Most of the time I watched aspects of the killing from my flat on the sixth floor which overlooks large sections of Nicosia. Eventually the British arranged a convoy for us to one of their bases on the island; a day later a helicopter lifted us onto an American warship, which finally deposited us in Beirut. Alitalia completed the job but by avoiding both Greece and Turkey and hence flying indirectly over most of the Middle East en route to Rome." Then he told her, "I now am a bit less ignorant—not false modesty, as you realize—concerning the subtle values that are to guide the decisions in which I shall participate."[54] He promised to keep in touch, which he did consistently throughout his tenure as trustee. The following year, he wrote to say that he had returned to Cyprus to see if he could revive his peacemaking mission (it was impossible

at the moment "while the unbelievable hatred persists, and no political settlement is in sight") and to tell Olga that he had dropped into the Tyrol on
his way back to New Haven. He and Mary were considering a new publishing project.[55]

He had already had ample opportunity to exercise the "subtle values" that
the Rudge-Pounds expected of him. In 1974, C. David Heymann submitted
a manuscript to the trustees for their approval. It immediately created a stir,
for Heymann had been granted access to the FBI files on Pound; he portrayed
Pound as a fanatical anti-Semite, and he broached the subject of Omar
Pound's birth. The trustees welcomed none of these perspectives, even though
one of their founding principles was that they should allow Pound scholarship to develop completely without impediment. Finally, Doob wrote to Doris Blazek of Covington and Burling, saying that Mary had had time to
examine the manuscript and that he agreed with her views. Just as Parker-
Hayden "examined the book to shield Omar and Dorothy, so I as Trustee
for the Pound Estate insist that the same courtesy be extended to Pound
himself." He brought up five issues: he wanted to know what facts supported
Heymann's summary of Pound's entire life as governed by "rabid anti-
Semitism, fascism and paranoia"; he wanted to know what evidence existed
that Pound himself had "insisted that his case be handled as here implied;
viz., that Dorothy withdraw the petition of habeas corpus and never attempt
such a petition again?" "This," he pointed out, "is the critical point in the
handling of Pound's legal status." He insisted that Pound's alleged marriage proposal to Marcella Spann in 1958 could not be corroborated and
thus constituted libel; he challenged Heymann to produce the photograph
of Pound leading "a neo-fascist, May Day parade" and asked him to prove
that he knew Pound's motive for being there; and he similarly challenged
Heymann's assertion that Dorothy had supported Pound for all the years of
their marriage. Pound, he pointed out, had continually earned money, particularly during World War II, when Dorothy's funds had been sequestered
in England.[56]

Already the members of the Literary Trust were casting about for ways
to shape the image of Pound's political and personal life. In this case, both
"sides" of the Trust wanted Heymann's manuscript to be revised. Soon the
two factions were working against each other, wanting posterity to hold
distinctive views about the "truth" of history. For Mary, this effort became a
lifetime goal, and as the years passed, she understood that she and Omar
could not reconcile their differences, if simply and profoundly because

Omar's inheritance rested on what Mary called the "myth" of filiation and further on his assertion of Pound's insanity. "My battle," she told her mother, "is to get the wording, the attitude to, the image of Babbo's legal status changed. To avoid litigation, yes, out of respect for The Law, but *not* because Omar deems Ezra Pound was incompetent does he get his 60%."[57]

The first move in this direction came from Mary. She proposed to publish a book of letters from her father to his parents, Homer and Isabel Pound. She knew that Pound had sent his parents her baby pictures; that Homer had met her in Gais when she was a small child; and that Isabel had eventually been told the truth. The letters would speak for themselves. Omar asked his representative, Walter Pilkington, to veto the proposal. To James Laughlin, Omar wrote to explain himself, saying that he would have to know a lot more before he could give the plan "any further thought." How many letters would there be? What years would be covered? Who would write the introduction, edit, and annotate the volume? "As you know," he pointed out, "under the Family Settlement Agreement (Paragraph VI), Olga, myself and Mary have equal veto powers over any book written by one another involving personal or family matters." The book was scotched.[58] Mary Barnard was visiting Brunnenburg when the news arrived in the first week of June 1978. She recorded in her Italian diary that she could see that Mary was "obviously going through [a] crisis . . . that morning she received letter saying Omar had vetoed the publication of the Family Letters that she has been working on."[59]

Four years later, Omar made a counterproposal. James Laughlin had introduced him to A. Walton Litz at Princeton; the two of them wanted to publish the early love letters of Pound and Dorothy Shakespear (1909–14): 250 letters, primarily from 1911–13, ending just before the beginning of the First World War. "The most interesting letters," in Omar's judgment, were "those of 1911 about Ezra Pound's visits to Milan and Turin libraries in search of manuscripts (Provençal and Cavalcanti materials) and 1912–13 about his visits to various troubadour centres in France." But the subtext of his endeavor seems also to have been the need to reinforce the image of Dorothy Pound as the great love of Pound's youth. He nonetheless wrote to Olga, at Leonard Doob's insistence.[60] Consent to publish personal material had to be unanimous. He was lucky, for Mary and Olga did not object to the project.

For Mary this constantly watchful, consistently strategic arrangement was increasingly wearing. She had tried to establish for herself a principle she identified as the "four f's": "freedom from family feuds," but by this point, she had been dealing with lawyers for nearly twenty years about every aspect of every possession ever owned by Dorothy, Pound, and Olga. The group, supported by various legal counsels, had considered the disposition of books, notebooks, paintings, sculptures, and even, as Mary put it, "clothes hangers." The problem of ownership was particularly acute with regard to Gaudier-Brzeska's hieratic head of Ezra Pound, for this marble sculpture seemed somehow to symbolize Pound's greatness, his youthful friendships, his position within the Vorticist movement, and his place, however fraught, in the hearts of the people who most loved him.

In anticipation of Pound's return to Italy in 1958, Mary had made a permanent mounting for the statue in the courtyard at Brunnenburg, but in the intervening years, with Pound's migration back to Venice, Olga had taken the head back to the Hidden Nest. In 1973 she spent over $2,000 to have a cast of the Gaudier bust made for Pound's grave on San Michele. She had also asked Isamu Noguchi to create a base for it with marble from the Henraux yard in Pietrasanta.[61] But this gesture did nothing to resolve the permanent disposition of the original. Omar wanted to sell it to the Tate Gallery; Olga herself mentioned the Hirshhorn or the Library of Congress as possible resting places.

Mary wrote on 6 April 1974 to ask Olga for specific directions about the Gaudier collection; four years later, she was still trying to find out her mother's desires. In January 1978 she wrote to inform Olga that the estate (as opposed to the Literary Trust) would be settled in February. "Could she, Olga, put in writing her wishes re the Head?" she asked. As far as Mary was concerned, the Head could stay in Venice, but she did not think that such an arrangement was a permanent solution. Olga procrastinated for over ten months before writing to Doris Blazek, "I seize this occasion to state that I have delivered to Mary and Omar Pound all articles belonging to them with the exception of the Gaudier-Brzeska Hieratic Head which belongs to Mary."[62] Her letter begged the question of an ultimate destination for the statue. As it turned out, she mooted the decisiveness of her own views by not bearing in mind the legalities governing the international transport of artwork. Anthony d' Offay came to visit both Olga and Mary in 1980 to arrange a Gaudier-Brzeska exhibition in London. The statue was duly shipped; Olga went to see it in d' Offay's studio in New Bond Street, thought it beautiful—"remarkably clean, white, absolute"—without considering the impossibly high fees that would be entailed in returning it to Italy.[63]

In the interim, even without knowing what Olga would do with the sculpture, Mary had considered it a possible bargaining chip with Omar in rearranging the terms of the Literary Trust. What she most wanted was to gain control over copyrights. "Concretely," she informed Olga, "I had proposed to Omar/Jones that *provided you are in agreement*, he can have all the Gaud-iers and W. Lewis and books at Yale (*not* those still in Br/ . . . IF he renounces the copyright. . . . However, even to this proposal Omar has said no: it would deprive his children of income."[64]

Seven years later, Leonard Doob was still trying to help her accomplish this goal. He had written to Walter Pilkington and to Doris Blazek about al-tering the ways in which Pound copyright was handled. But counsel upheld Pilkington's assertion that nothing could be changed during Olga's lifetime without her consent and approval of the Connecticut court. Blazek also cau-tioned that any new Trust would have to be governed by an impartial trustee—that decisions about copyright could never be handed directly to Mary. At most she could serve in a consulting role.[65] I am, Mary wrote, the "pawn of TWO committees, plus Trust, etc."[66]

She had no idea what Olga would do with her own papers. One day, while Mary was working at the Beinecke, Donald Gallup stopped by to tell her that he had heard that Robert Hughes was selling Olga's archive to Stanford.[67] By this time she had learned not to interfere, but she watched as Olga procras-tinated.

In 1982 Omar Pound made two decisions: he sold Dorothy's archive to the Lilly Library at the University of Indiana at Bloomington, and he left his own Pound archive to Hamilton College. He wrote to Olga trying to negate the painstakingly negotiated relationship of Ezra Pound with Yale Univer-sity. "It seems to me a good moment to tell you something that I think you shd. know, namely that I have left in my will, i.e., in *writing* my entire Wyndham Lewis collection of books magazines, pamphlets, etc. to be added to the EP collection there [Hamilton]." It occurred to him that Olga might feel a similar loyalty to the College and "want to formally find a happy home for some of your papers, books, and memorabilia there." He claimed that they would be properly attended to "unlike a certain other place we know" and that Pound would have supported such a decision. Having helped to obstruct the acquisition of Pound's papers for almost seven years, he com-plained that there was still no proper catalog at Yale.[68]

Olga waited once again. In 1988 Pat Willis, the curator for modern Amer-ican literature at the Beinecke, told Mary that she had written to her mother saying that Yale would like to buy "*your* archive since it is a part of Ezra Pound's 'cultural unity.'" Mary ventured to say that she hoped Olga would consider it.[69] At this point in time, Olga was prepared to act. That year, the Gaudier head went to the Nasher Sculpture Center in Dallas, Texas. In 1990, after evading a raft of other interested parties, she did sell her archive to the Beinecke Library, lying down, at least symbolically, with the material remains of Ezra Pound.

Who, then, remembered what Pound had written to Olga Rudge sixty-five years earlier when he had advised her that it didn't matter whether a piece of paper (a birth certificate) had false information on it, but whether it would hurt another person? He seemed then to think that the authorities would only care if the child eventually tried to claim a false inheritance. "That is WHY they have formalities, at least MOST law has property basis, and penalties are severe on THAT ground, NOT because the learned jurisconsults are shocked by bastardy."[70]

That perspective had cost two young people half a lifetime of grief. The master of paper records had failed to leave the only records that were of primary concern to his heirs. By the time these legal battles were underway, but long before they were resolved, Pound, it seems, had come to desire Mary's "four f's": "freedom from family feuds." He left a codicil to his will saying that he wished to be buried alone in Hailey, Idaho. "I am considering this arrangement, which obviously will take some time. If I die before its completion, I wish to be buried temporarily either in Sant' Ambrogio or in Venice, Olga to take charge of the arrangements. . . . I saw Joyce's grave in Zurich. A warning that also brought the matter to mind. I feel that nobody can contest my right to be buried in my birthplace."[71] But because this desire was not written on the right piece of paper, it too was ignored.

CHAPTER 8

Leonard Doob and Africa, 1965–72

I

During that time of dizzying legalities, something went terribly wrong. It is not clear exactly what happened, but there was an emotional breach of extraordinary severity, even for the fractious Rudge-Pounds. Olga wrote, with her usual unsparing acerbity, that Mary had jeopardized her standing with Ezra Pound by not coming to visit him. Mary replied with equal insistence, that the situation was the reverse. In February of 1969, she told her mother, "I am sorry, it is the other way round: 'your position has been weakened by your not seeing Babbo'—I stopped seeing Babbo *because* at a decisive moment, after three years struggle he knocked the little ground I had from under my feet."[1] What did Pound do? Is it the same event that Mary spoke of in 1975, when she wrote, "I had said right from the beginning, i.e., 1963 that I knew I could not work profitably with and for the committeé which at the time, nominally at least, was represented by Dorothy. But you and Babbo did not side with me, and so now I find myself a pawn of TWO committees, plus Trust, etc."?[2] In some ways, the exact incident or the exact moment of recognition does not matter. We are witnessing a cumulative effect. "Non Valeva la Pena." "It wasn't worth it," Mary finally admitted. One finds this poem in *Il Diapason*, the small volume of verses that Mary published with Giovanni Scheiwiller in 1965.

> Old one, it was not worth
> you walking
> a thousand kilometers on foot
> with boots, hat
> and the burdens of others

to tell me
a truth
if now you deny it.[3]

Rupture was everywhere in the 1960s. The distance between Mary and her parents had been widening for years. It manifested itself directly in letters and indirectly in verse. In her first book of original poems, she remembered Pound as a god disappearing over the water, leaving behind his women disciples; she remembered him as a ruddy, dusty apparition, visiting a small child, wearing a red jacket with golden buttons and carrying a miraculous invention: a "diapason": a tuning fork. She created images not only of greatness and godliness, but also of simple, overweening size. She saluted a crab "that doesn't touch small crabs/ or molest its companion or its ancestors or become malevolent," expressing a need for space and solitude, for freedom from advice and criticism. Big creatures should let small beings live in their own eddies of water. Then she forsook the safety of displacement to write directly about poets and their daughters:

These are the morals of the poets and their daughters:
. . .
To pulverize pedestrian students
And sweaty journalists
To be blond, paper mâché angels
Like those beside the whitewashed sepulchers
Of country churches at Easter.
He is risen! To the crying women with the ointments.
He has taken the way of the sea.

The god has appeared, and he has disappeared, leaving fake replicas with ridiculous tasks. The poems are bitter, sparse, and unsparing. They rebel against destiny and are at the same time the mark of it. She has received an artistic inheritance, even as she disparages its receipt. The allure of the "diapason" has been left behind. The tuning fork: Sing with form and accuracy. Be attuned to hidden harmonies. Listen. Her relationship with her father had been shattered by the fate of papers and decisions taken long ago, so she picked up the fork herself. She made modest claims for her accomplishments, but she made them.

She had also to face the breach between herself and Boris. There are love songs in *Il Diapason*, but they are not those of comfortable, married affection. Something else has happened, perhaps the result of living in a castle distant from the world. Peripheries require centers; remoteness demands supply. Domesticity needs tenaciousness and basic probity. It requires two. But Boris seemed ill-prepared for the real requirements of the castle he had conjured for a supposed tribe of magicians. He was gone most of the time.

During these years, while the shadow-life of literary legacy was being fought over, Mary's letters were filled with news of absences from home. Boris was working at the Pontificio Istituto Biblico (1951–55); Boris was attending the Accademia Vaticana—the Vatican Diplomacy School (1953); Boris was home for ten days in January but then "he went back to his work in Rome."[4] Boris acquired a new flat in Rome, the via de Monserrato 149;[5] he began to write on the letterhead of the Comitato Internazionale per l'universalità della Cultura; in 1955–56 his name can be found on a list of those with *Carriera politica militare e letteraria, Ordine di servizio* at the Fondazione Mondadori. None of these credentials indicate a clear career path, but they led to years of expeditions in Africa and the Near East and eventually to books about African and Egyptian art.

The letters reporting these activities continued through the years: in 1959 Mary told Olga that "Boris is in Rome."[6] Later in 1959 she wrote hopefully to Mary Barnard, who was planning a visit to Brunnenburg, "My husband will certainly be at home this time."[7] In January 1960 he returned to Egypt; in June he was "still in Rome." In 1961 he went to Syria, where he was received by King Hussein.[8] The following year he was back in Egypt where he went to see John Slocum, who had become the American cultural attaché in Cairo.[9] In 1963 he was back in Rome; in 1964 he planned and then had to postpone and refinance an expedition to Jordan.[10] In 1965 he was in Chicago and Houston, seeking sponsorship for his work. Then it was Egypt from January to March and again in November; two years later it was the Sudan.[11]

During the early years of their marriage, Mary got used to temporary loneliness. "The house looked very sad and empty, only now I am used again to my solitude," she told Mary Barnard in 1949.[12] Fifteen years later, she admitted to her mother that her life was "more and more that of a Trappist."[13] The other term she frequently chose for herself was "hermit." Curiously, as her trust in her correspondents (Mary Barnard, Sister Mary Bernetta Quinn, Christine Brooke-Rose, Eva Hesse) grew into a source of strength, she began to describe Boris's travel as something other than simple travel. "Boris did come for my birthday," she wrote to Sister Mary Bernetta in 1967, "but he's left again for Milan-Roma—actually is kept 'operating.'"[14]

What was Boris doing? Nothing is clear. Every track leads into silence. The books did appear, but the funding sources for the travel remain obscure. "Operating" for whom? Whatever was going on was a risky business, for in 1950, the year Patrizia was born, Brunnenburg was transcribed in Walter's name.[15] It wasn't just poverty. The family did not want to lose their home to the expense of Boris's forays into the Middle East. This was one way to avoid a basic and haunting insecurity. By 1969, Mary did not even know her husband's basic whereabouts. "If Boris is not at the castle . . . I have not yet heard about his going to Africa."[16]

Years ago, after the initial damage done by Pound's desertion of Brunnenburg, John Drummond had assessed Mary's situation by wishing that she cease to be her father's daughter and become more fully her husband's wife. But by the 1960s, even this thin, condescending vision of fate held little promise. Whatever else Boris was doing—serious scholarship or elusive magic or clandestine politics—it involved flirtation. Something about "secretaries." This, too, is obscure, known primarily by the mistrust it engendered. Mary could excuse the lost money—she could rationalize that Boris had as much right to Pound's resources as she did—but the effects of absence are as cumulative as grief itself. To Christine Brooke-Rose, she wrote, "And you are right, I have so much . . . but somewhere in *The Cantos* it says something to the effect: if there be not love in the house there is NOTHING. . . . Years ago, at the peak of happiness . . . I used to say: I have all I want—a husband, a son (plus a daughter) . . . a castle and even a father who is not only the best of all living men, the most glorious and beautiful, but the Poet I admire most, in short God Himself with not only an Angel on each shoulder but lots of little Angels who would alight on Brunnenburg, and all praise his verses. . . . And my joy was overwhelming. Then one fine day a little desk girl called GIOIA— joy herself—walked into our house and puff—all my happiness gone."[17]

During this time of loosening ties, she wanted to remain solidly behind Walter and Patrizia. Looking back in the 1970s, she told Olga that it hurt her to hear Boris repeatedly called "mafia." My problem, she said, "is how to make life bearable for his children."[18] It was time to consider their education. Each child, distinctive in talents and temperament, took steps toward the future. In 1965 Walter went to Rutgers University in the United States. He wanted a classical liberal arts curriculum and pursued it in the midst of the civic crises of the mid-1960s. Protests against American imperialism in Vietnam and segregation for Black Americans colored campus life; protests on behalf of women's rights were frequent; anti-establishment sentiment was high across the country. He participated in some of the protests and peace marches; but he did not like the university he had chosen. In 1967, he took a break, and returned primarily to complete a commitment.

In 1966–67 he was back in Italy under military service obligation. He studied in Bologna, came to Brunnenburg on weekends and holidays, engaged in translation work, and made plans for the castle and the farm. To Sister Bernetta Quinn, Mary explained the value of his company. "He is taking a little bit father's place, I mean his conversation and kindness are of the same quality."[19] To Mary Barnard, she reported that Walter was considering becoming an American citizen and that she wished he would.[20]

When he returned to Rutgers in 1968–69 she went, too. The two of them rented a small house in Piscataway. "I am mildly amused," she wrote to Christine Brooke-Rose, "by having landed myself finally in an American suburb." The house was "typical," comfortable, and she thought she could switch to something similar "for good" as long as a few bright people were not too distant. On the weekends, James Laughlin gave them use of his flat in New York while he went to the country. New York excited her; she thought it the place she would most like to live in the world and knew beyond doubt that it could never happen.[21]

Underlying the change of residence were further internal upheavals. The previous spring, she had been invited to a symposium on Ezra Pound and translation at the University of Texas at Austin and had continued her journey to southern California to see Robinson Jeffers country. To Mary Barnard she wrote, "believe it or not, I am still very much in love with America and still would like to spend at least six months a year there."[22] Rutgers offered her a small hold on a national identity whose more complete manifestations still eluded her. It also tantalized, for the real goal was New Haven with a secure role in the ever-deferred Ezra Pound Center. After years of convincing herself that she did not want what it seemed she could not have, Mary learned that the Beinecke Library might go forward with a Pound Center after all. Pound and Olga had included Yale in their recent American itinerary and the talk was now of a 30 October opening. This turn of events awakened dormant "flies." Less dormant were concerns about Walter himself and his occasional "fits of depression."[23] He was coping, she told Christine Brooke-Rose, but in the midst of unsettling life events spanning three generations, her role was now to be the "unswerving pivot." It was a role she played in appearance only.

Outside the walls of Yale and beyond the arms of her studiously well-heeled academic friends, she felt unprotected in America. Walter was teaching her to drive, an experience that she loved, but she had a small accident in a parking lot while practicing. The parking attendant called the police; calling the police involved producing identity papers; the papers showed clearly that she was not an American and she knew she could not act like one. Where at home she would have told the guy he was "an idiot," here she had to hold her tongue and reckon with the racial dynamics of an Irish cop and a Black man. It fascinated her, but it depressed her too. "Perhaps I am a European after all and this country will never, never accept me." After three years, she had just received a $15,000 legal bill for making her claim to the Pound archive. "It's all wrong," she said. "Here . . . oh, you are not on a lecture tour, you are not teaching, you are not working in the library . . . all so very gently with voices fading into the distance—oh you are not. No, I am NOT."[24]

By summer she was back in Brunnenburg. Walter weathered the year, stayed on as Mrs. e. e. cummings's chauffeur to earn money for a car, and returned to Italy with some of the air of American youth mixed with the formalities of his European upbringing. He chose the car, took a driving tour of Yugoslavia with his friend Peter, and showed up in Venice to see his grandparents unannounced and unkempt. Mary heard every critical detail: he wasn't clean; Olga wouldn't allow him a bath; she complained to him about Mary's poems. Letters flew.

Mary remembered a similar visit from her own newly married youth: she and Boris had paused to wash at the Fonte Branda after an all-night train trip from Rome, but could Olga not see any virtue in Walter's more natural behavior? Could she not see that her grandson was sensitive, clear-sighted, and highly reserved? Did she not recognize in him tolerance, pity, and a need, similar to Pound's and Mary's, for independence? He interpreted criticism as criticism of Boris as well as himself. His sensitivity might be "out of focus" and "excessive," but it stemmed from the desire young people harbored to have their elders be "happy spectators," and to be unobtrusive in their support.[25] To her delight, she learned that Walter had been accepted into graduate school at Harvard in comparative literature. He had regained his composure.

Patrizia, too, was making her way, though she chose a strictly European path. She completed her baccalaureate.

II

The changes in Mary's own life were breathtaking and unexpected. The summers had been filled with the usual rush of guests. "People & people & work & more work," as she put it. Dorothy, for one, stayed on until 1968. Marcella and Giuliana del Pelo Pardi came in 1967; Patrizia, Graziella, and Boris returned to the castle from their various pursuits; the MacNaughtons came. The summer of 1968 repeated the routine of people coming and going. This time it was the Corys, the Noel Stocks, and a German professor and his wife. But by 1969, the castle was not only the source of interesting companionship, but also the basis of economic survival. In June Mary admitted to Mary Barnard that "from now on, or at least from next year onwards, I'll be dependent on my own elbow grease entirely."[26] The breach with Boris was irrevocable.

At various times over the ensuing years, Christine Brooke-Rose would broach the subject of rapprochement. Originally a writing guest at Brunnenburg, Brooke-Rose had almost immediately become a close friend, intellectual companion, and confidant. By 1967, Mary was writing letters to her as a fellow member of MAC (Mutual Admiration Club) and relying on her friend's empathy and judgment. Like the enigmatic Natalie Troubetskoi, Brooke-Rose had been a member of the British WAAF during World War II, although she made no questionable pretenses about being something other than what she was. She had been stationed at Bletchley Park along with James Jesus Angleton and Norman Holmes Pearson and had worked in Hut 3, Block D. Her "hut" had been identified as the German army and Air Force Enigma Reporting Section, and her job had been to produce reports from signals decrypted by other intelligence units. Here she had met and married Rodney Bax, a British army Intelligence Corps captain, and had gone on after the war to Somerville College at Oxford and to University College London, where she had taken BA and PhD degrees in French literature. Her marriage to Bax had been short-lived, but her interest in "signals" remained for a lifetime. She was astute at recognizing them in human relationships and she spent the remainder of her life writing extraordinary experimental novels using them. Encryption was her specialty and complexity did not faze her. Could not Mary circumvent the difficulties of her marriage? She pointed out that she and her new husband, the poet Jerzy Pietkiewicz, had survived similar arguments, entanglements, and estrangements. Damages were often reparable. But Mary wrote that living with Boris again as a husband was unthinkable. It was also, at least by formality, unavoidable. They had married in the Catholic Church, and in Italy there was no divorce.

Mary's affair with Leonard Doob started somewhere around this time. One can imagine them meeting in Munich or Milan. One can imagine Mary's impassioned need for advice about the situation at Yale meeting Doob's more restrained desire to give it. One can envision clandestine trips. Perhaps the stopovers from his research turned into stopovers of other sorts. Doob first helped Mary with the Pound archive in 1964; by early spring of 1967, she mentioned missing the marvelous African sun to Sister Mary Bernetta Quinn. Had she gone there with Doob? The available records do not add up. But the consequences of this relationship were far-reaching. In her next 1967 letter to Quinn she wrote, "The nature of my sorrow (and predicament) I think you have intuited."[27]

By the summer of 1967, she had taken a decision. Instead of spending another Tyrolean winter in drafty isolation, she would close the castle. Sue Hilles had invited her to travel to Rome, Assisi, and Siena and she was going. She described the experience of Assisi to Sister Mary Bernetta Quinn as coming "too late—at a time of . . . internal struggles and rebellion." But it was a profound experience nonetheless. She went to the Saint Francis Church intending to look at the Giotto frescos. Instead, she descended to the tomb and stayed the entire morning, returning with a feeling of being "renewed and cleansed and serene." Then she and Sue Hilles visited Saint Clare's convent before going back to the church for a solemn high mass.[28]

The Italian trip was the prelude to more changes. She had broached the subject of writing a memoir with John Schaffner, the husband of H.D.'s daughter, Perdita, who was now a literary agent in New York. He had managed to get her a two-year advance for it. Tentatively called *Discretions*, she thought of the book as a counterpart to Pound's *Indiscretions*, and it had apparently been on her mind for months, since her letters to Christine Brooke-Rose were peppered with inquiries about other such daughter/father books—in particular those by the daughters of Yeats, Blunt, and Churchill.[29] In October 1967, Mary locked up Brunnenburg, put the key in her pocket, a bolt on her mouth, and flew to Tanzania to join Leonard Doob. She, who usually facilitated the writing of others by offering them still mountain air and clean European tablecloths, sought refuge for her own writing in Africa.

A cherished few people knew about her relationship with Leonard Doob. Most people did not, but those who did learned about events that altered her life even as they could promise only temporary respite. To Sister Mary Bernetta Quinn, Mary admitted simply that she was in East Africa, that she was working on her own writing and helping to assemble an anthology of African poetry.[30] Christina Brooke-Rose, who seems to have been in on the secret to a greater extent, received a letter toward the end of October saying that "the momentous decision" had been taken. "Don't put any questions as to how, why, etc. I got here . . . the agony has been great. It is an egotistical decision, but d-it, if I am to write a book about life without father I have to be egotistical, and it may at a certain point even be generous to stop torturing oneself and others. An interlude. This much is clear."

> I have for the past week discretely written *Discretions*. I have also swum every day in the Indian Ocean, watched the fishing boats come in, admired the Africans in every possible way, plus their incredibly beautiful flora and fauna, not to mention the beach. In my wildest fantasies I had never conjured up anything so white and blue and green palm trees . . . All the swimming and exploring I haven't had so far—concentrated—no responsibility—a servant who says *ndja-ndja*—which is supposed to mean yes, and he is supposed to understand English but understands not a word—so I stopped talking, just smile and nod and say *ma-suri* and he shops and cooks. Jambo. It's great. If I could conjure you and Eva (with Jerzy and Mike) to these shores and possibly Patrizia and Walter—the world would be perfect.[31]

Doob, whose work in the 1960s took him primarily to the developing countries of Africa, had offered her a choice between mountains—possibly Rwanda—and the coast. She discovered that Dar es Salaam means "Haven of Peace," which is what she sought, and that it was protected by a coral reef. It echoed Pound's "the coral face under wave-twinge." The decision was easy. Once there she found not only a coral reef but also a modern university standing in the bush with seven books by and on Ezra Pound.

The work was real, not just a pretext. One project was "claimed" by Leonard Doob. In his curriculum vita for 1967, one finds a book called *A Crocodile Has Me by the Leg: African Poems*, along with a piece written for *Public Opinion Quarterly*: "Scales for Assaying Psychological Modernization in Africa" (31, no. 3). Both people were doing serious writing along with the clandestine pleasures of being together in Dar es Salaam.

By the end of November, Mary reported that she had reached page ninety-nine (the year 1939) of her memoir. It didn't satisfy her, but she wrote from 7 a.m. until noon during the week and rested on the weekends. She had a wild sense of "fleeing what band of Tritons" back at home, and an equally wild exuberance about the natural life present for her inspection. She watched elephants, zebras, giraffes, and hundreds of gazelles and baboons "but above all LIONS—the beauty. The regal boredom of the lions in the morning sun—5:00 a.m.—worth a trip to Africa."

She was trying to write by memory, without notes, archives, theater programs, and documents. She was sick of papers. In a second draft of an introduction to *Discretions* written in the 1990s, she explained,

> The privilege I have availed myself of to the full is the quaint kind of memory that stems from affection: the having seen and judged with the eyes of a child, before I had any notion of who and what my parents were, before understanding their language, their poetry, their music. That my opinions were colored by my earliest surroundings, language, customs and beliefs is natural. Later memories may have been contaminated by the many books on the life, the work, the philosophy, the political and economic theories of Ezra Pound: a veritable "band of Tritons", I tried to flee from them and from archives, as well as the dictates of legal small print, in order to rescue "the coral face under wave-twinge/ Rose-paleness under water shift."[32]

She wanted to find some kind of truth without melodrama, some kind of peace without calculation. She wanted to write about Ezra Pound as if she were part of a tradition and not simply being impressed by it. Pound had once said,

> Remember that I have remembered/ mia pargoletta
> And pass on the tradition.

But she was not certain she could. He was beyond containment:

> In a way he still remains "The Gallant Foe/hiding behind a veil". I had
> knitted socks and pullovers for him, cooked and washed, treasured
> his old shoes and hats as well as his papers and books, hailed him as
> the source of all my happiness, branded him as the root of all sor-
> row, listened to his superb reading of poetry, his bitter and enlight-
> ened tirades against usury and all falsification, exchanged ordinary
> everyday topics as well as wild fantasies and phantoms, and still I
> asked: Who is he? What? Where?

She wanted to remember Pound as he had belonged to her and not as he had
been defined by military prisons, mental institutions, and public labels, and
to tell the story of her origins, reclaiming through memory what had been
sealed away in library file cabinets by law.

She used the time in Tanzania to finish a draft using copybooks of the
type Sister Mary Bernetta Quinn had used when she wrote *The Metamorphic
Tradition in Modern Poetry*. By Christmas she had filled up four books. She
expected to write, but she did not expect the other consequences of the trip.
As the New Year approached, she wrote to the sister that she had felt very
close to her at Christmas:

> The truest, most meaningful service I have participated in—only
> Assisi can compare with it. The church faces the bay—boats lit up
> looked like Christmas trees—the square & the steps to the church
> packed with singing Africans and it was only 11:30—early—I feared
> I would have to remain outdoors. Then I walked around the church,
> inspecting—a flitting white nun was entering a little side door I—
> followed her, probably she saw my pleading face—in a nice Irish ac-
> cent, God bless her! She said: it's not permitted, never mind, come
> in. And I found myself close to the altar and there was high Mass
> celebrated by the bishop—with beautiful singing and music in <u>Latin</u>
> and Swahili—Silent Night & other hymns in Swahili—it seemed to me
> the Irish nuns, the bishop and a few other priests were the only white
> faces! The miracle of all those dark women and men streaming to
> Holy Communion, with babies tied to their backs and little barefoot
> boys with bare navels. Whenever I think of it I feel so moved, as though

I had experienced the true Xmas <u>spirit</u> for the first time in my life. And all so surprising. I have not expected such an experience in Africa—But my life [is full] of blessings & I feel so peaceful and happy once more . . . I shall try and stay on here until spring comes to Brunnenburg.[33]

By March of 1968, the idyll was over. She told Christine Brooke-Rose that she felt old—the suntan had faded, the bags under her eyes had returned; she was back in the location where no one else could tolerate her "didactic tone" or her desire for order and decorum. Outside her windows, Tyroleans were once more marching in the streets. The issue of autonomy had still not been resolved. Negotiations between Italy and Austria had been going on for over ten years. On 11 July 1967, Lujo Toncic-Sorinj, Italy's foreign minister, described the situation (four people had been killed as the result of a bombing in Porzenscharte) as at "their lowest point since 1945."[34] The castle was "dilapidated," needed furious housekeeping, and she wanted to finish her translations of Robinson Jeffers's poetry. She was, she said, "obsessed with father's obsession—or rather obsessed by the obsession of his obsession. But is it a wonder? Can you understand the new gold standard?"[35] Christine Brooke-Rose told her to slow down. What had been the effect of her five months away?

Mary named the obvious things. She was rested and restored. Had she not had that respite, she might not have been able to deal with her depression and anger, but now she felt able to cope. She recognized what had helped her writing: not understanding the language, knowing no one, "watching people and things and animals all behaving according to a different logic from my square one—fields tilled differently, with patches here and there, no Tyrolean or Roman patterns."[36] She had grappled with "the Sire." She'd also had a taste of normalcy. The trip wasn't only about coming to terms with her father; it was also about loving Leonard Doob.

She had spent five months with a man she described as a "truly wonderful human being." He was not a genius or a god or a magician. He was thoughtful and generous; he understood that she needed to get back on her feet. He apparently fell in love with her, and he was married.

He was also part of the American academic establishment, a man who took the amenities of elite campus life for granted, and who expected and got substantial government support for his work. His first book on Africa, *Becoming More Civilized: A Psychological Exploration* (1960), which included studies of Ghana, Togo, and Nigeria, thanked the Carnegie Corporation of New York "for arousing my interest in Africa by means of a red-carpet trip in 1952; for enabling me to carry on research in East and South Africa in 1954–55 and for . . . advice ever since, especially from Alan Pifer." He also acknowledged the U.S. Public Health Service and the National Institutes of Health for a summer in 1957 in Jamaica; and Paul J. Bohannan and "our" committee functioning from the National Academy of Sciences, for going to Africa in 1959.[37]

The list of official supporters continued for decades. In 1969, when the Kenyan political leader Tom Mboya was assassinated, Doob was there, thinking about *Resolving Conflict in Africa* (1970). By this time, he was working for the United Nations Institute of Training and Research and getting money from the Academy for Educational Development.[38]

He was accustomed to keeping national identities secret, the purpose of international missions under wraps, and with Mary, too, he moved around the world with confident and illicit privilege. Years later, when she fictionalized a final encounter between lovers, she made the protagonist's name Hera: Her Existence Remains Anonymous.

Clandestine lovers appear in Mary's first book of poems (*Il Diapason*, 1965), in both rural and international settings. The verses are not about the thrill, but about the unexpected and foolish glory of loving in midlife. In "Stone Flints," she writes about transcendence through a pheasant "heavily and stupidly" stalking a gray bustard in a vineyard. "But when it rises in flight/ It is a ball of fire/ Which cleaves and tears apart/ The heavens with its cries." She writes with wry circumspection: even the "yokels of Völlau" understand that it is better to steal a cow than someone else's husband ("Battologia"). She writes about being blessed. "We are two slender white birch trees/ Kissing and bowing down on the mountain/ Under green conifers and dilapidated golden oaks" ("Birch"). The blessing is doubled for coming long after youth: "If you set fire to the cherries in the mountains/ (and in the vicinity of Tuscany)/ Ouch! 'We must have done something'/ To be loved in such a late season" ("In the Late Season").

But the poems also express displacement, poverty, and a kind of peasant's "reverse pride" in the face of others who are more privileged. The U.S. appears as a kind of Tantalus, shimmering but unattainable: "Lovingly I suspend myself in mid air/ It's not possible to exit or to enter" ("In Flight"). What she sees there are "Those Who Have Arrived":

Now we all have wonderful houses
Stuffed with Ming, Rosia and Picasso
From Sardinia, Saudi and Alaska
Or at least the project of an architect friend
And a piece of land in the Riviera or in San Zeno.
Come, my companions,
From so much art and so much gold.
We have lost friendship and decorum.

She experiences herself as a stranger to this system of American consumerism: "A thousand times poor/ Only snow on a straw hat belongs to me/ Slight gift of heaven/ In a strange country" ("Strangers"). And finally, she expresses what will become the subject of a whole novel: the inevitable solitary end to the journey of the adulterous outsider.

Here we must separate, in the midst of love and such.
Never let me continue on these rails
Lost in the fog and in the terror of the periphery. ("The Railroad")

A very deep displacement had been being acted out in Africa: she had been there with an American, remembering an American father walking half the length of Italy to speak candidly to a girl deposited in the Tyrolean mountains at birth, knowing that she was stuck in the Tyrol with no way to claim her American heritage, and only able to express the insight because she was temporarily outside of ordinary time and in a place free from her wonted "Tyrolean or Roman patterns."

She had not only loved Leonard Doob, but she had also understood that he embodied what she did not have: a world of copious resources, status, financial security, education, and effortless professional and social connection. He made her long even more for America, for a residence in New Haven, for a professional place in the world.

She didn't say any of these things overtly. To Sister Mary Bernetta Quinn she remarked only how lovely it had been to remember "Father" the way he had been before international history made its harsh claims. But Pound's famous walk had also been about secrets, mistresses, affairs of the heart, and more and more secrets until they all had all but obscured her place in the world. And here she was again part of a secret, with someone else's wife and three sons living securely beyond her imposed silence.

It could not last indefinitely, though the affection, respect, and physical attraction did last intermittently for years. The intervening periods of loneliness had to be coped with. Christine Brooke-Rose wrote to say that she would come to Brunnenburg in July 1969. Mary sent back a huge "HURRAAH-HHH." There would be other castle guests, but she could look forward to a gathering of the "select exclusive" MAC. She was certain that Eva Hesse and Mike would come for a long weekend; she told Christine about traveling to see Eva and Mike on Mljet, an island off the Dalmatian coast. The dread of "peripheries" expressed in her early poems turned to a kind of counteraction where she would arrange, as much as possible, for the literary world to come to her as if the castle could become a palazzo of the kind Pound imagined for himself while he was still in "exile" in St. Elizabeths. Christine and Eva encouraged her to work and to make herself the center of a world of endeavor. During these years, she began translating *The Seafarer*, translating Pound's Chinese poems, reading Chinese history, and finishing *Discretions*.

By 1969 she had sent drafts of it to Eva Hesse, Christine Brooke-Rose, and Hugh Kenner. Eva, at least, had known about Mary's plan to write *Discretions* since 1967, when she wrote to tell Christine Brooke-Rose of Mary's "momentous decision" and to describe the great inversion involved in the undertaking: "So the existing situation is about to be reversed and it will be *The Cantos* themselves that are to be used for exegesis!"[39] Each reader had decided views of the manuscript; some were artistic responses; others were rooted in pragmatism, and, at least on Eva Hesse's part, by the circumstance that she routinely dealt with lawyers for Omar and Dorothy in the course of her work translating *The Cantos* into German.

Christine Brooke-Rose went over the typescript carefully and wrote mostly words of encouragement. It was her judgment that Mary should be allowed to narrate her story exactly as she remembered it. Eva Hesse disagreed with her. For the most part, she found the writing excellent, but she viewed things as an outsider and worried that Mary's "imputations" against Dorothy would undercut financial support—which she supposed to come to Mary from the "committeé"—and would undermine any chances she retained, in the late 1960s, of obtaining any share of the Pound estate after Pound died. She objected to Mary's reading of *The Cantos*, claiming that it was wrong to personalize allusions that had more universal application. And she pointed out that legal issues were wrongly argued: Pound could never have been asked to "sign a chit acknowledging his insanity." The United States Justice Department would, of course, have known that such a document was without value. Her main objection was about the Pound/Olga/Dorothy triangle, for, she reasoned, Pound could have divorced Dorothy anytime over thirty years and he didn't. She also found that the "coda" took the wrong tone . . . it departed from the "digested," "filtered," and "beautiful" voice of the first part of the typescript and became, instead a foray into an "acquisitive, bourgeois" world.[40]

She didn't want to upset Mary with most of her criticisms, but with Christine Brooke-Rose she was more candid. She had opinions not only of what Mary should and shouldn't say in her memoir, but also of the life situation of all of the Rudge-Pound-Shakespears. Her view—that Mary and Omar should be joint heirs to the estate—was based on her conception of "moral and social justice." She rehearsed the history of the ménage, as she understood it, with the claim that Dorothy had supported Pound for over twenty-five years and even subsidized some of his publications. She reminded Brooke-Rose, once again, that Pound had chosen not to divorce Dorothy, and thought that a "provoked and condoned act of infidelity some 45 years ago" simply had to be overlooked. She was also afraid that the real danger was not Dorothy, who was in ill health and who, Hesse claimed, acknowledged that Mary had a moral claim to a share in Pound's estate, but Olga. Should Dorothy die, Olga would marry Pound. "If that ever happens, you can image what chances Mary and the children would have of inheriting anything."[41] She also told Brooke-Rose that Mary had fired all her lawyers and seemed to be giving up on the whole business of the archive. No amount of reasoning, she said, would convince Mary to accept a lifelong stipend from Omar. Mary had visited her with Patrizia and the subject was unapproachable—for Mary's reasons of moral and social justice.

Hugh Kenner was blunter. He told her that Omar would sue her for libel if she printed the typescript as it was.[42] He had visited the castle in November 1969. A week later Mary wrote to Brooke-Rose that she was so depressed that she had returned the contract to Little, Brown unsigned. Then there was a spate of further exchanges. John Schaffner, her agent, wrote to ask why it was important for her to mention the fact about Omar's parentage. Mary was flummoxed. "What have I written the . . . book for if people who read it don't know WHY it is important for me?"[43] John Schaffner wrote again, as did Patrick Gregory, her editor at Little, Brown. Then John Monteith from Faber and Faber in London wrote. Gregory had shown him the manuscript and he was interested in bringing out an English edition.[44]

By the beginning of 1970 Mary was cutting and revising. As she put it to herself, the law had intervened in her life again. She substituted Gais folklore and ellipses for the "objectionable" parts of her life story. But to Christine Brooke-Rose, she admitted that the excisions had taken a toll: she couldn't enter her study, avoided her room, her desk, her pen and paper. Brunnenburg received the attentions of a "hyena" with displaced pounding and scraping and painting and gluing. "I have now 'born' a book of my own," she wrote, but she had a horrible feeling. "It's a still-birth. One of my nurse's little boys. I weep over it. It's DEAD—yet, a beautiful blond blue-eyed book, and you have seen it and have even recognized that it looks like me. But the blue box containing the pages is a little coffin."[45] Patrick Gregory at Little, Brown helped her through the revisions and his attention assuaged some of the rage. By January she reported, "I think I am near clean cuts, which will eliminate tensions forever. I feel sad, but strong. I also feel grateful for your and Eva's friendship."[46]

She had little time to pause, and, indeed, *Discretions* had to be put away for a few weeks while she completed Pound's *Selected Poetry and Prose* for Mondadori. She had to go to Milan to discuss details, and she was faced with a bibliography, biographical notes, and over one thousand pages of proof for a June publication date.[47] By April she had finished both projects and expected a visit from Patrick Gregory and his wife. He wanted to change the title of the memoir to *What Thou Lovest Well*. She held firm, weathered his visit and then enjoyed the company of Denise Levertov, whose poetry she had translated into Italian for Mondadori in 1968.

Then the waiting began, with the lives of young people taking center stage. Walter's acceptance to Harvard arrived, but Patrizia, who had taken a French baccalaureate, was thrown out of university in Venice because her French degree was considered invalid. Christine Brooke-Rose offered to help her enroll at Vincennes, where she taught in Paris, but by September Patrizia decided to continue studying Japanese in Rome.[48] For her own part, Mary faced solitude. In October, she steeled herself for Pound's annual birthday celebration in Venice; she read the new novel, *Go When You See the Green Man Walking*, which Brooke-Rose sent as a gift. She listened to her friend's struggles with her partner, Jerzy, recognizing some of her own dilemma in dealing with a man whose "mystical" development she could not share. Brooke-Rose did not know her own heart. Mary empathized, but could offer no advice. She had finally come to understand what she did want, but she knew she could not have it. She spoke of old-fashioned Christian duty; she spoke of compromise. She reminded her friend that work was a kind of salvation.[49]

In March, she had a reprieve. Leonard Doob returned to Africa and she joined him once again. They went first to Legon, Ghana, and then at the end of the month to Togo. Their housing, offered to them by the Ford Foundation, was a basic, motel-style room. They had air-conditioning and comfort, but no privacy, and until they acquired a car, no way to go out to the villages or to the beach. Mary loved the heat, and with Leonard she found "the old magic." She was happy; she was peaceful, and she knew that their sojourn would end in June. While Leonard researched, she followed African studies classes and a course taught by Molly Mahood, newly arrived from Kent State, on the new African novel. To Christine Brooke-Rose she admitted that the publication of *Discretions* loomed as a "nightmare," but she tried to put it out of her mind.[50]

When she was back in Brunnenburg, "for good," as she put it, she spoke of acceptance. There had been no "grand gestures" on parting from Leonard, no "deep unhappiness." There was, she said, nothing to renounce. Walter, who understood something of his mother's life situation, wrote to his grandparents from Cambridge that his mother had enjoyed the African sun and added that he hoped "with the new laws that have been passed in Italy, she and father will be able to find a feasible solution."[51]

III

No feasible solution was immediately at hand. And the parting was in no way as simple as renunciation. Outwardly the summer was once again filled with guests and Mary looked forward to Christine's return to "the green grotto," the set of rooms she most loved to inhabit while writing. With good company in a close apartment, Mary began her own first novel. Its working title was *Kronos* or *Infinite Regress* and her idea was that prose should be written with the same care as poetry.

She had none of Christine Brooke-Rose's penchant for experimental form. The novel was, for her, an exploration of character, an examination of motives, and an inquiry into the hidden dynamics of human relationship. Ostensibly the story of two lovers parting after a week together in the lake district of northern Italy; ostensibly the story of prohibited love, the tale turns, finally, into a set of musings about the aftereffects of history, as if motive were, even years after an armistice, the engine of wartime duplicities. Explanation can, in this book, regress infinitely—"the loom forever pays the debts of the weaver"[52]—but the anxiety of the book is more immediate. There is an aspect of this novel that reveals a preoccupation with secrecy and with the need for revelation, as if the constant presence of people with double identities and covert missions had finally taken psychic seat in Mary's identity.

The moral complications most obviously explored are those, one can imagine, that were presented to Mary by her relationship with Leonard Doob, but they are not only that. They are the result of a life of illicit border crossings and they explore the deepest complexities of international, intergendered, interclassed existence. Through this story Mary named her place in the world and the contours of her interior life as she struggled with it. If the protagonist is named Hera (Hermina Roswita von Weber) because "Her Existence Remains Anonymous," she is also named after the goddess who, according to legend, regained her virginity every year.

There is a simple chronological structure, driven by seven days of travel and ten years of memory evoked by that voyage. The memories of the two lovers are of places in which they have lived in the interludes allowed by married life. They have swum in the Indian Ocean. "[Felt the] salty water off the African shore."[53] They have also gone from "Arusha to Zanzibar, starting at northern Passau"; they have met in Munich, traveled along the Danube, stayed in the Black Forest. Sometimes recollection takes a very particular, intimate form . . . a porch, a eucalyptus tree, a mango, a child playing in water . . . but it is summed up with: "Los Angeles—New York—Athens—Rome—Accra—Nairobi—Dar . . . Milan—Lagos—Munich . . . seven years through the skies."[54]

Their current meeting is in the vicinity of Milan, but the various places they stay are destinations of a Poundian heart revisiting its beloved landmarks. It is a heavily coded trip, dense with allusions to a father who is only named once—as a prisoner of war—but who has taken root in the very foundation of the mind. This inhabitation is displaced onto other historical figures, other works of art, other "saints" and personages, but the text is haunted by "bodies possessed by the spirit of others."[55]

As the lovers travel, their characters are measured by their responses to immediate experiences, and their sensibilities are sharply contrasted: Hera is "in harmony with beauty." Architecture, silent forests, the sea, her love for Hu Bruck are of an aesthetic piece. They call, they awaken, they rouse and satisfy her. She is a deeply religious woman, who now questions received teachings. Adultery is illegal and, according to the Catholic Church, it is a sin; yet to her, loving Hu seems sacred in the same way that Hester Prynne's love for her silent, sin-smoldering minister had "a sacrament of its own."[56] In this narrative, Hu asks her to marry him, has asked many times, and has suffered with her reply, "A Catholic marriage is insoluble. . . . I am inside an iron box."[57]

Once again, the law is pitted against THE LAW . . . a private sense of rightness and sacredness competes with behavior that is socially condoned, as if the lawyers for the archive and for the Ezra Pound estate had transformed themselves into the arbiters of the heart, as if the fictional Bruck wife, sitting inside her snug New Haven community, were a cipher for Dorothy Pound with her lawful position and her fateful status as "committeé"—the legal projection of Pound's personhood, both the blocking figure and the embodiment of what is desired. But it is also as if one's own heart had reseized a familiar dilemma in order to confront, once again, the intricacies of human existence. The position of "intruder without status" is replicated in affairs of the spirit, as once they had been in claiming the material world and one's right to an inheritance. The acceptance of this position, named to Christina Brooke-Rose as quiet and without "grand gestures" of renunciation becomes, through the cover of fiction, something perhaps more akin to the truth. Hera is jealously despairing. "For seven years [she] had howled like a coyote in pain."[58]

Hu Bruck is a professor carrying the desolations of age and professional diminishment in his emotional pockets. He is rational as if reason were itself a religion; his life's mission has been to subject human motivations to scientific scrutiny; and he is seen by Hera as a "stable professor with tenure, head of this, director of that" but more tellingly as "a trapped bird vibrating with energy, pessimism, shyness, joy and fear." Outwardly, at least by reputation, he is standing next to a woman "of strict moral standards, good sense, straight" and both of them need, for a mutual future to exist, to shed their social identities. "How, when, is the snail rid of its house?"[59]

For a week they are unhoused together: he with preoccupations about time and economics and the perfections of the disciplined intellect; she with intense responses to the indwelling spirits of monuments and symbols. In Ferrara she looks at Girolama Savonarola's statue and "reads" it in light of her own experience with both the greatness and the ignominy of Ezra Pound and even, one might imagine, with the Gaudier-Brzeska statue of Pound in mind, for its disposition was becoming as embattled as its subject. In her imagination, Savonarola is not a heretic or creator of the "bonfire of the vanities"; he is not the destroyer of art or the preacher of Catholic fundamentalism, but someone who challenged the status quo. "Anyone daring to attack bankers and popes gets twisted into knots and thrown into the fire."

> There had to be a Savonarola first . . . an explosion of energy and will power to generate the idea of him and another soul to catch a glimmer of that idea, catch the spirit and put it into clay. The sculptor's love for the subject and now her love for the artwork and the subject, gave this statue life.[60]

Hera's sympathies are for the heretic, as if challenge to wonted and condoned behaviors were itself a social good albeit a precarious and dangerous one. What did it mean for her to walk past the Gaudier-Brzeska hieratic head of her father each day as she went to market? It was, we can surmise, an emblem of life that, in this case, belonged distinctively to her, created and conveyed by Gaudier-Brzeska's prior recognition of Pound's "energy and will." Pound and Gaudier-Brzeska are never mentioned in the novel, but the transfer of sensibility offers a coded and moving parallel.

One sees this transference at another tourist site, the palazzo Schifanoja, where the Este family had called their dwellings *Delizie*—delights. The architecture and stately proportions of the rooms are not just that—stately and proportional—but are perceived as a "projection of paradise." Like Pound's project—to write Paradise—the Estes had, according to Hera, a transcendent mission, a compelling need to imagine a better, more perfect human situation, to use the beauty of architecture and landscaping as the momentary counterpart to harsh political realities. She does not see power expressed through materiality, but aesthetic intension inspired by the sacred. Thinking of the sculptures of Bernini and Michelangelo, she also feels an "overwhelming" recognition of "genius" and reverence for their gifts to history.

More telling, however, is the weight Hera gives to three women who had lived in the *Delizie* palace: Parisina Malatesta, Lucrezia Borgia, and Renata di Francia . . . all married in the fifteenth and sixteenth centuries to one or another of the d'Este noblemen, the Dukes of Ferrara. Where others might see women who were bartered in marriage to preserve the political alliances of their families, Hera sees "three beautiful, immortal women [whose fates] outlast and overshadow the glory and prowess of their Lords." Mary's text says, "there were no women, dead or alive, that Hera would have been happier to meet."[61]

But what inverse and unrecognized longing lies in this affiliation? Parisina Malatesta (1404–25) grew up in the court of her uncle, Carlo Malatesta, because her mother was poisoned; she was married to Niccolò II d'Este when she was ten years old, and when she had an affair with Niccolò's son, both were imprisoned in the castle and then beheaded. Lucrezia Borgia (1480–1519), the illegitimate daughter of Rodrigo Borgia (later Pope Alexander VI), was married first to Giovanni Sforza, second to Alfonso of Aragon, and third to Alfonso I d'Este. All were politically motivated marriages and none were without notorious infidelities. Renata di Francia (1510–75), the younger daughter of Louis XII of France, was married to the son Lucrezia Borgia bore to Alfonso I d'Este. Hera does not read their lives as pawns of calculated parental gain but as embodiments of the blessing of her own patron saint, Cunizza da Romano (c. 1198) who lived, according to Dante, under the influence of Venus. Cunizza, too, was married—to Riccardo di San Bonifacio, Lord of Verona—but she eloped with the court troubadour, the poet Sordello. She ended her life in the household of Cavalcanti, where Dante met her and memorialized her in the third sphere of Paradise. There, according to Dante, she told him that she had known love during each stage of her life and that she had nothing to regret.

Overtly these imaginative kinships bless and condone Hera's choice to shed possessions and stability to pursue a precarious liaison with Hu Bruck. They seem to speak about the power of love. Subliminally they acknowledge and resist something quite different: her role as pawn of another sort, the vehicle of her parents' sense of artistic nobility, and the purveyor of their desires. It is as if the silent darings of youth had extended into middle age where one might, with sufficient tenacity, "outlast and overshadow" the lords of the fraught emotional kingdom that was her birthright.

Subsequently she reads "translation," the task of her ordinary life, as if translating were the equivalent of interloping on the affairs of others. It is a tailbone: "All you have left is your work, translat[ing] other people's love stories while you yourself dry up in a broken home, drifting."[62] Hu Bruck is her story, her chosen narrative, the eventuality that needs no interpreter, but as she clearly sees, their meetings are "a couple of nights sandwiched in between one plane and another."[63] These nights assume, however, a defiant independence, for like Eva Hesse, like Christine Brooke-Rose, the lover sees her dilemma, her interiorization of damage. "Forget all the voices that have tyrannized your life."[64]

There is gain here, but the illegal aspect of her situation is never far submerged; its transitory nature announces itself at every swerve of the road: the two fail to stop at the scene of a crash for fear of having to give evidence; Hera's mind echoes with the words of an African border official: "We don't care what you white foreigners do . . . but . . . don't you dare lie to us. We are not stupid; we don't believe you; you are not married."[65] Their status at European hotels is the same. Both lovers, for different reasons, think their situation doomed: Hu because he will neither tell his wife nor commit fully to life with her in New Haven—his ambivalence is expressed in contradiction—thoughts of suicide, commitment to rationality, repeated proposals of marriage to Hera—all coexist in raucous mutiny. Hera despairs because of the prison of Italian marriage law and because of the insufferable waiting between rendezvous. She, too, contemplates suicide, then the convent, and settles finally on the resolution of faith. Remembering Swedenborg's idea of "marriage in Heaven," she realizes that their relationship can be a sacrament but not a social institution. Of one thing she is certain: that Hu is "one who loves you, a friend, who will never hurt you—forever your lover, on your side."[66] And of all the fictional episodes we are forced to decipher in this narrative, this is a statement that one understands to be true in Mary's life outside of art. Leonard Doob did remain a true and loyal friend throughout her life.

He also remained an enigma. What was he doing in Africa? "Argentina, Bolivia, Brazil, Colombia, Cuba"? Hu Bruck is represented as a man who is expertly able to repress, and, according to his wife, to rationalize. Hera only says that "he had responsibilities toward political bodies."[67] But her speculations tantalize. In the novel, Hu Bruck had been Victor Amour's wartime boss; that is, World War II had forged a bond between Hera's husband and her current lover. There is a hidden, predetermined link to this man or as she puts it, "there was a kind of shadow-play going on outside."[68]

Like other inquiries about Boris/Victor, questions posed in this novel lead nowhere; they remain at the level of speculation, so that incertitude becomes itself the subject. As the "shadow story" goes, Victor had never mentioned knowing Hu Bruck during the ten years of his marriage to Hera. He, too, had become reacquainted with Bruck, who had "suddenly" become the most important man in his life, "capable of rekindling old ambitions." By the time Hera had made the connection, it was too late to trust Victor's answers. Her initial response is to deny the importance of this coincidence. "That was wartime. They had lost track of each other. The wartime oaths, sworn secrecy, had nothing to do with it."[69] But the issue of this prior connection never goes away in the novel. The text is haunted by the unspoken. Although Hera lives with the impression that the war is over, Hu tells her, "If you worked in the Pentagon or even in West Point, you might have the impression there has been no change at all."[70]

He is articulating the political philosophy of the American cold war to a woman who has no idea of its existence, but who is astute enough to intuit duplicity and its pressure on ordinary relationships. Was there, in fact, a relationship between Boris de Rachewiltz and Leonard Doob? Or does the novel articulate the anxiety of distrust, projecting into fiction what had to remain unstated and unaddressed in life?

To the extent that one can read *Kronos* as a roman à clef, one can, at the least, understand that secrets, possibly, probably, political, have intervened in private life at Taufers/Brunnenburg for decades. One can see that the motive for living there is no longer love but the desire for truth. The "shadow-play" has episodes and evasions. "That shadow man she had seen in Capri on their honeymoon. . . . An illusion, Victor had said. . . . She was made to doubt it the day she heard strange voices and buzzing coming from the bathroom. . . . Then came the time when she thought Victor was making signals with his reading lamp. . . . She had mentioned the shadows and was laughed at."[71]

> There had once been heavy breathing over the wires and in the background, a noise like the ticking of a clock, no, slower, clearer, like the beat of a metronome. Victor-Hu. The split. What stood between them? Hera. Hera was the space between them. No, not the space, the time. The war time. Secrets, OSS and a young girl in the London W.A.A.F. All spies, weren't they? Cracking codes. What does W.A.A.F. stand for? Intelligence. English intelligence, sleeping with American Secret Service. That's what they both did in London while her own father was sent to die in a war he hated.[72]

The most chilling memory that grows from this veiled inquiry is of a tryst with Hu Bruck seven years ago in Rome, "a mystery never solved." A woman whose photo looked very much like her own, had been killed in the same hotel on the first night she and Hu had made love. Boris/Victor had known about it. He claimed that he had been told that someone had seen her coming out of the Hotel Napoleon. How, possibly, could he have known, when her "cover" had been a visit to her publisher in Milan? She, of course, denied that she was in Rome; it was stupid nonsense. But the suspicions of unseen, postwar maneuverings remain, and they are one of the most interesting constructions of the novel. Hera asks, "What has scared me so, exactly, in all those secret meetings with Hu?" And she remembers a phone line going dead at Taufers. "Hera saw WHY. Hera heard WHY in the time-space of the metronome. The answer. The split. An explosion."[73] Was the other woman in the hotel killed because she had been mistaken for Mary? Why should a love affair elicit fear? What is the full extent of the behavior that educes such anxiety? The text only alludes to an unspecified group of men. "All the names are in the books. But why do they continue to speak of secrets, secret assassins, drugs and alchemy?"[74]

She experiences herself as the link between Hu and Victor, knowing that there was once a wartime connection between them without understanding why there should be a continued link; she experiences fear, without knowing why dread should adhere to affection, and this is all that the novel reveals. One can see this constellation as a fictional representation of unresolved anxieties about being introduced to Boris by the Princess Troubetskoi, who was, in all probability, a British agent working at Rome radio; one can see it as the consequence of other suspicions—that the archeological expeditions were, like Doob's forays into places of world conflict, a cover for some other kind of work—or that his years in Rome with a separate apartment concealed unknown colleagues, unknown activities, and indecipherable connections. In the novel, there is no truth; as a cipher for life, there is even less certainty. But as a statement of preoccupation, the manuscript speaks clearly about a life of continued and occluded apprehension.

IV

In late 1971, while Mary worked on this project, *Discretions* came out. For over a year, reviews poured forth, each different, all of them mindful of a distinctive voice emerging to tell an extraordinary story. Among others, the *New York Times*, the *New Republic*, the *Wall Street Journal*, the *New Yorker*, *Esquire*, the *New Statesman*, the *Nation*, the *Economist*, and the *Times Literary Supplement* all took notice. Philip Toynbee, for one example, was an inattentive reader who got many of his facts wrong—he thought Mary was "farmed out" at age one or two; thought she went to live with Olga and Pound at twelve instead of going to the convent school and so forth. He read the book through his dislike of Pound's "perverse, even wicked" views of the world and thus looked at Mary's account of life with her father as deeply generous. In all, he found her story "shocking." "If a competition had been set by some black humorist . . . to see which couple could devise the worst . . . way of bringing up a child, I think Ezra Pound and Olga Rudge would have stood a good chance of winning it."[75]

Guy Davenport, to the contrary, found Pound, as a parent, to have the same genius that characterized his remarkable poetry. "It is difficult not to see in Mary de Rachewiltz's upbringing a wisdom far beyond the exigencies." He appreciated Mary's "insider" explanations of *The Cantos*, found her to be a rigorous scholar, a woman of character, and of such straightforward talent that she stood in nobody's shadow. He understood Brunnenburg to be the fulfillment of a Poundian idea—a place where people of like mind and gifts could gather, and he read as if rose-tinted glasses were horse blinders. "Henry James himself, if he had ever been disposed to write a story with a conventional happy ending, might have plotted Mary's life." He saw a shepherdess and a princess and, remarkably, that is all.[76]

To Christine Brooke-Rose, Mary wrote that she wished reviewers would quit criticizing her parents for giving her foster care. Gais was, she freely admitted, the best thing in her life. If she had any resentment it was for the role Pound and Olga played in cutting her off from America when she wanted to take her place there.[77] She also wrote to Mary Barnard to say that Hugh Kenner seemed to be the only reviewer who really understood the book[78] . . . as well he might, having helped to engineer its final manifestation.

He called his essay "Impassioned Reticence." "She doesn't want the reader to know what she is telling . . . and yet she does. Pressure, against constriction . . . makes *Discretions* art; art, not 'reminiscences.'" He admitted to his *National Review* readers that he was already part of the inner circle: he knew the dramatis personae; he had been to Brunnenburg; Mary was downstairs asleep in the castle when he first read the typescript. He set the scene of the brooding mountains; he tried to emphasize "the dream" in which a poet and violinist had conceived a child together; he tried, also, to indicate the raw antitheses that coalesced in Mary because of that dream. Who else could "think toward Homer" through *Puschterisch*? Kenner, unlike the other reviewers, knew that, despite the glimpses of Pound taking a child to see Tarzan films and *Snow White and the Seven Dwarfs*, despite the narrative line, which held tightly to the child's perspective, that this was no staunch "we have come through" account. He spoke of sunderings and of realities colliding with dreams. The publisher, he said, wanted an upbeat ending, which accounted for the abrupt "and ever since [Pound] and Mamile have been taking care of each other" final line.

The review was itself a masterful dissimulation. Like the redacted manuscript, it never mentioned what was being withheld or why. He said that the text was made of facts, "only of facts, selected facts." He alluded to "complications" but did not allude to what happened in the space between "facts." Mary's life had been "frayed" by her father's "melodramatic fate," but it had not been smashed. The book was, he concluded, proof of a "persistent heritage" from Pound. Mary was the tender of her father's "great dream, the work in which he 'tried to write Paradise.'"[79]

Behind the scenes, hell broke loose. To the self-contained Mary Barnard, Mary wrote in a similarly restrained fashion, "my parents, helas, did not like my book. . . . No miracle has happened. I am very sad about this but resigned."[80] Eva Hesse heard another version. Olga had written to Peter du Sautoy; Pound had denounced the book to du Sautoy as "'worse than Ronald Duncan's hogswill' or words to that effect."[81] When Eva next saw Mary in midwinter 1972, she found her in "great form," as if "all that chicanery" by her parents had finally freed her from "that awful fixation." But it was a brief respite. By May of 1972, Mary wrote to Christine Brooke-Rose saying that she hoped no more reviews would come out, for every time they depicted Olga in a severe light, "her vengeance is a bit more bitter—I can tell when she has seen or heard some comment by the 'retaliation.'"[82]

In the interim, life at the castle went on. Mary accepted a position teaching English at the local seminary—fifty-two boys aged fifteen to twenty. She read Hugh Kenner's *The Pound Era* during the winter months, startled to find her own conversations recorded in the book as well as an accurate inventory of manuscripts and furniture still in the castle. In March, Graziella married the grandson of an elderly man from Dorf Tirol. Boris arrived at the wedding with a Bengalese woman on his arm.[83]

In the same month, Eva Hesse reported to Christine Brooke-Rose that Mary had been "declared a U.P. (Unfit Person) to be any longer Custodienne of the Phallic Head, which last week was hijacked by two Venetian emissaries."[84]

On 1 November 1972, Ezra Pound died. There was a simple Mass, arranged by Olga on San Giorgio Maggiore; she planned the ceremony so abruptly that Boris and Walter arrived late and Omar not at all. He was buried in a small

Protestant corner of the cemetery called San Michele. Mary admitted that she felt "like weeping for the whole world—yet I am at peace because I know he is."[85]

A few months earlier, on 10 January 1972, Olga Rudge changed her will. There had been two previous wills, one made in 1955 and another in 1966, both of them virtually identical in wording: "I leave all of my property of all kinds and descriptions, real and personal . . . in fee simple to my daughter Mary de Rachewiltz." Then to Walter and Patrizia "to share and share alike." The new will, written in Italian and executed in Venice, said that she revoked all prior wills, that she was of sound mind, and that should she die, she left her house in Venice at Dorsoduro 252 to the "Fondazione Giorgio Cini." They were to use it to preserve and study *The Cantos* and other works of Ezra Pound. She named Giorgio Manera, resident of Venice, as her executor.[86]

CHAPTER 9

Transparency

Publishing the Rome Radio Speeches, 1973–76

I

In the fall of 1973, Mary received a fellowship to the Radcliffe Institute in Cambridge, Massachusetts. To Mary Barnard, she explained, "My activity at Radcliffe is no secret: TRANSLATING CANTOS. Of course, people will start asking WHY it is taking me so long—and the answer is: I try to read all EP has read, and more, and I am a slow reader. As you probably know it is impossible to live in this country without a family or a big income, unless one has some affiliation, and the Institute has provided just that."[1]

It was her second trip to the United States that year. In February she and Patrizia had spent time at Yale—she'd been given the use of a fellows' suite at Silliman College—but it was for the business of settling the Pound estate. To Christine Brooke-Rose she reported, "We have simply all (DP, OP, OR & M de R) signed a 50 page document, signed away I don't quite know what. Until Xmas I've experienced a period of deep devotion & peace. Now it's limbo."[2] She had to wait to find out if her curator's role at the Beinecke would materialize. Eva Hesse, who went down to Brunnenburg in mid-summer, after Mary's return, told Christine Brooke-Rose that she "seemed curiously vulnerable and troubled to me after her stay in the USA, which completely upset her balance. No wonder, it must have been nasty."[3] Several months later she added that she had "learned through L., Mary is having a very hard time indeed. Not financially, although the final installment of the sale of the archives was completely eaten up by lawyer's fees, but because this sticky arrangement of the 3 trustees links her doings constantly with Omar's. And her feud against Omar has become, more than ever, the main theme of her existence."[4]

But Omar was not the main theme. He was an extension of what Dorothy had been . . . part of the "Nessus shirt," a reminder of the power of the law, where she had always to make her own distinctive set of rules for conduct. Radcliffe affirmed her own legitimacy: she was a translator and a poet, and for once an institution offered her a place to do her work. It also gave her a stipend, an office, a view onto the Radcliffe courtyard, and the companionship of other accomplished women. The problems of the Pound archive did not go away, but they were supplanted by the satisfactions of the life of the mind.

She left for Cambridge on 20 September via Milan and Amsterdam, encouraged by her visit with Leonard Doob and Eva Hesse in Munich the previous month. Initially she stayed in the home of Susan Lyman, the dean of Radcliffe College, on Beacon Street in Boston; soon she moved to a Cambridge house-sitting stint for the Williams family at 2 Craigie Circle . . . an arrangement that alternated with staying in a Radcliffe efficiency apartment near the Institute (3 James Street) for the two years she was to spend in Cambridge. She liked the easy elegance of the houses she inhabited when she was in them; she liked the independence of the small apartments when house-sitting was not available. She liked all of her roles: translator, poet, colleague, and "mother of Sizzo" who, though doing military service in 1973, was still working on his degree at Harvard.

The young people she found always a joy, her relationship to them "a new one in fact, and so far the most rewarding & gay or perhaps simply new and funny. Again, and again, 'Oh! Are you Sizzo's mother?'"[5] Life among the Institute fellows was more complicated. She judged them to be first-rate; she enjoyed the lunchtime chats and the dining out . . . worried that she was trying too hard to be charming ("sing for your supper") and wanted to listen more than she wanted to talk. After the first month, she summed up her experiences. "Undoubtedly Cambridge is more pleasant than New Haven & suddenly I find myself with many more acquaintances (and friends) here than at Yale, and my 'role' is naturally much easier (also because I have no emotional complications here) having started out on my own, not as someone's guest, etc."[6]

The social life was the "extra." She was hard at work translating the Adams Cantos and, as she usually did, reading everything that Pound had first consulted in order to proceed. By the end of October, she was deeply immersed in Thomas Hart Benton's *Thirty Years' View*, which intrigued her because the two volumes were not among Pound's personal books. Christine Brooke-Rose sent her a personal reading list: Robbe-Grillet's *Toward a New Novel*, Bakhtin's *Dostoevsky*, and Wayne Booth's *The Rhetoric of Fiction*. She discovered the glories of Widener Library and sought help understanding its labyrinthine storage and retrieval system. She called it pure intellectual greed, admitted that one tended to stop "living" in the presence of such wealth and was perfectly happy. She immersed herself totally in the Adams Cantos and then moved on to the *Pisan Cantos*. This was her planned rhythm.

Each day began for her with a reading from Dante's *Paradiso*—her personal touchstone against "sinking" into academia or the women's movement. Raised in the Tyrol, where gender roles were essential for family survival—baked bread was just as important as raked hay—she failed to understand what American women sought for themselves. The movement did not resonate, even though the Radcliffe Institute had been founded, as had Radcliffe College itself, to address the very lack of educational opportunity that characterized her own life.

It was as if she could temporarily shield herself from tangible history, or at least suspend its demands. As it turned out, neither university politics nor "women's liberation" were the historical tides that pulled at her, but the extended machinations of Watergate and the FBI's response to the public finally learning of partisan intrigue and its cover-up.

In February of 1973 she herself had received disturbing news: she heard that Julien Cornell had given all of Pound's (non)trial papers to the Beinecke Library.[7] Even before the FBI decided to release its own batch of information, the issues of Pound and treason had been made live again after lying dormant for almost thirty years. She had been at Radcliffe for barely one month before she wrote to Olga that she planned to go to Washington to read "those FBI documents of which they gave copies to [David] Heymann and a number of other people." "My battle is to get the wording, the attitude to, the image of Babbo's legal status changed. . . . Basically, you have tried for the same goal and will go on doing it. It is hard, but it gives one a sense of dimension and of 'the possible.'"[8] Never in dream could she have imagined that the fate of the American president, Richard M. Nixon, would affect the course of her private efforts to clear her father's name.

At one point she and Olga discussed going to Washington, D.C., together, but Mary rejected the idea. She and her mother would talk rather than work and work needed to be done. It's not clear exactly when she did first go or how her initial visit corresponds with Eva Hesse's 5 February 1974 report to Christine Brooke-Rose: "Did you read about the ca. 100 letters of EP to Mussolini that the FBI have released from their files in America? It's sure to cause a big stink. Mary was told that this was a direct consequence of Watergate—the FBI not wanting another cover up on their hands! Also, in the files there are a lot of documents showing EP's friends, Laughlin, cummings, W.C. Williams, all acting scared. Williams even offered to perform as witness for the prosecution in the trial of EP. Susan, who saw Mary just when this broke, says she was phoning up everybody asking whether they really did say this or that at the time. Also, as a kind of counteraction, she is planning to publish the radio broadcasts."[9]

In any case, Mary's very first response to reading the FBI files was calm. She informed Olga that there was little contained in the government material not already knowable through the Pound archives. She found a few letters that she had written to her father in the past and reported that none of Olga's seemed to be in the collection. On 30 October, she went to Yale for a celebration of Pound's birthday, and from there she visited the FBI, a trip arranged by John B. Jones. Her first goal was to join the material with the rest of the Pound archive at the Beinecke and to claim copyright for it; and, second, as Eva Hesse had correctly surmised, to publish it. One day of her visit to Washington was devoted to examining the transcriptions of Pound's speeches made in the 1940s as the FBI built its case against Pound; the next was devoted to listening to the old mimeovox tapes, which still existed.[10] For her it was a pleasure to hear her father's voice. Gradually the plan to publish took form.

But Eva Hesse's connection of the release of the Pound tapes with Watergate was a savvy reading of the changed nature of the American political atmosphere. Where once the secrecy surrounding Pound's arrest and detention was an accepted maneuver, the outgrowth of techniques developed by the secret services of World War II and the ensuing cold war, now transparency assumed a previously unacknowledged public value. The hidden agendas, the spying, the secret transmissions of an earlier era had become the vehicle of government corruption. Where she had come to the United States with a completely private agenda—to translate the Adams Cantos—Mary's hand had been forced by an unprecedented public drama that acted out and made visible the damages to public discourse that adhered in the secret methods used not only by the Republican government but also by the FBI itself.

The 1970s saw the release of two sets of "tapes"—Nixon's White House tapes, with their controversial "gaps," and the texts of Pound's radio recordings. The FBI sought to conceal its behavior, its philosophy and, most of all, its myriad files on "suspect" individuals, whereas Mary sought to disclose supposedly damning texts and to bring philosophy and actions to light. One path led, inadvertently, to the virtual destruction of the agency that had hounded Pound throughout the '30s and '40s; but the other path did not lead, nor could it lead, to an unambiguous recuperation. Mary's goal was to provide the prerequisites for the public to judge Pound's words without the intervention of prior interpretations of those words. She meant to re-open the issue of free speech and treason outside of and beyond the postwar climate of opinion that had condemned Pound without looking at the evidence. She wanted his language to speak posthumously. Why the FBI wanted to release the radio texts in 1974, why the publication project came to a head at this date, is less easy to explain.

II

By the time Mary arrived at the Radcliffe Institute, the Watergate investigations had been underway, in one form or another, for over a year. The break-in at the Democratic National Committee that had so startled the press, the public, and the series of officials appointed to sort the matter out, had occurred on 17 June 1972. President Nixon had forestalled various inquiries about the five men involved; John Mitchell, the former attorney general, had denied all links to the burglars; but by October of that year, the FBI had established that Watergate was not an isolated incident but rather part of a pattern, an ordinary but undisclosed practice of political spying and sabotage used by the Nixon reelection campaign—and indeed by the FBI itself under J. Edgar Hoover. In effect, Watergate required the investigators to investigate themselves. This is why the FBI's examination of the Nixon administration's behavior was initially so focused and limited to the five burglars—the Bureau acted as if no one understood that some of the culprits had been former FBI and CIA agents whose techniques had first been learned in the secret services.

Whereas the Bureau had functioned, sometimes with tacit, sometimes with explicit authorization for break-ins, buggings, burglaries, stealing documents, opening mail, and installing hidden microphones for decades, the mechanisms that concealed those activities now failed. Dwight Eisenhower had authorized illegal espionage during his administration; Lyndon Johnson had done the same; Nixon had depended upon Hoover as had no other U.S. president. He had been in the FBI's camp ever since he entered Congress in 1947. Tim Weiner claims that Hoover's "tutelage in the political tactics of the war on communism had been Nixon's primal experience of power." When he came to office he had grandiose plans to get out of Vietnam and to end the cold war with Russia and China—plans that "hinged on secret government in America." "His policies and plans, from carpet bombings to the diplomacy of détente, were clandestine, hidden from all but a few trusted aides."[11]

Although Hoover himself was aging—indeed he was well beyond personal coherence—when Nixon assumed office, and although the FBI was filled with internecine power grabs, the White House and the agency still worked hand in hand to quell flaring political disturbances. Both were convinced that foreign financiers provoked American unrest; they thought that an international Communist conspiracy supported the far left and Black militants,[12] and they were prepared to do "anything it takes" to promote national security. Again, according to Tim Weiner, Nixon knew that opening mail was a federal crime and that "black bag" jobs were similarly culpable. But he also believed that "if a president did it, it was not illegal."[13]

When Hoover balked, the White House began to rely on William Sullivan, who expanded the Bureau's squad of informants to include agents as young as eighteen, who dressed in jeans, haunted American campuses, acted like members of the student movement, and called themselves the "Beards, Blacks, and Broads." The marches that Sizzo had participated in while at Rutgers had likely included FBI infiltrators; they were ostensibly about peace but were implicitly a means of counterintelligence. The various aspects of the program—called COINTELPRO—worked against whites, Blacks, and anyone in the New Left. The files from these secret programs joined Hoover's "diary"—his twenty-seven-year history of the cold war, his handwritten notes that record a "rage [that] was personal and political, bitter and implacable, barking and biting."[14]

The nation watched as one commission after another tried to wind its way through the collusions, omissions, and deals that protected these programs, joining them into a fabric that, had they known it, Watergate merely shadowed. But each investigation hit a stone wall until Mark Felt, a senior official in the FBI, decided to end the agency's cooperation with the White House cover-up by leaking information to the press, to prosecutors, and to federal grand juries. "There is a way to untie the Watergate knot," he told Bob Woodward of the *Washington Post* on 9 October 1972. From this moment, using this undisclosed source, Woodward and his collaborator, Carl Bernstein, slowly sussed out the hidden organization and the line of command that led to the president. "Gray knew," Tim Weiner writes, "The attorney general/CREEP [Committee to Reelect the President] chief, John Mitchell knew. If Mitchell knew, the president knew. And if the facts came out, they would 'ruin . . . I mean ruin' Richard Nixon."[15]

It can be argued that the tipping point in the investigation of Watergate came during L. Patrick Gray's confirmation hearings as Nixon's choice to replace Hoover as director of the FBI. Nixon counted on Gray to be a team player; instead, he handed over the FBI's raw files on the break-in, incurred the wrath of the Nixon administration, scotched his own nomination, and set in motion a series of events that brought down both the president of the United States and the FBI as Hoover had created it.

In 1973, still another candidate for FBI director was put forward. Clarence M. Kelley, chief of police in Kansas City, was confirmed quickly and was immediately confronted with problems as difficult as Nixon's impending impeachment. On his desk sat the history of his service's secret intelligence operations. Shocked and forewarned about the dangers of illegal surveillance, he dismantled Hoover's national security machine.

> By the time he was done, the FBI had eliminated 94 percent of its domestic intelligence investigations, erased more than nine thousand open cases from its books, transferred the roles and functions of national security cases to the Criminal Investigation Division, and reassigned at least 645 agents from chasing radicals to tracking common criminals.[16]

Kelley's redefinition of the function of his agency . . . or rather his return of his agency to the parameters of the law . . . did not preclude further trouble.

In December 1973, the Socialist Workers Party filed for legal disclosures under the Freedom of Information Act, only to discover that they had been "a target of a major COINTELPRO operation."[17] The FBI responded as it had with regard to Watergate by burning thousands of pages of files, once again repeating its own cover-up of illegalities; and once again, they found themselves the further subject of official investigation. Congress discovered that the FBI had bugged Martin Luther King and maintained a half-million pages of files on Americans. The Senate found that the FBI had misused its investigative power by spying on Americans without just cause. It found that the Bureau had violated the Constitution; it created the first guidelines to govern FBI intelligence; and Edward Levi, the next attorney general, said that they had been mandated because "government monitoring of individuals or groups because they hold unpopular or controversial political views is intolerable in our society."[18]

None of these events explain exactly why Ezra Pound's papers should have been released in 1974. It does seem likely, however, that the general housekeeping demanded by the revelation of a government agency with unsupervised powers can go some way toward clarifying it. One can imagine that Clarence Kelley's dismay over the disclosures on his desk prompted the release of Pound's files, or one can imagine that Congress itself, in poring over the thousands of cases it later deplored, felt the need for revelation. One can also imagine that litigation by the American Civil Liberties Union on behalf of a Smith College history professor, Allen Weinstein, might have served as a catalyst. Weinstein had used the Freedom of Information Act to press for the release of the FBI files on Alger Hiss and Whittaker Chambers, and Attorney General Elliot Richardson had ordered that the Hiss files be opened. The *New York Times* was only able to discover that "a Yale professor" had asked the see the Pound files.[19] That is, in 1974, given thirty years' perspective, Pound might have been seen as one of many, a victim of the U.S. "government monitoring of individuals or groups because they hold unpopular or controversial political views."

Or the Pound case could have served as a rather forlorn alibi, as if the agency were saying, "look, we have nothing to hide." If this is so, then the disclosure was, at best, strategic and partial, for it presented the case the FBI had built against Pound but not his self-understanding of his own behavior or his attempt to contact then Attorney General Biddle, or Julien Cornell's freedom of speech arguments that were later subsumed and then omitted under an insanity defense. It was a sleight of hand that seemed to say that even "treason" was now an open book; if a "traitor's" files could be released, then nothing else could possibly remain undisclosed. "Government monitoring . . . is intolerable in our society."

III

Mary could not have known any of this. For her, as for millions of Americans, Watergate was a series of newspaper and television reports that accumulated weight as the press and special investigative committees tried to sort out what was hidden behind the government's continued protestations of innocence. For her the narrative unfolded story by story as Carl Bernstein and Bob Woodward and others of the newspaper corps pressed forward. But it had meanings that were private and beyond the obvious threat to the collective good.

Secrecy had been ordinary food . . . from the hidden upheavals of her birth in Bressanone, to the "hidden nest" of her parents' love life, to the seemingly endless personal time with Boris and his deeply covered mysticisms and Leonard Doob with his obscure purposes in discerning how and why certain world populations behaved the way they did. Secrets explained why her father had been held in an army cage; secrets demanded that she not tell the truth about Omar's parentage, and they spelled out the legalities that prevented her from claiming her own material legacy.

For her there had been no "Deep Throat," no clandestine source waiting in a parking garage to give leads, but only the stark reality of a government reading room where she discovered that people she had considered lifelong friends of her family had, in fact, been the very persons first to cast aspersions upon her father. The "un-redacting" was, to her, a moment's worth of recognition, an unraveling of deceptions held long and close, a facing of grave incivilities, masked, for years, as literary friendship.

So Eva Hesse was right to pick up on the ultimate emotional fallout of Mary's going to the FBI; she was right to notice that the visit eventually led to a series of phone calls to see if the FBI had got it right, that the W. C. Williamses, for example, in whose home she had taken refuge, had offered to testify for the prosecution. She was made with a stern character, but the truth for her was bitter. More than ever, the Rome Radio Broadcasts book came to the fore as a necessity.

She approached Leonard Doob to help her. The request put him on the spot professionally. It was one thing to have a clandestine affair or to serve on a board of directors for the Pound estate; it was another to publish a book with his name on the cover. But he agreed and by the end of 1974 was reading the manuscripts with Mary and trying to sort out factual ambiguities.

He needed Olga Rudge's help, which could not be taken for granted, for Rudge had disapproved of Doob from the beginning, on the grounds that he knew almost nothing about Pound's writing. "I don't know what to do about your outburst against Doob," Mary had written on 6 October 1973. Six months later, she was still defending Doob to her snubbing mother. "Yes 'he does not know enough about Pound,' but by now he knows a great deal more about his ideas and values than Poundians . . . who *interpret* the work."[20] On this one, Olga lost. Doob, as has already been noted, was appointed a trustee of the estate. But her acrimony left Doob in a delicate negotiating position. Rudge had been the only one present when Pound wrote his radio speeches in the 1940s; she was the only living person who could answer some crucially important questions.

In August 1975, after Mary had returned from the Radcliffe Institute, he stopped by Brunnenburg on his return from Cyprus, where he had gone to see if any peacemaking efforts would now be possible. He wrote to Rudge from the Tyrol. In the face of the radio transcripts now in hand, he was trying to sort out a contradiction in public records; specifically, he was trying to answer the question "Did Pound continue broadcasting between July 26, 1942, and March 19, 1943, and, if not, what is the explanation for the gap?"

He spelled out the problem to Rudge: "At this moment we find the following asserted by Niccolò Zapponi ("EP e il fascismo" in *Storia Contemporanea* Anno IV, n. 3, settembre 1973, 423–479) whose article strikes us otherwise as scholarly and accurate: '*Finora, dei discorsi pronunciati al poeta da "Radio Roma" sono state pubblicate soltanto le transcrizioni curate negli Stati Uniti dalla Federal Communications Commission, le quali . . . riguardano il periodo 7 dicembre 1941–25 luglio 1943, con un' interruzione intermedia di circa sette mesi (dovuta presumibilmente a una sospensione temporanea delle transmissioni poundiane), fra il ventisei luglio 1942 et il quattro marzo 1943.'*"

Doob had been assiduous in calculating dates, reading Charles Norman's *The Case of Ezra Pound*, Julien Cornell's *The Trial of Ezra Pound*, and Noel Stock's biography, as well as the work of Eustace Mullins and Richard Chase. Nowhere could he find any transcripts of radio speeches in that seven-month period. But the treason indictment included charges (10–17 and 19) within that period; in fact, it stated "flatly" that Pound was broadcasting during the period between 26 July 1942 and 19 March 1943. He also discovered that Julien Cornell referred to a broadcast on 4 February 1943 . . . but it was only a reference, not a transcript. He spelled out what was at stake in the contradiction: "The statement by Zapponi could be true: Pound did not broadcast during these seven months; hence parts of the official indictment were false. Or the statement itself could be false; but then why do we have no transcripts from that period?"[21]

Rudge apparently did not or could not answer Doob's question, for the book, finally published by Greenwood Press in 1978, states that "neither the Italian Archives . . . nor . . . the papers at the Beinecke Library at Yale University have revealed why Pound ceased broadcasting between 26 July 1942 and 18 February 1943."[22] Nor did Doob explain why the cessation date of the "gap" changed from 19 March 1943 to 18 February 1943.

While the transcripts were being edited, Mary wrote an introduction to the book, which she called, "Fragments of an Atmosphere." Pound's radio speeches, she claimed, had never been "faced squarely." Now was the time to do it and she made her argument for her father's integrity, creating in essay form the defense that had never been made for him in a court of law. What did she care if it was not a message that could have saved him from death in a courtroom? No one had ever tested what the indictment meant: did "treason" consist of (1) the content of what Pound said, (2) taking a salary from the Italian government, or (3) the issue of speaking on a foreign radio in and of itself, regardless of the words that were spoken?

She did not take on the issue of taking pay from the Italian government. This was verifiably true. He did. She did not know how to construe its meaning. Did anyone who took money from a nation at war with the U.S. commit de facto treason? She did not know, nor did she ask, what legalities had governed the fates of other non-Italians who had routinely spoken on Rome Radio during the war, for there were many Allied foreigners—Natalie Troubetskoi for one—on the broadcasting payroll.

Instead, she went straight to what she thought was the heart of the matter: treason involved a clear intent to betray, and here she claimed that all evidence pointed to the contrary. She claimed she knew from years of personal knowledge as she also knew from reading *The Cantos* that Pound was an American patriot. Consequently, she drew a distinction between criticism of specific government actions and general disloyalty. Like conscientious objectors, whether to World War II or the Vietnam War, Pound had disapproved of certain policies but he had done so, she claimed, within the protective circle of the First Amendment's freedom of speech. To her, as to her father, this was the great, untested issue posed by Pound's indictment: could one speak according to conscience, and if so, did it matter on what media one aired those views? Pound was, she said, a man who adopted the Chinese ideogram for "sincerity": "man standing by his word." He did not believe in hiding the truth as he saw it. He said, "I don't know that it is the citizen's duty to whitewash who blundered."[23] This was another way for Pound to express his lack of faith in Roosevelt's policies and supposed motives for waging war. The question implicitly posed by this remark was whether Pound could blunder himself... that is, have mistaken or wrong or bad ideas... while still living and acting within his rights as a citizen. How would one know that one's ideas were mistaken if they were sincerely held? And what was the role of the medium itself? "He insisted that he believed the public assurance given by the Italian government (viz., he would not be asked to send *their* propaganda) absolved him of the crime of aid and comfort to the enemy, and that free speech in an age of radio is a farce if it doesn't cover free speech on the air."[24]

In relating the factual history of the broadcasts, she pointed out that it was James Jesus Angleton who had first interested her father in the radio when they met at Yale in 1939. "Maybe this will interest you," Angleton had written, "MacLeish is the innovator.... The idea is that every American has a couple of ears and that the ear is half poet. That by radio a vast crowd is reached which gets the muse by flicking a button. Hence whole masses can hear.... The poet chooses social subjects and whatever he pleases... the only part that we are concerned with is broadcasting on records and rebroadcasting until the proper effect has been attained."[25] She added that Natalie Barney had been the person who first gave Pound a radio as a gift and thus contributed to setting the whole idea of mass communication in motion.

When she spoke of the content of the broadcasts, Mary said that it was Pound's mistake to fail to see the point where Jeffersonian democracy and Mussolini's Fascism parted. "He kept hammering on parallels between our revolution of '76 and the Axis fight against international loan capital." It was wrong to focus so exclusively on economic reform; his tirades, as she summarized them, were primarily against usury and misinformation. This was not, in and of itself, incorrect—she cited a transcript—"The difference between being free from debt and being free to stay out of debt, is not mine at all, just a translation of the word AUTARCHIA.... Well, 'autarchia' is a Fascist idea, and it is the idea they call 'economic independence,' that's the word, a long phrase, and part of that autarchia is the liberty to stay out of debt" (5 May 1943)—but its fault lay in a misaligned focus on individual Jewish bankers and businessmen rather than the economic system in and of itself. That is, she distinguished between candor and candidly held mistakes in thought and rhetoric. The candor was undoubtedly there. So were the mistakes, although Pound himself did not see them. "If anyone takes the trouble to record and to examine the series of talks I have made over this radio it will be found that I have used three sorts of material: historical facts; convictions of experienced men, based on fact; and the fruits of my own experience."[26]

The question remained: were Pound's ideas—mistaken or correct, obnoxious or savvy, biased or provocative—the substance of the treason charge? If so, did it matter whether he spoke them in conversation, wrote them on paper, or aired them on a shortwave band? Were his ideas intended to incite Americans to cease their resistance to Hitler and Mussolini? Did he break ranks with his compatriots? Did he advise violence? These were not, Mary claimed, his intentions; nor were they in evidence in the broadcasts, which, when they did advocate action, advocated action within a clear government frame. "Use personal influence with Congressmen and particularly let your wishes be known to your senators" (30 March 1943). Or "If there are any New Englanders, if there are any Americans who have been American for three centuries or two centuries or one century, any whose forebears constructed the nation, it is time for 'em to get together and think" (26 February 1942).

In some sense, she acknowledged, Pound was flummoxed: "I know that for years," she quoted him as saying, "the American people were incited against an Italy which was not the Italy that I lived in. Before all wars, before any war, there arises a tide of misrepresentation" (15 May 1943). Mary could judge the ideas she felt were wrong and the rhetoric that she found excessive or offensive. There was no getting around the twisted names: Roosevelt became Rosenfelt; Chiang Kai-Shek became Chaing Kike Shek; "a fair exchange and no robbery" became "fair exchange and no kikery" (16 April 1942). This language was anti-Semitic. But never would she concede that her father's goals had been subversive. And she continued to claim that he had not forfeited the right to utter them even during wartime. Against the unproved accusations of the United States legal system, she reasserted the value of her father's self-defense: Pound spoke according to conscience and according to belief and without the coercion or even the cooperation of the Italian government. He could not, in so individual a capacity, have given "aid and comfort to the

enemy." A salary proved nothing to the contrary. She ended her essay by repeating Pound's assessment of his own material: historical facts, convictions
of experienced men, and personal experience. "What whiteness will you add
to this whiteness," she asked, "what candor?"[27]

It was a daughter's tribute and statement of faith. History would not share
her vision. Daniel Pearlman, one of the book's first reviewers, pointed out
that many of Pound's speeches had been quoted in other contexts. He, like
Mary, saw the value of assembling them as a strategic move. Face the worst,
he said: "This hefty volume—465 pages, including scholarly apparatus—
forces us, for the first time, to take a good long accurate and unexpurgated
look at Pound during the ugliest period of his career and to face again that
old issue so many of us would rather avoid: the seeming incompatibility between Pound the poet and Pound the man, between the servant of the Muse
and the champion of Mussolini, between the creative genius and the ideological fanatic." How could he "espouse so many lies, and how could he out
of love of humanity preach the most virulent form of racial hatred?"[28] According to Pearlman, the worst was there to be found.

A few years later, Tim Redman assembled a broader picture of Pound's
Fascist activities in the '30s and '40s. Correlating the language from the radio broadcasts with Pound's letters and articles, he found the pattern of anti-
Semitism to be indisputable. According to him, it reached its "most violent
and consistent form" in his radio broadcasts.[29] One could imagine, he argued, Pound's founding principle—that all wars benefited munitions manufacturers and loan capitalists—but not excuse his rhetoric. Earlier tendencies
grew more extreme, and Redman correlated their increased virulence
with the beginning of World War II. Where, for example, Pound had written articles for *Il Meridiano di Roma* with titles like "Jews and the War," "The
Jew: Pathology Incarnate," and "Anglo-Israel," Redman considered the views
expressed in them to be primarily economic with only "mild and . . . occasional"
anti-Semitism. This changed to "shrill (broadcast) hostility" that went well beyond name-calling.[30] Pound claimed, "The danger to the United States was
"NOT from Japan but from Jewry. . . . The danger is not that you WILL BE
invaded, it is that you HAVE BEEN invaded."[31] He reiterated the idea:
"The U.S.A. will be of no use to itself or to anyone else until it gets rid of the
kikes."[32] And again: "I think it might be a good thing to hang Roosevelt and a
few hundred yidds IF you can do it by due legal process, NOT otherwise."[33]

Eventually some of Pound's readers went still further, using the radio
broadcasts, in conjunction with all of Pound's writing, to make the case that

his entire life and work could be viewed through the lens of ever-deepening race hatred. Robert Casillo, writing at about the same time as Tim Redman, called his study *The Genealogy of Demons: Anti-Semitism, Fascism and the Myths of Ezra Pound*. In it he asserted that all Pound scholarship had suppressed Pound's malevolent worldview, and that anti-Semitism was a "necessary and indispensable" element of his thought. "Not only does it dwell manifestly within the text, but it figures within its verbal and especially its metaphorical economy . . . a cluster or tangle of varied images."[34]

Years later, in 2015, A. David Moody would see Pound's broadcasts as injuriously mistaken but not malevolent. In *Ezra Pound: Poet*, vol. 3, *The Tragic Years, 1939–1972*, he observed Pound's "habit of identifying and confusing the practice of usury with Jews and Judaism for rhetorical effect had become so ingrained that he could at times lose all sense of the error of doing so, and now the error was bringing him near to evil."[35] If one looked at the radio texts dispassionately, from a postwar vantage point, one had to see that Pound was "using the arguments and the language of Nazi anti-Semitic propaganda, and would almost certainly have been understood in Germany to be endorsing the Nazi measures to rid Germany of its Jews in the pursuit of 'racial purity.'"[36]

Mary could not have anticipated these views, although it would have been impossible to avoid the scholarship that developed in the wake of her publication. Her efforts did not have the effect she desired.

As it turned out, her essay was not included in the *Ezra Pound Speaking* book. In November 1976 the anonymous reader's report came back from Yale University Press, asking that it be withdrawn. Mary would use the essay in various university lectures, but it was not to be part of the scholarly, impartial, and analytical presentation of Pound's speeches. To Olga Rudge she wrote that the press demanded, instead, a series of appendices as the *sine qua non* of publication . . . both content analysis and a quantitative analysis. It was not, she said, that either she or Doob wanted introductions and explications, but that they were demanded so that the volume could fall within the parameters of current social science analyses of mass media. She consoled herself by telling Olga that, should she ever rework the essay, she need not be so "cautious." "By the end of my life I hope to have in *evidenza* all the letters and documents showing up slanderers and falsifiers in *malefede* or out of fears."[37]

Leonard Doob duly provided the scholarly apparatus demanded by the press. He made no judgments about the content of the speeches, saying only that they were part of Pound's legacy and that they revealed what one

American, broadcasting from an enemy radio station during World War II, thought his countrymen should hear. Because they were the basis of Pound's treason charge they could not be ignored. In answer to the question of why he, personally, had undertaken the project, he said only that he had been actively engaged in psychological warfare against Italy, Germany, and Japan during the war and that it had occurred to him that he could use the technique of content analysis that he had used during the war and later in analyzing Goebbels's diaries to organize "this vast collection of words."[38]

Thus, he and his collaborators identified the themes of Pound's speeches—the aims, causes, effects, and future outcomes of the war; the nature of usury, productivity, and regulation in economics; the history and preservation of culture; the nature of domestic policies, foreign policies, and constitutionality; the national referents—the U.S., the United Kingdom, Germany, Italy, the Soviet Union, Japan; the specific persons named and the categories of those persons. Once the themes were identified, they were quantified: what percentage of the broadcasts contained these themes and did the percentages change over time?

What is most interesting about Doob's work is what is *not* contained in his scholarly apparatus, for he did not analyze the principles that governed Pound's supposed propaganda; he did not ask what strategies and tactics Pound employed. Even though he named his work with Hitler's propaganda minister as his qualification for undertaking the Pound project; even though he considered Goebbels's diaries, like Pound's speeches, his "intellectual legacy"; there was almost no similarity between the two endeavors.

The reason for this discrepancy is probably simple: Pound was a rank amateur, and he had no clue that there was a "science of coercion." Those who monitored his broadcasts in the 1940s were among those inventing psychological warfare as "the purportedly scientific application of propaganda, terror, and state pressure as a means of securing an ideological victory over one's enemies." They were busy discussing "the conflict between the democratic values that are said to guide U.S. society, on the one hand, and the manipulation and deceit that often lay at the heart of projects intended to engineer mass consent."[39]

Doob knew how to analyze Germany's techniques of radio broadcasting because he had been part of a team trained to "sacrifice both truth and human individuality in order to bring about given mass responses to war stimuli."[40] He had knowingly "thought in terms of fighting dictatorship-by-force through the establishment of dictatorship-by-manipulation."[41] This wartime training and continued participation in the Rockefeller Foundation's programs on communication research, his affiliation with Hadley Cantril's Public Opinion Research Project at Princeton, and his knowledge of Paul Lazarsfeld's Office of Radio Research at Columbia University gave him the tools to recognize that Ezra Pound had no training, instinct, or personal skill for carrying out a campaign of mass manipulation.

Had he applied the same criteria to Pound's speeches that he used with Goebbels's program of propaganda, he would have discovered that Pound's broadcasts fit almost none of the criteria that would have made his speeches of interest as war information in the 1940s: Pound had no access to intelligence about military events; no information about enemy, Allied, or neutral nations gathered from spies or classified sources; he made no suggestions for action, aside from asking people to think or to discuss things with their congressmen. Pound didn't speak with the intention of damaging enemy morale, since the U.S. was not his enemy and he certainly was in no position to suppress desirable material that would have been useful to an enemy, goad anybody into revealing vital information, or discredit other people's activities. Pound warned against misinformation; he did not knowingly engage in it, and he certainly did not calculate whether his material should be purposefully true or purposefully false based upon credibility as the only standard. He didn't use material from enemy propaganda in his "operations" to diminish his enemy's prestige or lend support to his own objectives. He did not use "black" propaganda—material whose source is concealed from the audience—because he wrote his own narratives.

Of the nineteen criteria Doob used for measuring Goebbels's principles of propaganda, the only one that remotely fit Pound's broadcasts was the broadcasting in and of itself: "To be perceived propaganda must evoke the interest of an audience and must be transmitted through an attention-getting communications medium."[42]

This circumstance, that Pound used the radio, was, if one were to guess what was never revealed in a trial, the heart of the treason accusation. That Doob did not address the question of the medium remains one of the curiosities of his involvement with this project, for it was a kind of finesse, a dodging of a problem that he was well trained to handle. To have spoken of it would have been to tackle the question of Pound's guilt or innocence; it would have required him to take a stand and to demonstrate that Pound was not a propagandist, and if not a propagandist then not a traitor, based on the principles underlying the content of his speeches.

So the book that Mary and Doob put together in 1978 got the material out into the world with no judgments of any kind drawn. It would be years before anyone would tackle the question of "treason on the airwaves" or begin to unravel the reasons that radio was so fraught with dangers.

IV

Not many children need to understand the nature and uses of clandestine radio to evaluate their place in the world. Mary was not aware that she needed to know anything beyond the FBI files. Thus, it is highly unlikely that she could have disentangled the complex web of events and attitudes that had contributed to Pound's indictment for treason in 1943. It was likely she would have seen what was obvious: that, as Humphrey Carpenter reports, Pound was first named, along with seven other people, in a group indictment on 26 July 1943—which was, as it turned out, the day after Italian king Victor Emmanuel dismissed Mussolini as premier. The *New York Times* quoted Attorney General Francis Biddle as saying that the crimes of the defendants were not only "the lies and falsifications which were uttered, but also . . . the simple fact that these people have freely elected, at a time when their country is at war, to devote their services to the cause of the enemies of the United States."[43] The next day, after a grand jury hearing on 27 July, Biddle got what he wanted: a front page headline in the *New York Times*. That is, the indictment served an immediate function in the mass media, long before it could possibly have brought any one of the eight accused people to trial.

But to look at what was obvious was also to call attention away from what remained purposefully hidden. Pound had, ironically, learned of his political vulnerability on the BBC radio, in a public broadcast. He knew only what the public knew and also what was apparent to Italians on the streets of Rome in 1943: that the Germans seem to have taken over the city and that all of its institutions, including the radio station, were in disarray. Carpenter reports Pound wandering around the city after 10 September, the official day of the German takeover. One witness reported him searching the EIAR offices supposedly looking for the scripts of his broadcasts.[44]

In this general alarm, no private person in Italy, or in America for that matter, knew that on 3 September the Italian government had negotiated an unpublicized armistice and that it was the U.S. military rather than the Germans who had surreptitiously expropriated the airwaves of Rome radio to accomplish this goal. They had, in fact, been using these airwaves since May 1943 . . . and thus were in control of Rome Radio transmissions on some of the very dates that Pound had been named as uttering "lies and falsifications."[45] Another way to say this is that Pound's broadcasts, which warned Americans against the "lies and falsifications" of the American government at war, were true in a way that it was impossible for him to know. "Lies and falsifications" were part and parcel of psychological warfare and the military strategies it supported. Both Pound and the U.S. were broadcasting from Rome Radio wave bands at the same time.

Against this vast machine of cultural politics, indeed, unaware of its existence, Mary published a book with the evidence in the case. In quick order, she was defeated by what she did not know. No one seemed to want to hear what she succeeded in putting before the public. Certainly the U.S. government did not, but then, she had never seen the Department of Justice files that reveal that it was President Roosevelt himself who first aligned the concept of speaking on the radio with treason. On 1 October 1942, he had written a memo to the Attorney General planting the idea and implicitly asking for action. "There are a number of Americans in Europe who are aiding Hitler et.al. on the radio. Why should we not proceed to indict them for treason even though we might not be able to try them until after the war? I understand Ezra Pound, Best, Anderson and a few others are broadcasting for Axis microphones. FDR."[46] Nor was she ever to learn that Pound had spoken on airwaves secretly controlled by Americans, who labeled one use of the radio illicit while concealing their own duplicities.[47] In 1978, while reading page proofs in her Yale College guest rooms, she simply wrote to Olga about the long view. "I can only say: the more I read with documents, mss. and letters, the more I am convinced the Vatican's attitude of 100 years postmortem is the wisest."[48] History could judge. She had achieved her goal of transparency.

V

In the midst of sorting out these manuscripts and finding the proper route to publication of the radio speeches, Mary decided to take a trip across the country. She wanted to visit Pound's birthplace in Hailey, Idaho, and proposed to work her way to the West Coast. She had spent the 1973 holidays by herself in Cambridge. To Christine Brooke-Rose she admitted that December and January had been "BLACK, bleak" but she prided herself on having overcome Christmas "sentimentalities." She was beginning to have a sense of being displaced in Cambridge. Despite its friendship circle, despite its professional endorsement, she felt that she belonged either at the Pound Center at Yale or back home in Brunnenburg.[49] Nonetheless, when Radcliffe renewed her fellowship, she was glad . . . a happiness tempered in the fall by discovering that the stipends had been halved and that her beautiful office had been exchanged for a small cubicle with a window in the roof. In November, she gave a reading at the University of Buffalo at the invitation of Christine Brooke-Rose and Al Cook. By March of 1975, she found the tour shaping up. It included St. Andrews College in Laurinburg, North Carolina; Norfolk, Virginia; Washington, D.C. (the FBI files); Boulder, Colorado; and from there to Hailey, Idaho. Finally, she thought, she would visit Mary Barnard in Vancouver, Washington, and then consider going south to accept an invitation from the Robinson Jeffers family at Tor House in Carmel, California.[50]

She and Hugh Kenner were both guests of the English Department at the University of Colorado in mid-April; she used her fees for traveling to Hailey, Idaho, where, as she told her mother, the visit was quiet. Like her previous trip to Wyncote, Pennsylvania, to see Pound's childhood home, it was a private pilgrimage; she wanted no fanfare. "Hailey was," she told Brooke-Rose, "quite an experience—culminating in a two seater plane from Ketchum to Boise, endless snow ranges, in fact more, deeper, higher, whiter snow in three days than in my lifetime so far."[51] Her next engagement was at Simon Fraser University in British Columbia, but her great joy was to visit the Barnards and to give a reading at Reed College in Portland, Oregon.

By May, when she finally came to a standstill in New Haven, she looked back on that time as a chance to be with "a real mother & a real daughter" and especially appreciated the old Mrs. Barnard as a "sweet, courageous, wise old woman." From that moment, the Barnards became a surrogate family, serving as a model for a healthy mother/daughter relationship she could only conjure in imagination.[52] She sent news of her own family: Walter was in Morocco with Boris, having turned military service into civilian service by "saving monuments," and Patrizia had turned from the study of Japanese language to the study of Japanese painting and then gone on, in Breda, Holland, to study painting at the Academy of St. Joost.[53] She also sent a copy of her curriculum vita for Mary Barnard to critique. "Sadly, I am learning that I must now play the 'career game,' though I don't know the rules (and moreover must abide by the Laws set down in *The Cantos*)."[54]

By 1974, with no formal education beyond the prewar academy for young ladies in Florence, she listed her accomplishments: In book form: *The First Decade of Cantos*, 1952; *Three Cantos*, 1954; *Introduction to the Noh*, 1954; *Nishikigi, Introduction by W. B. Yeats*, 1957; *Brancusi, an Essay*, 1957; *Gaudier-Brzeska, an Essay*, 1957; *Canto XCVII*, 1958; *Cathay*, 1959; *The Chinese Written Character by Ernest Fenollosa and Ezra Pound*, 1960; *Canto XCIX*, 1960; *Certain Noble Plays of Japan with an Introduction by W. B. Yeats*, 1961; *Cantos I–XXX*, 1961; *Canto XC*, 1966; *The Noh Plays*, 1966; *Ezra Pound: Selected Poetry and Prose*, 1970; *Selected Cantos*, 1973; *Drafts and Fragments*, 1973. She had translated e. e. cummings's poetry into Italian between 1961 and 1967; she had translated Denise Levertov's poems into Italian in 1968 as well as the work of Ronald Duncan, Marianne Moore, and James Laughlin. She listed three books of her own poetry in Italian (*Il Diapason*, 1965, which won the Cervia Prize; *Di Reflesso*, 1966, and *Processo in Verso*, 1973). There were essays in *Esquire*, *Arion*, and the *Texas Quarterly* as well as the English and Italian versions of *Discretions*. She could now name herself as the curator of the Ezra Pound Archive, Center for the Study of Ezra Pound and His Contemporaries at the Beinecke Rare Book and Manuscript Library, and a second-year fellow at the Radcliffe Institute.

It was an impressive list of achievements, the record of a life devoted to the study of modernism and a life devoted in particular to Pound's cantos. None of it was ever to land her a formal, tenure-track job and, as she reported to Brooke-Rose, the curatorial position at Yale was slated to end in 1982. As her Radcliffe years drew to a close, she also faced the rejection of her novel— sometimes called *Infinite Regress*, sometimes referred to as *Kronos*. To her mind, James Laughlin had written an evasive letter saying that it was not "experimental" enough for New Directions—though Mary wondered how he measured experiments.

These experiences drew forth internal divisions that seemed as much a part of her birthright as bread and butter: she wanted to be part of academia as much as she wanted to dig potatoes; she was drawn to the life of the mind as strongly as she was held to the earth by its produce. How one could keep the spirit alive in both circumstances was a problem she discussed for years with Brooke-Rose. She found herself "buried" at the Beinecke Library; she considered the committee meetings for the Pound estate "painful and wasteful"; she valued Brooke-Rose's companionship because her friend never seemed to "succumb to academic routine." And yet she needed and wanted these aspects of existence. Those people under thirty, those who had passed through "the wandering stage," were the people she most identified with as she herself approached her fiftieth birthday. They understood "the urge to study science, architecture, biology, metallurgy etc. without hope of promotion within the system but for the poetry inherent."[55]

Suddenly Olga wrote to ask if she had been following the political situation in Italy. Then Mary heard news about Boris that shattered bone. "I am aware," she told her mother, "that a huge scandal may break out in Italy/Merano/Rome because of Boris. I hope I can finish my work here and return in May."[56] Boris had apparently leveraged Brunnenburg to finance his trip to Morocco. He had persuaded Walter to countersign the note. With renewed force, the instability of her position in America seized her. "To be alone in this country is bitter and now that Brunnenburg may be lost I have no anchor left," she admitted to Olga. Finances pressed at her from all sides; ironically, they seemed to be American rather than Italian finances. "There are no 'gods' in this country . . . this is, as Babbo used to say, a country for millionaires. The poor are destitute." Despite her worry, she defended Boris. In her eyes, he had more right to Pound's resources than Omar did, and she resisted Olga's insinuation that the Barattis ("they") had worked against her or married her only for money. "If anyone has been wronged, it is Boris."[57]

This spring she tried, despite her anxieties, to renegotiate control of copyright with Omar. Seeking Olga's support, she proposed to the Literary Trust that Omar receive all the Gaudier-Brzeska and Wyndham Lewis books at Yale if he would renounce copyright—noting, too, that one third of account money went into administration expenses. This was to no avail. Omar took the view that such a decision would deprive his children of future income, and the Trust took the view that no changes could be made in its structure while Olga Rudge was alive. The good news was that Sue Hilles had built a small, bucolic house in the woods outside of New Haven and had asked Mary to become a semi-permanent house-sitter. No ambiguities clouded the happiness that came with this suggestion. Mary took it with her when she returned to Brunnenburg that spring.

She and Walter took out a mortgage. The situation, as Eva Hesse surmised, was more complicated than Boris's debt, though that was problem enough. Walter had had to sign a guarantee with or for his father; funds had to be provided to keep Boris from prison, and part of the proceeds of the estate went to this use. It was at this point that Mary instigated divorce under the new laws that now permitted the dissolution of marriages in Italy. She and Boris were to remain loyal to one another—she told Olga that he had the skills and perseverance to negotiate with Omar—while at the same time drawing clear delineations in their private lives.

There were other issues with Brunnenburg having to do with the farmer who occupied part of its structure. Eva Hesse reported that Mary was trying to sell three parcels of land to some "rich Germans," but these plans were being thwarted by her tenant farmer who, under Italian law, had some claim to it by virtue of the long years he had worked the land. She was trying to buy "the tower" portion of the castle for Walter, put in plumbing throughout the buildings and provide for the farmer's greater comfort. The problems were multiple and she summarized them by saying that Brunnenburg had been "burning since Christmas" and by telling Hesse that she now loved Canto IV above all others since she identified Brunnenburg with Troy.[58] "Palace in smoky light/ Troy but a heap of smoldering boundary stones."

Olga's inquiry about politics more generally had been met with a sort of indifference. "I confess I have not followed Tyrolean politics," she told her mother. Among the Italians she said that she expected the neo-Fascists to win there—"which is better than communism I suppose but not much."[59] But soon she, like most Italians, retracted her cavalier attitude. In the previous December she had written, "I hope the newspapers are exaggerating the state of affairs in Italy."[60] But there were few exaggerations in those years of general social and political turmoil. In retrospect they would be referred to as *anni di piombo*—years of lead—and her return to Brunnenburg was preceded by multiple waves of terrorism and two bombings, one in May and one in August; the first in Brescia during an anti-fascist protest in Piazza della Loggia, the second in a train of the Ferrovie dello Stato. First eight people had been killed and over ninety wounded; then twelve people had been killed and forty-eight wounded. It would take years to sort out what groups held the responsibility for this strategy of tension, and Mary had no idea that these events, along with the Piazza Fontana bombing in Milan five years earlier, would also touch her life.[61]

CHAPTER 10

Safe House

Brunnenburg, 1976–84

I

First there was a respite when Mary returned to Brunnenburg. Years later, after another such homecoming, she described the castle as a place "with all its problems insoluble,"[1] but in 1976 she was hopeful about it. "Brunnenburg," she wrote, "is finally becoming what it was supposed to be."[2] After a month of furious work, she paused to observe that the "smoldering walls of Troy" were beautiful to her, and she wanted an internal landscape that matched her well-swept rooms. She wrote to Olga saying that she had been surprised by the various responses to the publication of *Discretions* and that she had been "heartbroken" that her mother didn't like the book. It was, she said, a "mistake" to have published it. Could they not live with each other on another plane "disobeying unto victory until we can also say, 'I hate no one.'"[3]

It was a hope as fond as it was futile, and Olga was not her only antagonist. Boris waited with long-covered secrets, immune to Mary's Christianity, living outside of her Confucian ideals. She proceeded alone. The idea of the useful as beautiful was always in her mind. She wanted Brunnenburg to be the strong stone house described in *The Cantos*, but she did not want it simply to be a place to be viewed, dramatic as that high-perched dwelling was. She wanted it to have clear functions. Working farm, yes, but more than that: a tribute to her mountain past; a tribute to her father's genius; a tribute to integration, as if her own gift for translation could find material in rock as well as words. Pound had written about art as a form of making, science, and production; he had said that the engineer was an artist whose "best form comes from the mathematics of strains."[4] He had admired the form and generative power of tools in and of themselves. She thought that Brunnenburg should grow out of those strains. It should become something new through the tensions of her own upbringing, united, reconfigured and made into an organic whole, a habitation as distinctive as any in the world of letters. W. B. Yeats had Thoor Ballylee in the west of Ireland; Robinson Jeffers had Tor House where the land met the Pacific Ocean in California. Mary had Brunnenburg.

As an idea, it was complicated; as a task, it was even harder going. "Dear old house," she wrote, "Corroded by worms/ Stone fungus/ Wood and mold/ Constructed on sand/ How much longer will/ I be able to keep/ You alive by love's fury/ And force of will?"[5] The battlements were crumbling; earthquakes threatened it periodically; it was cold. Sometimes it seemed like a solitary outpost on the periphery; sometimes it seemed like a hermitage; but she wrote about lovely occasions within its walls: It was a "mirror of my soul," maybe without carpets and protection from the elements, but heated from a real fire whose light could refract the beauty of beloved eyes.[6]

In 1972, Walter became part of the vision. He could see the divisions of his mother's life, the diverse longings precariously balanced through forays out into the literary world and return to the soil. He decided to make a farm museum at the castle. In the same way that his grandfather gathered photographs of machines, displaying their formal integrity as if they were worthy museum pieces, he gathered the farming implements of the Alto Adige, seeing that they carried the sundered parts of Mary herself. The tools were witnesses to her alpine, agrarian past; by framing them, Walter implied that the objects were art that obeyed distinctive rules. To frame was to value; it was to see that utility was beautifully at the core of life itself.

And so, with the help of fellow graduate students from Harvard, Walter began to build at Brunnenburg, slowly assembling and displaying the special equipment that made life on the steep alpine slopes possible. He reconfigured anecdotes and personal memories as a heritage for visitors. Gradually he made rooms devoted to ironwork, winemaking, cooking, and transportation, turning the museum into a resource for ethnology, folklore, and folk art. It opened officially on 14 September 1974 with a presentation of papers, formal speeches by local authorities, and music by the ensemble "Oswald von Wolkenstein." He also used the occasion to inaugurate the Ezra Pound room with an exhibition of work by Paul Floras. In 1975 Mary reported to Sister Bernetta Quinn that they had made a small chapel enclosed by a railing.

It was under a vault; it contained a crucifix and, in her mind, it made the courtyard into a basilica where the family lit candles at Christmas.[7] They finished the smithy in 1976.

By September Mary was able to write to Mary Barnard that Walter had definitely "opted for the Tyrol" versus the U.S. But the building projects did not address her own sense of displacement; her inner divisions were still too deep; she could not let go of wanting a house in New Haven.[8] It is not clear if she sensed that this would never happen. Brunnenburg was to be her last home. The high mountains slowly made their final claim.

It is certain that her thoughts still turned to Leonard Doob. "If your lover lives/ In another hemisphere/ Physical and mental/ Don't remain," she told herself. Where did she belong? Brunnenburg received all of Walter's loyalty. For her, the castle remained divided by time and continents.[9] International flights, traversing the heavens, coming and going from life at Yale still preoccupied her and presented an old series of dilemmas. Her own infidelities also weighed on her. She tried to confront them from a generational perspective, writing that her father used to say that "Marital fidelity/ Frequently skips/ A generation."

> But he excluded himself
> From the annotated list of grandfathers,
> Faithful and unfaithful.
> So, I arrived at the junction
> not knowing which way to go,
> Nor have I ever explained
> The mechanism for proving nine
> In mathematics.
> It is clear to me I am the only one
> Who is $\sqrt{}$
> In two.[10]

She wrote about the distance between herself and Doob; she wrote about waiting with a secret. Who could tell that she was loved from afar? "Love is a short season," she noted: "And I say:/ Why are you not here? / And in your letter you say:/ Why are you not here?"[11]

These ties to the U.S. colored her relationship to Brunnenburg, to Dorf Tirol, and indeed to the whole region in which she was born. Years later, in writing an introduction to *Gocce che contano*, Luca Cesari pointed out this dual allegiance: he saw in Mary's poetry a spiritual affinity with the cold mountain heights of the Alto Adige, but he saw it tempered by her American origins. "Think of the same language of Thoreau transposed into the valleys of Trentino. This is the America present in the depths of her upbringing, a mentality of colonial exploration that finds its own New World in mountain pastures."[12] His description glossed over the wrenching displacements of identity posed by two continents. She loved America, felt excluded from it, and experienced the Tyrol as both home and banishment. "After God and the Tyrol/ Land of exile/ One knows that I love you/ America, my country/ And I am intent on protecting/ The false names."[13] For her, the glacial Ahr River spoke to her of defeat: "Here lies the torrent of tears/ That was rejected by the country/ With the Schuylkill, the Potomac/ The Hudson and the laughing waters of Hiawatha."[14]

Gradually, over who knows how long a time, the castle became something more than a house, something more akin to St. Teresa of Avila's *The Interior Castle*, the measure of an inner journey. It became a metaphoric way to articulate the tension between the two halves of her life. Walter's projects excited her, but there was more: the weight of the past, the memory of discord, the sense that height itself contained danger. She wrote: "The dreams buried in my house overwhelm me/ More than a thousand tombstones and urns of alabaster/ Grand fathers bind me to this shrine."[15] As much as she embraced her fate as the daughter of a poet, as much as she saw Pound as an immensely great teacher, Mary understood that Brunnenburg also represented a choice that precluded other desires. She identified it as "the graveyard of dreams," seductively beautiful and damningly heavy. She understood herself to be burdened by family history, a caretaker of stones.

In the 1980s, she looked back and remembered a time when the castle's foundations had fallen apart.[16] Just as New Haven and the Tyrol stood in strained opposition, so the life of her mind clashed with the demands of the practical world, represented in her poems as a tension between contemplating the mountain heights and failing to notice flaws in the foundation. She accused herself of looking up, as if the air contained idealism, instead of attending to life's basic problems.

Ostensibly, she worked: translating, proofreading the Rome Radio broadcasts and improving the castle. Editing made her reflect on the clarifying role of time. As she sat at her desk, she admitted pain, conquered self-pity, searched for serenity. At the same time, she reshaped the gardens, the vineyards, and the guest apartments. One set of activities mirrored the others, and there was new reason to persist. She was helping Brunnenburg become the Pound Study Center that had failed to materialize at Yale.

In 1975 Ronald H. Bayes, a poet and teacher of creative writing at St. Andrews Presbyterian College in North Carolina, invited Mary to St. Andrews, and, with her encouragement, he began planning a five-week summer session at the castle. Six students were slated to come as part of a pilot project—something that might become, and did become, a permanent arrangement.[17] Later in the summer, she negotiated another summer seminar, announced by *Paideuma*, the newly established magazine for the study of Ezra Pound, in its January 1976 issue. The initial project, organized by Peter Way and William McNaughton, envisioned twenty-five people coming to Brunnenburg for three months. Mary thought the idea unworkable and recommended six students for five weeks.[18]

McNaughton and Way eventually assembled fifteen writers and scholars[19] who came to Brunnenburg from July to early September 1976. Sponsored by Arts and Letters: A Center for Classical Studies, which was located in Oberlin, Ohio, the group focused on "West Easternizing" and "East Westernizing," and it supported Pound for his "Kung/Dante/the Greeks" outline of *The Cantos*. Each morning the participants read between two and five cantos aloud, discussed how best to read the poems and then contributed specialized knowledge of Greek, Latin, Italian, and Chinese. Mary read the two "missing" cantos in Italian and offered insight into the autobiographical aspects of the tale of the tribe. Sister Mary Bernetta Quinn came; Giovanni Scheiwiller came and, remarkably, Leonard Doob visited several sessions, reading from his introduction to the radio broadcasts.

The gathering was, for many, a tribute to Pound in Europe, for they spent extra time visiting sites made famous by Pound's writing: Paris, Poitiers, Excideuil, Montségur, Verona, Rimini, and Ravenna were on the list. They made these excursions on their own, and then most of them spent the first week of July together in Venice. It was a time filled with music, recitations, and endless talk that extended well beyond the formal morning sessions. By the winter of 1976, McNaughton could report that the experiment had been such a success that the Center for Classical Studies would finance a second gathering in the summer of 1977.

These and other summer sessions grew for over thirty years. Mary's initial response was positive: the new Poundians were great assets, with "most admirable intentions-into-action."[20] Here, in her own environment, she taught, shared a lifetime of private insight, and gave voice to the years of dedicated study that informed her life. Eventually Guilford College, Green Mountain College, and the University of New Orleans joined the company of fledgling Poundians, bringing students to study creative writing, painting, and anthropology, as well as the poetry of Ezra Pound. The de Rachewiltzes rebuilt the farmhouse so that students could live at the castle instead of walking down from lodgings in Dorf Tirol. They established principles to guide the experience of their guests: practice, purpose, and production supported each student's experience of the Tyrol; these values stood in implicit contrast to theory, subjectivity, and usury. Many programs, but especially the program established by Philip Leist of Green Mountain College, emphasized environmental ethics, sustainable farming systems, and animal husbandry. For Philip, the three years (1993–95) he spent in the Tyrol were transformative: "The years at Brunnenburg were probably the most critical of my life," he wrote in 1995. "I had an ideal balance of duties in my role there as teacher and farmhand, and the environs suited me like no other. Part of my attraction to Südtirol has always been the fact that the slopes inhibit machines but foster technical innovation and intensive labor . . . one must work within nature's bounds and within one's own limitations."[21] Students who came to Brunnenburg were expected, like Philip, to work in the vineyards as part of their experience of life in the Alto Adige.

Over the years, the energy and focus and intellectual exchange generated by these university affiliations shifted Mary's feelings. Where once the castle had been both home and exile, a beautiful place located in a small village on the periphery, gradually it grew into a center for herself as well as a center for the study of Pound.

She did not entirely sever her ties to the U.S. In 1976 Mary flew to Yale and then to the West of the United States, going to Reed College, then to Stanford University; and Albert and Barbara Gelpi drove her to Carmel to see Robinson Jeffers at Tor House. Two years later in April, she was back at Yale, planning another great trip west, flying to Seattle, then to the University of Idaho in Moscow, where Marshall McLuhan was giving a lecture on Pound. Then she planned to go back to Yale with a return to Moscow in time for its commencement.

In 1978 on her annual pilgrimage to the Beinecke Library, she included a trip to Washington, D.C. "I am going . . . to Saint Elizabeths to look at Babbo's files. I probably won't understand much, but at least I will have an idea and be in a better position to veto (or perhaps encourage?) access to others. In effect, the case is NOT closed."[22]

There is no record of Mary's immediate response to this experience, but her open-mindedness and sense of relieved discovery can be glimpsed in the publication of E. Fuller Torrey's *The Roots of Treason: Ezra Pound and the Secrets of Saint Elizabeths*, which came out a few years later in 1984. Torrey's thesis was that Pound's insanity defense had been contrived from the beginning, a strategy trumped up by doctors and lawyers alike to avoid almost certain death from a guilty charge of treason. For Torrey, himself a psychiatrist at St. Elizabeths, this charade was anathema, both a perversion of justice and a blot on the integrity of his profession. He faulted Dr. Winfred Overholser for shielding Pound, and he faulted Pound for abandoning the intellectual honesty that had previously guided his life. He considered that Pound needed to be forgiven for not standing trial; he educed as evidence Pound's own cry for charity: "Let the gods forgive what I have made/ Let those I love try to forgive what I have made."[23]

Mary did not agree: the conclusions to be drawn from the opening of Pound's medical files were not at all straightforward to her. She took from them assurance that her father had not been insane. Dr. Overholser left few of his own files on record, but the yearly nursing reports and the doctors' "chronic notes" revealed a patient who was "quiet and cooperative [and] fully oriented," a person "correctly oriented in all spheres."[24]

Privately, and as she admitted publicly at a 1988 James Joyce Symposium in Venice, the experience had been extremely important to her; for it fit into her lifelong mission to reclaim Ezra Pound's reputation. The records of St. Elizabeths reassured her that the radio broadcasts, whatever else they might be, were not the rantings of a lunatic. She decided to make everything available for posterity to judge. Torrey's conclusions (he thought that St. Elizabeths served as a country club for Pound, providing comfort, good food, and even sex at the taxpayers' expense) probably distressed her, but she refused censorship.

To go to St. Elizabeths had required bravery, for the summer of 1978 was difficult. Mary Barnard had come to Brunnenburg in June, picking up an old and valued friendship. When she and her companion Mildred Cline left, Mary sat down and wrote: "The best gift/ An old friend/ Leaves behind: a myriad/ Of things/ Unsaid."[25] She regretted that they had not had enough time to discuss her current poems, but she was preoccupied. Her old nurse was in Martinsbrunn, the clinic that had cared for her father, after a year's stay in a hospital in Bruneck. Mary went daily, carrying private wounds from her recent interactions with Omar Pound.

He had written once again to remind her of her legal status: "My attention has been drawn to a recent article on EP . . . referring to yourself as 'EP's only offspring,' which surprises me since I am alive and well. I have taken the matter up with the Editor of *The Christian Science Monitor*."[26] Mary dealt with this by resolving never again to refer to herself as Pound's daughter and could do so by separating her personal feelings from her work. But her work, most importantly, was now to publish Pound's correspondence with his parents. In this way, she reasoned, she could demonstrate Pound's filial devotion both to parents and to country, and some of the truth of her birth could come to light. But in 1978, just at the end of Mary Barnard's visit, she received word that Omar had vetoed this project. It was a blow, especially since she had approved Omar's proposal to publish a book of courtship letters between Pound and Dorothy Shakespear.[27] Mary Barnard remembered the day: "Yes, I was there when you received word that Omar was blocking your publication. . . . We [Mildred Cline] both observed and commented to each other that you seemed to have relaxed and become more at peace with the world just during that short stay. . . . And then the morning we left you received that letter, so that we left you in SUCH a state."[28]

By the time Mary Barnard returned in 1980, the domestic scene at the castle was more tranquil on the surface. Mary had returned from the University of Toledo, where she had read from *Discretions* and *The Cantos*; there were plans afoot to commemorate Pound's ninety-fifth birthday; Patrizia had had a second son, and Walter was anticipating his own marriage in the fall. Noel Stock was in residence, and Brunnenburg was becoming more beautiful with the installation of iron gates—a birthday present to Mary—and the whitewashing of tower stairs that now extended up to the roof. When Barnard arrived, Mary was busy readying Patrizia's apartment, and Walter, Graziella, and Louis all joined in greeting Patrizia's arrival with the babies in what Barnard called a "beautiful homecoming scene."[29] The two boys, Demian and Cyril, were a joy. Dinners were preceded by companionable vermouth; both women worked and talked, agreed and disagreed, and through all the variation of days, they remained friends.

Under the surface, anxieties simmered. Mary fretted that "the Pound Industry" ignored the radio speeches. The entire "colony of Poundians" was silent. How could they remain mute when the speeches continued to be insulted as "bizarre aberrations"? In her judgment, her father was "wrong because of anger, bad temper, pride . . . yes, but despite all this he saw RIGHT in the main issues."[30] Mary Barnard noticed "tension, urgency, dogmatism" and worried that her friend seemed "at the bottom of a well."[31] The two women had genuinely divergent opinions on some subjects, one being Catholic, the other not, but both agreed that Mary should not go to the next Pound gathering in Orono, Maine, and they anticipated making a trip to Ireland together the following summer. Theirs was a friendship that survived moods, and indeed it deepened as they aged, for Mary Barnard, in searching for her own ancestors on Nantucket, discovered that the Pounds and the Barnards were distant cousins, "twelve times."[32]

The two Marys met again that fall at St. Andrews College in Laurinburg, North Carolina, where Mary quoted from *The Cantos*: "O God of silence make clean our hearts within us. Be men, not destroyers. Let the wind speak."[33] She brought the vatic parent with her, "the greatest, kindest and most marvelous father," and spoke about the poet's obligation to take risks, to love in original ways, to consider history and to view life from unexpected perspectives. She claimed that Pound "loved America more than anything," and that he didn't reject America. "America rejected him."[34] She was unwavering in this belief, and she later considered that she, too, had acquired that outcast status. "Feeling 'rejected' (that old inherited wound) by the USA; I have started to write in Italian again."[35]

II

In 1984 Boris was arrested and charged with gunrunning. On 2 February, Bruno Borlandi reported in *La Notta* that "his highness, the serene" prince was suspected of using archeological packing cases to smuggle guns into Libya. How, he asked, could a scholar, indeed, one of the foremost Egyptologists of his time, be implicated in clandestine arms trafficking? He pointed to Boris's tireless efforts to restore the historic Brunnenburg castle, to his search for "extraterritorial" status for his land (a protection, he claimed, should the cold war between the United States and the USSR turn into actual belligerence), and to the fact that Ezra Pound had lived there upon his release from St. Elizabeths. The story seemed like something out of a "yellow thriller." A prominent academician, a titled aristocrat, the founder of the noble order of Canossa could not be involved in such a mess. The reporter was incredulous.[36]

Nonetheless, the indictment was a fact. Vincenzo Mannino, a Roman prosecutor deeply involved in civil defense cases, pressed charges against Boris and twelve others, contending not only that Boris operated his African expeditions as fronts for arms passing into Libya, but also that he recruited mercenaries to fight there. He had, according to the indictment, used his "fragile" shipping boxes to avoid ordinary customs inspections. They were suspect because one might anticipate such cases to be imported with valuable archeological finds, but not exported, as they had been in this instance.

In the 1980s, this was not a light charge: tensions between the U.S. and Libya had escalated to the point of armed aggression. President Reagan had expelled all Libyan diplomats from the U.S.; he had evacuated U.S. citizens from the country, embargoed Libyan oil exports, and had shot down several SU-22s over the Gulf of Sidra. General Qaddafi, supported by Soviet armaments, had, upon first taking office, closed all U.S. military bases on his soil. If the U.S. or NATO needed arms on the ground for resistance, this was theoretically one way to do it.

Nothing in this case was clear-cut. Certainly no U.S. involvement in the shipments was ever uncovered, but the charges did not go away. Boris was arrested in his apartment in Rome and, in a terrible irony for Mary, imprisoned in Pisa. Later he was granted house arrest at Brunnenburg, but the actions of the Italian government were severe.

News traveled fast and it complicated Mary's life in the U.S. She reported to Olga that things at the Beinecke were somewhat tricky, and that James Laughlin had refused her telephone call. "Anne [Laughlin] . . . knew about Boris. 'Someone' who reads Italian papers told them Boris would be put on trial."[37] To Mary Barnard she first wrote simply that Boris was in "deep trouble and ill health." The following year, she expanded, explaining that he had been incarcerated for recruiting mercenaries and providing weapons. "Rzzzzomantic as the accusation may sound, I believe him; he did *not* DO any such thing. But he has been in jail for 18 months and one of the places was Pisa! When I visited him on August first—cement blocks worse than tents. Anyway, not for Christmas, the New Year they sent him here. And although I did everything I could to get him released, I am now unable to be kind and generous and it distresses me. If love be not in the house there is nothing—the line an obsession."[38]

This case seems to have hovered, unresolved, dismissed, and reinstated, for years. The venue was moved from Rome to Milan; the initial judge, Guido Salvini, was apparently unable to unearth sufficient evidence to proceed and dropped the charges, but not before it made headlines again. This time the *Corriere della Sera* reported the names of the gang that had attempted the gun running . . . all members of "clan Cutolo," a Nuova Camorra Organization (NCO): Antonio Moccia, Adriano Paschetto, Vincenzo Buffo, Dino de Benedet, Pierangelo Morando, Giorgio Fadel, Caterina Bonici, Maria Mestriner, Maria Pia Mostrochicco, Rino Pezzuto, Paolo Vada, Mario Mari, and Giorgio Santambrogio. This time the destination for the weapons was thought to be Senegal, Gambia, and Zimbabwe. The newspaper reported that Sten machine guns had been found in Pordenone in the Friuli-Venezia region in 1983.[39] This time Boris, identified as the Grand Master of the Order of the Iron Cross, was accused of working with the Neapolitan Mafia, in shipping the guns to Africa.

In 1994 the case was reopened by Domenico Chiaro, who got far enough in his investigation to ask that Boris be given an additional sentence of three years, eight months. The last hearing was set for 12 December 1994, the exact anniversary of the Piazza Fontana bombings in 1969, when thirteen people had been killed and over 100 injured after a bomb exploded in a Milanese bank. Finally, Boris was acquitted. The court, whose judgment was read by President Renato Semek, determined once again that "against de Rachewiltz there was no evidence but only faint clues."[40]

The further stories about Boris de Rachewiltz during these years are equally ambiguous. Suspicions about his life in the '60s and '70s and '80s persisted for years. Most of them concerned his role in the "strategy of tension" that clouded the political horizon of Italy in the post–World War II era. To follow these allegations is to enter a labyrinth and to find his name in an ever-widening and ever more dangerous network of associations, but to find no proof. At the least one can say that he spent years of his life under judicial investigation. He was suspected of being part of various right-wing groups, subversive structures always in the shadows, whose goals were the disruption of civic life, nominally in the interest of fighting communism.

To name these activities accurately is impossible. Like James Jesus Angleton, like Norman Holmes Pearson, and to a lesser extent, Leonard Doob, Boris seemed to thrive on secrecy. One recalls his correspondence with Pound in St. Elizabeths during the 1950s, and Pound's admonition to his son-in-law: take your esoteric groups "underground." Where did he go? What were these clandestine societies doing? Do we witness, as much as outsiders can witness anything, grown men experimenting with chivalric rituals or was something more dangerous going on?

The group that attracted most judicial attention was the Ludwig Keimer Foundation; the friend who excited most suspicion was Count Pio Filippani Ronconi. Boris's association with them dates from the 1960s; all of them—Boris, Filippani Ronconi, and the Keimer Foundation—were under judicial inquiry well into the 1990s and through the beginning years of the twenty-first century. Like so many Italian investigations about this period of civilian bombings, assassination attempts, and aborted coups, there seemed always to be sufficient reason to doubt the ostensible activities of these people and groups, but rarely definitive evidence of wrongdoing.

Boris founded the Ludwig Keimer Foundation in Basel, Switzerland, in 1969. A year later, as its president, he published several books to identify its raison d'être: he wanted to honor his mentor and to expand his methods of comparative archaeology and ethnology. On the surface, the group assembled to foster this research was stellar. Ludwig Keimer (1893–1957) had worked primarily in Egypt, but Boris invited scholars and dignitaries from Senegal, Iran, Great Britain, Belgium, Switzerland, Germany, Costa Rica, the Philippines, Lebanon, Uganda, Nicaragua, China, and the U.S. to join hands in this enterprise. Among those listed on the advisory board are S. E. Léopold Sedar Senghor, then president of the republic of Senegal, Count Pierre Baruzy of Switzerland, Count Philippe d'Arschot of Belgium, and the Honorable William W. Grosvenor of Great Britain. Numerous professors, presidents of research institutes, and directors of libraries and foundations are listed as affiliates.[41]

Among these names are some that seem to have no professional reason to support Boris's work, at least as that work is explained by the Ludwig Keimer Foundation statement of purpose. What was Norman Holmes Pearson doing on the board of advisers? How could a degree in American literature benefit the "scientific inheritance" of an Egyptologist whose primary investigation seems to have been the animal and plant life of ancient and modern Egypt? Why were Julius Evola and Dr. Elémire Zolla invited to join? Both of them were known for their idiosyncratic mysticism and for a distinctive metaphysics of war. According to Franco Feraresi, "Evola's thought can be considered one of the most radically and consistently antiegalitarian . . . systems in the Twentieth Century."[42] Such men could certainly bond over esoteric interests, but they were by no means archaeologists. The same question could be asked of Count Pio Filippani Ronconi, who was a linguist, adept at Turkish, Hebrew, Chinese, Tibetan, Sanskrit, and Persian.

On the surface, these affiliates show Boris to be a well-connected scholar. In the description of his role as president of the foundation, he listed his credentials: he reiterated his specialization in Egyptology at the Facoltà degli Studi dell' Oriente Antico of the Pontificio Istituto Biblico in Rome; he asserted that he had studied law at the University of Rome, specializing in diplomacy at the Pontificia Accademia Ecclesiastica and that he took courses in the Vatican Library. He received fellowships. He worked with famous professors; he made archaeological discoveries and published books. In 1969, the same year that he established the Ludwig Keimer Foundation, he was appointed professor of Oriental archaeology and ethnology at a university in Jordan.

But the organization was also suspect. By 2000, Count Pio Filippani Ronconi, who wrote for the *Corriere della Sera*, had been identified as a former Nazi storm trooper, the likely founding theorist of the "strategy of tension" in Italy, and as an agent of the secret services. He was recognized as Boris's colleague at the "mysterious" Keimer Foundation, which served, according to the report, as the hub of "secret agents, masons, Nazis, and dealers in mercenary arms."[43] He worked with Boris in Lugano at the Istituto ticinese di alti studi between 1970 and 1973, promulgating unorthodox discussions ranging from shamanism to Satanism.[44] He and Boris were members of an aristocratic organization called the Order of the Iron Cross.

By the 1990s, both men were under active investigation, their gnosticism, their forays into the Middle East, their penchant for elitist and esoteric codes suspected of providing cover for other clandestine activities. Dr. Dominic Tucci of the court in Milan questioned Boris about the Keimer Foundation and about his association with "Senegal Italy." Stefano Sakai of Italian public security also questioned Boris about the Keimer Foundation. What was his relationship with the secret services of the Italian state? What did he do for Servizio informazioni Defesa (SID)? For Servizio per le informazioni e la Sicurezza Mililtare (SISMI)? For Servizio informazioni delle Forze Armate (SIFAR)? The prosecutor's office in Rome picked up the inquiry. Even the Senegalese woman he lived with in Rome, Gioia Bruna Nali, was suspect.

Pio Filippani Ronconi fared no better. Years previously, during 3–5 May 1965, he had given a highly influential lecture at the Alberto Pollio Institute at the Parco dei Principi Hotel. That gathering was later considered to be the ground zero of the strategy of tension—a series of mysterious acts of terror—and many people thought that Filippani Ronconi's lecture had articulated its guiding principle. To fight the threat of communism, the professor contended, the state should acquire a secret structure consisting of three levels of commitment and three levels of knowledge.

Prosecutors recognized in this clandestine social organization an all too familiar pattern. Beginning in the 1970s and extending into the 1990s, the Italian judiciary began to uncover a network of secret organizations, most of them eventually connected to NATO, that became known in Italy as "Gladio." It was planned as a stay behind army, should the Russian military ever penetrate Italian soil, and its ideological counterpart was a series of steps to steer Italy to the political right. No communists should be voted into office, and an intimidated population . . . one frightened by seemingly random violence against civilians . . . was part of a larger strategy to defeat the Soviet bloc. Networks of communication, arms and explosives, and men trained to use them were all aspects of this scheme.[45]

The existence of a secret, state-sponsored structure was first hinted at by the right-wing terrorist Vincenzo Vinciguerra, imprisoned as a bomber at Peteano, who insisted in 1974 that this was accomplished with the assistance of the official secret services and political and military forces. Pio Filippani Ronconi worked for these services. He had theorized the need for a secret state; one of his students, Stefano della Chiaie, had been charged with involvement in the 1969 Piazza Fontana bombings. He had founded a conservative youth group, URRI, which had all the trappings of a training camp for paramilitary operations. He was, as his frequent inquisitions at tribunals attest, a suspicious person. Investigations of Pio Filippani Ronconi extended through the administration of Prime Minister Andreotti, who in 1990 exposed an elaborate matrix of people and organizations dedicated to this clandestine mission.

In 2014, Solange Manifredi, using court documents, commission documents, parliamentary documents and something called the Flamigni Archive assembled by Italian Senator Sergio Flamigni, put together the most comprehensive picture of what Boris, Pio Filippani Ronconi, and their associates might have been doing. She followed the proceedings of the Italian judiciary as it tried to untangle the many mysteries of the country's troubled post-World War II history. Her book presents documentation without drawing conclusions from it, and as such, it indicates the direction of official inquiry but does not judge the persons being investigated.

Boris appears frequently in these documents as a man whose life is clouded by distrust. He is presented in a network of dubious associations ranging from Pio Filippani Ronconi, whose friendship was widely known; to his allegedly Mafia father, Bruno Baratti; to Zorana Gaberscik, a suspected Russian agent; to Karl Hass and John Gehlen—both former Nazis thought to be agents who were "recycled" by the American intelligence services after World War II. The Keimer Foundation appears repeatedly, and Boris is referred to as "a collaborator" and as an affiliate of the Italian Military Service, working from office "R." He is identified as having a code name, "Brando," and he is especially noted for operating a radio station with a built-in recorder.

Manifredi weaves a tapestry of intrigue, clothed in tattered logic: events happen sometime "between the years 1960 to 1970"; the roles of individuals are "not yet clear"; circumstances are "mysterious"; people are "under careful observation"; they engage in "ambiguous activities." In tracing these networks of communication, especially those of former German intelligence officers working in Italy, Manifredi is only able to say, "behind these people [worked] Pons, Priori, Boris de Rachewiltz, Chaldyruan, Matschuk and others whose effective roles have not yet been highlighted."[46] In the end she, too, leaves us in shadows, suggesting that the chain of evidence is broken for a reason: it was protected or covered up by officials who did not want the judiciary to know that American secret agents were involved. In the 1960s the operative agent was Renzo Rocca, an officer of SIFAR, who had sponsored the Pollio Institute where Filippani Ronconi had theorized the strategy of tension. Later, it was Federico Umberto d'Amato who became the director of the Confidential Affairs Bureau of the Italian Ministry of the Interior. He was in charge of "Office R," for which Boris reputedly worked; he was also the Italian liaison with NATO. Both men, Rocca and d'Amato, were agents set in place by James Jesus Angleton in the 1940s before he left Italy to join the CIA.[47] Angleton's nebulous interference in the Pound/Rudge family extended for over forty years.

III

How much did Mary know? She understood enough about James Jesus Angleton to recognize that he was implicated in her family life. In 1986 she responded to Mary Barnard's mention of a new book about Angleton by remarking, "I have been trying to figure him out for so long!"[48] The few clues we have about her knowledge of Boris's activities come from *Infinite Regress.* "There was," she said in the novel, "a kind of shadow-play going on." She knew something was amiss: Of Boris (Victor) she said, "Clocks became his toys ... he is a useful wheel in the huge clockwork; the establishment hands him the crimson cloak." But there is a difference, as she acknowledges, between "to intuit, to know, to prove."[49]

The novel poses questions but does not answer them; it speculates but does not assert. "All the names are in the books. But why do they continue to speak of secrets, secret assassins, of drugs and alchemy?"[50] It seems fair to say that she intuited Boris's clandestine activities ... seeing them rise to the surface in suspicious clicks on the telephone, lamps sending light signals, radios recording unknown voices. But she rested there, short of knowledge and proof. We could observe, then, that *Infinite Regress* is written from a perspective close that of the Italian judiciary investigating the mysterious violence of the 1970s and '80s: neither can ever establish undisputable evidence; both are certain that it is there to find. Officially there was doubt; privately, for entirely different reasons, there was also doubt. Mary defended Boris's innocence before the law; she repeatedly referred to "false allegations" in her correspondence about him, but she also worried about the unknown and about the burden that she and Boris left on the shoulders of their children.[51] Mary Barnard reminded her of the weight she had borne in her own inheritance. All generations, according to her, did the same.[52]

What was there to do while the law delayed again? Olga advised Walter, who had apparently written to her about his father, to "know nothing definite." Boris had, she cautioned, probably acted for "good if mistaken motives." That is, he was trying to help friends who were in danger and who had, in the past, helped with his archeology.[53] Mary Barnard also recommended distance as a coping strategy. "I hope," she wrote, that you can "keep clear of too much involvement in the affair. You've had enough."[54]

The collective de Rachewiltzes seemed to follow Mary Barnard's advice. Their lives continued with literature, culture, and family at the heart of everything they did. In 1985, Mary published the completely translated Italian version of *The Cantos*, described by reviewers as "perhaps one of the most encyclopedic poetical works in the English language ... a way to sum up man's intellectual achievements for future generations should another great deluge come." Mary described this epic achievement as a quest ... not to devote a life to her father, but to her own education. "That is what I would like to give to the students: to go on seeking this idea that there is no end on the road to knowledge."[55] Privately she told Mary Barnard that the finished project had healed old wounds and, indeed, had restored her to the days before Pound had abandoned her. "I even have the impression that Pa would be proud of me—as he would have been before 1958."[56]

Her children followed suit. A few years later, Walter assumed a position as director of Schloss Tirol, where he organized excellent exhibitions of library manuscripts and other treasures. He became an expert on the history and folk practices of the Tyrol. Patrizia translated children's books like *Mr. Wind and Madame Rain*. Four healthy grandchildren ran around the castle grounds. Mary looked at Michael Ezra, Nicholas Thaddeus, Cyril, and Demian and realized that they made her laugh. No great artistic talent seemed latent in their antics, but she rested in their other abilities and enthusiasms. On one of her visits to Brunnenburg, Mary Barnard still noticed "tension, urgency, dogmatism" in her friend's conversation,[57] but Mary felt that things were as they should be: "Fortunately I have a feeling we are all doing the right thing, more and more meaningful is the summons in *The Cantos*: 'begin where you are.'"[58]

It took twelve years for Boris to be tried and "declared innocent."[59] In the interim, he was ill. Heart bypass surgery left him drained of energy. Mary thought his poor health to be the result of the extended and unresolved tension from judicial review. On the very day that his sentence was announced in 1995, he fell and broke his wrist and hand. He was in Rome, where his widowed sister cared for him. Two years later he was dead.[60] At the time, he was at Brunnenburg, which Mary thought fortunate for "this place gives dignity, almost an air of triumph to death."[61] Looking back, she summed up these circumstances tersely: "Strange destinies."[62]

She turned her attention inward and toward the future, writing in both Italian and English. In verse, she continued to be a "love forsaken daughter," who "must sing/ Dangling between two tongues." Although she could name the divisions of self implied by no mother tongue, she did not see Brunnenburg as a house divided against itself, with her own agenda standing at odds with Boris's clandestine motives. She did not speak of her ex-husband as someone operating in the same network of spies who had helped to bring down her father. That duality, one of the deepest of her life, remained unarticulated.

But the division had been there from the beginning of their relationship, even if she could not see it. The young Boris, coming from whatever dark, unseen background of family and wartime connections, had looked up at Brunnenburg and seen a place of extraterritorial neutrality. He wanted immunity from possible prosecution and a place of safety in an anticipated war on communism. The young Mary had looked up at the same parapets and envisioned extraterritorial neutrality because the conflicts of nation-states had torn apart her family's identity. Pound, she had hoped, could be free there; the castle could serve as an alternative to historical space and time, a private kingdom willed into existence by force of character and deep love.

She hoped that the children born into that space would not carry the same cross. One of her most beautiful poems, written to Walter, who was named for Walter von der Vogelweide, looked forward to what Brunnenburg could be for him.

We fought
Not only for bread
Or a piece of land [but also that]
You should be noble
In yourself and of your time
And no whim of others
Dare interrupt your urgent thoughts.

To give birth to the weight of stone pyramids
And words.
Your dreams do not change
In the spectrum of
Tired tomorrows.

O my mustard seed.
Firm your roots in the heavens
And on the branches of your mind.
Colorful birds will stand to sing
In counterpoint.[63]

Brunnenburg was not its land, not its castle, not its stone ramparts. It was not its vineyards, although the vineyards helped to sustain the life of the family. It did not, finally, exist in the Tyrol, even though the Tyrol had intimately shaped its contours. Walter's heritage should be a nobility of mind and spirit, a freedom from circumstance and from the intrusion of others. The foundations of his character should be "rooted" in "the heavens," as if trees could reverse the arc of their growth and spring forth from air.

In Mary's formulation, Boris has disappeared; the spies and betrayals are gone; Pound's perturbations of the political world have vanished. The winds of some imagined realm blow away the hazards of this life so that color and song can prevail. "We fought for this," she says. "This is it." What chilling defiance.

CHAPTER 11

The Right Frequency, 1985–2002

I

Nineteen eighty-five was the centenary of Pound's birth. It was a year of celebration, marked by honors and festivities in Hailey, Idaho; Orono, Maine; Zurich; and Venice. Mary went to all of them, pleased with the companionship and impressed by the various lectures. By November, she reported to Christina Brooke-Rose that the commemorations were over, all of them fine, but leaning a little too much toward psychology and politics.[1] Olga had amazed everyone with her vivacity and stamina, traveling to Orono with David Moody, conversing amiably, sharing memories, and granting an interview to the poet Desmond Egan.

Despite these celebrations, the major drama of the year, a series of events Mary called "the final blow," played itself out in Venice. Olga changed her will again. On 30 March 1985, she effectively disinherited Mary, leaving her house to the City of Venice, as well as all of her books, manuscripts, diaries, and private correspondence.[2] No one knew. Mary purposefully stayed out of Olga's affairs, but even a year later she was in the dark, writing a note to her mother about the confused state of her archive.[3] Three years later, in 1988, Patricia Willis wrote to Olga suggesting that her papers belonged at Yale as part of a "cultural unit," never guessing that Olga had already formed an "Ezra Pound Collection" that should remain under seal for thirty years. Even her artwork—a Max Ernst and a Fernand Léger hanging on the first floor of the Hidden Nest—were parceled out in this last testament to her desires.

The story that most people eventually pieced together about Olga's belongings had to do not with this will, but with the maneuverings of Philip and Jane Rylands in Venice during the 1980s. There the couple, who oversaw the Peggy Guggenheim Collection on the Grand Canal, befriended Olga, only to overstep the boundaries of friendship and to assume control of property that did not belong to them. Venice gossip had it that they had formed an Ezra Pound Foundation, ostensibly to help preserve Pound's legacy; but it was generally believed that Olga had been guided to act against her own interests.

Initially Mary had no reason to be suspicious. After Pound's death, Olga, always sociable, had flourished in the Rylands' company. Their invitations included a seminar at the Gritti Hotel in 1983 called "Ezra Pound in Italy," an elaborate ninetieth birthday party, and numerous daily kindnesses. Mary and Walter had participated in the seminar, and Mary's letters through the years often mentioned the Rylands as fond acquaintances. They made her life easier and took the edge off worry. Then came the incident of the missing trunks. Olga, not recognizing or even remembering what she had done, realized one day that all her papers were gone from calle Querini.

Some years later, John Berendt, a New York journalist, tried to sort out the story, writing a chatty account of Venetian intrigue centered on the declining memory of an old woman. "What was said?" he asked. "What was signed; who carried the boxes to whose storage area?" "Who was a knowing partner, who was manipulated and used?" In all it was "not a nice story."[4]

As the details of the affair emerged—one person after another suspecting dark motives behind the Rylands' behavior—Joan Fitzgerald and Liselotte Höhs finally called Mary. In return, in February 1988, Mary wrote to Olga saying very clearly, "DEfund your 'foundation' and make sure that the only place we can call home will be kept up by one daughter, two grandchildren, four great-grandsons. . . . If you want to entrust the 'technicalities' to Walter, I am sure he'll be ready to assume responsibility. At present you are tending the fire in a place that does not belong to you."[5] But by 1988, it was too late.

Walter and Boris went down to Venice to find out what had happened. They discovered contracts that Olga apparently did not remember signing. An Ezra Pound Foundation had indeed been formed two years earlier, on 17 December 1986, with Olga as president, Jane Rylands as vice-president, and a lawyer from Youngstown, Ohio, as secretary. Here Olga repeated her bequest of everything she owned to an organization—this time called a "foundation" rather than a "collection"—instead of her family. In one document, she had signed over her house to the foundation free and clear; in another she had given up "books, manuscripts, diaries, private correspondence, newspaper clippings, writings, papers, documents of any kind, drawings, books and albums of drawings and sketches, photographs, tapes and magnetic cassettes, and any objects that might be added to the collection before her death." In return she had received something in the neighborhood of $7,000. John Berendt estimated that these objects were worth millions of dollars.[6]

There was no way to revoke these contracts, for the rules of incorporation specified that two members of the executive board could override the wishes of a third member. That is, Olga had signed away control of everything she owned—and when she did try to dissolve the foundation two years later, claiming that she had never wittingly sold anything to anyone, neither Jane Rylands nor the lawyer sided with her.

Finding that the deed to the house had not yet been transferred, Boris and Walter succeeded in saving Olga's home. It had, in the interim, acquired a plaque honoring the Hidden Nest as Pound's former place of residence. Quite apart from the Rylands, it had become a monument. But the foundation refused to budge on Olga's papers. The Youngstown lawyer insisted that they could not be returned to Olga but could only be sold to another nonprofit institution. In 1990, Yale stepped up to buy the archive. The transaction was made under apparent duress to all parties. The Rylands received something on behalf of the foundation; the de Rachewiltzes received something; and no one was permitted to speak of the settlement. The Rylands were pushed to this move not by charity or ethical imperatives or even the entreaties of Maxwell Rabb, the American ambassador in Venice, but by the John Simon Guggenheim Foundation itself. Jim Sherwood, one of the Guggenheim trustees, insisted that Philip Rylands choose between his current position and the Ezra Pound Foundation. He chose to stay on the Grand Canal.

But for Mary, there it was again: the nightmare of possessions, the ire over inheritance, the need to argue for what should have been a clear line of succession. Mary reported that Walter had had some kind of "blow up" with Ralph Franklin and Pat Willis at the Beinecke about Olga's archive, and she herself was let go from her position as curator of the Ezra Pound collection at Yale.[7] James Laughlin saw the whole sorry affair with the perspective of a longtime family friend, understanding that Jane Rylands had moved with malignant ignorance, causing "more heartache and expense for a family that's already suffered for decades over this kind of thing." He knew the history of Pound's contested 1940s will; he knew the idealism with which Mary had battled legalities for many years. For Mary, the guiding principles of her life were wearing thin. She had lived with a clear distinction between the Law, conceived as eternal, and the law, construed as wearying nation-bound rules, for longer than she could remember. In 2002, she queried everything. "Whose World?" is it, she asked. "So stately, so pure the tyranny/ Legally established by pen and ink."[8]

II

In late 1988 Mary took Olga to live at Brunnenburg. Olga had been visiting more frequently, and the move was slow and measured. In September 1988, she was still not in permanent residence, for Mary wrote to Olga after her return from a T. S. Eliot celebration that the kitchen seemed empty and charmless without her mother's elegant touch.[9] But gradually, as Olga's memory faded, the transition was accomplished. Mary's plan had initially been to give Olga the independence of a self-contained apartment in the castle—a suite of rooms with bath and kitchenette. But Olga refused to stay in place, insisting on the room next to Mary's own. The view was magnificent, but so close a presence was disconcerting to Mary, who found the kitchen unexpectedly rearranged and her mother, at ninety-three, a person capable of "forgetting, not caring, not telling, hiding things."[10] She was also someone who sang and recited nursery rhymes.[11]

For Mary it was a time of worry about her own future, since her days were taken up by feeding Olga and taking her tea. Even with help five days a week, it was a burden and contributed to isolation. She wished repeatedly for the company of Mary Barnard "to have long talks with you about 'family,' hunches, theories, facts that surface, hints."[12] Her mother remained in the tower until she was 101. In 1996 she died quietly, slipping away during a nap in a large wicker chair. Mary carried her back to her wonted room, opened the windows to let the mountain air claim her, and later laid her in the small Brunnenburg basilica until the village priest came to say the rosary with the family.

III

Then there were the travels, which began before the commotion about Olga's papers. Where the Rylands affair brought with it all the dark associations of greed and possessions, Mary's voyages out, visiting Japan, China, and lovely locations in Italy were trips to a world made habitable by her father's mind. The travails of archives stood in opposition to the interior world of Pound's imagination. "The book I want to build," she wrote, as if language could mold the pages of creation, "[demands that you] give me of your own/ all you have." And, "still our longing to see all the Tai-shans mirrored in the holy Rock-Pool."[13] She had given "all you have," in defense of Pound; but nothing could blunt the allure of the creative father or the quest to dwell in the presence of his vision. It colored everything.

In 1986 Mary received an invitation to be in residence at Kansei University in Osaka, Japan. For two months she relished the quiet, the order, and her escape from the duties of home and profession. For all their joyfulness, the Pound centenary conferences had contained a share of vitriol; Mary had had to sit through a number of attacks; she had felt the stress and she was also still recovering from the different stresses of completing the bilingual *The Cantos* publication. The research scholars were put up in the Sun-Route Hotel in western-style comfort; the trains ran punctually. Although the rooms were small, they required no housekeeping. The hospitality she was shown made her "ashamed of how I treated all my guests at Brunnenburg," and in these circumstances, she flourished.[14]

Her Japanese hosts took her to Kyoto and to all the places mentioned in *The Cantos*. She attended Noh plays, Bunraku, and Kabuki. She experienced her first real Japanese tea ceremony, heard concerts with ancient instruments, and went to Fenollosa's grave, to Lake Biwa, and to the beach at Suma. She saw the ancient Pine Tree in Takasago. Though it had died fifty years ago, its black stump was enshrined and two young pines, the fourth generation of the legendary tree, were made to grow in a nearby enclosure. Peter Makin and Philip Gibbs, both Poundians who had been to Brunnenburg and who spoke Japanese, provided good food, good conversation and a respite from sitting through ceremonies whose words she could not understand. Through Sanehide Kodama, who was working on the manuscript that would become *Pound and Japan*, she learned that Pound, who had never set foot in the Far East, intended to visit the island in 1923. Mary wondered if Olga had planned to travel there as well.[15] She met Mrs. Katue Kitasono, who was indisposed and could not attend the dinner party commemorating "Pound-Nishiwaki-Kitasono-Vortex."[16] These events provided a glimpse of Pound's life in Paris before she was born, for Kitasono had been a poet writing with the ideas of Dada and visual Surrealism, whose publication, *Vou*, Pound had greatly

admired. In all, she found Japan "a marvel of efficiency, cleanliness, honesty
and courtesy," and for once she did not feel on the defensive, for everyone
treated Pound with respect and "without the usual digs." How much history
one was not aware of, she remarked. There were Japanese "holocausts"
never mentioned in the U.S. or Europe.[17]

From Japan, Mary flew to New Haven for her usual month in residence.
By 8 April 1986 she was home again, wondering at her "wandering gipsy life,"
and anticipating a teaching position at the University of Toledo for three
months in early 1987.[18] She went to Ohio simply because she was asked, and
because teaching at the graduate level appealed to her. She was given a very
Spartan apartment, enjoyed the three-hour seminars, went down to New Haven for her usual month and was back in Brunnenburg in time for Easter.[19]
She asked Olga to forgive her dull letters . . . she felt very cut off . . . but the
lectures she gave at the university show that she was grappling with big issues. Where Japan had been a matter of coordinating outer landscapes with
imaginative evocations of place, Ohio allowed her to reflect on *The Cantos* as
"The Tale of the Tribe."

While she was there, she gave several lectures. The last, "Feminine
Gaiety," evoked the historic American family that haunted Pound's epic—
showing that Pound had fled those ancestors in order to find his voice
and returned to them once they could become quiet shades. She looked
back and saw in the Wadsworths, the Westons, and the Thaddeus Cole-
man Pounds "the America Pound stood for, learnt from, and lamented
the loss of. An America of certain values and no usury." They were, according to *The Loomis Family History* (1906), men who "believed in doing some
little good, not in dreaming." They were lovers of freedom who thought
less of heaven in some dim and far-off future [than] getting themselves
into heavenly conditions just now. Here, in the American genealogy of
actual kinsmen, Mary saw the origins of Pound's "message made new in
The Cantos."

> Confucius . . . said nothing of life after death
> And that I tried to make a paradise
>   Terrestre.

She pointed out that "to the very end, Pound tried to improve man's lot in
this world. To make an earthly paradise."[20]

Mary was living in impersonal rented rooms, marking time and making money until she could return to the Tyrol at Easter. But she made her claim: the Pounds had origins on American soil. She traced her ancestry back to the *Mayflower*:

> Here from the beginning, we have been here
>   From the beginning.[21]

But she herself was deeply displaced. She had no home here. America did not welcome her. "Be of words a little bit/ more careful," she wrote, "if language/ in place of love and country/ is all you have."[22]

IV

China did open its arms. "Had Pound not re-created China in 'the wilds of the mind,'" she observed, "even before writing the *Pisan Cantos*, an extended Pound family would not in 1999 have climbed the sacred mountain [Taishan] and visited Confucius's birthplace and burial ground in Qufu."[23] Mary wrote about the experience after the Eighteenth International Pound Conference in Beijing (16–19 July 1999). She had been invited by her host, Professor Jian Zhang, to address the ninety participants, but she arrived in China so filled with the complexities of Pound's relation to the Far East that she abandoned her own words. Instead, she asked the audience to listen to a recording of Pound reading the Confucian Odes. And she reminded them that Confucius had, like her father in old age, wanted to do without language. Confucius's silence was, in her judgment, Pound's silence, his wisdom diffused *The Cantos* just as his wisdom filled the culture of China; the two were inseparable.

Having made this claim, when she later published the talk she had not given, Mary asked herself who had preceded her to China's high mountains? She remembered that the Jesuits had come and that, as much as Pound resisted their attempts to convert others to Christianity, they had also been the source of Pound's understanding of Asia. It was after all through the eyes of Father Joseph-Anne-Marie de Moyriac de Mailla's thirteen-volume *Histoire Générale de la Chine* that Pound had seen the origin and decline of the Chinese empire. The Jesuits were part of the vision of paradise on earth, for it was with use of their translations that Pound assembled a series of building blocks for imagining a new civilization. To understand *The Cantos*, one had to appreciate the Confucian teachings of "right conduct in this world," as well as Catholicism, which she understood to be a "luminous road" rather than a set of restrictive institutional practices. Pound had blended insights from the East with those of the West, with the intention of making "it cohere"; she did the same, finding Confucian thinking compatible with the religion of her own Tyrolean upbringing.

To Mary Barnard, she wrote that she had been happy to climb Taishan, despite the desperate heat, the crowds, and the ubiquitous hawkers. The experience had been overwhelming, and she was still incorporating the impression of the many thousand stairs to the South Gate of Heaven, the Temple of the God, Dai Miao, the Azure Clouds Temple, and the ancient grove of cypress trees. At this point in time, their friendship had lasted fifty years—Patrizia had not been born when they first met—and it gave her special pleasure to send a photograph of herself with her daughter at the tomb of Confucius.[24]

After the journey, Mary thought she would never again travel, except, perhaps to Hailey, Idaho, and then on to Vancouver. But then she reported with pleasure that Ezra Pound would be remembered, along with F. Scott Fitzgerald, in the Poets Corner at the Cathedral of Saint John the Divine in New York. She and Patrizia purchased their tickets, and she forwarded the announcement to Mary Barnard, with its news that Dana Gioia and Rachel Hadas would be the poets to install Pound.[25]

Then, unexpectedly, the invitation was withdrawn. The Very Reverend Harry S. Pritchette Jr. wrote to say that the cathedral could not commemorate Pound because he was an anti-Semite. A flurry of equivocal statements ensued, following the debate lines drawn decades earlier by literary people, who felt the need to distance themselves from their own decisions. Of course, Pound had been anti-Semitic, Tim Redman told *The New York Times*; Donald Hall was even more ambivalent: Pound had been "generous" to other writers, he allowed, "before he became a megalomaniac and paranoiac. I think that the malice of his madness is not relevant to his stature as a poet." Daniel Hoffman, the cathedral's poet in residence, admitted that Pound's anti-Semitism was "vituperative and incoherent," but said he had hoped that the general public would now agree that Pound's achievements were otherwise "heroic." Once the challenge was thrown—in this case initiated by Marsha Ra, a warden of the cathedral—no one defended his or her choice to honor Pound.[26]

Mary and Patrizia did not use their tickets, and Mary, staying in Italy, reported, "right now I feel we are truly all better off here." Her dear friend, the Italian publisher Giovanni Scheiwiller, died on 17 October 1999, so she went to his funeral in Milan instead. She found the church "packed with friends, writers, artists." Scheiwiller seemed the greater loss. Both American and Italian publishers were gone; she felt "[g]reat emptiness."[27]

The affair at the cathedral was like killing the dead twice over.[28] It left Mary in the position of Antigone, who asserted a law beyond "the decree of the throne." It was as if Creon had declared that no proper burial could take place, for honoring the dead is a way of laying their memory to earned and quiet rest. In Sophocles' ancient drama, the king had said that Polyneices, who fought against Thebes, be left "unwept, unburied, a lovely treasure for birds that scan the field and feast to their heart's content." Antigone had reminded the king that his actions were "an outrage [of what is] sacred to the gods." "Death longs for the same rites for all."[29] The exercise of full humanity requires judgment beyond the viewpoint of shifting political power. Antigone was willing to die for that cavernous allegiance, even when the chorus of public opinion sided with the king.

Who, in the American drama, would see that Pound should be remembered for accomplishments measured outside the boundary of the city-state? Who, in America, could gauge an imagination that dwelt outside the perspective of particular nationalisms? Who could see that militarisms were wrong, especially if they tore families apart, as World War II had torn Mary from her father? Who would remember that conquering powers could shift boundaries with pen and ink, as the Allies had traded the Tyrol, Mary's homeland, according to the exigencies of tactical political alliances? The Tyrol had been Austrian; the Tyrol had been Italian, the Tyrol had belonged to Mussolini, the Tyrol had been anything that the Allies wanted it to be, and Mary had lived through these forced and shifting allegiances; Pound had seen his daughter traded from nation to nation, and he had spoken about the meaning of it. War is different if you have a child born to the supposed enemy.

There was to be no American burial, as eventually there had been in Thebes when Creon realized that he had misjudged the most sacred of human obligations. Pound had written, "No wind is the king's wind."[30] There are limits that are arbitrary creations of national cultures; and there are sacred forces beyond them. Despite Pound's faults, beyond his hammering rhetoric, Mary could see that her father deserved the honor due his action, his intention, and his gift. She had felt the wind and read its broad message.

Instead of honor at the cathedral, there was a sundering. By this point, the various breaches with America were impossible to ignore. Mary counted the break with Yale as twenty-five years of wasted investment in an American institution: "And Juda becomes New Haven," she wrote. To her it had become a place of "scapegoat pastures" and "venomous" grass.[31] Where the de Rachewiltz family had once considered the Beinecke Rare Book and Manuscript Library the site of a reconstructed "cultural unity" for Pound studies, it no longer served that purpose. From this point, Pound's books, manuscripts, and memorabilia remained at Brunnenburg, symbolically living in the country that had sheltered Pound before the war and after he left the confines of St. Elizabeths Hospital. She now understood that there would be no plaque to commemorate Pound's childhood home in Wyncote, Pennsylvania. She was grateful for Great Britain's wider embrace, for in 2004, the English recognized Pound as the "poets' poet" and honored him with a blue plaque at his former house in Kensington Church Walk, where he had lived from 1909 to 1914. But England was Dorothy and Omar's country. It had no hard-won claim to Mary's affection.

In her heart, Pound needed no commemorative plaque. Her father had shaped her journey from the beginning of memory. In the end, she thought that Pound had got it right on the basic things: he saw the blindness of nationalisms, the ubiquity of usury, the destructiveness of war, the darkness of its financial imperatives that benefited few; the false rhetoric of international conflict. The people who had excluded him knew none of the scars of the battle he had waged; they saw only the unexamined labels. They lacked mercy.

There was still more to do. More conferences were on the horizon, more classes, more invitations, more struggles to defeat the misuse of Pound's name by Casa Pound Italia, the squatters' group that grew into an independent movement of the radical right.[32] But this is a good place to end the story. We never say all we know.

*   *   *

Omar Pound died on 2 March 2010. In the end, Mary felt sorry: "Pound" had been, after all, a difficult name to bear. The strife behind her, Mary reflected on the circumstances of their births: "The lie invented to/ Hide an earlier lie/ Where and when did it start/ And in whom to suit whom/ Has death killed a lie?"[33]

Leonard Doob died earlier on 29 March 2000. He might have, she felt, liked to end his years at the castle, but he had not come and had not really been invited. "You and I," she wrote, "have committed/ to ashes the greatest of/ loves."[34]

James Jesus Angleton went to his grave in 1987, holding the secrets of his craft as closely as the mystery of his preoccupation with Ezra Pound.

In the end, Mary trusted the ground she stood on. "My eyes hold many landscapes/ the heart but one, traversed/ by the singing river Ahr," she said in her last English-language book of poetry. In 2002 she remembered a child's feet in its glacial waters; she remembered turf in April, fresh grass in May, stubble in September, dry leaves in November, and the plow opening furrows for new plantings to begin it all again. "Wisdom rises through bare feet," she wrote, stepping firmly beyond division and regret.[35]

Epilogue, 2015

I last saw Mary de Rachewiltz in the summer of 2015. She and her entire family were hosting the twenty-sixth Ezra Pound International Conference at Brunnenburg, Dorf Tirol. She was sitting at tea with Patrizia and with many of the scholars and poets who had come, over the years, to form a close friendship circle. It was a ritual that had been established for a very long time. Indeed, one of her poetry books, *Whose World?*, had been dedicated to those many people who had joined her in this simple act of conviviality. She was waiting with anticipation for the group to expand. When would John Gery arrive? When would Richard Sieburth get there? The list of guests was impressive and it represented those people who understood the meaning of many years of imposed silence or what Hugh Kenner had called Mary's "impassioned reticence." Recently David Moody had completed a three-volume biography of Pound, which had, for the first time, acknowledged her status as Ezra Pound's child. David and Joanna Moody had also helped her publish *Ezra Pound to His Parents: Letters 1895–1929*, which they jointly edited, with Oxford University Press. An Ezra Pound Research Center had been established at the Academy of German-Italian Studies in Merano. It welcomed international collaborations and joint projects. Finally the truths so long hidden were emerging, and with them, a new lightness of spirit. 2015 was Mary's ninetieth birthday year, and many celebrations were planned.

The conference was matchless in organization and in hospitality. Guests moved easily from rooms fitted for presentations to a newly built area for coffee and conversation. Brunnenburg was at its most beautiful: it was open to the clear air as well as to the voices of eager scholars. If Pound had not found its shelter sufficient to his needs, a later generation certainly did. As everyone could see, he had established a gifted and generous family.

The events of the week included many tributes to Mary, but they also contained another homage. On Friday, 10 July, the guests were taken to Tschengls, where there was a small castle in the Ortler Mountains overlooking the Val Venosta or Vinschgau. Traveling west from Merano, along the Adige riverbed, buses brought us past alpine farms, winding up a hillside until the road ended. There, at the site of another ancient stronghold that Walter had bought some years ago, the de Rachewiltz family had erected a monument to the memory of Pound and Olga. Made from marble, its three pillars mirrored an ideogram from Canto XCVII, each column rising evenly against the sky. It was clear what meaning lay encased in its stone: "The temple is holy because it is not for sale." The consecration was heralded by two alpine horn players in lederhosen and by the enunciation of cantos. Champagne was handed round and then we were free to walk the grounds.

I struggled to take it in. My own parents live in quiet circumstances. For many years, the tepid rooms of assisted living have framed my family memories. We are a modest clan. This penchant for annunciation bothered me. Why such drama? I thought about it as I listened to a companion recount the history of the mountains. Peace surrounded us, troubled only by the ragged wind, but it had not always been so. Not far from here and in similar terrain, World War I had reaped a terrible harvest. Half the casualties of the Italian army had occurred on this eastern front; 300,000 soldiers had died; the Austrians had occupied higher ground; offensives had to be carried out while climbing; avalanches had claimed the lives of 10,000 men on both sides. One assault after another failed before the Austrians lost heart. The valley I looked out on had been nothing but carnage, where all sides had used destructive stratagems. Now it was farmland. Once, too, there had been more personal landscapes for this family: secret services of foreign governments and cages and accusations that were never proved. There had been overwhelming adversaries. We need history to be a palimpsest, always covering its prior devastations. Perhaps proclamations were now in order. Perhaps cantos should offer the final words: we all live in a wind that no one can own.

I realized that my imagination had been shaped neither by exclusions that demanded recompense nor by battles that needed to be turned into a green world. I had to see from a wider perspective: this was not only the Tyrol; it was also the burial that Antigone did not live to see, writ large and witnessed by a new kind of chorus. Mary had done her job. We were there. It was time for everyone to rest.

NOTES

List of Abbreviations

Frequent correspondents are cited in the notes by initials:

B de R	Boris de Rachewiltz
CBR	Christine Brooke-Rose
CLS	Carol Loeb Shloss
DG	Donald Gallup
DP	Dorothy Pound
EH	Eva Hesse
EP	Ezra Pound
H.D.	Hilda Doolittle
JJA	James Jesus Angleton
LD	Leonard W. Doob
MB	Mary Barnard
M de R	Mary de Rachewiltz
NHP	Norman Holmes Pearson
OP	Omar Pound
OR	Olga Rudge

University libraries and special collections are noted by the name of the university, with these exceptions:

Beinecke	Beinecke Rare Book and Manuscript Library, Yale University
Berg	Henry W. and Albert A. Berg Collection at the New York Public Library
British National Archives	National Archives of the United Kingdom, Kew
Burke	Special Collections of the Daniel Burke Library, Hamilton College
HRHRC	Harry Ransom Humanities Research Center, University of Texas at Austin
Lilly	The Lilly Library, Indiana University Libraries, Bloomington
NARA	National Archives and Records Administration, College Park, MD
YCAL	Yale Collection of American Literature

Preface

1. Mary de Rachewiltz, *Ezra Pound, Father and Teacher: Discretions* (New York: New Directions, 2005), 257.

2. Ezra Pound, Canto LXXVI.

3. Canto CX.

4. Notes for Canto CXVII.

5. M de R, *Discretions*, 279.

6. Ibid., 295.

7. FBI file on Ezra Pound, microform (Wilmington, DE: Scholarly Resources, 2000). Unredacted by author.

8. Seamus Heaney, *The Burial at Thebes: A Version of Sophocles' Antigone* (New York: Farrar, Straus and Giroux, 2005), 39.

9. Ibid., 26.

10. Ibid., 21.

11. Ibid., 26.

12. Ibid., 46.

13. M de R, *Discretions*, frontispiece.

Chapter 1

1. OR to EP, 20 July 1925, OR Papers, YCAL MSS 54, Beinecke.

2. M de R, *Ezra Pound, Father and Teacher: Discretions* (New York: New Directions, 2005), 8.

3. OR notes, personal papers in Anne Conover, *Olga Rudge and Ezra Pound: "What Thou Lovest Well . . ."* (New Haven, CT: Yale University Press, 2001), 60.

4. OR to EP, 22 July 1925, OR Papers, YCAL MSS 54, Beinecke.

5. EP to OR, 18 April 1925, OR Papers, YCAL MSS 54, Beinecke.

6. OR to EP, 18 April 1925, OR Papers, YCAL MSS 54, Beinecke.

7. EP to OR, 19 April 1925, Ezra Pound Papers, YCAL MSS 43, Beinecke.

8. EP to OR, 9 June 1925, EP Papers, YCAL MSS 43, Beinecke.

9. EP to OR, 12 June 1925, EP Papers, YCAL MSS 43, Beinecke.

10. EP to OR, 9 June 1925, EP Papers, YCAL MSS 43, Beinecke.

11. EP to OR 12 June 1925, EP Papers, YCAL MSS 43, Beinecke.

12. OR to EP, 18 July 1925, OR Papers, YCAL MSS 54, Beinecke. See also M de R, unpublished manuscript: "Domenica le tre. Well after 48 hours of it and an operation to finish she knows what it feels like-though that was *not* why she went in for it—her figliolin is a lina-very confusing—ride gia come un orso-cosi dotter stamattina pesa 4 kili etc. I've only just met it ma ha una bocca bellissima—being fascied could not find the hands—but ears all right—still— as they're coming for a name in a moment-and I was only prepared with nome maschili-am making 'Mary Quite Contrary' do—good lesbian—if he remembers poem—and expressing *my* feelings—but it *deserves* a beautiful name—e bella sense dubbio—la piccinina—He *might* help her out with some- & quickly- after all e suo mestiere-no?-trovare nome- e voglio nome per una *mia* figlia-not addata a anyone else—Ciao, stanca [tired]. Olga." Polyxena was the daughter of Priam and Hecuba, the lover of Achilles. Pound identifies her in Canto IX as the second wife of Sigismundo Malatesta. De Rachewiltz Archives, Brunnenburg.

13. OR to EP, 22 July 1925, OR Papers, YCAL MSS 54, Beinecke.

14. EP to OR, 16 August 1925, EP Papers, YCAL MSS 43, Beinecke. Anne Conover, Olga Rudge's biographer, asserts that Olga went to Katherine Dalliba-John's villa in Florence in August. She may have done this, but Pound's letters to her by 16 August are addressed to 2 rue Chamfort, Paris XLI, France. See Conover, *Olga Rudge and Ezra Pound*, 62; EP to OR, 30 August 1925, OR Papers, YCAL MSS 54, Beinecke.

15. M de R, *Discretions*, 10–11.

16. OR to EP, 22 October 1925, OR Papers, YCAL MSS 54, Beinecke.

17. OR to EP, 27 November 1925, OR Papers, YCAL MSS 54, Beinecke.

18. Richard Aldington, *Soft Answers* (London: Chatto and Windus, 1932), 160.

19. OR quoted by M de R, unpublished manuscript. Olivia Shakespear was the lover of W. B. Yeats.

20. EP to Homer Pound, 24 December 1925, EP Papers, YCAL MSS 43, Beinecke.

21. See also Humphrey Carpenter, *A Serious Character: The Life of Ezra Pound* (New York: Dell, 1988), 450–51.

22. The truth of Omar's paternity is part of what Pound revealed to Mary de Rachewiltz in 1943 when he walked from Rome to Gais on the eve of Italy's entry into the war. Fear of reprisals made the first publisher of *Discretions* delete the full account of what Pound said to her, and she then substituted "The Goat Song" in her book for full disclosure of the truth. M de R, interview by Carol L. Shloss, 4 October 2004.

23. See Carpenter, *A Serious Character*, 453.

24. Humphrey Carpenter recounts a Richard Aldington short story called "Nobody's Baby," which articulates what many literati in Paris suspected. "Was it possible that the child was really Ophelia's [Dorothy's] but not Charlemagne's [Pound's], and that all the curious hanky-panky in Paris which had perplexed us so much was simply a clumsy but generous plot on the part of Charlemagne and Maggie [Olga] to shield the erring but repentant wife?" *A Serious Character*, 455.

25. EP to HP, 11 September 1926, EP Papers, YCAL MSS 43, Beinecke.

26. EP to HP, 23 November 1926, in Carpenter, *A Serious Character*, 454.

27. EP to OR, 7 and 8 January 1927, EP Papers, YCAL, MSS 54, Beinecke.

28. James Joyce, *Ulysses*, ed. Hans Walter Gabler (New York: Random House, 1984), 9:301.

29. M de R, *Discretions*, 14.

30. OR notes, personal papers, in Conover, *Olga Rudge and Ezra Pound*, 62.

31. Johann Wolfgang von Goethe, *Italian Journey: 1786–87* (New York: Penguin, 1992), 102.

32. M de R, *Discretions*, 15.

33. Ibid., 34.

34. EP to OR, 24 July 1927, EP Papers, YCAL MSS 43, Beinecke.

35. EP to OR, 17 August 1927, EP Papers, YCAL MSS 43, Beinecke.

36. OR to EP, 19 January 1928, in Conover, *Olga Rudge and Ezra Pound*, 74.

37. OR to EP, 19 November 1929, OR Papers, YCAL MSS 54, Beinecke.

38. M de R, "Beauties of the Tirol" (unpublished manuscript, trans. Ezra Pound), EP Collection, HRHRC.

39. EP to OR, 26 December 1929, EP Papers, YCAL MSS 43, Beinecke.

40. M de R, *Discretions*, 20.

41. Ibid.

42. HP to EP, 3 August 1939, private collection.

43. Isabel Pound to EP, 30 July 1939, private collection.

44. OR to EP, 8 November 1928, OR Papers, YCAL MSS 54, Beinecke.

45. EP to OR, 10 November 1928, EP Papers, YCAL MSS 43, Beinecke.

46. EP to OR, 9 December 1928, EP Papers, YCAL MSS 43, Beinecke.

47. EP to OR 12 December 1928, EP Papers, YCAL MSS 43, Beinecke.

48. OR to EP, n.d. [1928], OR Papers, YCAL MSS 54, Beinecke.

49. OR to EP, 25 January 1929, OR Papers, YCAL MSS 54, Beinecke.

50. M de R, *Discretions*, 23.

51. Ibid., 22.

52. OR, *I-Ching Notebooks*, OR Papers, YCAL MSS 241, Beinecke.

53. Rolf Steininger, *South Tyrol: A Minority Conflict of the Twentieth Century* (New Brunswick, NJ: Transaction, 2003), 5.

54. Ibid.

55. Eduard Reut-Nicolussi, *Tirol unterm Beil* (Munich: Beck, 1928), 30.

56. Ibid., 118–19.

57. In Steininger, *South Tyrol*, 21–22.

58. Ibid., 29.

59. Ibid., 32.

60. Ibid., 22.

61. M de R, *Discretions*, 70.

62. Ibid., 38.

63. Ibid., 15, 34.

64. In Conover, *Olga Rudge and Ezra Pound*, 108.

65. OR to EP, 18 May 1932, OR Papers, YCAL MSS 54, Beinecke.

66. OR to EP, n.d. [January 1935], in Conover, *Olga Rudge and Ezra Pound*, 121.

67. Ibid., 123.

68. OR, *I-Ching Notebooks*, OR Papers, YCAL MSS 241, Beinecke.

69. Steininger, *South Tyrol*, 49.

70. M de R, preface to *Discretions* (unpublished), given to CLS at Brunnenburg, October 2004.

71. M de R, *Discretions*, 45.

72. Ibid., 52.

73. M de R, preface to *Discretions*.

74. M de R, *Discretions*, 67.

75. Ibid., 68.

76. EP, "Rules for Maria," EP Papers, YCAL MSS 43, Beinecke.

77. EP, in M de R, *Discretions*, 70.

78. Ibid., 66.

79. OR to EP, 31 October 1938, OR Papers, YCAL MSS 54, Beinecke.

Chapter 2

1. OR to EP, 12 November 1936, OR Papers, YCAL MSS 54, Beinecke.

2. M de R, *Ezra Pound, Father and Teacher: Discretions* (New York: New Directions, 2005), 98.

3. OR Papers, YCAL MSS 54, Beinecke.

4. OR to EP, 18 October 1937, OR Papers, YCAL MSS 54, Beinecke.

5. M de R, *Discretions*, 104.

6. EP to OR, 28 October 1937, EP Papers, YCAL MSS 43, Beinecke.

7. M de R to EP, 22 November 1937, EP Papers, YCAL MSS 43, Beinecke.

8. OR to EP, 7 July 1937, OR Papers, YCAL MSS 54, Beinecke.

9. M de R, *Discretions*, 105.

10. OR to EP, 29 December 1937, OR Papers, YCAL MSS 54, Beinecke.

11. M de R, *Discretions*, 107.

12. Rolf Steininger, *South Tyrol: A Minority Conflict of the Twentieth Century* (New Brunswick, NJ: Transaction, 2003), 48.

13. Ibid., 51.

14. OR to EP, 16 March 1938, OR Papers, YCAL MSS 54, Beinecke.

15. Richard Aldington to H.D., 15 January 1937, in *Richard Aldington and H.D.: The Later Years in Letters*, ed. Caroline Zilboorg (Manchester: Manchester University Press, 1995), 60.

16. H.D., undated statement, H.D. Papers, YCAL MSS 24, Beinecke.

17. In *The Later Years in Letters*, 65.

18. H.D., *End to Torment: A Memoir of Ezra Pound* (New York: New Directions, 1979), 8.

19. EP to H.D., n.d. [1938], H.D. Papers, YCAL MSS 24, Beinecke.

20. H.D. to EP, 16 March 1938, H.D. Papers, YCAL MSS 24, Beinecke.

21. I wish to thank Jacob Korg, whose book *Winter Love: Ezra Pound and H.D.* (Madison: University of Wisconsin Press, 2003) alerted me to H.D.'s constellation of feelings about children in relation to Pound.

22. Bryher to Richard Aldington, 1925 [before April], H.D. Papers, YCAL MSS 24, Beinecke.

23. Richard Aldington, "Nobody's Baby," in *Soft Answers* (London: Chatto and Windus, 1932), 124.

24. Ibid., 125.

25. Ibid., 126.

26. EP to OR, 7 October 1938, OR Papers, YCAL MSS 54, Beinecke.

27. OR to EP, 27 October 1938, EP Papers, YCAL MSS 43, Beinecke.

28. OR to EP, 31 October 1938, EP Papers, YCAL MSS 43, Beinecke.

29. DP to EP, 29 October 1938, Pound MSS II, Lilly.

30. OR to EP, 2 November 1938, EP Papers, YCAL MSS 43, Beinecke.

31. OR to EP, October 1938, EP Papers, YCAL MSS 43, Beinecke.

32. M de R to EP, 9 February 1939, EP Papers, YCAL MSS 43, Beinecke.

33. EP, "Rules for Mary," OR Papers, YCAL MSS 54, Beinecke.

34. M de R, *Discretions*, 99.

35. Ibid., 138.

36. EP to M de R, 17 November 1940, ibid., 139.

37. EP to M de R, 12 March 1940, EP Papers, YCAL MSS 43, Beinecke.

38. M de R, *Discretions*, 138.

39. Ibid., 114.

40. OR to EP, 4 July[?] 1939, EP Papers, YCAL MSS 43, Beinecke.

41. M de R, *Discretions*, 116.

42. Ibid.

43. EP to J. H. Cochran, 16 May 1939, in E. Fuller Torrey, *The Roots of Treason: Ezra Pound and the Secrets of St. Elizabeths* (New York: McGraw-Hill, 1984), 312.

44. EP to OR, 27 June 1939, OR Papers, YCAL MSS 54, Beinecke.

45. OR to EP, 4[?] July 1939, EP Papers, YCAL MSS 43, Beinecke.

46. OR to EP, 6 or 7 July 1939, EP Papers, YCAL MSS 43, Beinecke.

47. EP to OR, 5 July 1939, OR Papers, YCAL MSS 54, Beinecke.

48. OR to EP, 23 July 1939, EP Papers, YCAL MSS 43, Beinecke.

49. OR to United States Supreme Court, 1939, OR Papers, YCAL MSS 54, Beinecke.

50. M de R, *Discretions*, 135.

51. EP to OR, 1 September 1939, OR Papers, YCAL MSS 54, Beinecke.

52. EP to OR, 3 September 1939, OR Papers, YCAL MSS 54, Beinecke.

53. EP to OR, 12 September 1939; 3 July 1940, OR Papers, YCAL MSS 54, Beinecke.

54. EP to OR, 9 September 1939, OR Papers, YCAL MSS 54, Beinecke.

55. JJA to EP, 23 August 1939, EP Papers, YCAL MSS 43, Beinecke.

56. Robin W. Winks, *Cloak and Gown: Scholars in the Secret War, 1939–1961* (New Haven, CT: Yale University Press, 1987), 329.

57. JJA to EP, 28 December 1939, Furioso Papers, YCAL MSS 75, Beinecke.

58. JJA to EP, n.d., Furioso Papers, YCAL MSS 75, Beinecke.

59. Winks, *Cloak and Gown*, 339.

60. JJA to EP, 31 May 1940, Furioso Papers, YCAL MSS 75, Beinecke.

61. DP to EP, 28 September 1940, Pound MSS II, Lilly.

62. OR to EP, 28 November 1939, EP Papers, YCAL MSS 43, Beinecke.

63. OR to EP, 30 July 1940, EP Papers, YCAL MSS 43, Beinecke.

64. EP to OR, 18 July 1940, OR Papers, YCAL MSS 54, Beinecke.

65. M de R, *Discretions*, 143.

66. Clark's visiting card reads "Comm. Dott. Prof. Charles U. Clark, Ex-Direttore, Scuola Classica America. Yale Club, New York."

67. EP to OR, 11 October 1940, OR Papers, YCAL MSS 54, Beinecke.

68. The Agenzia Stefani was a press organization, originally created to further the public image of Italy abroad, but as taken over by the Fascists, it became an arm of Fascist propaganda. Under the guise of promoting Italian culture, its real agenda was political. Pound's work for this agency gives a further reason for his decision to go to America; and (this is speculation), if the assignment was withdrawn or didn't come through as expected, it may contribute to understanding why Pound decided not to repatriate in 1940.

69. OR to EP, 14 and 15 October 1940, EP Papers, YCAL MSS 43, Beinecke.

70. M de R, *Discretions*, 147.

71. Ibid.

72. Ibid., 147, 151.

73. EP to OR, 3 October 1941, OR Papers, YCAL MSS 54: ". . . am now full blooded Maltese cat with at least two tails . . . if the Maltese committee gits back the island; I spoke Chig's unkle will be Lord protector?" [His Highness Prince Sigismundo Chigi, Grand Master of the Order of Malta]; EP to OR, 8 October 1941, OR Papers, YCAL MSS 54: "Did she get letter saying he was a Maltese cat?"

74. EP to OR, 3 October 1941, OR Papers, YCAL MSS 54, Beinecke.

75. EP to OR, 5 October 1941, OR Papers, YCAL MSS 54, Beinecke.

76. EP to Adreano Ungaro, 5 and 9 March 1942, EP Papers, YCAL MSS 43, Beinecke.

77. EP to OR, 6 July and 29 November 1941, OR Papers, YCAL MSS 54, Beinecke.

78. EP to Adreano Ungaro, 9 December 1942, EP Papers, YCAL MSS 43, Beinecke.

79. EP to OR, 21 October 1941, OR Papers, YCAL MSS 54, Beinecke.

80. J. J. Wilhelm claims that the initial monitoring of Pound's broadcasts was simply part of the Federal Communications Commission's general monitoring of all Axis communications, but the letters to Biddle from the "Listening Post" and Biddle's forwarding of these letters for criminal investigation in July 1941 clearly indicate that this was not the case. See *Ezra Pound: The Tragic Years, 1925–1972* (University Park: Pennsylvania State University Press, 1994), 182ff.

81. EP to JJA, 7 July 1940, Furioso Papers, YCAL MSS 75, Beinecke.

82. EP to Adreano Ungaro, n.d. [1941], EP Papers, YCAL MSS 43, Beinecke.

83. M de R, *Discretions*, 156ff.

84. Confucius, *The Great Digest; The Unwobbling Pivot; and The Analects* (New York: New Directions, 1969), 29–33.

85. EP to OR, 12 May 1943, OR Papers, YCAL MSS 54, Beinecke.

86. See Princess Troubetzkoi to EP, 4 August 1941, and his reply, 7 August 1941, EP Papers, YCAL MSS 43, Beinecke.

87. EP to OR, 23 June 1943, OR Papers, YCAL MSS 54, Beinecke.

88. See Robert Katz, *The Battle for Rome: The Germans, the Allies, the Partisans, and the Pope, September 1943–June 1944* (New York: Simon and Schuster, 2003).

89. "Mary's Notebook," 1943–45, OR Papers, YCAL MSS 54, Beinecke.

90. Steininger, *South Tyrol*, 68.

91. In Wilhelm, *Ezra Pound*, 202–3.

92. M de R, interview by CLS, October 2004.

93. M de R, *Discretions*, 187.

94. M de R, preface to *Discretions*, unpublished (version 1), given to CLS in 2004.

95. Isabel Pound, 30 July 1939; Homer Pound, 3 August 1939, EP Papers, YCAL, MSS 43, Beinecke.

96. M de R, *Discretions*, 191.

97. EP to Francis Biddle, 4 August 1943, EP Papers, YCAL MSS 43, Beinecke.

Chapter 3

1. Rolf Steininger, *South Tyrol: A Minority Conflict of the Twentieth Century* (New Brunswick, NJ: Transaction, 2003), 69.

2. M de R, *Ezra Pound, Father and Teacher: Discretions* (New York: New Directions, 2005), 189.

3. Ibid., 222.

4. Ibid., 224.

5. EP to M de R, 3 December 1943, EP Papers, YCAL MSS 43, Beinecke.

6. M de R, *Discretions*, 198.

7. EP to M de R, 6 March 1944, EP Papers, YCAL MSS 43, Beinecke.

8. In Tim Redman, *Ezra Pound and Italian Fascism* (Cambridge: Cambridge University Press, 1991), 263.

9. In Humphrey Carpenter, *A Serious Character: The Life of Ezra Pound* (New York: Dell, 1988), 634.

10. EP to OR, 30 November and 2 December 1943, OR Papers, YCAL MSS 54, Beinecke.

11. In Redman, *Ezra Pound*, 250.

12. EP, "Race or Illness," *Il Popolo di Alessandria*, 12 March 1944.

13. M de R, *Discretions*, epigraph.

14. EP to Fernando Mezzasoma, 15 March 1944, FBI files, NARA, trans. CLS.

15. EP to Mezzasoma, 14 September 1944, FBI files, NARA, trans. CLS.

16. Ibid.

17. OR, "Letter book, 1945," OR Papers, YCAL MSS 54, Beinecke.

18. Quoted in Robert Spoo and Omar Pound, introduction to *Ezra and Dorothy Pound: Letters in Captivity, 1945–46* (New York: Oxford University Press, 1999), 5.

19. M de R, *Discretions*, 258.

20. OR to Count Guido Chigi Saracini, 11 January 1944, OR Papers, YCAL MSS 54, Beinecke.

21. M de R to OR, 20 February 1945 and 1 March 1945, OR Papers, YCAL MSS 54, Beinecke.

22. OR to M de R, 30 April 1945, OR Papers, YCAL MSS 54, Beinecke.

23. M de R, *Discretions*, 237.

24. Donald Hall, "Ezra Pound: An Interview," *Paris Review*, no. 28 (Summer–Fall 1962): 45.

25. For an excellent and painstaking account of Pound's capture, see Spoo and Pound, introduction to *Letters in Captivity*.

26. EP to M de R, 13 January 1974, copy in OR's research notebook, OR Papers, YCAL MSS 54, Beinecke.

27. M de R, *Discretions*, 244.

28. "Ramon Arrizabalaga's Memoir (1956)," in *Letters in Captivity*, 375.

29. M de R, *Discretions*, 245.

30. M de R to OR, 9 August 1945, OR Papers, YCAL MSS 54, Beinecke.

31. M de R to OR, 2 August 1945, OR Papers, YCAL MSS 54, Beinecke.

32. See Allen W. Dulles, *The Secret Surrender: The Classic Insider's Account of the Secret Plot to Surrender Northern Italy During WWII* (Guilford, CT: Lyons, 2006), 125ff., and Silvia Bertoldi, *I Tedeschi in Italia* (Milan, 1964), 186ff.

33. 22 May 1945, in C. David Heymann, *Ezra Pound: The Last Rower* (New York: Citadel, 1992), 159–60.

34. Walter A. Hardie, Colonel, CMP, Provost Marshal General to DP, 24 August 1945, in *Letters in Captivity*, 81.

35. M de R, *Discretions*, 247.

36. DP to EP, 29 September 1945, in *Letters in Captivity*, 99.

37. OR to DP, 2 June 1945, OR Papers, YCAL MSS 54, Beinecke.

38. DP to EP, 15 October 1945, in *Letters in Captivity*, 133.

39. OR to EP, 9 October 1945, EP Papers, YCAL MSS 43, Beinecke.

40. See EP to DP, 24, 25, and 30 October 1945, in *Letters in Captivity*, 158.

41. OR to James Laughlin, 11 November 1945, OR Papers, YCAL MSS 54, Beinecke.

42. Homer Somers, telephone interview by CLS, August 2007.

43. COMGENMED to AGWAR, 22 October 1945, U.S. Department of Justice, NARA.

44. M de R, *Discretions*, 257.

45. Ibid., 258.

46. EP to DP, 4 November 1945, in *Letters in Captivity*, 173.

47. DP to EP, 28 October 1945, ibid., 163.

48. J. Edgar Hoover, Urgent message to Communications Section, 27 December 1945, FBI document 100-34099-417, NARA.

49. M de R, *Discretions*, 260.

50. DP to EP, 22 December 1945, in *Letters in Captivity*, 225.

51. EP to M de R, 10 February 1946, EP Papers, YCAL MSS 43, Beinecke.

52. M de R, "Notebook 1943–45," OR Papers, YCAL MSS 54, Beinecke.

53. DP to EP, 16 January 1946, in *Letters in Captivity*, 241.

54. DP to EP, 20 January 1946, ibid., 245.

55. DP to EP, 23 January 1946, ibid., 247.

56. M de R. to EP, "Notebook 1943–45," OR Papers, YCAL MSS 54, Beinecke.

57. EP to DP, 25 May 1946, in *Letters in Captivity*, 345.

58. Homer Somers to M de R, 15 December 1945, OR Papers, YCAL MSS 54, Beinecke.

59. Homer Somers to M de R, 11 January 1946, OR Papers, YCAL MSS 54, Beinecke.

60. Homer Somers to M de R, 1 May 1946, OR Papers, YCAL MSS 54, Beinecke.

61. Homer Somers, interview by CLS, August 2007.

62. EP to DP, 14 and 16[?] November 1945, in *Letters in Captivity*, 189.

63. Gerald Brenan, *Personal Record 1920–1972* (London: Cape, 1974), 346.

64. Ronald Duncan, *Journal of a Husbandman* (London: Faber and Faber, 1944), 18, 25.

65. M de R. to EP, "Notebook 1943–45," OR Papers, YCAL MSS 54, Beinecke.

66. EP, *Confucius* (New York: New Directions, 1951), 51.

67. M de R, *Discretions*, 266.

68. M de R to CLS, 2 December 2007.

69. M de R to CLS, 8 December 2007.

70. M de R, *Discretions*, 266.

71. Ibid., 265.

72. EP to OR, n.d. [1946], OR Papers, YCAL MSS 54, Beinecke.

73. William Shakespeare, *Merchant of Venice* (New York: Signet, 1998), act 2, scene 5.

Chapter 4

1. M de R to OR, 20 February 1946, OR Papers, YCAL MSS 54, Beinecke.

2. Homer Somers to M de R, 4 April 1946, OR Papers, YCAL MSS 54, Beinecke.

3. DP to EP, 2 April 1946, in *Ezra and Dorothy Pound: Letters in Captivity*, ed. Robert Spoo and Omar Pound (New York: Oxford University Press, 1999), 307.

4. Julien Cornell, *The Trial of Ezra Pound: A Documented Account of the Treason Case by the Defendant's Lawyer* (London: Faber and Faber, 1966), 41.

5. M de R to OR, 10 April 1946, OR Papers, YCAL MSS 54, Beinecke.

6. M de R to EP, n.d., EP Papers, YCAL MSS 43, Beinecke.

7. EP to Julien Cornell, 1 January 1946, in Cornell, *The Trial of Ezra Pound*, 75.

8. M de R to OR, 16 April 1946, 9 May 1946, OR Papers, YCAL MSS 54, Beinecke.

9. Minutes Cope and Ronald, 5 March 1946; and UK Delegation, Paris, Brief No. 15, 19 April 1946. PRO, FO 371/55118/C5001 in Rolf Steininger, *South Tyrol: A Minority Conflict of the Twentieth Century* (New Brunswick, NJ: Transaction, 2003), 152.

10. Top Secret, Charles to Under Secretary of State Oliver Harvey, 26 June 1945. PRO, FO 371/50780/U 5163, in Steininger, *South Tyrol*, 78–79, 151.

11. M de R, *Ezra Pound, Father and Teacher: Discretions* (New York: New Directions, 2005), 264.

12. See Alessandro de Felice, "L'intelligence U.S.A. spia il 'rinnegato' Ezra Pound durante la seconda Guerra mondiale: alcuni documenti statunitensi inediti," www.alessandrodefelice .it/rassegnastampa/Articolidoc/Ezra%20Pound.doc.

13. RG 226, entry 125, box 44, NARA.

14. RG 226, entry 165, box 35, NARA.

15. Alessandro de Felice. "L'intelligence U.S.A. spia il 'rinnegato' Ezra Pound." Although this letter is not dated, Scamporino was recalled to the U.S. in June 1944. We can assume therefore that it was written between 2 December 1943 and June 1944.

16. Frank L. Amprim to Liaison Section, 23 January 1944 and 3 February 1944. Communication No. 70 and Communication No. 81. FBI Microfiche Files.

17. Ranieri de San Faustino to Frank L. Amprim, n.d., FBI Microfiche Files. The identities of Amprim's informants have been deduced from heavily redacted FBI files by working with the remaining evidence and cross-referencing it with other sources. In this case, San Faustino's statement was also found among declassified documents in the British National Archives file on Ezra Pound, without the name deletion. See Ranieri de San Faustino, "Statement," WO 204/12602, 7 June 1945, British National Archives.

18. Frank L. Amprim, Report [illegible], FBI Microfiche Files.

19. Frank L. Amprim to Director, FBI, 12 June 1945, FBI Microfiche Files.

20. Frank L. Amprim to J. Edgar Hoover, 29 May 1945, FBI Microfiche Files.

21. Frank L. Amprim to J. Edgar Hoover, 22 August 1945, FBI Microfiche Files.

22. Sidney L. Henderson, Major, M.I. (G-2) (C-I) to Frank L. Amprim, 8 September 1945, British National Archives.

23. AGWAR G-2 TO Frank L. Amprim, Message W-37061, British National Archives. Also J. Edgar Hoover to Frank L. Amprim, 25 June 1945. "Nowhere has two witnesses to same overt act of treason been developed. Discontinue all general investigation in the case and concentrate on development of two witnesses." FBI Microfiche Files.

24. Frank L. Amprim to Director, FBI, 25 September 1945. "[Redacted] were only in a position to observe Pound speaking until January, February or March of 1942. They reemphasized their inability to recall any other dates. It is not believed that either of these two men would make competent witnesses, especially since it would appear that the Department of Justice is only interested in acts committed after Pearl Harbor." FBI Microfiche Files.

25. Frank L. Amprim to Director, FBI, 25 September 1945, FBI Microfiche Files.

26. Frank L. Amprim to Director, FBI, 7 September 1945. "There is set forth hereinafter an analysis of the evidence developed to prove overt acts by the Subject." FBI Microfiche Files.

27. John Drummond to Asst. Judge Advocate General, 24 August 1945, FBI Microfiche Files.

28. Lt. Col. M. R. Irion to G-2 (Counter Intelligence), 3 September 1945 (Log: JA-13,165), WO 204/12602, British National Archives.

29. Frank L. Amprim to Director, FBI, 14 September 1945, FBI Microfiche File.

30. McNarney (G-1) to AGWAR WASHINGTON, 21 June 1945, Ref No FX-96763, WO 204/12602, British National Archives.

31. James Jesus Angleton to EP, 31 May 1939, EP Papers, YCAL MSS 43, Beinecke.

32. JJA to EP, 7 July 1940, EP Papers, YCAL MSS 43, Beinecke.

33. Ibid.; and JJA to EP, 3 July 1939, EP Papers, YCAL MSS 43, Beinecke.

34. JJA to EP, 19 January 1939, EP Papers, YCAL MSS 43, Beinecke.

35. JJA to EP, 31 May 1940, EP Papers, YCAL MSS 43, Beinecke.

36. Angleton was first interviewed just after he was at Harvard Law School on 13 January 1943. His identity is inferred from the following unredacted facts in the FBI document: he admits meeting Pound in the summer of 1937 in Rapallo; he explains that he was educated

abroad because of his father's business interests; he mentions arranging a dinner for Pound in New Haven in 1939; he mentions returning to Italy with Pound on the same trans-Atlantic ship in 1939; he tells of taking Pound's photograph and of the photographs being used in an article about Pound in *Time* magazine before the outbreak of the war.

37. See, for example, James Jesus Angleton to Ezra Pound, 28 December 1939. "The press carries all the accounts from the British sources on the war and leaves Berlin out. Everything is definitely British and the jews [sic] cause a devil of a lot of stink. Here in New York will be the next pogrom and they do need about a thousand ghettos in America. Jew Jew Jew." EP Papers, YCAL MSS 43, Beinecke.

38. FBI Interview of JJA, Boston Office, 13 January 1941, FBI Microfiche File.

39. Ibid.

40. James Jesus Angleton. Military Personnel Records, NARA. Some of the dates that follow in this account of Angleton's activities in Rome and London disagree with dates in two of the most extensive sources on Angleton's activities in the OSS: Robin W. Winks, *Cloaks and Gown: Scholars in the Secret War, 1939–1961* (New Haven, CT: Yale University Press, 1987), and Timothy Naftali, "X-2 and the Apprenticeship of American Counterespionage, 1942–1944" (PhD diss., Harvard University, 1993). However, since my narrative is derived directly from Angleton's personnel files, with all letters of requisition, travel, and reports for duty, I am confident that the chronology presented here is correct. I wish to thank Larry Macdonald at the National Archives for pulling these files for me, along with all the military personnel records for Angleton's father.

41. James Hugh Angleton, Military Personnel Records, NARA.

42. Memorandum for Puritan, From Saint and Cardinal, 16 September 1943, RG 226, box 50, file 4, NARA.

43. JJA to EP, 19 January 1939, EP Papers, YCAL MSS 43, Beinecke.

44. In Naftali, "X-2," 566.

45. In the Norman Holmes Pearson papers at the Beinecke Library, one can find the OSS organizational chart that shows the duties of the various OSS divisions and the flow of traffic among them: "exchange of intelligence with ONI, G-2, FBI, State Department, OEW, X-B."

46. JJA to EP, 19 January 1939, EP Papers, YCAL MSS 43, Beinecke.

47. See Naftali, "X-2," 611ff., and Max Corvo, *The OSS in Italy, 1942–1945* (New York: Praeger, 1990), 226ff.

48. See Naftali, "X-2," 613. His information is derived from documents in the National Archives, Record group 226/174. In the Ezra Pound files declassified by the British National Archives, one can observe the initials "JA" on most of the documents up to 1945.

49. Angleton's father, James Hugh Angleton, had also been interviewed by the FBI and had stated that "he would be quite happy to testify in any trial which might be had concerning subject." His identity in the redacted document is easily inferred from the statement that "his son, presently a student at the Harvard Law School, Cambridge, Massachusetts, had . . . made a special visit to Rapallo in order to meet POUND and had taken quite a number of pictures of subject." FBI Microfiche. There is no date, but Angleton Jr. was at Harvard "presently" in 1941.

50. In *Between History and Poetry: The Letters of H.D. and Norman Holmes Pearson*, ed. Donna Krolik Hollenberg (Iowa City: University of Iowa Press, 1997), 40.

51. Ibid., 18.

52. Perdita MacPherson to H.D., 1 June 1941, H.D. Papers, YCAL MSS 24, Beinecke.

53. NHP to H.D., 25 August 1943, in *Between History and Poetry*, 28.

54. See Donna Krolik Hollenberg, introduction to *Between History and Poetry*, 1.

55. Perdita MacPherson to H.D., 16 July 1943, H.D. Papers, YCAL MSS 24, Beinecke.

56. Winks, *Cloaks and Gowns*, 261.

57. Hollenberg, introduction to *Between History and Poetry*, 7.

58. Ibid., 4.

59. H.D. to NHP, 12 July 1943, unpublished letter at www.imagists.org/hd/hdchron4.

60. Winks, *Cloaks and Gowns*, 263.

61. Ibid., 346.

62. Ibid.

63. Ibid.

64. H.D., *The Sword Went Out to Sea* (Gainesville: University Press of Florida, 2007), 57.

65. Ibid., 58.

66. Ibid., 83.

67. Ibid., 109.

68. Ibid., 90.

69. See H.D., *The Sword Went Out to Sea*: Her unease still not settled, the spiritual map of her life not completed, she explored still other layers of her experience with Pound by recasting him in the role of Robert Devereux, the Earl of Essex (1566–1601), who was at one and the same time the favorite of Queen Elizabeth I and her betrayer. The historical Devereux had been introduced at court when he was twenty and evoked in the Queen a love that hovered tempestuously between maternal solicitude and Eros. Devereux played on this affection, using it to engender support for expeditions into Spain and Ireland, pushing the boundaries of her concern until they broke in 1599. After he had engineered an unauthorized truce in Ireland, Elizabeth stripped him of his command and placed him under house arrest. He handled his disgrace by an armed rebellion against her, and when it failed, she sent him to the Tower, where he was beheaded on 25 February 1601.

In retelling the tale, H.D. pretends to watch these events unfold, as if through the perceived parallels with herself and Pound, she can work out the intricacies of personal affection and loyalty to the state. "We had tried to imagine the reason for his plot, his insurrection," she remarks, adding, clearly, "I could not think of Robert Devereux as a traitor. In her imagination, which superimposed one set of relationships upon another, seeing Devereux's joining forces with Oliver Cromwell is analogous to Pound's support of Mussolini; and the key event is not Devereux's misjudgment of a treaty, but his disloyalty to the person of the Queen . . . a disloyalty provoked by the Queen's prior dismissal of him. "The blow that ended three years later, in the Queen's death, had been delivered before I met Geoffrey. But the Queen really died when she said, 'We dismiss you.'" In the fluidity of this dreamscape, H.D. understands the female to have brought about the demise of her own heart by a refusal that ends in a retaliatory abandonment. "There is still the Queen. He has killed her." But the interest of the trope, considered as a way to think about allegiance that is owed to the State as well as to a person, is its refusal to consider rebellion as an unmotivated uprising. The Queen bears the responsibility for the seeming disloyalty of her subject, and by analogy, H.D. poses the question of what aspect of United States policy had provoked a similar rebellion in Pound. "But the Queen really died when she said, 'we dismiss you.'" There must have been, she thought, a previous alienation that had led "the dismissed" Pound to his ideological positions. He was both victim and abuser of power; actor in a plot that involved multiple perspectives and motives. And in 1945, when she was working on the manuscript, she did not know where the historical Pound was. "Where is Essex? Will they wait? Will they take him to the Tower? Has it already happened?"

70. H.D. to Bryher, 13 and 15 October 1948, in *Between History and Poetry*, 110.

71. Rebecca West, *The Meaning of Treason* (London: Phoenix, 1982), 13.

72. H.D. to NHP, 22 September 1949, in *Between History and Poetry*, 92.

73. H.D. to NHP, 29 January 1946, ibid., 54.

74. NHP to H.D., 12 January 1959, ibid., 257.

75. NHP to William Carlos Williams, 9 January 1946, unpublished letter, ibid., 110–11.

Chapter 5

1. EP to OR, 8 May and 22 May 1946, OR Papers, YCAL MSS 54, Beinecke.

2. EP to OR, 22 March 1946, OR Papers, YCAL MSS 54, Beinecke.

3. M de R, *Ezra Pound, Father and Teacher: Discretions* (New York: New Directions, 2005), 268.

4. Ibid., 269–70.

5. M de R to OR, 15 June 1946, OR Papers, YCAL MSS 54, Beinecke.

6. Ibid.

7. Ibid.

8. OR to EP, 19 October 1946, EP Papers, YCAL MSS 43, Beinecke.

9. M de R to CLS.

10. See FBI files.

11. FBI files. The identity of the Princess Troubetzkoi is of more than passing interest. One of the major questions raised by the charge of treason against Ezra Pound is why Pound was prosecuted and not, for example, George Nelson Page, another American who had started the *American Hour* program in Rome, or James Barnes, who also broadcast. Of equal interest is why the British did not prosecute Natalie Troubetzkoi—whose anti-British and anti-Russian radio scripts were translated, at Pound's suggestion, into Italian by Signora Rosetti Agresti. One unverifiable conclusion is that Troubezkoi was an agent in place. At the least, the FBI files reveal that Natalie Troubetzkoi's address on 17 December 1945, was c/o Government Communications Bureau, 14 Ryder Street, London SW I. This conjecture would also explain another mystery: James T. Quirk's 1940s letters mention a Russian Princess in British uniform riding with Frank Amprim to the Disciplinary Training Center.

12. John Drummond to OR, 24 October 1946, OR Papers, YCAL MSS 54, Beinecke.

13. Ibid.

14. OR to EP, 19 October 1946, EP Papers YCAL MSS 43, Beinecke.

15. OR to EP, 11 and 23 November 1946, EP Papers, YCAL MSS 43, Beinecke.

16. Quoted in M de R to OR, 22 June 1946, OR Papers, YCAL MSS 54, Beinecke.

17. M de R, *Discretions*, 275.

18. Ibid.

19. EP to M de R, 7 January 1947, OR Papers, YCAL MSS 54, Beinecke.

20. M de R to OR, 10 April 1947, OR Papers, YCAL MSS 54, Beinecke.

21. M de R to OR, 3 February 1948, OR Papers, YCAL MSS 54, Beinecke.

22. Anne Conover, *Olga Rudge and Ezra Pound* (New Haven, CT: Yale University Press, 2001), 180.

23. OR to EP, 14 February 1948, EP Papers, YCAL MSS 43, Beinecke.

24. See Conover, *Olga Rudge and Ezra Pound*, 181.

25. OR to EP, 10 May 1948, EP Papers, YCAL MSS 43, Beinecke.

26. M de R to EP, 4 March 1948, Ezra Pound Collection, HRHRC.

27. OR to EP, 22 February 1951, EP Papers, YCAL MSS 43, Beinecke.

28. M de R, *Discretions*, 282.

29. M de R, conversation with CLS, October 2004.

30. OR to EP, 21 June 1950, EP Papers, YCAL MSS 43, Beinecke.

31. Quoted in Conover, *Olga Rudge and Ezra Pound*, 196.

32. M de R, *Discretions*, 289.

33. John Drummond to OR, 29 May 1948, OR Papers, YCAL MSS 54, Beinecke.

34. OR to EP, 2 June 1948, EP Papers, YCAL MSS 43, Beinecke.

35. M de R, *Discretions*, 280.

36. Hugh Kenner, *The Pound Era* (Berkeley: University of California Press, 1971), 537–38.

37. M de R, *Discretions*, 283.

38. Ibid.

39. Monsignor Prof. Gustavo Tulli, "The Royal Descendents of the Arodij across the Centuries: A Genealogical History" (unpublished manuscript, 1955).

40. Boris's controlling intellectual romance was with an extraordinary medieval woman whose life had been chronicled by a Benedictine monk named Donizone. His *Vita Mathildis*, composed in 1046, documents a tale of medieval intrigue among rich feudal princes who ruled northern Italy on behalf of the German kings. Mathilde was of the fourth generation and the final heir of a dynasty dating back to 940, when Atto Adalberto constructed an impregnable castle on the unapproachably steep mountains of Canossa—a place that commanded prospects of the Po River plain—not unlike the location of Brunnenburg, which, like Castle Tyrol above it, looks out over the Adige River and its surrounding valleys.

Mathilde's father died when she was eight; then her older brother and sister also died, and she and her mother, Beatrice, were banished from the family seat in Mantua. All Bonificio's lands, income, and property were claimed by the German king, Henry III. From this point, Mathilde's life can be seen as an extended maneuver to reclaim her father's property, a play of the Church against the State, which, in her time, struggled to establish the ascendancy of one institution over the other. Her ties were understandably and irrevocably to the Church, and this loyalty was intensified by a particularly close bond to Pope Gregory VII. It was Gregory who extended the first excommunication of a king by a pope, and it was Mathilde who negotiated the meeting between Henry IV and Gregory at the fortress at Canossa that sought to resolve this sundering. The issues of ascendancy were not decided at Canossa—there was to be further treachery—but it was from this point Mathilde claimed her inheritance from Bonificio in the name of St. Peter and the Roman church. "She left then the part of the king . . . and gave all her goods to Saint Peter who held the keys as the divine doorkeeper, making him her heir and she the heir of Peter." This Act of Donation—however ambiguous its legal status (could women own property in the eleventh century under any circumstances?)—won her (and Gregory) the temporary loyalty of Rome, a place in history, and ultimately, the imaginative allegiance of Boris Baratti. Mathilde assumed that her entitlement depended on the church and not the king, and whatever significance this story had for Boris, it resonated, if only subconsciously, with Mary, who had also, since her father's imprisonment, and for very different reasons, come to distinguish between and depend upon the claims of various kinds of law. See Michele K. Spike, *Tuscan Countess: The Life and Extraordinary Times of Matilda of Canossa* (New York: Vendome, 2004).

41. EP to OR, 21 October 1949, OR Papers, YCAL MSS 54, Beinecke.

42. EP to M de R, 18 November 1948, OR Papers, YCAL MSS 54, Beinecke.

43. OR to EP, 13 November 1949, in Conover, *Olga Rudge and Ezra Pound*, 199.

44. M de R to OR, 29 September 1949, OR Papers, YCAL MSS 54, Beinecke.

45. M de R, *Discretions*, 279.

46. EP, Canto XLV, in *The Cantos of Ezra Pound* (New York: New Directions, 1969), 229.

47. EP, Canto XLV.

48. OR to EP, 10 April 1950, EP Papers, YCAL MSS 43, Beinecke.

49. Mary Barnard, *Assault on Mount Helicon: A Literary Memoir* (Berkeley: University of California Press, 1984), 263.

50. EP to M de R, 21 July 1950, OR Papers, YCAL MSS 54, Beinecke.

51. M de R to OR, 13 July 1950, OR Papers, YCAL MSS 54, Beinecke.

52. M de R to OR, 2 March 1951, OR Papers, YCAL MSS 54, Beinecke.

53. OR to EP, 22 February 1951, EP Papers, YCAL MSS 43, Beinecke.

54. EP to M de R, 24 July 1950, OR Papers, YCAL MSS 54, Beinecke.

55. EP to M de R, 10 August 1952, OR Papers, YCAL MSS 54, Beinecke.

56. EP to M de R, 7 July 1951, OR Papers, YCAL MSS 54, Beinecke.

57. M de R, interview by CLS, 23 June 1994.

58. EP to M de R, 23 December 1952, OR Papers, YCAL MSS 54, Beinecke.

59. EP to M de R, 30 July 1952, OR Papers, YCAL MSS 54, Beinecke.

60. M de R, interview with CLS, October 2004; OR to EP, 26 May 1952, EP Papers, YCAL MSS 43, Beinecke; and Conover, *Olga Rudge and Ezra Pound*, 205.

61. M de R, introduction to second edition of *Discretions*, draft, private collection.

62. M de R, *Discretions*, 288.

63. Ibid., 290–91.

64. M de R to OR, 12 April 1975, OR Papers, YCAL MSS 54, Beinecke.

65. FBI files.

66. FBI files, 3 July 1945.

67. These names have been deduced from the information remaining after the redacted FBI files were made public. Anyone who wishes to know how this list was assembled—the "clues" about dates, places, and degree of acquaintance with Pound can contact the author. Information like: [] went with Pound to Harvard in 1939 and heard him lecture, or [] first met Pound in Paris in 1933, or [] first met Pound in England in 1911, or [] was himself in Rapallo in winter/spring 1928–29, or [] saw Pound at Olga Rudge's place in Paris in 1930, and so forth.

68. When Pound gave Harry Meacham a list of people to contact who might help with his release in 1957, he included W. C. Williams, Norman Holmes Pearson, Ernest Hemingway, and e. e. cummings. See Harry M. Meacham, *The Caged Panther: Ezra Pound at Saint Elizabeths* (New York: Twayne, 1967), 32–33.

69. M de R, *Discretions*, 292.

70. Ibid., 295.

71. Archibald MacLeish, review of *Section: Rock-Drill*, by Ezra Pound, *New York Times*, 16 November 1956, quoted in Meacham, *The Caged Panther*, 32–33.

72. M de R, *Discretions*, 293.

73. M de R to OR, 12 March 1953, OR Papers, YCAL MSS 54, Beinecke.

74. M de R to OR, 20 March 1953, OR Papers, YCAL MSS 54, Beinecke.

75. EP, Canto LXXXIV, in *The Cantos*, 569.

76. EP to M de R, n.d., OR Papers YCAL MSS 54, Beinecke. "Then they sit round yelling for EP to get into some TOTALLY useless legal tangle that will cost $5000 a week and get NO where/instead of getting on with the job of getting his most important work into print as fast as possible."

77. Meacham, *The Caged Panther*, 52.

78. M de R to OR, 20 March 1953, OR Papers, YCAL MSS 54, Beinecke.

79. H.D. imagined Martinelli as a young, inexperienced counterpart to her twenty-one-year-old self. In fact, Martinelli was middle-aged, divorced, the mother of a ten-year-old child (left in the custody of its father), and by the 1950s an experienced literary groupie. She had been part of the circle of "transparent children" surrounding Anaïs Nin; later she became a fixture of the Greenwich Village scene, remembered in Anatole Broyard's memoir, *Kafka Was the Rage*, and fictionalized as Esme in William Gaddis's novel *The Recognitions*. She was thirty-three when she met Pound in 1952.

80. H.D., *End to Torment: A Memoir of Ezra Pound* (New York: New Directions, 1979), 40.

81. EP, Canto LXXIX, in *The Cantos*, 503.

82. H.D., *End to Torment*, 96.

83. Sheri Martinelli, *Undine's Little Book* (Milan: Scheiwiller, 195?).

84. David Rattray, "Weekend with Ezra Pound," *The Nation*, 16 November 1957, 343–49.

85. Quoted in H.D., *End to Torment*, 57.

86. See http://www.williamgaddis.org/recognitions.

87. M de R, *Discretions*, 293.

88. M de R to OR, 10 May 1953, OR Papers, YCAL MSS 54, Beinecke.

89. She reasoned that Italy would be more open-minded since it did not have the apparatus of state invested in Pound's case; she did not know that some people in Italy had thought that Pound was, if anything, a spy for the U.S. government (Pellizi interview), and that others had, for their own purposes, supported Pound's broadcasting as beneficial to the Italian propaganda efforts against the Allies. See FBI Memo, 27 May 1945, quoting a letter dated 22 December 1941, marked "Urgent" by the Italian Ministry of the Interior to the Royal Prefecttura of Genoa and the Rome Police department. "The Ministry of Foreign Affairs has communicated as follows: 'The Ministry of Popular Culture is advised that the American citizens [redacted] and Ezra Pound, residing at Rapallo, Via Marsala 12, are collaborators of the Ministry of Popular Culture and have manifested the desire to continue their collaboration (broadcasting to North America). This Ministry, considering the desirability of maintaining the aforesaid in their service for the purpose of propaganda against North America, asks that we consider the possibility of excepting them from the restrictions imposed upon American citizens, and that they be authorized to continue their work on behalf of Italy for the Ministry of Popular Culture.' It is requested that this demand on the part of the Ministry of Popular Culture be granted." This memo is of interest for at least two reasons: 1. It indicates that several American citizens were broadcasting on Rome Radio (the other was named as Lida Lacey Fleitmann Bloodgood) but that the FBI pursued only Pound, and 2. It indicates that, although Pound thought he was speaking according to conscience and his right of free speech, the Italians quite clearly understood that they were using him for their own purposes.

90. Conover, *Olga Rudge and Ezra Pound*, 207.

91. M de R to OR, 15 July 1953, OR Papers, YCAL 54, Beinecke.

92. M de R to OR, n.d. 1950s, OR Papers, YCAL MSS 54: "About the 'legal right.' It's a notarized declaration from D. that I am authorized to sign contracts and to attend to all matters

concerning the publication of Italian translations of EP's writings. It applies also to any text written by EP in Italian."

93. M de R to OR, 14 November 1954, OR Papers, YCAL MSS 54, Beinecke. "Babbo sent us the first installment for the land—so it's now ours! And you know how much that means for us."

94. M de R to OR, 10 January 1955, OR Papers, YCAL MSS 54, Beinecke.

95. M de R to OR, 15 December 1953, OR Papers, YCAL MSS 54, Beinecke.

96. EP to M de R, 6 November 1953, OR Papers, YCAL MSS 54, Beinecke.

97. *In the Rose of Time* was published in 1956.

98. Robert Fitzgerald, "Memorandum for Mary," accompanied by twenty-four pages of abstracts from the broadcasts, 24 August 1954, Robert Fitzgerald Papers, YCAL MSS 222, Beinecke.

99. M de R, "Broken Promises Are as Good as a Lie," in *Whose World? Selected Poems* (Laurinburg, NC: St. Andrews College Press, 1998), 18.

100. Norman Holmes Pearson to H.D. quoted in H.D., *End to Torment*, 37.

101. In July 1955 there were thirty people in the house. She mentioned Bill and Gloria French, Ingrid Davies and her husband, Igor de Rachewiltz, Miss Cora Felcioni, Signora Agresti and her sister. In the next several months, she mentions Maria Britneva, the Prodans, and Lady St. Just.

102. EP to M de R, 19 October 1954 and 5 August 1954, OR Papers, YCAL MSS 54, Beinecke.

103. EP to M de R, 21 November 1956, OR Papers, YCAL MSS 54, Beinecke.

104. M de R to OR, 6 September 1957, OR Papers, YCAL MSS 54, Beinecke.

105. EP to M de R, 7 July 1955, OR Papers, YCAL MSS 54, Beinecke.

106. EP to M de R, 5 January 1956, OR Papers, YCAL MSS 54, Beinecke.

107. EP to M de R, 27 March 1956, OR Papers, 54 YCAL MSS 54, Beinecke.

108. EP to M de R, 7 July 1955, OR Papers, YCAL MSS 54, Beinecke.

109. EP to M de R, 17 April 1956, OR Papers, YCAL MSS 54, Beinecke.

110. EP to M de R, 5 January 1956, OR Papers, YCAL MSS 54, Beinecke.

111. EP to M de R, 30 September 1955, OR Papers, YCAL MSS, Beinecke.

112. EP to M de R, 7 April 1956, OR Papers, YCAL MSS 54, Beinecke.

113. "Aus ihr Trümmern treibt er die Synthese von American und Europa hervor. Sie ist sein Werk, ganz allein, Seine 84 Cantos sind die One World der Poesie . . . grossten lebenden Lyrikers." *Weltwoche*, quoted in EP to M de R, 25 January 1954, OR Papers, YCAL MSS 54, Beinecke.

114. EP to M de R, 26 March 1955, OR Papers, YCAL MSS 54, Beinecke.

115. EP to M de R, 9 July 1955, OR Papers, YCAL MSS 54, Beinecke.

116. EP to M de R, 14 and 17 November 1955, OR Papers, YCAL MSS 54, Beinecke.

117. EP to M de R, 12 July 1955, OR Papers, YCAL MSS 54, Beinecke.

118. EP to M de R, 19 July 1955, OR Papers, YCAL MSS 54, Beinecke.

119. EP to M de R, 1 December 1955, OR Papers YCAL, MSS 54, Beinecke.

120. M de R to OR, 25 June and 30 July 1956, OR Papers, YCAL MSS 54, Beinecke.

121. M de R to OR, 14 September 1956, OR Papers, YCAL MSS 54, Beinecke.

122. EP to M de R, 8 October 1956, OR Papers, YCAL MSS 54, Beinecke.

123. EP to M de R, 17 May 1955, OR Papers, YCAL MSS 54, Beinecke.

124. M de R to OR, 14 February 1957, OR Papers, YCAL MSS 54, Beinecke.

125. M de R, *Discretions*, 301.

126. In J. J. Wilhelm, *Ezra Pound: The Tragic Years, 1925–1972* (University Park: Pennsylvania State University Press, 1994), 303.

127. *Life* magazine, 6 February 1956.

128. M de R to OR, 13 March 1957, OR Papers, YCAL MSS 54, Beinecke.

129. M de R to OR, 26 February 1958, OR Papers, YCAL MSS 54, Beinecke.

130. M de R to OR, 19 April 1958, OR Papers, YCAL MSS 54, Beinecke.

131. M de R to OR, 9 May 1958, OR Papers, YCAL MSS 54, Beinecke.

132. M de R, *Discretions*, 303.

133. EP to M de R, 12 January 1956, OR Papers, YCAL MSS 54, Beinecke.

Chapter 6

1. M de R to OR, 13 May 1958, OR Papers, YCAL MSS 54, Beinecke.

2. Ibid.

3. M de R to OR, 3 August and 27 August 1958, OR Papers, YCAL MSS 54, Beinecke.

4. M de R to OR, 19 December 1958, OR Papers, YCAL MSS 54, Beinecke.

5. M de R, *Ezra Pound, Father and Teacher: Discretions* (New York: New Directions, 2005), 305–6.

6. EP to M de R, 9 July 1955, OR Papers, YCAL MSS 54, Beinecke.

7. Quoted in J. J. Wilhelm, *Ezra Pound: The Tragic Years: 1925–1972* (University Park: Pennsylvania University Press, 1994), 324.

8. B de R to OR, 25 February 1959 (trans. CLS), OR Papers, YCAL MSS 54, Beinecke.

9. M de R to OR, 26 March 1959, OR Papers, YCAL MSS 54, Beinecke.

10. M de R to OR, 20 March 1959, OR Papers, YCAL MSS 54, Beinecke.

11. M de R to OR, 2 March 1959, OR Papers, YCAL MSS 54, Beinecke.

12. M de R to OR, 10 March 1959, OR Papers, YCAL MSS 54, Beinecke.

13. D. G. Bridson, "My Reading," and "An Interview with Ezra Pound," *New Directions in Prose & Poetry* 17 (1961): 165ff.

14. M de R to OR, 29 April 1959, OR Papers, YCAL MSS 54, Beinecke.

15. M de R to OR, 18 May 1959, OR Papers, YCAL MSS 54, Beinecke.

16. Sophocles, *Women of Trachis: A Version by Ezra Pound* (New York: New Directions, 1957), 25.

17. M de R to OR, 31 May 1959, OR Papers, YCAL MSS 54, Beinecke.

18. EP, Canto CXIII.

19. M de R, *Discretions*, 305.

20. Arthur Moore to James Laughlin, 28 September 1959, James Laughlin Papers, YCAL MSS 654, Beinecke.

21. EP, Canto IV.

22. M de R to OR, 27 October 1959, OR Papers, YCAL MSS 54, Beinecke.

23. M de R to OR, 1 August 1959, OR Papers, YCAL MSS 54, Beinecke.

24. M de R to OR, 20 February 1960, OR Papers, YCAL MSS 54, Beinecke.

25. John Drummond to OR, 18 April 1960, OR Papers, YCAL MSS 54, Beinecke.

26. M de R to OR, 20 April 1960, OR Papers, YCAL MSS 54, Beinecke.

27. M de R to OR, 19 July 1960, OR Papers, YCAL MSS 54, Beinecke.

28. M de R to OR, 1 August 1960 and 10 March 1961, OR Papers, YCAL MSS 54, Beinecke.

29. M de R to OR, 9 March 1961, OR Papers, YCAL MSS 54, Beinecke.

30. M de R to OR, 31 May 1959, OR Papers, YCAL MSS 54, Beinecke.

31. Henry James, *The Turn of the Screw and The Aspern Papers* (New York: Penguin, 1986), 51.

32. Ibid., 71.

33. Ibid., 46.

34. M de R to OR, 1 August 1959, OR Papers, YCAL MSS 54, Beinecke.

35. Perdita Schaffner to H.D., Paris, March 1945. H.D. Papers, YCAL MSS 24, Beinecke.

36. NHP to EP, 31 January 1961, Za Pearson, Beinecke

37. NHP to EP, 20 March 1955, Za Pearson, Beinecke.

38. M de R to OR, 27 February 1961, OR Papers, YCAL MSS 54, Beinecke.

39. Eveline Bates Doob, "Some Notes on E.P.," *Paideuma* 8, no. 1 (Spring 1979): 74.

40. Ibid., 72.

41. Ibid., 70.

42. Ibid., 74.

43. He also belonged to the American Assembly ("illuminating issues of public policy"), the African Studies Association, and Harvard's Center for Russian Research. In 1961, he had not yet begun serving as the executive editor of the *Journal of Social Psychology*, a position he would occupy for over thirty years, but he was a frequent contributor to the *Public Opinion Quarterly*. By 1961, he had published books on *Propaganda: Its Psychology and Technique* (1935), *Frustration and Aggression* (1939), *Public Opinion and Propaganda* (1948), *Social Psychology: An Analysis of Human Behavior* (1952) and *Becoming More Civilized: A Psychological Exploration* (1960).

44. LD, "The Utilization of Social Scientists in the Overseas Branch of the Office of War Information," *American Political Science Review* 41 (August 1947): 653.

45. Ibid., 654.

46. "OWI Aid in Dissemination of Rumors," Memo, 4 October 1943, OSS Morale Operations, NARA.

47. He was also linked in with the heads of the Viking Press, Harper & Brothers, and Farrar, Straus and Young; among them were two Hollywood Oscar winners; a two-time Pulitzer Prize winner; the board chairman of CBS and a dozen key network executives; President Eisenhower's chief speech writer; and the editor of *Reader's Digest* international edition. Edward Barrett, Doob's boss at OWI (he was overseas director of psychological warfare) served as the chief of the U.S. government's overt psychological warfare effort from 1950–52 before becoming dean of the Columbia Graduate School of Journalism and founder of the *Columbia Journalism Review*. Other of his cohort left the war to take over major funding agencies: Charles Dollard became president of the Carnegie Foundation; Donald Young left the presidency of the Social Science Research Council to oversee the Russell Sage Foundation; Leland DeVinney went from Harvard to the Rockefeller Foundation.

48. LD, "The Utilization of Social Scientists," 652.

49. See LD, "Goebbels' Principles of Propaganda," *Public Opinion Quarterly* 14 (Fall 1950): 419–42.

50. LD, "The Strategies of Psychological Warfare," *Public Opinion Quarterly* 13 (Winter 1949): 635–44.

51. Austrian Foreign Minister Bruno Kreisky brought the problem before the UN on 21 September 1959.

52. U.S. nuclear missile bases in the Tyrol are located at Aviano Air Base and Ghedi-Torre Air Base.

53. See three books by Rolf Steininger on the Tyrol: *South Tyrol: A Minority Conflict of the Twentieth Century* (New Brunswick, NJ: Transaction, 2003); *Austria, Germany and the Cold War: From the Anschluss to the State Treaty, 1938–1955* (New York: Berghahn Books, 2008); and *Süd Tyrol im 20. Jahrhundert* (Innsbruck: Studien Verlag, 1997).

54. Steininger, *South Tyrol*, 123.

55. E. Doob, "Some Notes on E.P.," 75–76.

56. James Laughlin to Winfred Overholzer, 31 January 1963, Library of Congress.

57. M de R to OR, 28 May 1961, OR Papers, YCAL MSS 54, Beinecke.

58. M de R to OR, 26 June 1961, OR Papers YCAL MSS 54, Beinecke.

59. E. Doob, "Some Notes on E.P.," 77.

60. NHP to EP, 23 November 1961, EP Papers, YCAL MSS 43, Beinecke.

61. EP to NHP, 23 March 1957, EP Papers, YCAL MSS 43, Beinecke. "I don't get the feel that NHP DOES companionate or talk to any INDIVIDUALS."

62. Perdita Schaffner, "Mary de Rachewiltz, Discretions," *Paideuma* 4, nos. 2–3 (Summer–Fall 1975): 517.

63. Steininger, *South Tyrol*, 124–26.

64. LD, *Patriotism and Nationalism: Their Psychological Foundations* (New Haven, CT: Yale University Press, 1964), 263.

65. Ibid., 262.

66. E. Doob, "Some Notes on E.P.," 78.

67. OR to Ronald Duncan, 24 November 1961, OR Papers, YCAL MSS 54, Beinecke.

68. Ronald Duncan to EP, 6 November 1961, EP Papers, YCAL MSS 43, Beinecke.

69. M de R to OR, 23 January 1962 and 14 April 1962, OR Papers, YCAL MSS 54, Beinecke.

70. M de R to OR, 23 January 1962.

71. M de R to OR, 15 November 1961, OR Papers, YCAL MSS 54, Beinecke.

72. M de R to OR, 2 November 1962, OR Papers, YCAL MSS 54, Beinecke.

73. H.D., *End to Torment: A Memoir of Ezra Pound* (New York: New Directions, 1979), 43.

74. Ibid., 48.

75. Ibid., 48.

76. Ibid., 49.

Chapter 7

1. H.D., *End to Torment: A Memoir of Ezra Pound* (New York: New Directions, 1979), 49.

2. M de R to OR, 23 October 1968, OR Papers, YCAL MSS 54, Beinecke.

3. Herbert P. Gleason to M de R, 2 June 1964, OR Papers, YCAL MSS 54, Beinecke.

4. Lt. Col. Paul M. Hart to NHP, 16 March 1955, NHP Papers, Za Pearson, Beinecke.

5. NHP, introduction to *The Double Cross System*, typescript, 1971, NHP Papers, Za Pearson, Beinecke.

6. He mentions Compton Mackenzie's *Water on the Brain* (1933), Graham Greene's *Our Man in Havana* (1958), Edward Weismiller's *The Serpent Sleeping* (1962), Lt. Commander Ewen Montagu's *The Man Who Never Was* (1953), and Sir Alfred Duff Cooper's *Operation Heartbreak* (1950).

7. NHP, introduction to *The Double Cross System*.

8. Ibid.

9. NHP to DP, 9 October 1947, NHP Papers, Za Pearson, Beinecke.

10. DP to NHP, n.d., NHP Papers, Za Pearson, Beinecke.

11. DP to M de R, 27 June 1949, OR Papers, YCAL MSS 54, Beinecke.

12. D. D. Paige to OR, 14 July 1949, OR Papers, YCAL MSS 54, Beinecke.

13. DG, *Pigeons on the Granite: Memories of a Yale Librarian* (New Haven, CT: Beinecke Rare Book and Manuscript Library, 1988), 191.

14. Ibid.

15. Ibid.

16. NHP to EP, 9 January 1949, EP Papers, YCAL MSS 43, Beinecke.

17. DG, *Ezra Pound: A Bibliography* (Charlottesville: University Press of Virginia, 1983).

18. NHP to OR, 31 March 1953, OR Papers, YCAL MSS 54, Beinecke.

19. NHP to EP, 10 November 1954, EP Papers, YCAL MSS 43, Beinecke.

20. NHP to EP, 7 December 1954, EP Papers, YCAL MSS 43, Beinecke.

21. EP to NHP, 23 March 1957, NHP Papers, Za Pearson, Beinecke

22. M de R to OR, ? September 1959, OR Papers, YCAL MSS 54, Beinecke.

23. M de R to OR, 14 January 1963, OR Papers, YCAL MSS 54, Beinecke.

24. M de R to OR, 19 February 1964, OR Papers, YCAL MSS 54, Beinecke.

25. M de R to OR, 16 March 1964, OR Papers, YCAL MSS 54, Beinecke.

26. Bertram Rota, 3 July 1964, OR Papers, YCAL MSS 54, Beinecke.

27. Herbert Gleason to M de R, 29 June 1964, OR Papers, YCAL MSS 54, Beinecke.

28. Ibid.

29. M de R to James Laughlin, 19 June 1964, OR Papers, YCAL MSS 54, Beinecke.

30. M de R to OR, 4 August 1964, OR Papers, YCAL MSS 54, Beinecke.

31. M de R to OR, 29 August 1964, OR Papers YCAL MSS 54, Beinecke.

32. DG, *Pigeons on the Granite*, 195.

33. Bruce Nichols to Sister Mary Bernetta Quinn, 8 June 1970, Sister Mary Bernetta Quinn Papers, YCAL MSS 177, Beinecke.

34. Ibid., 197.

35. DG to DP, 23 March 1965, EP Papers, Lilly.

36. DG to DP, 17 October 1968, EP Papers, Lilly.

37. M de R to OR, 18 July 1965, OR Papers, YCAL MSS 54, Beinecke.

38. M de R to OR, 10 July 1964, OR Papers, YCAL MSS 54, Beinecke.

39. M de R to OR, 2 May 1966, OR Papers, YCAL MSS 54, Beinecke.

40. M de R to OR, 23 February 1967, OR Papers, YCAL MSS 54, Beinecke.

41. In DG, *Pigeons on the Granite*, 267.

42. M de R to Thurman Arnold, January 1967, OR Papers, YCAL MSS 54, Beinecke.

43. M de R to Sister Mary Bernetta Quinn, 19 July 1968, Mary Bernetta Quinn Papers, YCAL MSS 177, Beinecke.

44. M de R to Sister Mary Bernetta Quinn, 9 November 1975, Mary Bernetta Quinn Papers, YCAL MSS 177, Beinecke.

45. M de R to Sister Mary Bernetta Quinn, n.d., Mary Bernetta Quinn Papers, YCAL MSS 177, Beinecke.

46. DG to DP, 11 June 1973, EP Papers, Lilly.

47. M de R, interview by CLS, October 2004; OR to EP, 26 May 1952, EP Papers, YCAL MSS 54, Beinecke; and Anne Conover, *Olga Rudge and Ezra Pound: "What Thou Lovest Well . . ."* (New Haven, CT: Yale University Press, 2001), 205.

48. M de R, interview by CLS, October 2004.

49. The archive "is hedged about with a considerable number of rather stiff restrictions . . . no personal or family letters can be looked by anyone until ten years after Dorothy's death." James Laughlin to Noel Stock, 17 July 1973 in Conover, *Olga Rudge and Ezra Pound*, 266.

50. EP, n.d., EP Papers, YCAL MSS 43, Beinecke.

51. Minutes of the Meeting of Trustees, 11 October 1975, OR Papers, YCAL MSS 54, Beinecke.

52. OR to John Jones, n.d., OR Papers, YCAL MSS 54, Beinecke.

53. M de R to OR, 6 April 1974, OR Papers, YCAL MSS 54, Beinecke.

54. LD to OR, 28 July 1974, LD Papers, YCAL MSS 651, Beinecke.

55. LD to OR, 9 August 1975, LD Papers, YCAL MSS 651, Beinecke.

56. LD to Doris D. Blazek, 22 January 1975, LD Papers, YCAL MSS 651, Beinecke.

57. M de R to OR, 28 March 1974, OR Papers, YCAL MSS 54, Beinecke.

58. OP to James Laughlin, 1 August 1978.

59. MB, "Italy Travel Diary 1978," MB Papers, YCAL MSS 524, Beinecke.

60. OP to OR, 23 May 1982, OR Papers, YCAL MSS 54, Beinecke.

61. Conover, *Olga Rudge and Ezra Pound*, 266.

62. OR to Doris Blazek, 22 November 1978, OR Papers, YCAL MSS 54, Beinecke.

63. M de R to OR, 11 May 1980, OR Papers, YCAL MSS 54, Beinecke; and Conover, *Olga Rudge and Ezra Pound*, 278.

64. M de R to OR, 24 March 1975, OR Papers, YCAL MSS 54, Beinecke.

65. Doris Blazek to LD, 1 April 1982, LD Papers, YCAL 651, Beinecke.

66. M de R to OR, 24 March 1975, OR Papers, YCAL MSS 54, Beinecke.

67. M de R to OR, 3 April 1975, OR Papers, YCAL MSS 54, Beinecke.

68. OP to OR, 21 December 1982, OR Papers, YCAL MSS 54, Beinecke.

69. M de R to OR, 26 April 1988, OR Papers, YCAL MSS 54, Beinecke.

70. EP to OR, 9 June 1925, OR Papers, YCAL MSS 54, Beinecke.

71. EP, n.d., OR Papers, YCAL MSS 54, Beinecke.

Chapter 8

1. M de R to OR, 22 February 1969, OR Papers, YCAL MSS 54, Beinecke.

2. M de R to OR, 24 March 1975, OR Papers, YCAL MSS 54, Beinecke.

3. M de R, *Il Diapason* (Milan: All' Insegna del Pesce d'Oro, 1965).

> Vecchio, non valeva la pena
> tu facessi
> mille chilometri a piedi
> con scarponi cappello
> e fardello altrui
> per venirmi a dire
> una verità
> se ora la renneghi.

4. M de R to MB, 10 January 1954, MB Papers, YCAL MSS 524, Beinecke.

5. B de R to OR, 26 January 1955, OR Papers, YCAL MSS 54, Beinecke.

6. M de R to OR, 26 March 1959, OR Papers, YCAL MSS 54, Beinecke.

7. M de R to MB, 17 April 1959, MB Papers, YCAL MSS 524, Beinecke.

8. B de R to OR, 18 April 1961, OR Papers, YCAL MSS 54, Beinecke.

9. B de R to OR, 12 June 1962, OR Papers, YCAL MSS 54, Beinecke.

10. M de R to MB, 5 December 1963 and 21 January 1965, MB Papers, YCAL MSS 524, Beinecke.

11. M de R to MB, 25 May 1967, MB Papers, YCAL MSS 524, Beinecke.

12. M de R to MB, 4 July 1949, MB Papers, YCAL MSS 524, Beinecke.

13. M de R to OR, 1 March 1965, OR Papers, YCAL MSS 54, Beinecke.

14. M de R to Sister Mary Bernetta Quinn, 15 July 1967, Mary Bernetta Quinn Papers, YCAL MSS 177, Beinecke.

15. M de R to OR, 13 July 1950, OR Papers, YCAL MSS 54, Beinecke.

16. M de R to OR, 10 March 1969, OR Papers, YCAL MSS 54, Beinecke.

17. M de R to CBR, 19 August 1967, CBR Papers, HRHRC.

18. M de R to OR, 19 February 1975, OR Papers, YCAL MSS 54, Beinecke.

19. M de R to Sister Mary Bernetta Quinn, 27 April 1967, Mary Bernetta Quinn Papers, YCAL MSS 177, Beinecke.

20. M de R to MB, 18 January 1967, MB Papers, YCAL MSS 524, Beinecke.

21. M de R to CBR, 10 February 1968, CBR Papers, HRHRC.

22. M de R to MB, 18 January 1967, MB Papers, YCAL MSS 524, Beinecke.

23. M de R to CBR, 9 October 1968, CBR Papers, HRHRC.

24. M de R to CBR, 27 February 1969, CBR Papers, HRHRC.

25. M de R to OR, 30 October 1968, OR Papers, YCAL MSS 54, Beinecke.

26. M de R to MB, 18 June 1969, MB Papers, YCAL MSS 524, Beinecke.

27. M de R to Sister Mary Bernetta Quinn, 27 April 1967, Mary Bernetta Quinn Papers, YCAL MSS 177, Beinecke.

28. M de R to Sister Mary Bernetta Quinn, 6 October 1967, Mary Bernetta Quinn Papers, YCAL MSS 177, Beinecke.

29. M de R to CBR, 19 August 1967 and 25 October 1967, CBR Papers, HRHRC.

30. M de R to Sister Mary Bernetta Quinn, 24 October 1967, Mary Bernetta Quinn Papers, YCAL MSS 177, Beinecke.

31. M de R to Sister Mary Bernetta Quinn, 25 October 1967, Mary Bernetta Quinn Papers, YCAL MSS 177, Beinecke.

32. M de R, "Second Draft to Introduction," given to CLS.

33. M de R to Sister Bernetta Quinn, 29 December 1967, Mary Bernetta Quinn Papers, YCAL MSS 177, Beinecke.

34. Rolf Steininger, *South Tyrol: A Minority Conflict of the Twentieth Century* (New Brunswick, NJ: Transaction, 2003), 128.

35. M de R to CBR, "Spring" [1968], CBR Papers, HRHRC.

36. M de R to CBR, 18 April 1968, CBR Papers, HRHRC.

37. Two years later, in 1961, when he published *Communication in Africa: A Search for Boundaries*, he thanked the National Academy of Sciences, the Guggenheim Foundation, and the National Research Council [contract number DA 19-129-AM-1309 with the Quartermaster Research and Engineering Command of the U.S. Army] for their support.

38. He thanked Edward W. Barrett, the director of the Academy's International Mediation Study Group, along with Averell Harriman, the James Marshall Fund, the Concilium on International Studies of Yale, Oscar Schachter of UNITAR, G. A. Bayne of the American Universities Field Staff in Rome and said that "some, especially those connected with governments, must, alas, remain nameless as, here, at least must be the African participants."

39. EH to CBR, 29 September 1967, CBR Papers, HRHRC.

40. EH to CBR, 15 January 1970, CBR Papers, HRHRC.

41. EH to CBR, 16 November 1971, CBR Papers, HRHRC.

42. EH to CBR, 32 [*sic*] October 1969, CBR Papers, HRHRC.

43. M de R to CBR, 5 November 1969, CBR Papers, HRHRC.

44. M de R to CBR, 13 November 1969, CBR Papers, HRHRC.

45. M de R to CBR, 5 June 1969, CBR Papers, HRHRC.

46. M de R to CBR, 8 January 1970, CBR Papers, HRHRC.

47. M de R to CBR, 1 February 1970, CBR Papers, HRHRC.

48. M de R to CBR, 15 September 1970, CBR Papers HRHRC.

49. M de R to CBR, 27 January 1971, CBR Papers, HRHRC.

50. M de R to CBR, 1 March 1971 and 31 March 1971, CBR Papers, HRHRC.

51. Walter de Rachewiltz to OR, 1 April 1971, OR Papers, YCAL MSS 54, Beinecke.

52. M de R, untitled typescript given to CLS, 171.

53. Ibid., 21.

54. Ibid., 109.

55. Ibid., 36.

56. Nathaniel Hawthorne, *The Scarlet Letter* (New York: Penguin, 2015), 172.

57. M de R, untitled typescript, 25.

58. Ibid., 30.

59. Ibid., 47.

60. Ibid.

61. Ibid., 65.

62. Ibid., 88.

63. Ibid., 22.

64. Ibid., 140.

65. Ibid., 54.

66. Ibid., 51.

67. Ibid., 77.

68. Ibid., 162.

69. Ibid., 22.

70. Ibid., 41.

71. Ibid., 162.

72. Ibid., 165.

73. Ibid., 166.

74. Ibid., 169.

75. Philip Toynbee, "Pound as a Parent," *The Observer*, 21 November 1971.

76. Guy Davenport, "Three Books in One," *Virginia Quarterly Review* 47, no. 4 (August 1971): 638–40.

77. M de R to CBR, 8 December 1971, CBR Papers, HRHRC.

78. M de R to MB, 12 July 1971 MB Papers, YCAL MSS 524, Beinecke.

79. Hugh Kenner, "Impassioned Reticence," *National Review* 13, no. 33 (August 1971): 933–35.

80. M de R to MB, 12 July 1971, MB Papers, YCAL MSS 524, Beinecke.

81. EH to CBR, 7 December 1971, CBR Papers, HRHRC.

82. M de R to CBR, 19 May 1972, CBR Papers, HRHRC.

83. M de R to CBR, 12 March 1972, CBR Papers, HRHRC.

84. EH to CBR, 2 March 1972, CBR Papers, HRHRC.

85. M de R to Sister Mary Bernetta Quinn, 14 November 1972, Mary Bernetta Quinn Papers, YCAL MSS 177, Beinecke.

86. OR, OR Papers, YCAL MSS 54, Beinecke.

Chapter 9

1. M de R to MB, 21 November 1974, MB Papers, YCAL MSS 524, Beinecke.

2. M de R to CBR, 6 February 1973, CBR Papers, HRHRC.

3. EH to CBR, 14 June 1973, CBR Papers, HRHRC.

4. EH to CBR, 5 January 1974, CBR Papers, HRHRC.

5. M de R to CBR, 10 November 1973, CBR Papers, HRHRC.

6. Ibid.

7. M de R to OR, 21 February 1973, OR Papers, YCAL MSS 54, Beinecke.

8. M de R to OR, 28 March 1974, OR Papers, YCAL MSS 54, Beinecke.

9. EH TO CBR, 5 February 1974, CBR Papers, HRHRC.

10. M de R to OR, 24 March 1975, OR Papers, YCAL MSS 54, Beinecke.

11. Tim Weiner, *Enemies: A History of the FBI* (New York: Random House, 2012), 277.

12. Ibid., 289.

13. Ibid., 291.

14. Ibid., 140, 292.

15. Ibid., 315.

16. Ibid., 328.

17. Ibid., 331.

18. Ibid., 335–56.

19. Lesley Oelsner, "FBI Opening files on Alger Hiss and Whittaker Chambers," *New York Times*, 12 November 1973, 341.

20. M de R to OR, 6 April 1974, OR Papers, YCAL MSS 54, Beinecke.

21. LD to OR, 9 August 1975, OR Papers, YCAL MSS 54, Beinecke.

22. EP, *Ezra Pound Speaking: Radio Speeches of World War II*, ed. LD (Westport, CT: Greenwood, 1978), xiv.

23. M de R, "Fragments of an Atmosphere," *Agenda* 17–18, nos. 1–3 (1979–80): 157.

24. Ibid., 158.

25. Ibid., quoted but not attributed on 161.

26. Ibid., 170.

27. Ibid.

28. Daniel Pearlman, "Ezra Pound: America's Wandering Jew," *Paideuma* 9, no. 3 (1980): 461.

29. Tim Redman, *Ezra Pound and Italian Fascism* (Cambridge: Cambridge University Press, 1991), 217.

30. Ibid., 198.

31. Broadcast 23, 9 April 1942, quoted ibid., 224.

32. Broadcast 66, 24 March 1943, quoted ibid., 224.

33. Broadcast 80, 27 April 1943, quoted ibid., 224.

34. Robert Casillo, *The Genealogy of Demons: Anti-Semitism, Fascism, and the Myths of Ezra Pound* (Evanston, IL: Northwestern University Press, 1988), 22.

35. A. David Moody, *Ezra Pound: Poet*, vol. 3, *The Tragic Years, 1939–1972* (Oxford: Oxford University Press, 2015), 9.

36. Ibid.

37. M de R to OR, 1 November 1976, OR Papers, YCAL MSS 54, Beinecke.

38. LD, introduction to *Ezra Pound Speaking*, xv.

39. Christopher Simpson, "'Worldview Warfare' and the Science of Coercion," in *Science of Coercion: Communication Research and Psychological Warfare, 1945–1960* (New York: Oxford University Press, 1994), 89.

40. Donald Slesinger, quoted ibid., 90.

41. Ibid.

42. LD, "Goebbels's Principles of Propaganda," *Public Opinion Quarterly* 14, no. 3 (1950): 419–42.

43. Humphrey Carpenter, *A Serious Character: The Life of Ezra Pound* (New York: Dell, 1988), 621–22.

44. Ibid., 627.

45. Lawrence C. Soley, *Radio Warfare: OSS and CIA Subversive Propaganda* (New York: Praeger, 1989), 102.

46. Gerd Horten, *Radio Goes to War: The Cultural Politics of Propaganda During World War II* (Berkeley: University of California Press, 2003), 61.

47. These secret tactics had been in place since the beginning of the war; first in Britain, then in the U.S. After the war of Italy against the United States was announced on 11 December 1941, and particularly after the last enemy troops in Tunisia surrendered on 15 May 1943, the circumstance that put Allied troops in position to land on Italian soil, psychological warfare tactics against Italians escalated. The Morale Operations Branch of the OSS took charge of "the execution of all forms of morale subversion by diverse means including "false rumors, 'freedom stations,' false leaflets and false documents." (U.S. Joint Chiefs of Staff Directive 155/11/D). One clandestine radio plan, invented by Gen. Dwight Eisenhower, was to claim on Rome Radio's frequency that Italy had asked for and received an armistice." Eisenhower reasoned that a bogus armistice, referred to by code name "Helga," even if believed for a short time before being countermanded, would still give the Allies a psychological edge with local populations.

At the last minute, Winston Churchill opposed the plan on the grounds that such transmissions would undermine the credibility of future broadcasts. It was soon replaced with Radio Italo Balbo, supposedly operating within Italy, although the transmitter was really located at Cape Bon in Tunis. It too used Rome Radio's frequency and interrupted newscasts with coded messages, spreading rumors and news that undermined "Axis military capacity by driving wedges between Fascist groups, between Fascists and Italians, and between Fascists and Nazis." The British supplemented these broadcasts with their own "Radio Matteotti" a month before the invasion of Sicily began. It claimed to be operated by Italian army deserters in Greece, but was really located in Cairo, as was another British Political Warfare Executive program called "Giustizia e Libertà." In all, there were thirty-two Italian language programs each day during May 1943, all calling for sabotage and resistance against German troops and often using enemy nationals to convey the Allied message. It was in light of this Allied practice that the American secret services knew to suspect Axis powers of using people like Ezra Pound for a reverse but similar strategy.

Leonard Doob might have understood more than most people why radio was at the heart of the war effort, but he knew little and the American and British public knew even less. Only the most notorious cases of broadcasting for the Axis eventually received attention—William Joyce and John Avery in Britain, Charles Cousens in Australia, and Iva Toguri (Tokyo Rose) in the United States. But at least forty British individuals had made pro-Nazi broadcasts from Berlin and there was little or no official consistency in their treatment. Some, like William Joyce and John Avery, were executed; others received suspended or commuted sentences; still others, like P. G. Wodehouse, were never charged. In the United States eleven civilians were arrested as suspected traitors; nine had been employed as broadcasters on German shortwave networks based in Berlin; five were convicted of treason and again received inconsistent sentences. Judith Keene, who wrote *Treason on the Airwaves*, points out that the most severe judgments seem to have been those handed down closest to the end of the war, but even her detailed inquiry into individual cases does not reveal J. Edgar Hoover's preoccupation with the radio and its role in psychological warfare, espionage, and in crime detection.

During and after the war, Hoover wrote dozens of memoranda about the radio. "Communication is the heart and soul of espionage activities," he wrote in 1944. "Since radio stations do not have to be pretentious and since short transmission periods may escape detection, many spies have tried to use the radio wave to send messages to headquarters." And he went on with examples from the war, particularly ones that used counterespionage, where Germans or Russian were persuaded by the FBI that they were sending or receiving information to their own operators when, in fact, their signals were going directly to their enemies. "On May 22, 1940," he reported, "the FBI operator cracked the airwaves with the first message to the German Intelligence in Hamburg, signing the message with the name of the 'spy' the Nazis had trained so well. The Germans were jubilant. They had no idea they were trafficking directly with the FBI. From that day until August 1941, almost daily, the FBI was in contact with Hitler's German intelligence. A total of 500 messages were exchanged."

Radio, as Hoover knew, participated in a huge propaganda machine, used, in its overt or "white" mode for persuasion and politics, for advertising, and for news broadcasting. It had been used to unite the American population in agreeing to join the war effort in the first place and it was used continually to create an "imagined [national] community." It kept the population's morale tempered toward optimism and good will; it sold the foreign war just as it sold the products that shaped domestic living. At least 90 percent of Americans owned radios during World War II and most of them listened to four to five hours of radio each day. See Soley, *Radio Warfare*.

48. M de R to OR, 29 January 1978, OR Papers, YCAL MSS 54, Beinecke.

49. M de R to CBR, 28 February 1974, CBR Papers, HRHRC.

50. M de R to CBR, 5 March 1975, CBR Papers, HRHRC.

51. M de R to CBR, 21 April 1975, CBR Papers, HRHRC.

52. M de R to MB, 3 May 1975, MB Papers, YCAL MSS 524, Beinecke.

53. M de R to MB, 21 November 1974, MB Papers, YCAL MSS 524, Beinecke. Patrizia passed her baccalaureate in 1969, studying English literature and Japanese at the University of Venice and Vienna.

54. M de R to MB, 7 December 1974, MB Papers YCAL MSS 524, Beinecke.

55. M de R to CBR, 5 March 1975, CBR Papers, HRHRC.

56. M de R to OR, 19 February 1975, OR Papers, YCAL MSS 54, Beinecke.

57. Ibid.

58. EH to CBR, 13 June 1975, CBR Papers, HRHRC.

59. M de R to OR, 10 December 1974, OR Papers, YCAL MSS 54, Beinecke.

60. M de R to OR, 8 December 1974, OR Papers, YCAL MSS 54, Beinecke.

61. Both Philip Willan and Daniele Ganser claim that the violence of these years was a continuation of strategies put in place during James Jesus Angleton's postwar Italian tenure, where paramilitary groups or "stay behind armies" were organized and positioned all over Europe, but particularly in Italy, in anticipation of Communist expansion to the West. See Philip Willan, *Puppetmasters: The Political Use of Terrorism in Italy* (London: iUniverse, 2002) and Daniele Ganser, *NATO's Secret Armies: Operation GLADIO and Terrorism in Western Europe* (New York: Routledge, 2005).

Chapter 10

1. M de R to CBR, 22 June 1986, CBR Papers, HRHRC.

2. M de R.

3. M de R to OR, 1 November 1976, OR Papers, YCAL MSS 54, Beinecke.

4. EP, "Machine Art," in *Machine Art and Other Writings: The Lost Thought of the Italian Years*, ed. Maria Luisa Ardizzone (Durham, NC: Duke University Press, 1996), 45.

5. M de R, "The Old House," in *Il Diapason* (Milan: All'Insegna del Pesce d'Oro, 1965), 59.

6. M de R, "My House," ibid., 51.

My house endures
Without fancy things,
Shaped as a
Mirror of my soul.
You are not tended:
The hall passage is open,
There are no carpets,
Because I prefer straw.
Cold in winter
Freezing in summer
The wind blows
Between the double glazing
And the rain patters on the granite.
Yet a real fire burns
In the kitchen.
And branches and crystals
Refract the light of your eyes.

7. M de R to Mary Bernetta Quinn, 15 July 1975, Mary Bernetta Quinn Papers, YCAL MSS 177, Beinecke.

8. M de R to MB, 2 September 1976, MB Papers, YCAL MSS 524, Beinecke.

9. M de R, "Space Age," in *Processo in Verso* (Milan: All' Insegna del Pesce d'Oro, 1973), 25.

True reality is high.
I know there is the world of factories

But one does not need
To stop
In the periphery
In quotidian life.
The suburbs are deserts
To cross hurriedly to reach
The ivory tower, the launch tower
And span oceans
With Beethoven and Bach in stereo.

10. M de R, "Fidelity," ibid., 55.

11. M de R, "Short," ibid., 61.

12. Luca Cesari, introduction to *Gocce che cantano*, by M de R (Rimini: Raffaeli Editore, 1994), 14.

13. M de R, "Variations on e. e. cummings," ibid., 22.

14. M de R, untitled, ibid., 55.

15. M de R, "Graveyard of Dreams," ibid., 27.

16. M de R, "Bad Luck," ibid., 38.

After months of sun and drought,
The air became heavy and humid and
Under the weight of fog,
Piles of stones collapsed and rolled
To the bottom of the valley. Old trees
And shrubs were broken without
Wind blowing or snow or rain falling.
Portents certainly at a time when
The gods were with us. Now skeptical,
I wonder if I was not too intent gazing at the azure
And the diamantine points of ice
To notice the shambles at the base.

17. M de R to MB, 1 January 1976, MB Papers, YCAL MSS 524, Beinecke.

18. M de R to OR, 11 January 1976, OR Papers 54, YCAL MSS 54, Beinecke.

19. The participants were Dr. Vianney Devlin, Eric Fridman, Patrick O'Dowd, Kathi J. Patterson, Tim Redman, Richard Reid, Andrew Rosenbaum, Randy Scott, Dr. Ann Shaver, Don Tinker, John Vogt, Martha Peitzke Wilson. See William McNaughton, "The 1976 'Summer at Brunnenburg': Reading *The Cantos*," *Paideuma* 5, no. 3 (Winter 1976): 457–60.

20. M de R to OR, 13 July 1976, OR Papers, YCAL MSS 54, Beinecke.

21. Philip Leist to CLS, February 1995.

22. M de R to OR, 23 November 1978, OR Papers, YCAL MSS 54, Beinecke.

23. This canto was labeled CXX and used by James Laughlin to end the 1972 version of *The Cantos*. The date of its composition and its placement as the final canto have been disputed. See James Laughlin, "Bulletin Board," *Paideuma* 11 (1982): 187–88.

24. E. Fuller Torrey, *The Roots of Treason: Ezra Pound and the Secrets of Saint Elizabeths* (New York: McGraw-Hill, 1984), 243.

25. M de R to MB, 14 July 1978, MB Papers, YCAL MSS 524, Beinecke.

26. M de R to MB, 25 May 1976, MB Papers, YCAL MSS 524, Beinecke.

27. *Ezra Pound and Dorothy Shakespear: Their Letters 1909–1914*, ed. Omar Pound and A. Walton Litz (New York: New Directions, 1984).

28. MB to M de R, 25 March 1984, MB Papers, YCAL MSS 524, Beinecke.

29. MB, 1 June 1984, "Travel Diary Italy, 1980s," Uncat. 740, Beinecke.

30. M de R to MB, 26 January 1979, MB Papers, YCAL MSS 524, Beinecke.

31. MB, 18 June 1984, "Travel Diary Italy," Uncat. 740, Beinecke.

32. MB to M de R, 20 April 1995, MB Papers, YCAL MSS 524, Beinecke.

33. EP, Canto CXX.

34. M de R, undated news clipping, ca. 1980, OR Papers, YCAL MSS 54, Beinecke.

35. M de R to MB, 13 March 1990, MB Papers, YCAL MSS 524, Beinecke.

36. Bruno Borlandi, "Arrestato un Principe Spediva Armi in Libia in Casse Archeologiche," *La Notta*, 2 February 1984, newspaper clipping, OR Papers, YCAL MSS 54, Beinecke.

37. M de R to OR, 19 February 1984, OR Papers, YCAL MSS 54, Beinecke.

38. M de R to MB, 16 March 1985, MB Papers, YCAL MSS 524, Beinecke.

39. *Corriere della Sera*, 15 January 1992.

40. Paul Blondani, *Corriere della Sera*, 13 December 1994, 46.

41. Ludwig Keimer Foundation for Comparative Research in Archaeology and Ethnology, "Board of Advisers," in *Background and List of Members* (Basel, 1972).

42. Franco Ferraresi, "The Radical Right in Postwar Italy," *Politics and Society* 16 (1988): 84.

43. "Chi è Pio Filippani Ronconi?," Archivo storico dell' informazione, http://societacivile.it.

44. Hans Thomas Hakl, *Eranos: an Alternative Intellectual History of the Twentieth Century* (London: Routledge, 2014), 42.

45. Daniele Ganser, *Nato's Secret Armies: Operation Gladio and Terrorism in Western Europe* (London: Frank Cass, 2005), 7.

46. Solange Manifredi, *CIA e Nazisti uniti per destabilizzare l'Italia: Il ruolo dell' Organizzazione Gehlen in Italia negli anni della "strategia dell tensione"* (self-published, 2014), 42.

47. Philip Willan, *Puppetmasters: The Political Use of Terrorism in Italy* (London: iUniverse, 2002), 40–42; see also Ganser, *Nato's Secret Armies*, 75–77. See also the interview of Federico d'Amato on his friendship with James Jesus Angleton in *Il Borghese*, 12 July 1987.

48. M de R to MB, 27 January 1986, MB Papers, YCAL MSS 524, Beinecke.

49. M de R, untitled typescript, n.d., given to CLS, 155, 19.

50. Ibid., 169.

51. M de R to MB, 8 March 1984, MB Papers, YCAL MSS 524, Beinecke.

52. MB to M de R, 25 March 1984, MB Papers, YCAL MSS 524, Beinecke.

53. OR to Walter de Rachewiltz, 3 March 1984, OR Papers, YCAL MSS 54, Beinecke.

54. MB to M de R, 2 March 1984, MB Papers, YCAL MSS 524, Beinecke.

55. Unidentified newspaper clipping, undated in MB Papers, YCAL MSS 524, Beinecke.

56. M de R to MB, 27 January 1986, MB Papers, YCAL MSS 524, Beinecke.

57. MB, "Travel Diary Italy," 1980s, Uncat. 740, Beinecke.

58. M de R to MB, 19 June 2000, MB Papers, YCAL MSS 524, Beinecke.

59. M de R to MB, 25 January 1995, MB Papers, YCAL MSS 524, Beinecke.

60. M de R to MB, 18 February 1997, MB Papers, YCAL MSS 524, Beinecke.

61. Ibid.

62. M de R to MB, 25 January 1995, MB Papers, YCAL MSS 524, Beinecke.
63. M de R, "Walter von der Vogelweide," in *Il Diapason*, 57.

Chapter 11

1. M de R to CBR, 5 November 1985, CBR Papers, HRHRC.
2. OR, "Will," 30 March 1985, OR Papers Addition, YCAL MSS 241, Beinecke. "The house in Venice, 252 calle Querini, Dorsoduro, . . . I wish to leave (as a memorial of Ezra Pound) to the City of Venice—called the "Ezra Pound Collection" which also consists of books by Ezra Pound and by his contemporaries—also galley proofs of his works, manuscripts of published works, all letters from Ezra Pound to Olga Rudge to remain under seal for 30 years before publication—with certain exceptions: if I have time to list them—if not they must all be under seal as also the letters of Olga Rudge to Ezra Pound—I also leave paintings by Venetian painters—to be left hung on walls of the first floor—also my Max Ernst and my Fernand Léger (gifts to me by Ezra Pound). Duplicates of Ezra Pound's works to be offered as mementos to valued friends: Tsami Noguchi, Valerie Eliot, Prof. Ghayam Singh, Gabriel Stocchi and his wife Luisa Stocchi, John Drummond, duplicates of posters of concerts organized by Ezra Pound in Rapallo."
3. M de R to OR, 26 April 1986, OR Papers, YCAL MSS 54, Beinecke.
4. Arrigo Cipriani, in John Berendt, *The City of Falling Angels* (New York: Penguin, 2005), 204.
5. M de R to OR, 24 February 1988, OR Papers, YCAL MSS 54, Beinecke.
6. Berendt, *The City of Falling Angels*, 208.
7. M de R to MB, 13 March 1990, MB Papers, YCAL MSS 524, Beinecke.
8. M de R, untitled, in *Whose World? Selected Poems* (Laurinberg, NC: St. Andrews College Press, 1998), 55.
9. M de R to OR, 11 September 1988, OR Papers, YCAL MSS 54, Beinecke.
10. M de R to CBR, 20 November 1989, CBR Papers, HRHRC.
11. M de R to MB, 17 November 1993, MB Papers, YCAL MSS 524, Beinecke.
12. M de R to MB, 10 January 1990, MB Papers, YCAL MSS 524, Beinecke.
13. M de R, untitled, in *For the Wrong Reason* (New York: Edgewise, 2002), 47.
14. M de R to MB, 27 January 1986, MB Papers, YCAL MSS 524, Beinecke.
15. M de R to CBR, 26 February 1986, CBR Papers, HRHRC.
16. M de R to OR, 2 February 1986, OR Papers, YCAL MSS 54, Beinecke.
17. M de R to CBR, 26 February 1986 CBR Papers, HRHRC.
18. M de R to CBR, 16 June 1987, CBR Papers, HRHRC.
19. M de R to OR, 28 January 1987, OR Papers, YCAL MSS 54, Beinecke.
20. M de R, "Feminine Gaiety," unpublished manuscript, in OR Papers, YCAL MSS 54, Beinecke; and EP fragment, in OR Papers, YCAL MSS 54, Beinecke.
21. EP, Canto CXII.
22. M de R, "Broken Promises Are as Good as a Lie," in *Whose World?*, 18.
23. M de R, "Kung Is to Pound as Is Water to Fishes," in *Ezra Pound and China*, ed. Zhaoming Qian (Ann Arbor: University of Michigan Press, 2003), 283.
24. M de R to MB, 21 September 1999, MB Papers, YCAL MSS 524, Beinecke.
25. Ibid.
26. Dinitia Smith, "Cathedral Bars Ezra Pound from Its Poets' Corner," *New York Times*, 23 October 1999, B12.

27. M de R to MB, n.d. [November 1999], MB Papers, YCAL MSS 524, Beinecke.

28. Sophocles, *Antigone*, in *The Three Theban Plays: Antigone, Oedipus the King, Oedipus at Colonus*, trans. Robert Fagles (New York: Penguin, 1984), 112.

29. Ibid., 85.

30. EP, Canto IV.

31. M de R, "Juda Becomes New Haven," in *For the Wrong Reason*, 17.

32. Tom Kingston, "Ezra Pound's Daughter Fights to Wrest the Renegade Poet's Legacy from Fascists," *Guardian*, 14 January 2012.

33. M de R, untitled, in *For the Wrong Reason*, 35.

34. M de R, "Chiaro Scuro," ibid., 20.

35. M de R, untitled, ibid., 61.

BIBLIOGRAPHY

Agresti, Olivia Rossetti. Papers, 1947–1963. YCAL MSS 173. Beinecke Rare Book and Manuscript Library, Yale University.

Alcock, Antony Evelyn. *The History of the South Tyrol Question*. Geneva: Michael Joseph,
1970.

Aldington, Richard. *Soft Answers*. London: Chatto and Windus, 1932.

Angleton, James H. "Duty Assignment Completed as of 2400 hours, 29 July 1945." Rome X-2
Branch Records, 4 August 1945. Record group 226, box 120. National Archives and Records Administration, College Park, MD.

Angleton, James Jesus. Furioso Papers. YCAL MSS 75. Beinecke Rare Book and Manuscript
Library, Yale University.

———. "Letters to Ezra Pound." Ezra Pound Papers. YCAL MSS 43. Beinecke Rare Book and
Manuscript Library, Yale University.

———. "Report of Activities of the Italian Mission from 1–31 October 1945." Record group
226, box 260. National Archive and Records Administration, College Park, MD.

Arrizabalaga, Ramon, and Ezra Pound. Ramon Arrizabalaga Collection of Ezra Pound 1945–
1996. YCAL MSS 161. Beinecke Rare Book and Manuscript Library, Yale University.

Bachelard, Gaston. *The Poetics of Space*. Translated by Maria Jolas. Boston: Beacon, 1969.

Barnard, Mary. *Assault on Mount Helicon: A Literary Memoir*. Berkeley: University of California Press, 1984.

———. Papers. YCAL MSS 524. Beinecke Rare Book and Manuscript Library, Yale University.

Berendt, John. *The City of Falling Angels*. New York: Penguin, 2005.

Bernstein, Carl, and Bob Woodward. *All the President's Men*. New York: Simon and Schuster,
1974.

Bertoldi, Silvio. *I Tedeschi in Italia*. Milan: Rizzoli Libri, 1994.

Bettini, Emanuele. *Gladio: al repubblica parallela*. Rome: Ediesse, 1996.

Bok, Sissela. *Secrets: On the Ethics of Concealment and Revelation*. New York: Vintage, 1989.

Borlandi, Bruno. "Arrestato un principe spediva armi in Libia in casse archeologiche." *La
Notta*, 2 February 1984.

Breitman, Richard, and Timothy Naftali. *Report to the IWG on Previously Classified OSS Records*. June 2000. www.archives.gov/iwg/reports/june-2000.

Brooke-Rose, Christine. Papers, 1893–1992. Harry Ransom Humanities Research Center, University of Texas at Austin.

Brown, Anthony Cave, ed. *The Secret War Report of the OSS*. New York: Berkley, 1976.

Bryher. Papers, 1912–1980. GEN MSS 97. Beinecke Rare Book and Manuscript Library, Yale
University.

Byatt, A. S. *The Shadow of the Sun*. New York: Harcourt, 1991.

Carpenter, Humphrey. *A Serious Character: The Life of Ezra Pound*. New York: Dell, 1988.

Chalou, George, C., ed. *The Secrets War: The Office of Strategic Services in World War II*. Washington, DC: National Archives and Records Administration, 1994.

Charles, Norman. *The Case of Ezra Pound*. New York: Funk and Wagnalls, 1968.

"Chi è Pio Filippani Ronconi?" Archivo storico dell' informazione. http://societacivile.it.

CIA. "Government Affairs." Report CIA-RDP77-00432R000100350004-5. *News, Views and Issues* 1 (3 January 1975). National Archives and Records Administration, College Park, MD.

———. "James Jesus Angleton." Report CIA-RDP77-00432R000100340001-9, 3–20. National Archives and Records Administration, College Park, MD.

———. "James Jesus Angleton." Report CIA-RDP77-00432R000100350002-7, 16–25. National Archives and Records Administration, College Park, MD.

———. "James Jesus Angleton." Report CIA-RDP80R01731R002600470001-6, 25–192. National Archives and Records Administration, College Park, MD.

———. "James Jesus Angleton." Report CIA-RDP88-01315R000100500001-1, 34, 153. National Archives and Records Administration, College Park, MD.

Conover, Anne. *Olga Rudge and Ezra Pound: "What Thou Lovest Well . . ."* New Haven, CT: Yale University Press, 2001.

Cornell, Julien. Papers Relating to Ezra Pound, 1945–1965. YCAL MSS 176. Beinecke Rare Book and Manuscript Library, Yale University.

———. *The Trial of Ezra Pound: A Documented Account of the Treason Case by the Defendant's Lawyer*. London: Faber and Faber, 1966.

Corriere della Sera. Clipping. 8 January 1992. Olga Rudge Papers. YCAL MSS 54. Beinecke Rare Book and Manuscript Library, Yale University.

———. Clipping. 23 November 1994. Olga Rudge Papers. YCAL MSS 54. Beinecke Rare Book and Manuscript Library, Yale University.

———. Clipping. 18 December 1994. Olga Rudge Papers. YCAL MSS 54. Beinecke Rare Book and Manuscript Library, Yale University.

Corvo, Max. *The OSS in Italy, 1942–1945*. New York: Praeger, 1990.

Davenport, Guy. "Three Books in One." *Virginia Quarterly Review* 47, no. 4 (August 1971): 638–40.

Diamond, Sigmund. *Compromised Campus: The Collaboration of Universities with the Intelligence Community, 1945–1955*. New York: Oxford University Press, 1992.

Doob, Eveline Bates. "Some Notes on E. P." *Paideuma* 8, no. 1 (Spring 1979): 69ff.

Doob, Leonard W. *Becoming More Civilized: A Psychological Exploration*. New Haven, CT: Yale University Press, 1960.

———. *Communication in Africa: A Search for Boundaries*. New York: Praeger, 1979.

———. *A Crocodile Has Me by the Leg: African Poems*. New York: Walker, 1967.

———. *"Ezra Pound Speaking": Radio Speeches of World War II*. Westport, CT: Greenwood, 1978.

———. "Goebbels's Principles of Propaganda." *Public Opinion Quarterly* 14, no. 3 (1950): 419–42.

———. *Pathways to People*. New Haven, CT: Yale University Press, 1975.

———. *Patriotism and Nationalism: Their Psychological Foundations*. New Haven, CT: Yale University Press, 1964.

———. *Patterning of Time*. New Haven, CT: Yale University Press, 1971.

———. *Personality, Power, and Authority*. New York: Praeger, 1983.

———. *Public Opinion and Propaganda*. New York: Henry Holt, 1948.

———. *Social Psychology*. New York: Henry Holt, 1952.

———. "The Strategies of Psychological Warfare." *Public Opinion Quarterly* 13 (Winter 1949).

———. "The Utilization of Social Scientists in the Overseas Branch of the Office of War Information." *American Political Science Review* 41 (August 1947).

Doolittle, Hilda [H.D.]. *End to Torment: A Memoir of Ezra Pound*. New York: New Directions, 1979.

———. Papers, 1887–1977. YCAL MSS 24. Beinecke Rare Book and Manuscript, Library, Yale University.

——— [Delia Alton, pseud.]. *The Sword Went Out to Sea*. Gainesville: University of Florida Press, 2007.

———. *Trilogy*. New York: New Directions, 1998.

Drummond, John. "Letters to Olga Rudge." Olga Rudge Papers. YCAL MSS 54. Beinecke Rare Book and Manuscript Library, Yale University.

Dulles, Allen W. *The Secret Surrender: The Classic Insider's Account of the Secret Plot to Surrender Northern Italy During WWII*. Guilford, CT: Lyons, 2006.

Duncan, Ronald. *Journal of a Husbandman*. London: Faber and Faber, 1944.

FBI. "FBI File on Ezra Pound (microform). Guide to the Microfilm Edition of the FBI File on Ezra Pound." Wilmington, DE: Scholarly Resources, 2000.

———. "FBI File Relating to the Trial of Ezra Pound, 1943–1958. Depositions, Memoranda of Agents in Italy." BANC MSS 75/622. Bancroft Library, University of California at Berkeley.

———. "Memorandum: Re Radio in Crime Detection." 16 September 1944. ("Radio and the Spy"). Record group 65, box 121, folder 66-1723. National Archives and Records Administration, College Park, MD.

Feldman, Matthew. "The 'Pound Case' in Historical Perspective: An Archival Overview." *Journal of Modern Literature* 23, no. 2 (2012): 83–97.

Fettarappa-Sandri, Giulio. "Report on the Organization and Activities of the Italian CS Service, January 1941–September 1943." Norman Holmes Pearson Papers, Za Pearson. Yale University Library.

Fitzgerald, Robert. "Memorandum for Mary." August 1954. Robert Fitzgerald Papers, YCAL MSS 222. Beinecke Rare Book and Manuscript Library, Yale University.

———. Papers. YCAL MSS 222. Beinecke Rare Book and Manuscript Library, Yale University.

Freind, Bill. "'Why Do You Want to Put Your Ideas in Order?' Re-thinking the Politics of Ezra Pound." *Journal of Modern Literature* 23, nos. 3–4 (Summer 2000): 545–63.

Friends of the University of Toledo Libraries. "Mary de Rachewiltz Appointed First Canady Center Fellow." *The Deckle* 5, no. 2 (Winter 1987).

Gallup, Donald. *A Curator's Responsibilities*. New Brunswick, NJ: Graduate School of Library Services, 1976.

———. *Ezra Pound: A Bibliography*. Charlottesville: University Press of Virginia, 1983.

———. *On Contemporary Bibliography: With Particular Reference to Ezra Pound*. Austin: University of Texas Press, 1971.

———. *Pigeons on the Granite: Memories of a Yale Librarian*. New Haven, CT: Beinecke Rare Book and Manuscript Library, 1988.

Ganser, Daniele. *NATO's Secret Armies: Operation GLADIO and Terrorism in Western Europe.* Contemporary Security Studies. New York: Routledge, 2005.

Gleason, Herbert. Letters to Princess Mary de Rachewiltz, 2 June 1964 and 29 June 1964. Olga Rudge Papers. YCAL MSS 54. Beinecke Rare Book and Manuscript Library, Yale University.

Goethe, Johann Wolfgang. *Italian Journey, 1786–87.* New York: Penguin, 1996.

Gross, Feliks. *Ethnics in a Borderland: An Inquiry into the Nature of Ethnicity and Reduction of Ethnic Tensions in a One-Time Genocide Area.* Westport, CT: Greenwood, 1978.

Hakl, Hans Thomas. *Eranos: an Alternative Intellectual History of the Twentieth Century.* London: Routledge, 2014.

Hawthorne, National. *The Scarlet Letter.* New York: Penguin, 2015.

Heaney, Seamus. *The Burial at Thebes: A Version of Sophocles' Antigone.* New York: Farrar, Straus and Giroux, 2005.

Hesse, Eva. Letters to Christine Brooke-Rose. Christine Brooke-Rose Papers, 1893–1992. Harry Ransom Humanities Research Center, University of Texas at Austin.

——, ed. *New Approaches to Ezra Pound: A Co-ordinated Investigation of Pound's Poetry and Ideas.* Berkeley: University of California Press, 1969.

Heymann, C. David. *Ezra Pound: The Last Rower, a Political Profile.* New York: Citadel, 1992.

Hollander, John. *Reflections on Espionage: The Question of Cupcake.* New Haven, CT: Yale University Press, 1974.

Hollenberg, Donna Krolik. *Between History and Poetry: The Letters of H.D. and Norman Holmes Pearson.* Iowa City: University of Iowa Press, 1997.

Holzman, Michael. *James Jesus Angleton, the CIA, and the Craft of Counterintelligence.* Amherst: University of Massachusetts Press, 2008.

Hoover, J. Edgar. "Radio and the Spy 66-1723-54." 28 October 1944. Record group 65, box 121. National Archives and Records Administration, Washington, DC.

Horten, Gerd. *Radio Goes to War: The Cultural Politics of Propaganda During World War II.* Berkeley: University of California Press, 2003.

Hubatschek, Erika. *Vom Leben am Steilhang: Bilddokumente 1939–1960.* Innsbruck, 1995.

James, Henry. *The Turn of the Screw and The Aspern Papers.* New York: Penguin, 1986.

Jordan, Viola Baxter. "H.D." Papers. YCAL MSS 175. Beinecke Rare Book and Manuscript Collection, Yale University.

Joyce, James. *Ulysses.* Edited by Hans Walter Gabler. New York: Random House, 1984.

Katz, Robert. *The Battle for Rome: The Germans, the Allies, the Partisans, and the Pope: September 1943–June 1944.* New York: Simon and Schuster, 2003.

Kenner, Hugh. "Impassioned Reticence." *National Review* 13, no. 33 (August 1971): 933–35.

——. *The Pound Era: The Age of Ezra Pound, T. S. Eliot, James Joyce and Wyndham Lewis.* Berkeley: University of California Press, 1971.

Kington, Tom. "Ezra Pound's Daughter Fights to Wrest the Renegade Poet's Legacy from Fascists." *Guardian,* 14 January 2012.

Korg, Jacob. *Winter Love: Ezra Pound and H.D.* Madison: University of Wisconsin Press, 2003.

Kutler, Stanley. *The Wars of Watergate.* New York: Norton, 1990.

Latour, C. F. "Germany, Italy and South Tyrol, 1938–1945." *Historical Journal* 8, no. 1 (1965): 95–111.

Laughlin, James. "Bulletin Board." *Paideuma* 11 (1982): 187–88.

Lerner, Daniel, ed. *Propaganda in War and Crisis*. New York: George Stewart, 1951.

Ludwig Keimer Foundation for Comparative Research in Archeology and Ethnology. *Background and List of Members*. Basel, 1972.

———. *Ludwig Keimer and the Keimer Foundation*. Basel, 1970.

MacLeish, Archibald. Review of *Section: Rock Drill*. *New York Times*, 16 November 1956.

MacPherson, Nelson. *American Intelligence in War-Time London: The Story of the OSS*. London: Frank Cass, 2003.

Malcolm, Janet. *In the Freud Archives*. New York: New York Review Books, 1984.

Manifredi, Solange. *CIA e Nazisti uniti per destabilizzare l'Italia: Il ruolo dell'Organizzazione Gehlen in Italia negli anni della "strategia della tensione."* 2014.

McBride, Stewart. "Ezra Pound's Daughter Defends His Reputation as a 'Prophet.'" *Christian Science Monitor*, 26 December 1975.

McNaughton, William. "The 1976 Summer at Brunnenburg: Reading *The Cantos*." *Paideuma* 5, no. 3 (Winter 1976): 457–60.

———. "The Secret History of Saint Elizabeths." In *Ezra Pound and Poetic Influence*, edited by Helen M. Dennis, 256–74. Amsterdam: Rodopi, 2000.

McWhirter, Cameron, and Randall L. Ericson, eds. *Ezra Pound: A Selected Catalog from the Ezra Pound Collection Hamilton College*. Clinton, NY: Hamilton College Library, 2005.

Meacham, Harry M. *The Caged Panther: Ezra Pound at Saint Elizabeths*. New York: Twayne, 1967.

Melchior, Claus. *Ezra Pound and Europe*. Internationle Forschungen zur Allgemeinen und Vergleichenden Literaturwissenschaft, 2. Amsterdam: Rodopi, 1993.

Moody, A. David. *Ezra Pound: Poet*. Vol. 1, *The Young Genius, 1885–1920*. Oxford: Oxford University Press, 2009.

———. *Ezra Pound: Poet*. Vol. 2, *The Epic Years, 1921–1939*. Oxford: Oxford University Press, 2014.

———. *Ezra Pound: Poet*. Vol. 3, *The Tragic Years, 1939–1972*. Oxford: Oxford University Press, 2015.

Naftali, Timothy. "X-2 and the Apprenticeship of American Counterespionage, 1942–44." PhD diss., Harvard University, 1993. University Microfilms International.

National Archives of the United Kingdom. "Italy, Pound, Ezra." September 1943–November 1945.

———. Press cuttings re Ezra Pound; extracts of intercepted letters by Ezra Pound to various recipients; intercepted letters mentioning Ezra Pound. Reference number KV 2/875, job 215665.

———. Press cuttings re Ezra Pound. Reference number KV 2/876. Job 215665.

Netting, Robert. *Balancing on an Alp: Ecological Change and Continuity in a Swiss Mountain Community*. Cambridge: Cambridge University Press, 1981.

Norberg-Schutz, Christian. *The Concept of Dwelling: On the Way to Figurative Architecture*. New York: Rizzoli, 1985.

Norman, Charles. *The Case of Ezra Pound*. New York: Funk and Wagnalls, 1968.

Nuti, Leopoldo. "The Italian 'Stay-Behind' Network: The Origins of Operation 'Gladio.'" *Journal of Strategic Studies* 30, no. 6 (December 2007): 955–80.

O'Donnell, Patrick K. *Operatives, Spies and Saboteurs: The Unknown Story of the Men and Women of World War II's OSS*. New York: Free Press, 2004.

Oelsner, Wesley. "FBI Opening Files on Alger Hiss and Whittaker Chambers." *New York Times*, 12 November 1973.

Office of Strategic Services. "Bi-Monthly Reports of Italian S.I. Desk Forward, September 1944–April 1945." Record group 226, box 268. National Archives and Records Administration. College Park, MD.

———. "Files on Captain James Jesus Angleton." Record group 226, job 57-102, box 148. National Archives and Records Administration. College Park, MD.

———. "Information from Italy, 1943–1945." Record group 226, box 379. National Archives and Records Administration. College Park, MD.

———. "Italy 1945." Record group 226, box 64. National Archives and Records Administration. College Park, MD.

———. "Memo Regarding Synthesis of SIM (Italian Intelligence Service). Reports of August-September 1944." Record group 226, box 287. National Archives and Records Administration. College Park, MD.

———. "Message to Rome about Lower Level Operatives in Italy. 13 May 1945." Record group 226, box 5. National Archives and Records Administration. College Park, MD.

———. "Monthly Report for May 1945." Record group 226, box 127. National Archives and Records Administration. College Park, MD.

———. "Monthly Report of X-2 Activity in Italy. 31 August 1944." Record group 226, box 379. National Archives and Records Administration. College Park, MD.

———. "OSS MO Operations in Italy, 1944–45." Records group 226, box 140. National Archives and Records Administration. College Park, MD.

———. "Report from the Intelligence and Counter-Espionage Service of the General Command of Occupied Italy, 24 October 1944." Records group 226, box 15. National Archives and Records Administration. College Park, MD.

———. "Report on Sozzani Monarchist Group in Northern Italy." 2 August 1946. "Memo on South Tyrol. February 1946." "Report on Political Trends Among German Speaking Population of South Tyrol, 23 May 1946." Record group 226, box 47. National Archives and Record Administration. College Park, MD.

———. "Reports from SI Sources Around Milan, Italy, 23 December 1943–5 July 1946." Records group 226, box 212. National Archives and Records Administration. College Park, MD.

———. "Reports on Activities of Foreign Agents including Russian in Italy, 1946." Record group 226, box 9. National Archives and Records Administration. College Park, MD.

———. "Rome X-2 Branch Records." Record group 226, box 120. National Archives and Records Administration. College Park, MD.

———. "Vincent Scamporini." Record group 226, box 44. National Archives and Records Administration. College Park, MD.

Pearson, Norman Holmes. "Changes in British SIS. To 'Saint.' 12 December 1945." Norman Holmes Pearson Papers, 1909–1975. Za Pearson. Yale University Library.

———. "Counter-Espionage: X-2." Norman Holmes Pearson Papers, 1909–1975, Za Pearson. Yale University Library.

———. Foreword to *The Double-Cross System: The True Story of Nazi Spies, Double Agents, and the Men Who Outwitted the Third Reich*, by John C. Masterman. New York: Skyhorse, 2011.

———. "London Station Status, 30 April 1946." Norman Holmes Pearson Papers. Za Pearson. Yale University Library.

———. "Outline of American Counterintelligence and Security Activities in World War II." Norman Holmes Pearson Papers. Za Pearson. Yale University Library.

——. "Propaganda Against the Enemy and Against Neutral and Friendly States." Norman Holmes Pearson Papers, Za Pearson. Yale University Library.

——. "Report on the Organization and Activities of the Italian CS Service." Norman Holmes Pearson Papers, Za Pearson. Yale University Library.

Persico, Joseph E. *Roosevelt's Secret War: FDR and World War II Espionage.* New York: Random House, 2001.

Pound, Dorothy. Papers. Lilly Library, University of Indiana at Bloomington, Indiana.

——. "To Mary de Rachewiltz, 24 June 1949." Olga Rudge Papers. YCAL MSS 54. Beinecke Rare Book and Manuscript Library, Yale University.

Pound, Ezra. *ABC of Reading.* New York: New Directions, 2010.

——. *The Cantos of Ezra Pound.* New York: New Directions, 1970.

——. *Confucius: The Unwobbling Pivot; The Great Digest; The Analects.* New York: New Directions, 1969.

——. *Ezra Pound Speaking: Radio Speeches of World War II.* Edited by Leonard W. Doob. Westport, CT: Greenwood, 1978.

——. *Ezra Pound to His Parents, Letters 1895–1929.* Edited by Mary de Rachewiltz, A. David Moody, and Joanna Moody. New York: Oxford University Press, 2010.

——. *"I Cease Not to Yowl": Ezra Pound's Letters to Olivia Rossetti Agresti.* Edited by Demetres P. Tryphonopoulos and Leon Surette. Urbana: University of Illinois Press, 1998.

——. *Literary Essays of Ezra Pound.* New York: New Directions, 1968.

——. *Machine Art and Other Writings: The Lost Thought of the Italian Years.* Edited by Maria Luisa Ardizzone. Durham, NC: Duke University Press, 1996.

——. Papers. YCAL MSS 43. Beinecke Rare Book and Manuscript Library, Yale University.

——. Papers Addition. YCAL MSS 53. Beinecke Rare Book and Manuscript Library, Yale University.

——. *Selected Letters of Ezra Pound 1907–1941.* Edited by D. D. Paige. New York: New Directions, 1971.

——. *Women of Trachis.* New York: New Directions, 1985.

Pound, Ezra, and Dorothy Pound. *Ezra and Dorothy Pound: Letters in Captivity, 1945–46.* Edited by Robert Spoo and Omar Pound. New York: Oxford University Press, 1999.

Pound, Ezra, and Dorothy Shakespear. *Ezra Pound and Dorothy Shakespear: Their Letters, 1909–1914.* Edited by Omar Pound and A. Walton Litz. New York: New Directions, 1984.

Prouty, L. Fletcher. *The Secret Team: The CIA and Its Allies in Control of the United States and the World.* New York: Skyhorse, 2011.

Qian, Zhaoming, ed. *Ezra Pound and China.* Ann Arbor: University of Michigan Press, 2003.

Rachewiltz, Boris de. *Amuleti dell-antico Egitto.* Rome: Sigma, 1966.

——. *Black Eros: Sexual Customs of Africa from Prehistory to the Present Day.* London: Lyle Stuart, 1964.

——. *Egitto magico religioso.* Milan: Edizioni della Terra di Mezzo, 2008.

——. *Egyptian Art: An Introduction.* London: Readers Union, 1963.

——. *Gli antichi egizi. Immagini, scene et documenti di vita quotidiana.* Rome: Edizioni Mediterranee, 1987.

——. *Introduction to African Art.* London: John Murray, 1966.

——. *Vita nell' antico Egitto.* G. C. Sansoni Editore, 1958.

Rachewiltz, Boris de, and Valenti Gomez I. Oliver. *L'occhio del faraone*. Rome: Newton Compton, 1990.

Rachewiltz, Mary de, trans. *Brancusi/Ezra Pound*. Milan: All' Insegna del Pesce d'Oro, 1957.

——. *Canzoniere*. Rimini: Raffaelli Editore, 2002.

——. *A Catalogue of the Poetry Notebooks of Ezra Pound*. New Haven, CT: Yale University Press, 1980.

——, trans. *Certain Noble Plays of Japan* (*Alcuni nobili drammi dei Giappone dai manuscritti di Ernest Fenollosa, scelti e finite da Ezra Pound*). Introduction by W. B. Yeats. Milan: All' Insegna del Pesce d'Oro, 1961.

——. "Chronicle: The Brunnenburg Tapestry." *Paideuma* 37 (2010): 153–72.

——. Collection, 1973–1975. MSS 049. Ward M. Canaday Center for Special Collections, University of Toledo.

——, trans. *Denise Levertov: La Scala di Giacobbe e altre poesie*. Milan: A. Mondadori, 1968.

——. *Di Riflesso*. Milan: All'Insegna del Pesce d'Oro, 1966.

——, trans. *Ezra Pound: Cantos 1–30*. Milan: Lerici-Scheiwiller, 1963.

——, ed. *Ezra Pound: Cathay (Catai)*. Milan: Libri Scheiwiller, 1987.

——. *Ezra Pound, Father and Teacher: Discretions*. New York: New Directions, 2005.

——, trans. *Ezra Pound: Gaudier-Brzeska: Con un Manifesto Vorticista*. Milan: All' Insegna del Pesce d'Oro, 1957.

——, ed. *Ezra Pound: Opera scelte*. Milan: A. Mondadori, 1970.

——, ed. *Ezra Pound: The Cantos*. Milan: A. Mondadori, 1985.

——. "Feminine Gaiety." Unpublished typescript. Olga Rudge Papers, YCAL MSS 54. Beinecke Rare Book and Manuscript Library, Yale University.

——, trans. *Fenollosa: Chinese Written Character as a Medium for Poetry*. Milan: Libri Scheiwiller, 1987.

——. *For the Wrong Reason*. New York: Edgewise, 2002.

——. "Fragments of an Atmosphere." *Agenda* 17–18, nos. 1–3 (1979–80): 157.

——. "Gais, the Beauties of the Tyrol." *Paideuma* 37 (2010): 97–136.

——. *Gocce che contano*. Edited by Luca Cesari. Rimini: Raffaelli Editore, 1994.

——, ed. *H.D. Poems: Selections Italian and English*. Milan: Trenna per gli Amici, 1986.

——. *Il Diapason*. Milan: All'Insegna del Pesce d'Oro, 1965.

——, ed. *James Laughlin: Quello che la matita scrive*. Parma: Guanda, 1970.

——. "Kung Is to Pound as Is Water to Fishes." In *Ezra Pound and China*, edited by Zhaoming Qian. Ann Arbor: University of Michigan Press, 2003.

——. *Maschere Tirolesi*. Milan: All' Insegna del Pesce d'Oro, 1957.

——. "New Preface to *Discretions*." Unpublished typescript given to Carol Loeb Shloss, n.d.

——, ed. *Nishikigi*. Adapted by Ernest Fenollosa and Ezra Pound. Introduction by W. B. Yeats. Milan: All' Insegna del Pesce d'Oro, 1957.

——. *Omaggio a Marianne Moore*. Milan: All' Insegna del Pesce d'Oro, 1964.

——, trans. *Poesie di e.e. cummings*. Milan: All' Insegna del Pesce d'Oro, 1963.

——, trans. *Poesie e lettere di e.e. cummings*. Turin: Einaudi, 1974.

——. *Polittico: Poesie, 1985–1995*. Milan: All'Insegna del Pesce d'Oro, 1996.

——. *Processo in Verso*. Milan: All'Insegna del Pesce d'Oro, 1973.

——. *Robinson Jeffers: La bepenne e alre poesie*. With facing text edited by Mary de Rachewiltz. Parma: Guanda, 1969.

——, trans. *The Seafarer*. By Ezra Pound. Poiano: Franco Riva, 1980.

———. Untitled typescript. Given to Carol Loeb Shloss, 2004.

———. *Whose World? Selected Poems*. Laurinburg, NC: St. Andrews College Press, 1998.

Rachewiltz, Mary de, and Giovanni Scheiwiller, eds. *Il Natale: Antologia di poeti del' 900*. Milan: All'Insegna del Pesce d'Oro, 1961.

Rachewiltz, Mary de, and Brigitte Widner. *This House Is Made to Last and Last Forever in the Mind*. Merano: Offizin S, 1995.

Rainey, Lawrence S. *Ezra Pound and the Monument of Culture: Text, History and the Malatesta Cantos*. Chicago: University of Chicago Press, 1991.

Redman, Tim. *Ezra Pound and Italian Fascism*. Cambridge: Cambridge University Press, 2009.

Reut-Nicolussi, Eduard. *Tirol unterm Beil*. Munich: Beck, 1928.

Roosevelt, Kermit. *War Report of the OSS (Office of Strategic Services)*. New York: Walker, 1976.

Rota, Bertram. Letters to Princes Mary de Rachewiltz, 3 July 1964 and 6 July 1964. Olga Rudge Papers. YCAL MSS 54. Beinecke Rare Book and Manuscript Library, Yale University.

Rsch. #1. "Col. Angleton." Record group 226, E 125, box 54, Caserta-SI-INT-40. National Archives and Records Administration. College Park, MD.

Rsch. #4. "The Mafia." In "Agent Reports," folder 725. Record group 226, E 125, box 59, Caserta-SI-INT-56. National Archives and Records Administration. College Park, MD.

Rudge, Olga. Papers. YCAL MSS 54. Beinecke Rare Book and Manuscript Library, Yale University.

———. Papers Addition. YCAL MSS 241. Beinecke Rare Book and Manuscript Library, Yale University.

Shakespeare, William. *The Merchant of Venice*. New York: Signet, 1998.

Sieburth, Richard. "Mary de Rachewiltz in Conversation with Richard Sieburth." *Paideuma* 37 (2010): 7–58.

Simpson, Christopher. *Science of Coercion: Communication Research and Psychological Warfare, 1945–1960*. New York: Oxford University Press, 1994.

Soley, Lawrence C. *Radio Warfare: OSS and CIA Subversive Propaganda*. New York: Praeger, 1989.

Somers, Homer. Interview by Carol Loeb Shloss, June 2007.

———. Letters to Mary de Rachewiltz. Yale Collection of American Literature, Beinecke Rare Book and Manuscript Library, Yale University.

Sophocles. *The Three Theban Plays: Antigone, Oedipus the King, Oedipus at Colonus*. Translated by Robert Fagles. New York: Penguin, 1984.

———. *Women of Trachis: A Version by Ezra Pound*. New York: New Directions, 1957.

Spann, Marcella. Letters to Ezra Pound. Olga Rudge Papers, YCAL MSS 54. Beinecke Rare Book and Manuscript Library, Yale University.

Spike, Michele K. *Tuscan Countess: The Life and Extraordinary Times of Matilda of Canossa*. New York: Vendome, 2004.

Stacul, Jaro. *The Bounded Field: Localism and Local Identity in an Italian Alpine Valley*. New York: Berghahn Books, 2003.

Steiner, George. *Antigones*. New Haven, CT: Yale University Press, 1996.

Steininger, Rolf. *Austria, Germany and the Cold War: From the Anschluss to the State Treaty, 1938–1955*. New York: Berghahn Books, 2008.

———. *South Tyrol: A Minority Conflict of the Twentieth Century*. New Brunswick, NJ: Transaction, 2003.

———. *Süd Tyrol im 20. Jahrhundert*. Innsbruck: Studien Verlag, 1997.

Sussman, Barry. *The Great Cover-Up: Nixon and the Scandal of Watergate*. New York: New American Library, 1974.

Taylor, Welford Dunaway. *Amelie Rives (Princess Troubetzkoy)*. New York: Twayne, 1973.

Torrey, E. Fuller. *The Roots of Treason: Ezra Pound and the Secrets of Saint Elizabeths*. New York: McGraw-Hill, 1984.

Toynbee, Philip. "Pound as a Parent." *The Observer*, 21 November 1971.

Troubetzkoi, Natalie. "Confessions." *Commonweal* 28, no. 4 (July 1938): 368–70.

———. "Russian Exile." *Commonweal* 29, no. 2 (November 1938): 33–34.

Tulli, Gustavo. *La Stirpe reale degli arodij a traversoi secoli: Studio storico-genealogico*. Rome: Tipografia Poliglotta Vaticana, 1955.

Tye, Larry. *The Father of Spin: Edward L. Bernays and the Birth of Public Relations*. New York: Henry Holt, 1998.

Weiner, Tim. *Enemies: A History of the FBI*. New York: Random House, 2012.

West, Rebecca. *The Meaning of Treason*. London: Phoenix, 1949.

Wilhelm, J. J. *Ezra Pound: The Tragic Years, 1925–1972*. University Park: Pennsylvania State University Press, 1994.

Willan, Philip. *Puppetmasters: The Political Use of Terrorism in Italy*. London: iUniverse, 2002.

Winks, Robin W. *Cloak and Gown: Scholars in the Secret War, 1939–1961*. New Haven, CT: Yale University Press, 1987.

X-2. Progress Reports re James Jesus Angleton. Record group 226, boxes 21 and 22; The Italian Desk, box 23; The Italian Desk and Angleton's Unit, box 24; Angleton Mentioned by Name, box 25; All items related to Special Counterintelligence Zed (SCIZ). National Archives and Records Administration, Washington, DC.

Zilboorg, Caroline. *Richard Aldington and H.D.: Their Lives in Letters*. Manchester: Manchester University Press, 2003.

INDEX

Plates are indicated by *pl* and plate number.

ACKNOWLEDGMENTS

Writing this book has taken me to many places, the journey marked by help and encouragement along the way. Early work on the manuscript began at the Humanities Center at Stanford University. For this year of quiet concentration, I wish to thank John Bender and the staff of the Humanities Center and to remember especially conversations with Michael Bratman and James Clifford, who both offered me interdisciplinary ways to look at my project. Other Stanford professors helped with more specific questions: Tino Cuellar talked to me about international law during wartime, and Martin Schneider discussed the economics of the Federal Reserve System. Barbara and Al Gelpi and Arnold Rampersad all offered a more general but consistent, and consistently appreciated, support. The students in my class on *The Cantos* kept me focused and inspired. The Cecil H. Green Library at Stanford contained a surprisingly full and rounded collection about the history of the Tyrol and perspectives on life in the high Alps.

Other libraries played a big role in this project. The largest archives were, understandably, at the Beinecke Rare Book and Manuscript Library at Yale University. There I could read the files of Mary de Rachewiltz, Ezra Pound, Olga Rudge, H.D., Mary Barnard, Sister Bernetta Quinn, Robert Fitzgerald, Norman Holmes Pearson, and James Jesus Angleton. Patricia C. Willis, then the curator of American literature manuscripts, was of great help, especially in trying to locate Ezra Pound's missing will. I would also like to thank Helen Varney Burst and Margaret Ann Corbett for their hospitality while I was in New Haven.

I consulted manuscripts at the Lilly Library at Indiana University in Bloomington, Indiana, the Harry Ransom Humanities Research Center at the University of Texas at Austin, the Berg Collection at the New York Public Library, the New York Center for Visual Literacy, and works held by the Special Collections and Archives of the Daniel Burke Library at Hamilton College. At the National Archives and Records Administration in Bethesda,

Maryland, Larry MacDonald, an expert on the OSS in World War II, went far beyond duty in helping me discover the activities of James Jesus Angleton during his posting in Italy during the war. The National Archives of Great Britain, Kew, Richmond, Surrey, sent me their James Jesus Angleton and Ezra Pound holdings in a package that notably arrived ripped up, disassembled, and then stuffed into a clear plastic bag.

Various individuals offered me specific encouragement or advice about the manuscript as it took shape. Richard Sieburth sent me an advance copy of his interview with Mary de Rachewiltz before it was published in *Paideuma* ("Mary de Rachewiltz in Conversation with Richard Sieburth," 2010). Vincent Sherry, Philip Leist, Homer Somers, John Gery, Mary Luisa Ardizzioni, and Laura Barnes all offered personal memories of Mary and life and happenings at Brunnenburg. Penelope Doob sent me a photograph of Leonard Doob. Alessandra McCarthy and Sara Gelmetti taught me Italian at Stanford.

Those to whom I owe the deepest gratitude are the people who read my manuscript and offered perspective and suggestions about the whole, long project. These people include Brian Fay at Wesleyan University for his comments about the preface. It also and especially includes Jean-Michel Rabaté at the University of Pennsylvania and Marjorie Perloff, a former Stanford colleague, who both read the book in its entirety. When I moved to Philadelphia, I learned immensely from those in my nonfiction writing group: Nancy Moses, Darl Rastofer, David Barnes, and Margie Patlak, who all persevered with me over the years of preparing for publication. Thanks to Adriana de Palma for checking Italian references; thanks to Casey Horgan for general help with photographs and providing a current photograph of Mary; thanks to Irmtraud Hubatschek for permission to use her mother's photographs of the Tyrol. Special thanks to Jerry Singerman for his belief in the book. Noreen O'Connor-Abel at the University of Pennsylvania Press was of immense help. Walter Biggins was a superb editor. To my personal friends, the ones who support me in life as well as writing, I offer manifold quiet, but profound thanks. To Mary herself, whose generosity was great and whose presence I will never forget, the most thanks of all.